D0233029

LANDMARKS IN Rhetoric AND Public Address

LANDMARKS IN Rhetoric AND Public Address

David Potter, *General Editor*

ESSAYS FROM

Select British Eloquence

BY

Chauncey Allen Goodrich

EDITED BY

A. Craig Baird

FOREWORD BY

David Potter

Southern Illinois University Press CARBONDALE

Library of Congress Catalog Card No. 63–7978
Printed in the United States of America by Kingsport Press, Inc.,
Kingsport, Tenn.

DESIGNED BY ANDOR BRAUN

FOREWORD

By David Potter

SCHOLARS IN AMERICA have turned increasingly to the study of several score of British, European, and American works that have been recognized as classics in the history of rhetoric and public address. Unfortunately, the majority of these titles, when available, are preserved in rare book rooms or on scarcely more accessible rolls of microfilm, and are, hence, unobtainable for classroom use or for the scholar's personal library.

To make carefully edited editions of these works available, the general editor has enlisted the assistance of an advisory board consisting of A. Craig Baird and Ralph A. Micken, of Southern Illinois University, Douglas Ehninger, of the University of Iowa, Waldo Braden, of Louisiana State University, Carroll Arnold, of Cornell University, Ernest Wrage, of Northwestern University, Frederick Haberman, of the University of Wisconsin, Harold Harding, of Ohio State University, Lester Thonssen, of City College, New York, Richard Murphy, of the University of Illinois, Mary Margaret Robb, of the University of Colorado, and Horace Rahskopf, of the University of Washington.

The advisory board has established a priority of publication for a list of volumes, each to be edited by a specialist in the particular period or subject. Essays from *Select British Eloquence* by Chauncey Allen Goodrich is our first issue.

It was with good reason that our advisory board decided upon a one-volume edition of Goodrich as the first of the Landmarks series. Few books written or edited by an American have had the continued impact of *Select British*

Eloquence upon students of public address. No single volume on British orators or oratory is more frequently referred to in our classes. No single volume is more avidly or more vainly sought after in our bookstores.

The reader will observe that this edition does not contain the orations compiled by Goodrich. Of more immediate concern to the scholarly community are the essays. Consequently, this volume contains all of each essay as originally published and, in addition, a careful evaluation of Goodrich's theory and application of rhetorical criticism by a prime authority in the area of British Public Address.

Because of its historical importance Goodrich's Preface to *Select British Eloquence* is herewith reprinted in its entirety following this Foreword. The reader will observe that Goodrich's references to the size and contents pertain only to the original edition.

The editor of this edition is A. Craig Baird, Emeritus Professor of Public Address at the State University of Iowa, Distinguished Visiting Professor of Speech at Southern Illinois University, director of more than a hundred masters theses and more than forty doctoral dissertations, and author, co-author, or editor of such important contributions to the field of speech as *Public Discussion and Debate, Essays and Addresses Toward a Liberal Education, Discussion, General Speech, Essentials of General Speech, Speech Criticism, Argumentation, Discussion and Debate, American Public Address: 1740–1952,* and *Representative American Speeches.*

Drawing upon more than a half-century of research in British rhetoric and oratory, Dr. Baird has contributed a copious and carefully developed introductory essay. The resultant volume is an important example of the scholarship of Baird as well as a treasury of Goodrich.

AUTHOR'S PREFACE

MR. HUME has somewhere remarked, that "he who would teach eloquence must do it chiefly by *examples*." The author of this volume was forcibly struck with this remark in early life; and in entering on the office of Professor of Rhetoric in Yale College, more than thirty years ago, besides the ordinary instructions in that department, he took Demosthenes' Oration for the Crown as a *text-book* in the Senior class, making it the basis of a course of informal lectures on the principles of oratory. Modern eloquence came next, and he endeavored, in a distinct course, to show the leading characteristics of the great orators of our own language, and the best mode of studying them to advantage. His object in both courses was, not only to awaken in the minds of the class that love of genuine eloquence which is the surest pledge of success, but to aid them in catching the spirit of the authors read, and, by analyzing passages selected for the purpose, to initiate the pupil in those higher principles which (whether they were conscious of it or not) have always guided the great masters of the art, till he should learn the *unwritten* rules of oratory, which operate by a kind of instinct upon the mind, and are far more important than any that are found in the books.

Such is the origin of this volume, which contains the matter of the second course of lectures mentioned above, cast into another form, in connection with the speeches of the great British orators of the first and second class. A distinct volume would be necessary for American eloquence, if the lectures on that subject should ever be published.

The speeches selected are those which, by the general suffrage of the English public, are regarded as the masterpieces of their respective authors. They are in almost every instance given *entire,* because the object is to have each of them studied as a complete system of thought. Detached passages of extraordinary force and beauty may be useful as exercises in elocution; but, if dwelt upon exclusively as models of style, they are sure to vitiate the taste. It is like taking all one's nutriment from highly-seasoned food and stimulating drinks.

As to the orators chosen, Chatham, Burke, Fox, and Pitt stand, by universal consent, at the head of our eloquence, and to these Erskine may be added as the greatest of our forensic orators. Every tolerably reported speech from Lord Chatham is of interest to the student in oratory, and all that I thought such are here inserted, including eight never before published in this country. All of Burke's speeches which he prepared for the press have also found a place, except that on Economical Reform, which, relating to mere matters of English finance, has less interest for an American. In room of this, the reader will find most striking passages in his works on the French Revolution, so that this volume contains nearly every thing which most persons can have any desire to study in the pages of Mr. Burke. Six of Fox's great speeches are next given, and three of Pitt's with copious extracts from the early efforts of the latter; together with nine of Erskine's ablest arguments, being those on which his reputation mainly rests. Among the orators of the second class, the reader will find in this volume four speeches of Lord Mansfield; two of Mr. Grattan's, with his invectives against Flood and Corry; Mr. Sheridan's celebrated speech against Hastings; three of Mr. Curran's; Sir James Mackintosh's famous speech for Peltier; four of Mr. Canning's; and five of Lord Brougham's, including his instructive discourse on the study of eloquence in the Greek orators. Some of the most finished letters of Junius are given in their proper place, with remarks on his style as an admirable model of condensation, elegance, and force. In the first fifty pages will be found nearly all the celebrated speeches before the days of Lord Chatham, from Sir Robert Walpole, Lord Chesterfield, Mr. Pulteney, Lord Belhaven, Sir John Digby, the Earl of Strafford, and Sir John Eliot.

The selections in this volume extend through a period of two hundred years, and embrace a very large proportion of the most powerful eloquence of Great Britain.

The following are the aids afforded for the study of these speeches:

(1) A memoir of each orator, designed to show his early training in eloquence, the leading events of his public life, the peculiar cast of his genius, and the distinctive characteristics of his oratory. It ought to be said, in justice to the author, that these sketches were completed in every essential particular, long before the publication of Lord Brougham's work upon British Statesmen.

(2) A historical introduction to each of the speeches, explaining minutely the circumstances of the case, the state of parties, and the exact point at issue, being intended to place the reader in the midst of the scene as an actual spectator of the contest. These introductions, with the memoirs just mentioned, form a slight but continuous thread of political history, embracing the most important topics discussed in the British Parliament for more than a century.

(3) An analysis of the longer speeches in side-notes, giving the divisions and subdivisions of thought, and thus enabling the reader to perceive at once the connection and bearing of the several parts.

(4) A large body of explanatory notes, bringing out minuter facts. A few of these, on Chatham's early speeches, are from the Modern Orator, and also some definitions of law terms in two of Erskine's, pp. 637–83.

(5) Critical notes, as specimens of the kind of analysis which the author has been accustomed to apply to the several parts of an oration, and which every student in oratory should be continually making out for himself.

(6) Translations of the passages quoted from the ancient and foreign languages, with the poetry rendered into English verse. The passages are usually traced to their sources, and the train of thought given as it appears in the original, without a knowledge of which most quotations have but little force or beauty. For the same reason, the classical and other allusions are traced out and explained.

(7) A concluding statement of the way in which the ques-

tion was decided, with occasional remarks upon its merits, or the results produced by the decision.

Great compression has been used in preparing this volume, that all who are interested in the study of eloquence may be able to possess it. Each page contains the matter of three ordinary octavo pages in Pica type; and the whole work has in it one sixth more than Chapman's Select Speeches, or Willison's American Eloquence, in five octavo volumes each.

In conclusion, the author may be permitted to say, that while he has aimed to produce a volume worthy of lying at all times on the table of every one engaged in speaking or writing for the public, he has hoped it might prove peculiarly useful to men of his own profession; since nothing is more desirable, at the present day, than a larger infusion into our sacred eloquence of the freedom, boldness, and strength which distinguish our secular oratory.

September 1, 1852

CONTENTS

INTRODUCTION

By A. Craig Baird

CHAUNCEY GOODRICH'S VOLUME on British public addresses was published by Harper and Brothers in 1852, under the title *Select British Eloquence; Embracing the Best Speeches Entire, of the Most Eminent Orators of Great Britain for the Last Two Centuries; with Sketches of Their Lives, An Estimate of Their Genius, and Notes, Critical and Commentary.*[1]

Goodrich had designed this volume for Yale and other college students. Its favorable reception was immediate. S. Austin Allibone, a Goodrich contemporary, in his *Critical Dictionary of English Literature,* said of *Select British Eloquence,* "No student of history, biography, political, forensic or sacred eloquence, should be without this work." And relative to Goodrich's own statement that he might later publish a companion volume on American Eloquence, Allibone commented: "We trust the 'distinct volume' will be published, and also the author's lectures on Demosthenes' Orations for the Crown. Such contributions to the cause of public education are beyond price."[2]

The Harper publication was quickly duplicated by Sampson Low, Son, and Marston, in London, "under their own title page," announced as a "copyright edition." Several Harper reprintings were made as late as 1887. With the steadily increasing university research during the past half century in speech criticism and the history and criticism of British and American public address, the demand for the Goodrich edition has progressively increased. To help meet the demand for *Select British Eloquence,* Professor Carl Pitt, of the University of Illinois, Chicago Undergraduate Division, had printed a Microcard edition in 1956. Professor Richard Murphy provided the introduction and adapted his essay for publication during that year.[3]

Students of rhetorical theory and practice have steadily recognized the high place of Goodrich as a rhetorical critic. Murphy's judgment is that, "As a specimen of what a rhetorical critic can do in selecting speeches, and in giving them fine and discriminating analysis and appraisal, Goodrich's *Select British Eloquence* is supreme.[4] Dr. W. Norwood Brigance, in his study of the direction of research in rhetoric, stated: "I think we should recognize that critics of prose literature and biographies have failed, almost without exception, to understand this distinctive purpose, and scope of rhetorical literature. England has produced but four or five rhetorical critics who have not so failed—notably Lecky, Trevelyan, Bryce, and Morley. America, since Chauncey Allen Goodrich wrote in 1852, has produced none to my knowledge."[5] Lester Thonssen, in *Speech Criticism,* characterized Goodrich as "The Master of the nineteenth century," and observed that "no name in the history of rhetorical criticism has been more favorably received during the recent revival of interest in this field than that of Chauncey Goodrich, Professor of Rhetoric at Yale fron 1817 to 1839."[6] Dr. Donald Bryant concludes that the *Select British Eloquence* "is still the most valuable single resource book for the study of British Public Address of the eighteenth and early nineteenth centuries. So excellent is it—and so convenient—for both texts and historical-critical-biographical commentary—that many students of public address hardly go beyond it."[7]

To meet the increasing demand by students of public address for further accessibility to the Goodrich criticisms in his *Select British Eloquence,* the present volume is issued.

i

Chauncey Allen Goodrich, (1790–1860), educator, editor, lexicographer, and clergyman, of substantial New England ancestry, was born in New Haven, Connecticut. His father, Elizur Goodrich (1761–1849), a descendant of the

Goodriches who settled in Connecticut in 1643, a graduate of Yale, was a tutor there, studied law, and practiced law in his home town through the years. He was a member of Congress for one term (1799–1801), professor of Law at Yale, Secretary of the Yale corporation from 1818 to 1846, and briefly, Collector of the Port of New Haven.[8]

Chauncey Allen's grandmother was Catherine Chauncey of an old New England family that included the Boston preacher, Charles Chauncy. His mother, whose maiden name was Anne Willard Allen, also came of an early New England family, the Willards.

Chauncey entered Yale in 1806 and was graduated with "distinguished honors" in 1810, a member of Phi Beta Kappa. Chief among his teachers was President Timothy Dwight (1752–1817), stout conservative Congregationalist, who taught classes in rhetoric, logic, metaphysics, and ethics. He was generally conceded to have been a great teacher.[9] Dwight, a grandson of Jonathan Edwards, was a defender of Calvinistic determinism against metaphysical freedom of choice that to him threatened on one hand Methodism and on the other Unitarianism. Dwight was also a strong interpreter of Federalist political doctrines. Goodrich's graduation oration was on "The Influence of Novelty."

The young Yale graduate was rector of the Hopkins Grammar School in New Haven for two years. He then returned to Yale as tutor in Latin and Greek.[10]

At the suggestion of President Dwight, the young instructor in classics prepared and printed *The Elements of Greek Grammar* (1814). It both helped impecunious Goodrich and supported the teaching of classical education.[11] Later he prepared and published *Lessons in Greek Parsing* (1829) and *Lessons in Latin Parsing* (1832). The grammar went through various editions (the fourth in 1828), and *Greek Parsing* had its 29th edition in 1857.

The New Haven Association of Ministers in 1814 licensed Goodrich to preach. Resigning his tutorship, he was an itinerant minister for several months and was invited as permanent pastor at several New England churches. He accepted a call July 24, 1816, to the Middletown (Connecticut)

Congregational Church. In that year he married Julia Frances, daughter of Noah Webster. A year later, his health impaired, he resigned and accepted the first professorship of rhetoric at Yale, a position he held until 1839.

Meantime he continued his active religious leadership. He made possible in 1822 the establishment of a theological department at Yale. In 1825, to restore his health, he spent several months in Europe.[12] He purchased the *Christian Spectator* in 1828 and edited it as the *Quarterly Christian Spectator* until 1836. Through this journal, given to theological and literary discussion and criticism, he expounded the New Haven school of theology. The leader of this movement, Dr. Nathaniel Taylor, was professor of didactic theology at Yale. Taylor's doctrines were in the tradition of Jonathan Edwards with the modifications developed by President Dwight and other early nineteenth century Congregational leaders. Goodrich contributed at least fifteen articles to this magazine, in which he defended the philosophical concepts of determinism as opposed to metaphysical freedom. These polemic differences among New England churchmen led to the breach in the Presbyterian church in 1838.[13]

In 1838 Goodrich became Professor of Pastoral Charge at Yale, in which office he trained students in preaching and pastoral work. This post he retained until his death, from a cerebral hemorrhage, in 1860. He wrote and published such pamphlets as "Can I Conscientiously Vote for Henry Clay?" (New Haven, 1844), and "What Does Dr. Bushnell Mean?" (New Haven, 1849). He also spoke and wrote much in support of the temperance movement. Goodrich was "an enthusiastic and effective teacher, an active and energetic college editor, and a fervent promoter of all social reforms."[14]

T. D. Woolsey, President of Yale at the time of Goodrich's death, in his commemorative address, reviewed his career as teacher.[15] According to Woolsey, Goodrich taught the freshmen in declamation; the sophomores, in Jamieson's *Rhetoric;* the juniors, in declamations and exhibitions for public commencements. For the seniors, Goodrich, as he says in his preface, "took Demosthenes' Oration for the Crown as a textbook, making it the basis of a course of informal lectures on the principles of oratory."

The seniors also read compositions before him which he afterward criticised in private. Said President Woolsey:

> After a time, with the growth of a number of students, the business of his department became too great for any one man, and he was allowed to employ an assistant in declamation. . . .
>
> The tone and tendency of the teaching of Dr. Goodrich was not so much aesthetical as rhetorical, and this harmonized with the practical end which he had in view. His aim was to form vigorous, effective writers, men who by their eloquence should be able to move and lead their fellowmen. Eloquence, therefore, the forcible statement of arguments, occupied the front place. It will not be doubted that he did a good work for the College, and that he laid those foundations in his department on which the system pursued by his successor has been rewarded.[16]

Another of Goodrich's contributions to rhetoric was his report of the final words of Webster's peroration in the Dartmouth College case. Goodrich, who heard the final argument before the Supreme Court, 1818, stated in a letter to Rufus Choate, that a final sentence, not thus far included, should be added: "It is a small college. Yet there are those who love it." The letter containing also the bulk of Choate's eulogy of Webster was dated November 25, 1852.[17]

The work on which this Yale rhetorician spent much labor was the revision of the *Dictionary of the English Language*, compiled by his father-in-law, Dr. Noah Webster. In 1828, in co-operation with Dr. Joseph E. Worcester, and under the general supervision of Dr. Webster, Goodrich helped produce an abridged edition in octavo of the original quarto in two volumes. In 1846, Webster and Goodrich began the revision of both editions, the abridged and the unabridged. In 1847, Goodrich edited a new edition with a memoir of his father-in-law. In 1856 the University edition of the same work was published. In the 1859 revision, Goodrich added a detailed treatise on the principles of pronunciation. Kingsley commented that "the sound judgment and the exhibition of scholarly culture which he displayed did much to maintain the extensive popularity which Dr. Webster's dictionary has so long enjoyed."[18] F. B. Dexter, in his biography of Goodrich, states that "His work on Webster's Dictionary was largely original though nominally only editorial."[19]

ii

Goodrich wrote and lectured not only on the criticism of orators but embodied the theory of public address in his lectures at Yale. During the century after Goodrich's death, his notes on his lectures were assumed to be either nonexistent or lost. John Hoshor's search for these lectures led to their discovery in a Pasadena, California, attic, and to their deposit in the Yale Library. Hoshor partly reprinted them in the *Speech Monographs* and used them as the basis of his doctorate, completing the degree in 1947.[20]

Goodrich's most permanent contribution to American education was his *Select British Eloquence*. In this work, Goodrich applies his theory of oratory to the criticism of twenty important figures of British parliamentary and forensic address. His teaching philosophy underlying these criticisms he explains in the preface as based on his experience at Yale:

> My object was not only to awaken in the minds of the class that love of genuine eloquence which is the surest pledge of success, but to aid them in catching the spirit of the authors read, and, by analyzing passages selected for the purpose, to initiate the pupil in those higher principles which (whether they were conscious of it or not) have always guided the great masters of the art, till he should learn the *unwritten* rules of oratory, which operate by a kind of instinct upon the mind, and are far more important than any that are found in the books.

The speeches selected are those which, "by the general suffrage of the English public are regarded as the master-pieces of their respective authors."

With an eye to the instructional use of his text, he provides a brief biography of each orator, "designed to show his early training in eloquence, the leading events of his public life, the peculiar case of his genius, and the distinctive characteristics of his oratory." He also explains in an introduction to each speech the immediate situation and issues at stake. The longer speeches he also accompanies with side notes to indicate divisions and subdivisions of the thought; a considerable body of explanatory notes and critical comments, "specimens of the kind of analyses which the author has been accustomed to apply to the several parts of an oration"; the tracing of passages "usually to their sources"; the translation of quotations from ancient or other foreign languages; and a statement concerning the immediate and larger outcomes of the oration. The summaries of each speaker under the general "Contents" also list the topics to be treated in detail.

Goodrich's orators include Sir John Eliot, Earl of Strafford, Lord Digby, Lord Belhaven, Sir Robert Walpole, William Pulteney, Lord Chesterfield, Lord Chatham, Lord Mansfield, Junius, Edmund Burke, Henry Grattan, Richard Brinsley Sheridan, Charles James Fox, William Pitt, Lord Erskine, John Philpot Curran, Sir James Mackintosh, George Canning, and Lord Brougham.

The range covers two hundred years from Eliot (1592–1632) to Brougham (1778–1868), the last named still alive when Goodrich wrote. Of almost one thousand pages composing the book, only the first fifty deal with the century or more before Walpole and Chatham. The final one hundred pages treat Canning and Brougham. Thus four-fifths of the collection concentrate on the parliamentary speakers of the later eighteenth century. The orators given most space and detailed criticism are Chatham, Burke, Pitt, and Erskine. Goodrich is obviously more interested in speakers of his own times than in the Elizabethans or Tudors. Although some like Erskine were forensic leaders, all were also parliamentary orators.

Goodrich entered Yale (1806), the year of the deaths of Pitt and Fox. Sheridan died (1816) six years after Goodrich's graduation; John Philip Curran, in 1817; Henry Grattan, in 1820; Erskine, in 1823; Canning, in 1827; and Mackintosh, in 1832. Eleven of the twenty lived during Goodrich's life. Since Goodrich was still assembling his volume after 1845, he was no doubt well acquainted with important speakers of the early Victorian period other than Canning and Brougham. Other active Goodrich contemporaries not included were Lord Macaulay (whose essays Goodrich quotes), Robert Peel, Richard Cobden, Benjamin Disraeli, and Daniel O'Connell. Earlier parliamentary speakers excluded were Francis Bacon, William Wilberforce, and such controversial personalities as John Wilkes.

The volume might well have been entitled *Select British Parliamentary Eloquence*. Goodrich passed by, for example, such preachers as Jeremy Taylor, John Donne, John Wesley, and George Whitefield. He may have felt that the Yale undergraduates, for whom the compilation was assembled, would be primarily interested in these political figures, or that a larger volume would be impracticable. Practically all addresses were delivered in parliamentary or courtroom situations. A particular exception was Lord Brougham's "Inaugural Discourse."

iii

Goodrich, as critic, applied a philosophy and method of criticism almost unique among his contemporaries. He was relatively thorough, systematic, and comprehensive in his evaluation of individual speakers and of the group. His principles and standards of judgment were heavily classical. He knew intimately Aristotle, Cicero, Quintilian, and their fellows, as well as Demosthenes and other great orators. He was familiar with ancient literature of these nations. He knew also earlier and later philosophy, literature, and other areas of the humanities.

How well equipped was Goodrich in his Yale training for his role as critic? The Yale curriculum of 1800–1810, derivative like those of Harvard, Oxford, and Cambridge, was still largely humanistic, with some modifications after the Revolution to adjust to practical and professional trends. Its curriculum still stemmed from the seven liberal arts. The courses, required for the most part, included history of civil society, rhetoric, mathematics, logic, natural philosophy, ethics, theology and metaphysics, Latin, Greek, geography, and anatomy. President Dwight taught several of those subjects. Professor Benjamin Silliman led in the beginnings of science. The Linonian Society, Phi Beta Kappa, and Brothers in Unity flourished to stimulate forensic discussion and debate, oratory, and essays.[21]

Goodrich then was disciplined in ancient and English languages; ancient, medieval and later history; in the history and issues of the young American Republic; in the eighteenth century literature (e.g., Johnson, Addison, Swift); in ancient and British philosophy (e.g., Locke, Hume); in the elocutionary movement (e.g., Sheridan, Walker); in contemporary rhetoric (e.g., Campbell, Blair); in current psychology (the Scotch school of "Common Sense"). As an advanced student of theology, as tutor in Greek and other subjects, as occasional preacher, the Yale rhetorician knew well the art of communication and the theories of speech criticism.

Goodrich's scope of treatment is comprehensive. He keeps clearly before his readers the historical background and immediate social forces influencing the speaker; the audience and its reflection of the age and reaction to the speaker; the factors in the training and development of the speaker that partly explain the character of his later public discourses; the specific traits of his thought, forms of support, organization, language, and oral adjustments to the Parliamentary or other audience. His philosophical approach to the communicative case study and his interpretation of the interplay of speaker, occasion, audience, speech, and the communicative process itself have set off this critic as an outstanding guide for the twentieth century students of speech and speech criticism.

Goodrich's position as critic proceeds from his concept of communication as both spoken and written. He is obviously under the influence of the later eighteenth and early nineteenth century European and British literature as academic studies. This belles lettres movement of Kames and Blair meant also increased attention to literary and rhetorical criticism. Goodrich, like Aristotle, Bacon, and especially Blair whose text was used at Yale, assumes that all persuasive communication has oral qualities whether or not the document is delivered. To this American critic, British "eloquence" included the letters of Junius, excerpts of *Burke's Reflections on the French Revolution,* and Sir James Mackintosh's essay on the *Character of Charles J. Fox.* States Goodrich of Junius (see pp. 79–80 of this volume): "The letters of Junius have taken a permanent place in the eloquence of our language. Though often false in statement and malignant in spirit, they will never cease to be read as specimens of powerful composition; for the union of brilliance and force, there is nothing superior to them in our literature. Nor is it for his style alone that Junius deserves to be studied. He shows great rhetorical skill in his mode of developing a subject." Goodrich calls Junius an "orator." "It is, therefore, only as an orator—for such he undoubtedly was in public life and such he truly is in these letters—that we are now to consider him."

Goodrich then proceeds to analyze every trait of Junius as a communicator except that of voice and bodily action. With less justification he includes Burke's *Reflections.* This document Goodrich treats primarily as a literary composition. "In a literary view there can be but one opinion of this work. Though desultory in its character, and sometimes careless or prolix in style, it contains more richness of thought, splendor of imagination and beauty of diction than any volume of the same size in our language." Goodrich here, as a literary critic, is matching this extended essay with the best of Carlyle, Arnold, and Milton.

To Goodrich rhetoric is synonymous with public speaking, the end of which was to "address just and pertinent remarks on the subject under contemplation." The aim is not that of eloquence designed to enhance the speaker's prestige. Genius is not necessary, but rather "sound sense, knowledge, clear arrangement, a satisfactory style, and vivacity." Persuasive public speaking is that in which oratory (eloquence) holds sway. To Goodrich it is "The power of rapidly impressing on others the strong emotions which agitate our minds with a view to convince or persuade." Oratory is not to please but "to overpower and direct the soul—to enforce truth—direct to duty."[22]

The highest qualities of eloquence Goodrich summarizes

in his comment (pp. 11–12) on the Earl of Strafford's speech at the conclusion of his trial for treason, April 13, 1641:

> There is in it a union of dignity, simplicity and force—felicity in the selection of topics—a dexterity of appeal to the interests and feelings of his judges—a justness and elevation in every sentiment he utters—a vividness of illustration in every sentiment he utters, a freshness of imagery, an elasticity of and airiness of diction—an appearance of perfect sincerity, and a pervading depth of passion breaking forth at times in a passage of startling power or tenderness, which we find only in the highest class of oratory.

As Goodrich differentiates public speaking and oratory, so does he mark off the debater from the orator.

> The English distinguish between an Orator and a Debater. Promptitude of thought, sagacity in discerning the weak and strong points of our antagonist's cause, dexterity in evading difficulties, quickness in anticipating objections, and sturdiness in refuting them, the power of retort—these are the qualities of a debater.
>
> The adaptation of his matter to the temper of his audience is one of the great arts of a public speaker. Readiness in applying general principles to particular occasions, copiousness and felicity in illustration, earnestness in enforcing, vehemence in refuting, plainness of language without vulgarity and grandeur without bombast are the constituents of the orator. Also in this respect should be mentioned unclouded perspicuity of statement, undisturbed regularity of reasoning, correctness, fertility, and originality of conception.[23]

Goodrich regards the function of the critic chiefly that of estimating the methods that the speaker followed in adapting his ideas and methods to a particular audience and occasion, and of judging the extent to which the results of the speech could be assigned to such methods. For him, as for present-day rhetorical critics, the speech is a configuration of the factors of speaker, occasion, audience, and speech with the voice or bodily activity as transmission agents. His proposed plan of analysis and criticism, as outlined, contains seven steps. The first deals with the speaker; the second, chiefly with the occasion; the third, fourth, fifth, and sixth, with the speech; and the seventh, with the audience. Goodrich's methodology embodies the focussing on each of these aspects, enlarging on the one or more that chiefly mark the given speaker in action. At every point he assumes that the process is a unitary one of communication.

He refuses to categorize his critical judgments into Ramean dichotomies or into the more conventional subdivisions that reflect a rigid, critical mold. He would fix upon ideas or delivery or other traits. Sometimes he fuses them into a unified impression; at others, he stresses the major clue to the speaker's effectiveness; but always he indicates the relation of a given trait to the over-all communicative process.

Thus the Goodrich perspective centers in the speaker's ideas, his forms of support (emotional, imaginative appeals), his personality as a persuasive factor, his language, speech structure, and delivery. These divisions, however, are in no sense discrete employments, but rather aspects of the total oral activity under examination.

iv

Goodrich constantly concerns himself with the problems of textual authenticity. Despite Karl Wallace's comment that Goodrich rarely tells us what his texts represent (Wallace is referring only to the Tudor-Stuart period),[24] Goodrich, in most instances, discusses the sources of the speech. He reprints the entire text, "because [as he states in the preface] the object is to have each of them studied as a complete system of thought. Detached passages of extraordinary force and beauty may be useful as exercises in elocution; but if dwelt upon exclusively as models of style, they are sure to vitiate the taste. It is like taking all one's nutriment from highly seasoned food and stimulating drinks."

He well recognizes that the most important speeches of the eighteenth century and earlier were often inaccurate, incomplete, and sometimes misleading. He usually follows the texts found in *Parliamentary History;* for example, those of Eliot, Strafford, Digby, Belhaven, Walpole, but recognizes that prior to the later Lord Chatham days, "reporters of that day made little or no attempt to give the exact words of a speaker. They sought only to convey his sentiments, though they might occasionally be led, in writing out his speeches, to catch some of his marked peculiarities of thought or expression." (p. 67) Reporters, as Loren Reid reminds us, were not given space in the House of Commons until 1834. Before that time they were often ejected. Reid analyzes the uncomfortable conditions for accurate reporting in the eighteenth century House of Commons.[25]

Of the speech by the Earl of Strafford when impeached for high treason, April 13, 1641, Goodrich reports, "There are in *Parliamentary History* two reports of this speech, one by Whitelocke and the other by some unknown friend of Strafford. . . . They are here combined by a slight modification of language."[26] Of Lord Belhaven's speech, November 2, 1706, against legislative union of England and Scotland, Goodrich states "It is obviously reported in a very imperfect manner" (p. 18).

Although Samuel Johnson reported various speeches as allegedly uttered in the House of Commons, the great lexicographer apparently did not attend the sessions. Goodrich notes the case of Johnson and the reporting of the speeches of Lord Chesterfield. States Goodrich: "Lord Chesterfield made two speeches on this subject [granting licenses to gin shops] . . . It has been hastily inferred, from a conversation reported by Boswell, that these speeches, as here given, were written by Johnson. Subsequent inquiry, however, seems to prove that this was not the fact; but the contrary, that Lord Chesterfield prepared them for publication himself." (p. 29)

Goodrich in turn notes the varying degrees of accuracy of the important speeches under his analysis. Chatham's speeches were sometimes quite poorly reported; one at least was revised by Chatham himself. Burke's debates were more authentic in that he left six speeches written by himself. Thus this American critic looks at the speech texts of most of the other speakers, including Sheridan, Grattan, Fox, Mackintosh, and Mansfield, to suggest the extent to which what is reprinted represents what was actually said.[27] Goodrich apparently accepts a revision by the author as proper stamp of textual accuracy. At any rate, the New Haven editor-critic regards a text approved by the speaker as preferable to a garbled, unauthorized version.

He thus recognizes at every turn the critic's obligation to deal with the authenticity of the texts—to determine the best possible text by such investigative methods as may be open. He is interested in working from a copy as faithful to the original as possible. He does not always cite the source of his document, but does reveal an awareness of the problems of textual accuracy. In any case, he frankly indicates here and there the limitations of his critical methods as related to the handling of these written speeches.[28]

v

What type of judgment did Goodrich make as critic? What measures of effectiveness? One of these judgments is historical; a second, logical; a third, philosophical; a fourth, ethical; and a fifth, rhetorical.[29]

Goodrich as a historian concentrates on the social setting, the speaker's background, and rhetorical training. To Goodrich the speakers selected are outstanding in their impress on their day. They do not often succeed in House of Commons votes or even invariably in the judicial decisions following their pleas, but their larger influence is implied and here and there directly stated. Fox, for example, Goodrich rates as the "world's greatest debater" and certainly so in his contribution to the evolution of British democracy and stability—even though the votes were usually against his party and his individual argument. Goodrich is in the rhetorical tradition of Aristotle, Cicero, Quintilian, and the later rhetoricians who pronounce the influence of the orator as decisive in public affairs.[30]

As a historian, Goodrich selects the facts and trends that bear most directly on the speaker-speech-audience-occasion activity. He cites now and then from the contemporary historians and biographers on whom he chiefly relies. These include Macaulay, the historian and essayist; Wraxall, with his *Historical Memoirs;* the *Annual Register;* Howell's *State Trials;* Thomas Moore, with his *Memoirs of Sheridan;* Lord John Campbell, *Lives of the Lord Chancellors;* Lord Brougham and his comments on Athenian and later orators; and a considerable list of other contemporary authorities.

Like some other historians, Goodrich is politically and socially biased. He is often limited in his source materials. He is a strong New Englander, while he is also a moral and religious American, a Victorian, a congregationalist. He believes in Yale and preaches it. These attitudes of Goodrich's explain his interpretation of events and the personal politics of the speakers. He defends at length Burke's position on the French Revolution. Here Goodrich sounds more like a good Tory than a nineteenth century Whig philosopher.

His treatment of the election of 1784, as Lloyd Watkins reminds us,[31] is to glorify the personal leadership of Young Pitt throughout the nation. Goodrich oversimplifies the factors at work. Historians have long recognized that the King's Friends, the powerful Placemen and other supporters, turned the tide much more than popular clamor.

Despite these limitations of Goodrich's historical methodology, he has come out well. The many facts of the thousand pages and the historical factors and movements still stand even though his interpretations often call for considerable correction, in view of the later data and perspectives. The biases of Goodrich as historian are those of Carlyle, Macaulay, Gibbon, and the other British historians of that era.

Goodrich's chief validity in his historical treatment of oratory lies in the completeness of his overview of British eloquence. In this work he was more systematic and comprehensive than almost any other writer who dealt with a period of public discourse.

Cicero in his *Brutus* also contributed significantly in his critical and historical perspective of Greek and Roman oratory. Richard Jebb, in his *Attic Orators,* produced a highly readable, accurate, and mature analysis of Attic orators before Demosthenes. But in the history of rhetorical criticism, equivalents of the Goodrich edition with its combination of texts and detailed evaluations are few and fragmentary. The histories and appraisals of American public address before 1900 suffer from such sketchy and surface treatment. Works of limited historicity include William Matthews' *American Eloquence,* E. L. Magoon's *Living Orators in America,* Henry Hardwicke's *History of Oratory and Orators,* and Lorenzo Sears' *History of Oratory.*[32]

John Morley in his *Life of Richard Cobden* and George M. Trevelyan in his *Life of William Ewart Gladstone* and his *Life of John Bright* have reinforced sound biographical treatment with penetrating rhetorical analysis. But no British critic of the nineteenth century or later has produced the over-all view of British Public Address of 1750–1800 as effectively as was done in the Goodrich collection.

Typical of the Yale critic's historical technique was his development of a "memoir" of each orator. These were uneven in length. The author made no pretense at biographical completeness. Some were brief and perfunctory, explained either by lack of source data or by the critic's lack of interest in the immediate speaker. Some accounts were here and there eulogistic. All were governed by the rhetorician's conviction that important speakers were moulders of history. The best of these writings—those on Burke, Fox, Chatham, Pitt the Younger—were controlled by valid historical-biographical methodology.

The facts and influences were selected to highlight each as a public speaker. The items chosen were to explain the formative speaking methods and developments. The public career centered in the speaking record of the man. Goodrich minimizes details, economic, domestic, social, that contribute little to the speaker's public personality and platform methods.

The factors of early life included family influence, formal education, reading, writing, speaking, travel, early associates, listening to speakers, and analysis of the speaker's personality traits. Chatham, for example, was the product of a family "of high respectability." He was a superior student at Eton, a lover of the classics, a scholar at Oxford where he experienced a "severe course in rhetorical training" with vigorous exercises in "elocution," a traveler on the Continent. Burke, Fox, and Pitt the Younger were similarly analyzed. Goodrich's assumption is that superiority on the platform would refer not only to natural abilities but to (a) strong family background, (b) early and later familiarity with Greek and Latin language and literature, (c) wide reading in later history, philosophy, and literature, (d) ample training in essay writing and translating, (e) early experience in debate, discussion, extempore speaking, and occasional theatricals, (f) and attendance at parliament or elsewhere to study speakers in action.

Some biographies, as I suggested above, were brief and perfunctory. The "memoirs" of Sheridan's early life, for example, threw little light on his later practices. Thomas Sheridan, the father, is mentioned—but without evidence that this teacher of elocution had direct influence on the son's training. Some four sentences dispose of Richard Sheridan's career before his advent as a dramatist.

Burke, by contrast, receives much more space and analysis. Edmund's early training at Ballitore under Abraham Shakleton is cited; his six years at Trinity College; and his studies at Middle Temple. Details of Burke's readings are included to show his philosophical bent and his mastery of composition.

Goodrich systematically breaks the public career of his orators into logical periods and interprets in each phase the major political, military, and other events that call forth the speaker's eloquence. But Goodrich also implies that often the orator initiates or directs the evolving "forces of history."

How does Goodrich fare in the light of later historical and rhetorical scholarship? The research in twentieth century American universities in public address and the social, political and other historical investigations of the past one hundred years have obviously provided a flood of new materials and new insights to modify Goodrich. His essays are dated, but they are by no means factually misleading.

Inevitably the gaps in his facts and conclusions need much completion and revision—as is true of every older historian.[33] Goodrich's *Burke* illustrates the need for enrichment from later studies. A. P. Samuels in his study of Burke's early life and correspondence adds much to our knowledge of the Trinity College Curriculum of 1740, the procedures of the Historical Club, the early Burke essays, and his correspondence of early student years.[34]

What other later contributions are suggested? The list includes John Morley's *Burke;* Thomas Copeland's *The Correspondence of Edmund Burke,* in eight volumes (1958–59); Carl B. Cone's *Burke and the Nature of Politics* (1957); and such researches as those by Donald Bryant, American authority on Burke as a parliamentary speaker.[35]

Goodrich traced Fox in detail from his unbridled childhood to his dramatic last days and his vain attempt to promote peace with Napoleon. Like Burke, Fox had various later biographers, commentators, editors, and research students of rhetoric and public address. Among these contributors have been the Countess of Ilchester and Lord Stavirdale's *Life and Letters of Lady Sarah Lennox,* 1745–1826 (London, 1901) 2 vols.; John Drinkwater's *Charles James Fox* (New York, 1928); Christopher Hobhouse, *Charles James Fox* (London, 1934); William Lecky's, *A History of England in the Eighteenth Century,* new edition (New York, 1892–93); Lord John Russell's *Life and Times of Charles James Fox* (London, 1859–66) 3 vols.; and George Otto Trevelyan's *Early History of Charles James Fox,* 3d edition (London, 1881). Loren Reid has contributed highly important research on "The Education of Charles James Fox"[36] and "The Public Speaking Career of Charles James Fox."[37]

For new resources on the orators included in the Goodrich edition, Karl Wallace, in his review of "Tudor-Stuart speakers," cites a considerable list of modern biographers and students of parliamentary audience of that period; analyzes the weakness of Goodrich in his use of texts ("Goodrich rarely tells us what his text represents"); and states that, "As for knowledge of Tudor-Stuart audiences, of their attitudes and beliefs, a modern critic encounters such wealth as would have amazed Goodrich."[38]

Wallace's analysis concerning the first fifty pages of Goodrich is sound. The Yale rhetorician, it is true, hurried over this earlier century to concentrate on the second half of the eighteenth century—about which he knew much more. He was, moreover, proportioning his materials and emphasis to the interests of the Yale students of 1818 and later.

Other commentators have indicated the shortcomings of Goodrich in handling his materials, and have cited the more recent studies that would supercede or strengthen this work. Jerome Landfield, author of a dissertation on Sheridan (unpublished, University of Missouri, 1958), lists many recent post-Goodrich works on Richard Brinsley Sheridan as a speaker and concludes, "when we have a biography that evaluates all sources, accounts for contradictions, and penetrates the surface of the man, together with historical research that assess his political career, we can then clearly evaluate Sheridan as a speaker. Until that time we will continue to need qualified Goodrich."[39]

Similarly Lloyd I. Watkins, author of a dissertation on Lord Brougham (unpublished, University of Wisconsin, 1954), notes the more recent researches and writings on William Pitt. Merrill T. Baker, contributor of a dissertation, "a rhetorical analysis of Thomas Erskine's courtroom defenses involving seditious libel" (unpublished State University of Iowa, 1952), comments on later Erskine materials. Carroll Arnold analyzes "Goodrich Revisited."[40] Concludes Arnold, "Goodrich used the histories and psychologies of his time. We have our own and we think they are nearer the truth than his. Goodrich did not write definitive history or biography. He did not pretend to do so. . . ."

vi

What were Goodrich's logical judgments as critic? Consistent with Campbell, Blair, whom he quotes, and Whately (the texts of all three were used at Yale), Goodrich regards reason as all important in effective rhetoric. States he, "A powerful understanding appealing to the sense of truth is the chief instrument to be relied on. The rest should be subsidiary to this. It is then to the understanding of men that eloquence should be chiefly addressed."[41]

Thus this Yale critic analyzes Burke as superior in communication by reason of his "intellectual independence." "In the structure of his mind he had a strong resemblance to Bacon, nor was he greatly inferior in the leading attributes of his intellect." He had "remarkable comprehensiveness." He had "amplitude of mind" and "subtlety of intellect." Among the most active principles of his reasoning were "the association of resemblance," and use of "cause and effect."

Another characteristic of Burke's mind was his "remarkable power of generalization." These intellectual traits he continually exemplified in his debates. He was "a philosopher in action." (pp. 153, 154) States Goodrich: "In his *reasonings* (for he was one of the greatest masters of reason in our language, though some have strangely thought him deficient in this respect) Mr. Burke did not usually adopt the outward forms of logic. He has left us, indeed, some beautiful specimens of dialectical ability, but his arguments, in most instances, consisted of the amplest enumeration and the clearest display of all the facts and principles, the analogies, relations, or tendencies which were applicable to the case, and were adapted to settle it on the immutable basis of the nature and constitution of things." (p. 155) Thus the case to support Burke's intellectual processes is complete.

Goodrich looks upon the author of the Junius letters as an "orator," because of his argumentative robustness. "His mind, in early life, had clearly been subjected to the severest logical training." His composition was the creation of a system of thought, in which "everything is made subordinate to a just order and sequence of ideas. His reasonings often take the form of a syllogism, though usually with the omission of one of the terms; and we never find him betrayed into that careless diffusion of style so common with those who are ignorant of the principles of logic." Goodrich urges the study of Junius as a means of entering into the "Logic of Thought."

Similarly Goodrich singles out as basic the power of Mansfield's reasoning. What of Fox? "Reasoning was his forte and his passion." Pitt the Younger dominated Parliament by the force of his "logic and argument," derived partly from his close study of Aristotle's Logic.

Goodrich in his criticism shows his familiarity with the typical forms of argumentative reasoning—deductive, syllogistic, cause to effect, sign, analogy, example, and fallacies. In his Yale lectures, according to Hoshor, Goodrich lists at least fifteen specific rules for the speaker in refutation. "Each of these rules is carefully illustrated in his critical comments on the British orators."[42]

Even though Goodrich sharply discriminates between the components of the logical system, Aristotelian and later, he avoids the critical trend to dichotomize conviction and persuasion and the disposition of some later Ramists to view the parts as discrete. Goodrich illustrates his own method in his comment on Chatham's speaking (pp. 64–65):

> Thirdly, his mode of reasoning, or, rather, of dispensing with the forms of argument, resulted from the same cause. It is not the fact, though sometimes said, that Lord Chatham never reasoned. In most of his early speeches, and in some of his later ones, especially those on the right of taxing America, we find many examples of argument; brief, indeed, but remarkably clear and stringent. It is true, however, that he endeavored, as far as possible, to escape from the trammels of formal reasoning. When the mind is all a-glow with a subject, and sees its conclusions with the vividness and certainty of intuitive truths, it is impatient of the slow process of logical deduction. It seeks rather to reach the point by a bold and rapid progress, throwing away the intermediate steps, and putting the subject *at once* under such aspects and relations, as to carry its own evidence along with it. . . . It was so with Lord Chatham. The strength of his feelings bore him directly forward to the *results* of argument. He affirmed them earnestly, positively; not as mere assertions, but on the ground of their intrinsic evidence and certainty.

vii

Chauncey Goodrich approaches criticism not only as historian and logician, but as a philosopher-rhetorician. He looks at Edmund Burke's rhetorical training and decides that this English debater had a "philosophical cast of mind and should be evaluated accordingly." Says Goodrich, "Such were his habits of thought to which his [Burke's] mind was tending in his college days, and they made him pre-eminently the great Philosophical Orator of our language." (p. 97)

Each detail of Burke's ideas, logic, language, and delivery, Goodrich related to these philosophical overtones. Goodrich identified Burke's philosophical attributes with the comprehensiveness of this orator's treatment. Goodrich himself as critic had somewhat the outlook he attributed to Burke: "He looked upon a subject like a man standing on an eminence, taking a large and rounded view of it on every side, contemplating each of its parts under a vast variety of relations, and these relations often extremely complex or remote. There was no subject on which he had not read, no system relating to the interests of man as a social being which he had not thoroughly explored." (p. 152)

Goodrich's enthusiasm is here almost unrestrained as he interprets Burke's philosophical habits; including his method of penetrating into causes and results.

For both Burke and Goodrich the universe had order and consistency of explanation. Burke's role as historian, logician, psychologist, and speaker all moved him to trace these causitive activities. Burke continually asked, "Why?" "Whence?" and "By what means?" In his thinking and modes of public speaking, he attempted to answer these questions in respect to man "in all his multiple relations as the creature of society, to trace out the workings of political institutions, to establish the principles of wise legislation, to lay open the sources of national security and advancement." (p. 153)

Equally significant in Burke as philosophical speaker and Goodrich as a critic with philosophical discernment was Burke's power of generalization. Burke, as communicator, was able to "gather all the results of his thinking . . . around appropriate centers, and knowing that truths are valuable just in proportion as they have a wider reach, to rise from particulars to generals, and so to shape his statements as to give them the weight and authority of universal propositions." (pp. 153–54) This ability to reason from the simple to the complex, from the concrete to the abstract, through alternate inductive and deductive steps, marked both the superior speaker and the more capable critic. Such investigator applies a standard of epistemological and ontological ends.

Goodrich no doubt overplayed the philosophical genius of Burke as the latter lectured, debated, and persuaded. But much in Burke, as the American critic pointed out, would support such analysis. The speech on American taxation, as Goodrich illustrates it, proceeds first on the narrow ground of direct rebuttal concerning repeal and then moves to the wider historical ground. As Goodrich observes, "It would be harder to find any oration, ancient or modern, in which the matter is more admirably arranged."[43]

Concludes Goodrich, after his reflections on the details of Burke's methodology in the various speeches: "Without paradox, since oratory is only one branch of the quality we are now considering, that while Mr. Burke was inferior as an orator to Lord Chatham and Mr. Fox, he has been surpassed by no one in the richness and splendor of his eloquence." (pp. 156–57)

In reverse fashion Goodrich views from this same perspective Charles James Fox and finds him wanting. Fox, according to the Yale rhetorician, was "all English, plain, practical, of prodigious force. Facts were the staple of his thoughts. . . . He took everything in the concrete. If he discussed principles, it was always in direct connection with the subject before him. Usually, however, he did not even discuss a subject—he grappled with an antagonist." In other words, Fox communicated not as a philosopher, but as a debater.

viii

Goodrich's critical outlook and method involves a moral judgment. His philosophical analysis is closely identified with his estimate of these British speakers as revealed in their moral character as communicators. Like Aristotle and later rhetoricians, Goodrich sets great store by the personality of the orator, both his general reputation and his handling of his proofs in the speech itself. Goodrich, like Aristotle, expected intellectual integrity, social sensitivity, and good will, and especially virtue as revealed in the speaker's wisdom, moral and spiritual courage and commitment.

Out of his own background this Yale rhetorician weighs the British speakers by moral and religious standards of his New England inheritance. Robert Walpole, according to Goodrich, had great force and penetration of intellect; clear judgment, and knowledge of human nature. But he also had perfectly "unscrupled freedom" in the adoption of every means that seemed necessary to accomplish his designs." Despite his high abilities as an orator, he failed as speaker and leader. As Goodrich puts it, "He was the minister of the Present, not of the Future." (p. 23)

Lord Chatham, by contrast, was a powerful speaker, chiefly because of his moral stature. "Eloquent as he was," said Goodrich, "he impressed every hearer with the conviction that there was in him something higher than all eloquence."

Edmund Burke, too, comes in for high praise by Goodrich for this Irish orator's moral integrity. His source of effectiveness lay not in his ideas, delivery, language, or even his logical soundness, but in his moral and religious vigor. He was a man of principles; "of high moral sentiment and strong sense of religion." Goodrich concluded that "while Mr. Burke was inferior as an orator to Lord Chatham and Mr. Fox, . . . he has left us something greater and better than all eloquence in his countless lessons in moral and civil wisdom." (p. 157)

Sheridan, Goodrich concedes, was a tremendous orator in his denunciation of Warren Hastings in the speeches of 1787 and 1788. But Sheridan, as Goodrich repeatedly reminds his readers, had "massive, habitual indolence and continual rounds of conviviality." He always lived beyond his means, betrayed by his habits into "gross intemperance." Goodrich gives specific references to these derelictions, and concludes, "He died on the 7th of July, 1816, at the age of sixty-four, a melancholy example of brilliant talents sacrificed to a love of display and convivial indulgence." Sheridan, we conclude from Goodrich, lived too loosely to ascend the oratorical heights. Less Puritanical critics, like Macaulay, would give Sheridan a higher rating despite these moral lapses.

Fox, too, comes under Goodrich's condemnation. Goodrich generously assigns to Fox a position as the world's greatest debater. This critic, nevertheless, would have rated Charles James Fox among the elect with the Pitts and Burke had Charles avoided the loose life of London. His rise as parliamentary speaker and leader, Goodrich concedes, occurred despite the "irregularities of his private life." Goodrich lingers over the Fox-North coalition as a blot on the character of the great man. He was guilty of "laxity of principle." Then, too, his early advocacy of the French Revolution was a mark against his moral rectitude, "a great misfortune of his subsequent life." Gradually, however, he had "outworn his vices." Concluded Goodrich of Fox: "The life of Mr. Fox has this lesson for young men, that early habits of recklessness and vice can hardly fail to destroy the influence of the most splendid abilities and the most humane and generous dispositions. Through thirty-eight years in public life, he was in office only eighteen months." (p. 218)

Pitt the Younger, like his father, elicits Goodrich's moral praise. Pitt is superior to Fox or Sheridan through his moral and religious stability. The Yale critic, after detailed review of the chief speeches and speaking occasions of the younger Pitt, sums up Pitt by quoting George Canning: "Unallured by dissipation, and unswayed by pleasure, he never sacrificed the national treasure to the one, or the national interest to the other. To his unswerving integrity the most authentic of all testimony is to be found in that unbounded public confidence which followed him throughout the whole of his political career. . . . His talents, superior and splendid as they were, never made him forgetful of that Eternal Wisdom from which they emanated."

Goodrich in the last analysis assesses each orator by his moral and religious personality. Some, although great speakers, were morally sterile. Consistent with classical rhetorical principles of "ethics," Goodrich remoulds that concept to include his New England congregationalism. His persistence at this point is almost a blind spot in his otherwise high critical competency.

ix

Goodrich's historical, logical, philosophical, and ethical approaches are incorporated in his rhetorical judgment and evaluation. His criticism is based upon his appreciation of the power of public address; his concept of its aims and techniques; his understanding of the contributions of ancient, medieval and modern theorists to its development; his familiarity with the methods of its historical critics; his insight into the standards of oral discourse style and delivery; and his judgment concerning effectiveness. Goodrich obviously falls short of the ideal critic. However, more than most of his American and English predecessors or contemporaries, he possesses a desirable judgment of excellence in public address in its historical milieu.

In full accord with the rhetoricians since Aristotle, he views the elements or parts of rhetoric as comprising invention, with its divisions of logical, pathetic and ethical "proofs"; disposition, or structure; style or language; and delivery.

Goodrich's interest in logical approach, as I indicated above, leads him at every turn to rate high the speaker's thoughts and supports in fact and inference—the element of conviction, but conviction as incorporating feeling and imagination. According to Goodrich in his essay on Lord Chatham, "The leading characteristic of eloquence is force; and force in the orator depends on the action of strongly excited feeling on a powerful intellect."

(a) Emotion. The key to eloquence as Goodrich views it lies in deep emotion by which the basic reasoning and thought can be transferred to the audience. Such emotion, as he suggests, is to be accompanied or initiated by imagination, vivid pictures presented to the listeners, or by summoning for them a "sense of sublimity," or by awakening the gentler feelings of pathos, or by a strong appeal to "the sense of truth."[44]

Goodrich comments on the emotional power of John Philpot Curran, the great Irish orator, which "lay in the variety and strength of his emotions. . . . He turned the courtroom into . . . a place of tears, by a tenderness and pathos which subdued every heart; he poured out in invective like a stream of lava, and inflamed the minds of his countrymen almost to madness by the recital of their wrongs."

The faults of Curran, Goodrich adds, arose from the same source as those excellencies. They were the faults of "excess; intense expressions, strained imagery, overwrought passion." Goodrich recognizes that in Ireland Curran spoke for and to the people. "The power he sought was over the Irish mind." Thus Goodrich seems to condone this emotional exuberance as it applies to this Irish audience. (p. 293)

Henry Grattan, another Irishman of great power, was also overexcited by emotionalism. "His forte was reasoning, but it was 'logic on fire.' . . . He wanted that calmness and self possession which mark the highest order of minds . . . When he mastered his subject, his subject mastered him. His great efforts have too much the air of harangues." (pp. 163–64)

Goodrich thus warns against such excesses and cites Erskine as highly effective in the courtroom through his control of passion. The advocate "took care to impress his hearers in his most impassioned passages, with the feeling that all he said was in the exercise of severest judgment—that he was never borne away by mere emotion in his most fervent appeals. This gave great weight to his more glowing passages."[45]

In Chatham, Goodrich finds the most complete combination of high intellect and motivational expression. "But his intellect never acted alone. All the operations of his mind were pervaded and governed by intense feeling. . . . All went together, conviction and persuasion, intellect and feeling, like chain-shot."

(b) Disposition. What of Goodrich's criticism of disposition? It is based on the Ciceronian concepts as partly expounded in the Yale lectures, and as continually applied in his analysis of the British speakers. Blair's lectures on *Rhetoric and Belles Lettres* were used by Goodrich in his senior classes. Blair and Goodrich saw eye to eye concerning the principles of speech organization.[46]

Goodrich, for example, commends Junius for the clear organization of his letter of January 21, 1769. The letter develops an exordium, a transition, a proposition, proof, and recapitulation. Concludes Goodrich: "There is great regularity in the structure of this letter."[47] The Yale rhetorician in further enthusiasm for Junius's organization of his letters observes that "each of these letters was the result of severe and protected labor." Goodrich enlarges on this statement: "Yet it is certain that by far the greater part of all this toil was bestowed, not upon the language, but on the selection and arrangement of his ideas. His mind, in early life, had clearly been subjected to the severest logical training. Composition, with him, was the creation of a *system* of thought, in which everything is made subordinate to a just order and sequence of ideas. One thought grows out of another in regular succession."

The Yale critic disparages Chatham's failure in orderly evolution of his topics. On the other hand, Burke's speech on taxation of the American colonies is highly approved. Says Goodrich, "It would be difficult to find any oration, ancient or modern, in which the matter is more admirably arranged. The several parts support each other and the whole forms a complete system of thought."[48]

(c) Language. Basic in Goodrich's rhetorical judgment was his estimate of language in communication. His stressing of language effectiveness was the logical outcome of his training and experience, his classical education, his teaching of Greek, Latin, and the English languages, his lecturing and preaching, his considerable editorial writings, editorship, his pamphleteering, and his many years as lexicographer. To him the human family owed its progress and uniqueness to its use of language. He singled out with satisfaction Pitt the Elder who, as a youth, "went twice through the folio dictionary of Bailey . . . examining each word attentively, dwelling on its peculiar import and modes of construction." (p. 31)

What was Goodrich's standard of good style? He refers to Burke's style as furnishing such measure: "a clearness of statement, purity of language, and ease and variety in the structure of sentences, and an admirable rightness of imagery, which place it in the foremost rank of our elegant literature."

Junius also measures up well to Goodrich's standards, for Junius is particularly happy in his choice of words. "He gives you the exact word, he brings out the most delicate shadings of thought, he throws it upon the mind with elastic force, and you say, 'what is written is written!' " (p. 84) Contradictory to this impression that Goodrich demands a literary style for his "orators," he notes that Junius's style, in fact, originates in his oral approach to his theme and audience. Goodrich then, in reviewing Junius, analyzes the nouns, verbs, adverbs, adjectives, the use of contrast and antithesis that sometimes runs away with his judgment and "sinks into epigram."

Burke's language, though copious, is not verbose. Yet to Goodrich, Burke overloads his sentences. He is at times more careless and inaccurate than might be expected of so great a writer. Goodrich contrasts the style of Burke with that of Brougham. The latter "sometimes disgusts with his use of Latinized English and seems never to have studied our language in the true sources of its strength—Shakespeare, Milton, and the English Bible. His greatest fault lies in the structure of his sentences." His style is cumbersome and perplexing. (p. 321)

Although Goodrich, like Campbell and Blair, looks for vivacity and imagery as marks of an effective style, he recognizes that such exuberance and figurative abandon might mar the language effectiveness. Burke, for example, gave his figures "too bold a belief," and dwelt "on them too long, so that the primary idea" was "lost sight of in the image." Goodrich, nevertheless, concludes that Burke's language on the whole expresses a union of thought, feeling, and imagery. He is a superior artist in the handling of the English language. (p. 156)

Henry Grattan's style "abounds in metaphors which are always striking, often grand." His style is "full of antithesis and epigrammatic turns . . . which give it uncommon point and brilliancy, but have often an appearance of labor and affectation. His language is select. . . . His rhythmus is often uncommonly fine." In one Grattan speech our critic suggests that "we have one of the best specimens in our language of that admirable adaptation of sound to sense which distinguished the ancient orators." (p. 164)

He condemns oral language that fails to adapt to the audience. He commends Burke for his adjustment to his Bristol listeners,[49] but indicts him for poorly adjusting his language on one occasion to the House of Commons:

> It may be doubted whether this amplification, and the more graphic one which follows in respect to the fisheries of New England, are not out of place in an argument of this kind before the House of Commons. They would have been perfectly appropriate in an address like that of Daniel Webster on the landing of the Pilgrims at Plymouth, since the audience had met for the very purpose of being delighted with rich trains of thought, beautifully expressed. We who read the speech at the present day, dwell on such passages with unmingled gratification, because we peruse them much in the same spirit. But they would certainly be unsafe models for a business speaker.[50]

For Goodrich, language (or style) is highly functional. It demands accuracy, clarity, appropriateness (adjustment to the audience, occasion, and to the personality of the speaker), oral quality, and vividness through imagery, phrasing, and sentence construction.

(d) Delivery. Delivery, the equivalent of *pronuntiatio* and *actio,* Goodrich examined in detail as suggested by the title of his book. He assesses his speakers in each case with respect to their "elocution." His critical view of these processes of communication accords with his classical training. He, however, is also heavily influenced by the elocutionary authorities, Walker, Sheridan, Rush, and others, and makes clear in his lectures that these and other elocutionists have developed dependable standards for the training and criticism of delivery. The "moral and intellectual principles of our nature" he believes are important, "but scarcely less so is elocution."[51]

Lord Chatham's domination of the British Parliament was due in large part to his "personal advantages." These, Goodrich makes clear, are the "outward qualifications of the orator"—a tall erect figure, an imposing attitude, energetic gestures, power of his eye, glowing countenance, a full, clear voice, controlled rate, vocal intensity, proper pitch. The prevailing character of his delivery was "majesty and force." These physical attributes in action were only the outward attributes of Chatham's real power "which lay in his character—his lofty bearing, his generous sentiments," his commitment to the "intense spirit of liberty, which was the animating principle of his life" and to his political integrity in "an age of shameless profligacy."

Thus Goodrich's appraisal of Chatham's delivery encompasses voice (quality, rate, pitch, intensity), articulation, body activity, and speaking personality.

Conversely, Fox had serious vocal limitations. Although he was a bold champion against Chatham, "the keenness of his saber was blunted by the difficulty with which he drew it from the scabbard, I mean, the hesitation and ungracefulness of his delivery took off from the force of his arguments."

Note, however, that Goodrich gives great credit to Fox for his adaptation of his materials to the occasion. Observes Goodrich, Fox "added the most perfect sincerity and artlessness of manner. His very faults conspired to heighten the conviction of his honesty. The broken sentences, the choking of his voice, his ungainly gestures, his sudden starts of passion, the absolute scream with which he delivered his vehement passages—all showed him to be deeply moved and in earnest, so that it may be doubted whether a more perfect delivery would not have weakened the impression he made." (p. 216) Such penetrating and balanced criticism of delivery has not often been expressed.

Erskine, too, rates high for superior delivery. His oratory "owed much of its impressiveness to his admirable delivery. He was of medium height with a slender but finely-turned figure, animated and graceful in gesture, with a voice somewhat shrill, but beautifully modulated, a countenance beaming with emotion, and an eye of piercing keenness and power." (p. 283)

Pitt the Younger was tall and slender—with animated gestures—but devoid of grace. "His articulation was remarkably full and clear, filling the largest room with the volume of sound." (p. 267)

According to Goodrich, superior delivery is conversational. Walpole's effectiveness in debate was partly explained by his conversational skills.

Edmund Burke had his severe limitations in delivery. "As an orator he derived little or no advantage from his personal qualifications. He was tall, but not robust; his gait and gesture were awkward; his countenance, though intellectual, was destitute of softness, and rarely relaxed into a smile; and as he always wore spectacles, his eye gave him no command over an audience. 'His enunciation,' says Wraxall, 'was vehement and rapid; and his Irish accent, which was as strong as if he had never quitted the banks of the Shannon, diminished to the ear the effect of his eloquence on the mind.'" (p. 150)

"We see then in the philosophical habits of his mind (admirable as the results were in most respects) why he spoke so often to empty benches" while Fox "never failed to carry the House with him in breathless attention." (p. 155) Goodrich is evidently assuming here the theory that Burke's speaking became a signal for his bored audience to go to dinner.

Henry Grattan, the Irish orator, despite his vocal slovenliness, succeeded well (p. 164):

> Hence, a distinguished writer has spoken of his eloquence as a "combination of *cloud, whirlwind, and flame*"—a striking representation of the occasional obscurity and the rapid force and brilliancy of his style. But his incessant effort to be strong made him sometimes unnatural. He seems to be continually straining after effect. He wanted that calmness and self-possession which mark the highest order of minds, and show their consciousness of great strength. When he had mastered his subject, his subject mastered him. His great efforts have too much the air of harangues. They sound more like the battle speeches of Tacitus than the orations of Demosthenes.

John Philpot Curran, the great Irish orator, starting with many vocal handicaps, overcame them all: "His voice was bad and his articulation so hasty and confused that he went among his school fellows by the name of 'stuttering Jack Curran.' His manner was awkward, his gesture constrained and meaningless, and his whole appearance calculated only to produce laughter, notwithstanding the evidence he gave of superior abilities. All these faults he overcame by severe and patient labor." (p. 287)

Thus the author of *British Eloquence* discriminates sharply between his speakers in their skills of delivery.

(e) Effectiveness. Goodrich rounds out his evaluation of a speech by recapitulation of its effect on the immediate or later audiences. Sometimes he does little more than record the House of Commons vote after a major Burke, Fox, or Pitt the Younger speech. On Burke's Conciliation speech, for example, Goodrich merely notes that the vote was against Burke, 270 to 78. The parliamentary audiences, according to Goodrich's notes, were heavily influenced by the king's favors, bribery, Lord North's strategies, and strict Tory party control.

Goodrich sometimes dramatizes the immediate situation after a speech. After Chatham had finished his speech on American affairs, April 17, 1778, and had listened to a reply by the Duke of Richmond, he "made a sudden and strenuous attempt to rise, but as if laboring under the pressure of painful emotions. He seemed eager to speak, but after repeated efforts, he suddenly pressed his hand to his heart, and sunk down in convulations. Those who sat near him caught him in their arms. His son William Pitt, then a youth of seventeen, who was standing without the bar, sprang forward to support him. It is the moment which Copley has chosen for his picture of the death of Lord Chatham."

Sometimes Goodrich traces the wider results. Pitt the Younger, arguing against Fox on the issue of Negotiations with Napoleon, February 3, 1800, carried the day, 265 to 64. According to our critic, "Pitt's political adherents could not desert him on a question of this nature. Not to have passed the address approving his conduct would have been the severest censure." An adequate historian, however, Goodrich reports that "these results painfully disappointed the expectations of Mr. Pitt." Pitt expected a more unanimous support.

Pitt and Fox in this clash debated without victory. "The reader will see at the conclusion of Mr. Fox's speech . . . a slight sketch of events which followed during the two subsequent years—the entire discomfiture of the allies, their withdrawal from the contest, the resignation of Mr. Pitt, and the peace of Amiens" which ironically was only a pause in the long contest.[52]

Lord Belhaven gave an historic appeal against the legislative union of England and Scotland in the Parliament of Scotland, November 22, 1706. Goodrich reports: "The fervid appeal had no effect. The Treaty of Union was ratified, by a majority of thirty-three out of two hundred and one members. That it carried by bribery is now a matter of history." Goodrich cites facts concerning the distribution of £20,000 and the names of those to whom the money was given.[53]

Similarly, Henry Grattan's speech "impressive in its boldness, sublimity and compas of thought," in the Irish House of Commons, April 16, 1782, supported the declaration of Irish rights that England should no longer make the laws for Ireland.

The motion was passed with hardly a dissenting voice. "The Parliament of Ireland was now free; but the beneficial results so glowingly depicted by Mr. Grattan were never realized." This American rhetorician shows in detail how the good results were defeated through the combined English-Irish protestant minority machinations.[54]

Goodrich defends Burke's arguments in the East India case against Hastings (e.g., The East India Bill of Mr. Fox, December 1, 1783, and the Nabob of Arcot's Debts, February 28, 1785) even though Hastings was acquitted by the House of Lords. Goodrich clearly supports the role of Burke and assumes Hastings as the indirect villain. "This, however, does not imply that the atrocities so eloquently described by Mr. Burke were understated. . . . They are now matters of undisputed history." (p. 129)

Similarly Goodrich stoutly defends Burke's condemnation of the French Revolution. "While we cannot," contends Goodrich, "for these reasons give our sympathy or assent to every part of this volume, facts have shown that Mr. Burke was in the right far more than Mr. Fox as to the main point at issue, the character and prospects of the Revolution in France." (p. 140)

Thus, Goodrich is concerned both with immediate effects and the wider range of the speaker's influence. His assumption is that the effectiveness of eloquence is a function of audience adaptation; that it is to be regarded in the light of people's conduct as the result of hearing a speech. He is concerned with immediate response; with the speaker's judgment concerning the later ramifications of the position; with the responses derived from the audience changes in belief and attitude; and with the long-range effects of the social-political group. Goodrich applies a combination of such standards in his estimate of the speaking influence. His is the credit for the postulate that a speech is justified if "it achieves a response consistent with the speaker's purpose—if that purpose is consistent with the dictates of responsible judgment and solicious regard for the positive good of an enlightened society."[55] These principles of speaking effectiveness are unmistakable in his analysis of these successive British debaters and orators.

What, then, of Goodrich as a critic of the first rank? Present-day speech scholars appropriate much knowledge of the "new logic," semantics, psychology, electronic transmission, sociology, aesthetics, propaganda, mass society, space and other sciences, and other insights and experiences of the later twentieth century. Despite these later contributions, principles and details not dreamed of by Goodrich, an exclusive concentration on these modern techniques and methods may produce only poorly disciplined and superficial judges of communication. The substantial background of principles derived from Greece, Rome, and the later Western civilization, must continue to furnish the foundations of mature judgments. In that stream of communicative interpretation Chauncey Goodrich, American rhetorician, will continue to take a foremost position.

I AM ESPECIALLY INDEBTED to Dr. John Hoshor, Chairman of the Department of Speech and Assistant Dean at the University of Hawaii, for his permission to quote from his doctoral dissertation, unpublished, at the State University of Iowa, on the rhetorical lectures of Goodrich. Hoshor's study, based upon his unearthing of the Goodrich lectures on rhetoric at Yale, and partly reprinted in *Speech Monographs,* is a definitive record of Goodrich as a lecturer.

Professors Richard Murphy, Donald Bryant, Karl Wallace, Lloyd Watkins, Merrill Baker, Jerome Landfield, and Carroll

Arnold have published fresh insights into the Goodrich collection. I have made specific acknowledgments in my introduction.

I am also grateful to my colleagues at Southern Illinois University, Dean Horton Talley and Professor Ralph Micken, for their encouragement and co-operation. Professor Alan Cohn of the Southern Illinois University Library, and the humanities staff of the library also were major helpers. I also appreciate much the co-operation and good judgment of Mr. Vernon Sternberg and his staff of the Southern Illinois University Press.

Especially has Professor David Potter, editor of the Landmarks Series, guided wisely and well the successive versions of the introduction.

Essays from Select British Eloquence

SIR JOHN ELIOT

JOHN ELIOT was descended from a family of great respectability in Cornwall, and was born on the 20th of April, 1590. After enjoying the best advantages for education which England could afford, and spending some years in foreign travel, he was elected to Parliament at the age of thirty-three, and became one of the most prominent members in the House of Commons under Charles I.

The House embraced at this time some of the ablest and most learned men of the age, such as Sir Edward Coke, John Hampden, Selden, St. John, Pym, &c. Among these, Sir John Eliot stood pre-eminent for the force and fervor of his eloquence. The general style of speaking at that day was weighty, grave, and sententious, but tinctured with the pedantry of the preceding reign, and destitute of that warmth of feeling which is essential to the character of a great orator. Eliot, Wentworth, and a few others were exceptions; and Eliot especially spoke at times with all the enthusiasm and vehemence of the early days of Greece and Rome.

Hence he was appointed one of the managers of the House when the Duke of Buckingham was impeached in 1626, and had the part assigned him of making the closing argument against the Duke before the House of Lords. This he did with such energy and effect as to awaken the keenest resentment of the Court; so that two days after he was called out of the House, as if to receive a message from the King, and was instantly seized and hurried off by water to the Tower. The Commons, on hearing of this breach of privilege, were thrown into violent commotion. The cry "Rise! Rise!" was heard from every part of the hall. They did immediately adjourn, and met again only to record their resolution, "Not to do any more business until they were righted in their privileges." This decisive measure brought the government to a stand, and reduced them to the humiliating necessity of releasing Sir John Eliot, and also Sir Dudley Diggs, another of the managers who had been arrested on the same occasion. Eliot and his companion returned in triumph to the House, which voted that "they had not exceeded the commission intrusted to them."

In consequence of this defeat, and the backwardness of the Commons to grant the supplies demanded, Charles soon after dissolved Parliament, and determined to raise money by "forced loans." Great numbers resisted this imposition, and among them Eliot and Hampden, who, with seventy-six others of the gentry, were thrown into prison for refusing to surrender their property to the Crown; while hundreds of inferior rank were impressed into the army or navy by way of punishment. The King found, however, that with all this violence he could not raise the necessary supplies, and was compelled to call another Parliament within eight months. Eliot, Hampden, and many others who had been lying under arrest, were elected members of the new House of Commons while thus confined in prison, and were released only a few days before the meeting of Parliament.

These violent invasions of the rights of property and person, naturally came up for consideration at an early period of the session. The Commons, as the result of their discussions, framed, on the 27th of May, 1628, that second Great Charter of the liberties of England, the Petition of Right; so called because drawn up, in the humble spirit of the day, in the form of a petition to the King, but having, when ratified by his concurrence, all the authority of a fundamental law of the kingdom. This document was prepared by Sir Edward Coke at the age of seventy-eight, and was one of the last public acts of that distinguished lawyer. It provided that no loan or tax might be levied but by consent of Parliament; that no man might be imprisoned but by legal process; that soldiers might not be quartered on people contrary to their wills; and that no commissions be granted for executing martial law. On the 2d of June, Charles returned an evasive answer, in which he endeavored to satisfy the Commons without giving a legal and binding assent to the petition. The next day, Sir John Eliot made the following speech. It breathes throughout that spirit of affection and reverence for the King's person which was still felt by both houses of Parliament. It does not dwell, therefore, on those recent acts of arbitrary power in which the King might be supposed to have reluctantly concurred; and the fact is a striking one that Eliot does not even allude to his late cruel imprisonment, a decisive proof that he was not actuated by a spirit of personal resentment. The entire speech was directed against the royal favorite, the Duke of Buckingham. Its object was to expose his flagrant misconduct during the preceding ten years, under the reign of James as well as Charles; and to show that through his duplicity, incompetency, and rash counsels, the honor of the kingdom had been betrayed, its allies sacrificed, its treasures wasted, and those necessities of the King created which gave rise to the arbitrary acts referred to in the Petition of Right. The facts which Eliot adduces in proof are very briefly mentioned, or barely alluded to, because they were fresh in the minds of all, and had created a burning sense of wrong and dishonor throughout the whole kingdom. They will be explained in brief notes appended to the speech; but, to feel their full force, the reader must go back to the history of the times, and place himself in the midst of the scene.

There is in this speech, a union of dignity and fervor which is highly characteristic of the man. "His mind," says Lord Nugent, "was deeply imbued with a love of philosophy and a confidence in religion which gave a lofty tone to his eloquence." His fervor, acting on a clear and powerful understanding, gives him a simplicity, directness, and continuity of thought, a rapidity of progress, and a vehemence of appeal, which will remind the reader of the style of Demosthenes. His whole soul is occupied with the subject. He seizes upon the strong points of his case with such absorbing interest, that all those secondary and collateral trains of thought with which a speaker, like Burke, amplifies and adorns the discussion, are rejected as unworthy of the stern severity of the occasion. The eloquence lies wholly in the thought; and the entire *bareness* of the expression, the absence of all ornament, adds to the effect, because there is nothing interposed to break the force of the blow. The antique air of the style heightens the interest of the speech and will recommend it particularly to those who have learned to relish the varied construction and racy English of our early writers.[1]

THE EARL OF STRAFFORD

THOMAS WENTWORTH, first Earl of Strafford, was descended from an ancient family in Yorkshire, and was born at the house of his maternal grandfather, in London, on the 13th of April, 1593. At St. John's College, Cambridge, where he received his education, he was distinguished not only for the strength and versatility of his genius, but for his unwearied efforts to improve his mind by the severest discipline, and especially to prepare himself for the duties of public life, as an orator and a statesman. The leading features of his character were strongly marked. He had an ardor of temperament, a fixedness of will, a native impetuosity of feeling, and a correspondent energy of action, which united to make him one of the most daring and determined men of the age. To those who rendered him the deference he expected, who were ready to co-operate in his plans or become subservient to his purposes, he was kind and liberal. But he was quick and resentful when his will was crossed; and even Clarendon admits that "he manifested a nature excessively imperious."

He was trained from childhood, to a belief in those extravagant doctrines respecting the royal prerogative, which were so generally prevalent at that day. It was therefore natural that Wentworth, in entering on public life, should seek employment at Court. The King seems, from the first, to have regarded him with favor; but Buckingham, who was then in power, was secretly jealous and hostile. Hence he was treated at times with great confidence, and raised to important offices, and again stripped suddenly of his employments, and subjected to the most mortifying rebuffs. Under these circumstances, he came out for a time as a "patriot," and joined the popular party.

That he did so, however, only in opposition to Buckingham, as the most effectual means of putting down a rival—that there was no change in his principles, no real sympathy between him and the illustrious men who were resisting the tyranny of Charles, is obvious from his subsequent conduct, and from the whole tenor of his private correspondence, as afterward given to the world.[1] But such was the strength of his passions, and the force of imagination (so characteristic of the highest class of orators) with which he could lay hold of, and for the time being, appropriate to himself, all the principles and feelings which became his new character, that he appeared to the world, and perhaps even to himself, to have become a genuine convert to the cause of popular liberty. In the Parliament of 1627–8, during the great discussion on the public grievances, he came forth in all his strength, "amid the delighted cheers of the House, and with a startling effect on the Court." After entering upon the subject with a calm and solemn tone befitting the greatness of the occasion, he rose in power as he advanced, until, when he came to speak of forced loans, and the billeting of soldiers upon families he broke forth suddenly, with that kind of dramatic effect which he always studied, in a rapid and keen invective, which may be quoted as a specimen of his early eloquence. "They have rent from us the light of our eyes! enforced companies of guests, worse than the ordinances of France! vitiated our wives and children before our eyes! brought the Crown to greater want than ever it was in, by anticipating the revenue! and can the shepherd be thus smitten, and the sheep not scattered? They have introduced a Privy Council, ravishing at once the spheres of all ancient government! imprisoning without bail or bond! They have taken from us—what shall I say? Indeed, *what have they left us?* They have taken from us all means of supplying the King, and ingratiating ourselves with him, by tearing up the roots of all property; which if they be not seasonably set again into the ground by his Majesty's hand, we shall have, instead of beauty, baldness!"

He next, in the boldest language, proposes his remedy. "By one and the same thing hath the King and the people been hurt, and by the same must they be cured: to vindicate—

what? New things? No! Our ancient, lawful, and vital liberties, by re-enforcing the ancient laws, made by our ancestors; by setting such a stamp upon them, that no licentious spirit shall dare hereafter to enter upon them. And shall we think this a way to *break* a Parliament?[2] No! Our desires are modest and just. I speak truly for the interests of the King and the people. If we enjoy not these, it will be impossible to relieve him." "Let no man," said he, in conclusion, "judge this way 'a break-neck' of Parliaments; but a way of honor to the King, nay, of profit; for, besides the supply we shall readily give him, suitable to his occasions, we give him our hearts—*our hearts,* Mr. Speaker; *a gift that* GOD *calls for, and fit for a King.*"

In the same spirit, he united with Eliot in urging forward the Petition of Right; and when the Lords proposed an additional clause, that it was designed "to leave entire that *sovereign power* with which his Majesty is intrusted," he resisted its insertion, declaring, "If we admit of the addition, we leave the subject worse than we found him. These laws are not acquainted with 'Sovereign Power!' "

The Court were now thoroughly alarmed. But they knew the man. There is evidence from his own papers, that within *ten days* from this time, he was in negotiation with the speaker, Finch; and "almost before the burning words which have just been transcribed, had cooled from off the lips of the speaker, a transfer of his services to the Court was decided on." In a few days Parliament was prorogued; and shortly after, Sir Thomas Wentworth was created Baron Wentworth, and appointed a member of that same Privy Council which he had just before denounced, as "ravishing at once the spheres of all ancient government!" The death of Buckingham about a month after, placed him, in effect, at the head of affairs. He was made a Viscount, and Lord President of the North; and at a subsequent period, Lord Deputy, and Lord Lieutenant of Ireland, and Earl of Strafford.

The twelve years that followed, during which Charles undertook to reign without the aid of Parliaments, were filled up with arbitrary exactions, destructive monopolies, illegal imprisonments, and inhuman corporal punishments, which Strafford was known to have recommended or approved; while his presidency in the North was marked by numerous acts of high-handed injustice, and his government of Ireland carried on with such violence and oppression as "gave men warning," in the words of Clarendon, "how they trusted themselves in the territories where he commanded."

In 1640 Charles was compelled by his necessities to convene another Parliament. The day of retribution had at length arrived. The voice of three kingdoms called for vengeance on the author of their calamities; and not a man was found, except Charles and Laud, to justify or excuse his conduct. Even Digby, who sought only to save his life, speaks of Strafford, as "a name of hatred in the present age by his practices, and fit to be made a name of terror to future ages by his punishment." At the moment when, governed by his accustomed policy, he was preparing to strike the first blow, and to impeach the leaders of the popular party, as the surest means to avert the coming storm, he was himself impeached by the House of Commons, stripped of all his dignities, and thrown into the Tower. The 22d of March, 1641, was fixed upon for his trial. The great object of his accusers was to establish against him the charge of "attempting to subvert the fundamental laws of the realm." In doing so, they brought forward many offenses of inferior magnitude, as an index of his intentions; and they never pretended that more than two or three of the articles contained charges which amounted strictly to high treason.

In conducting the impeachment, they had great difficulties to encounter. They could find precedents in abundance to justify the doctrine of *constructive* treason. Still, it was a doctrine which came with an ill grace from the friends of civil liberty; and it gave wide scope to the eloquence of Strafford, in some of the most powerful and touching appeals of his masterly defense. In addition to this, the time had not yet arrived when treason against the state, as distinguished from an assault upon the life or personal authority of the king, was distinctly recognized in England. Strafford had undoubtedly, as a sworn counselor of Charles, given him unconstitutional advice; had told him that he was absolved from the established rules of government, that he might use his simple prerogative for the purpose of raising money, above or against the decisions of Parliament. Such an attempt to subvert the fundamental laws of the kingdom, if connected with any overt act, would now be treason. But the doctrine was a new one. The idea of considering the sovereign as only the *representative* of the state, of treating an encroachment on the established rights of the people as a crime of equal magnitude with a violation of the King's person and authority, had not yet become familiar to the English mind. We owe it to the men who commenced this impeachment; and it is not wonderful that Strafford, with his views, and those of most men at that day, could declare with perfect sincerity that he was utterly unconscious of the crime of treason.

The trial lasted from the 22d of March to the 13th of April, 1641, during which time the Earl appeared daily before the court, clothed in black, and wearing no badge or ornament but his George. "The stern and simple character of his features accorded with the occasion; his countenance 'manly black,' as Whitlocke describes it, and his thick hair cut short from his ample forehead." He was tall in person, but through early disease had contracted a stoop of the shoulders, which would have detracted from his appearance on any other occasion; but being now ascribed to intense suffering from the stone and the gout, which he was known to have endured during the progress of the trial, it operated in his favor, and excited much sympathy in his behalf. During eighteen days he thus stood alone against his numerous accusers, answering in succesion the twenty-eight articles of the impeachment, which of themselves filled two hundred sheets of paper, examining the witnesses, commenting on their evidence, explaining, defending, palliating his conduct on every point with an adroitness and force, a dignity and self-possession, which awakened the admiration even of his enemies. On the last day of the trial, he summed up his various defenses in a speech of which the report given below is only an imperfect outline.[3] It enables us, however, to form some conception of the eloquence and pathos of this extraordinary man. There is in it a union of dignity, simplicity, and force—a felicity in the selection of topics—a dexterity of appeal to the interests and feelings of his judges—a justness and elevation in every sentiment he utters—a vividness of illustration, a freshness of imagery, an elasticity and airiness of diction—an appearance of perfect sincerity, and a pervading depth of passion breaking forth at times in passages of startling power or tenderness, which we find only in the highest class of oratory. The pathos of the conclusion has been much admired; and if we go back in imagination to the scene as presented in Westminster Hall—the once proud Earl standing amid the wreck of his fortunes, with that splendid court around him which so lately bowed submissive to his will; with his humbled monarch looking on from behind the screen that concealed his person, unable to interpose or arrest the proceedings; with that burst of tenderness at the thought of earlier days and of his wife, the Lady Arabella Hollis, "that saint in heaven," to whose memory he had always clung amid the power and splendor of later life; with his body bowed down under the pressure of intense physical suffering, and his strong spirit utterly subdued and poured out like water in that startling cry, "My Lords, my *Lords,* my LORDS, something more I had intended to say, but my voice and my spirit fail me"—we can not but feel that there are few passages of equal tenderness and power in the whole range of English eloquence. We are strongly reminded of Shakspeare's delineation of Wolsey under similar circumstances, in some of the most pathetic scenes which poetry has ever depicted. We feel that Strafford, too, with his "heart new opened," might have added *his* testimony to the folly of ambition, and the bitter fruits of seeking the favor of a king, at the expense of the people's rights, and the claims of justice and truth.

"Cromwell, I charge thee, fling away ambition!
By that sin fell the angels; how can man, then,
The image of his Maker hope to win by 't?
Love thyself last! Cherish those hearts that hate thee!
Corruption wins not more than honesty!
Still in thy right hand carry gentle peace,
To silence envious tongues! Be just and fear not!
Let all the ends thou aim'st at be thy country's,
Thy God's, and Truth's! Then if thou fallest, O Cromwell,
Thou fallest a blessed martyr."

LORD DIGBY

GEORGE DIGBY, oldest son of the Earl of Bristol, was born at Madrid in 1612, during the residence of his father in that city as English embassador to the Court of Spain. He was educated at Magdalen College, Oxford; and entered into public life at the age of twenty-eight, being returned member of Parliament for the county of Dorset, in April, 1640. In common with his father, who had incurred the displeasure of the King by his impeachment of Buckingham in 1626, Lord Digby came forward at an early period of the session, as an open and determined enemy of the Court. Among the "Speeches relative to Grievances," his, as representative of Dorsetshire, was one of the most bold and impassioned. His argument shortly after in favor of triennial Parliaments, was characterized by a still higher order of eloquence; and in the course of it he made a bitter attack upon Strafford, in showing the necessity of frequent Parliaments as a control upon ministers, declaring "he must not expect to be pardoned in this world till he is dispatched to the other."

From the ardor with which he expressed these sentiments, and the leading part he took in every measure for the defense of the people's rights, Lord Digby was appointed one of the managers for the impeachment of Strafford. Into this he entered, for a time, with the utmost zeal. He is described by Clarendon as a man of uncommon activity of mind and fertility of invention; bold and impetuous in whatever designs he undertook; but deficient in judgment, inordinately vain and ambitious, of a volatile and unquiet spirit, disposed to separate councils, and governed more by impulse than by fixed principles. Whether the course he took in respect to the attainder of Strafford ought to be referred in any degree to the last-mentioned traits of character, or solely to a sense of justice, a conviction forced upon him in the progress of the trial that the testimony had failed to sustain the charge of treason, can not, perhaps, be decided at the present day. The internal evidence afforded by the speech, is strongly in favor of his honesty and rectitude of intention. He appears throughout like one who was conscious of having gone too far; and who was determined to retrieve his error, at whatever expense of popular odium it might cost him. Had he stopped here, there would have been no ground for imputations on his character. But he almost instantly changed the whole tenor of his political life. He abandoned his former principles; he joined the Court party; and did more, as we learn from Clarendon, to ruin Charles by his rashness and pertinacity, than any other man. But, whatever may be thought of Digby, the speech is one of great manliness and force. It is plausible in its statements, just in its distinctions, and weighty in its reasonings. Without exhibiting any great superiority of genius, and especially any richness of imagination, it presents us with a rapid succession of striking and appropriate thoughts, clearly arranged and vividly expressed. In one respect, the diction is worthy of being studied. It abounds in those direct and pointed forms of speech, which sink at once into the heart; and by their very plainness give an air of perfect sincerity to the speaker, which of all things is the most important to one who is contending (as he was) against the force of popular prejudice. Much of the celebrity attached to this speech is owing, no doubt, to the circumstances under which it was delivered. The House of Commons must have presented a scene of the most exciting nature when, at the moment of taking the final vote on the bill, one of the managers of the impeachment came forward to abandon his ground; to disclose the proceedings of the committee in secret session; and to denounce the condemnation of Strafford by a bill of attainder, as an act of murder.[1]

LORD BELHAVEN

THE author of this speech belonged to the Hamilton family. He was one of the old Presbyterian lords, of high education, especially in classical literature; lofty in his demeanor; dauntless in spirit; and wholly devoted to the peculiar interests of his country. The speech owes much of its celebrity to the circumstances under which it was delivered. It embodies the feelings of a proud and jealous people, when called upon to surrender their national independence, and submit to the authority of the British Parliament.

A century had now elapsed since the union of the English and Scottish crowns in the person of James I, and Scotland still remained a distinct kingdom, with its own Parliament, its own judicial system, its own immemorial usages which had all the force of law. This state of things, though gratifying to the pride of the Scottish people, was the source of endless jealousies and contentions between the two countries; and, as commonly happens in such cases, the weaker party suffered most. Scotland was governed by alternate corruption and force. Her nobility and gentry were drawn to England in great numbers by the attractions of the Court, as the seat of fashion, honor, and power. The nation was thus drained of her wealth; and the drain became greater, as her merchants and tradesmen were led to transfer their capital to the sister kingdom, in consequence of the superior facilities for trade which were there enjoyed.

It was now apparent that Scotland could never flourish until she was permitted to share in those commercial advantages, from which she was debarred as a distinct country, by the Navigation Act of England. The Scotch were, therefore, clamorous in their demands for some arrangement to this effect. But the English had always looked with jealousy upon any intermeddling with trade on the part of Scotland. They had crushed her African and India Company by their selfish opposition, and had left her Darien settlement of twelve hundred souls to perish for want of support and protection; so that few families in the Lowlands had escaped the loss of a relative or friend. Exasperated by these injuries, and by the evident determination of the English to cut them off from all participation in the benefits of trade, the Scotch were hurried into a measure of alarming aspect for the safety of the empire. Noble and burgher, Jacobite and Presbyterian, were for once united. There was one point where England was vulnerable. It was the succession to the crown. This had been settled by the English Parliament on the Protestant line in the house of Hanover, and the fullest expectations were entertained that the Parliament of Scotland would readily unite in the same measure. Instead of this, the Scotch, in 1704, passed their famous Act of Security, in which they threw down the gauntlet to England, and enacted, that "the same person should be *incapable* of succeeding in both kingdoms, unless a free communication of trade, the benefits of the Navigation Act, and liberty of the Plantations [*i.e.*, of trading with the British West Indies and North America] was first obtained." They also provided conditionally for a separate successor, and passed laws for arming the whole kingdom in his defense.

It was now obvious that concessions must be made on both sides, or the contest be decided by the sword. The ministry of Queen Anne, therefore, proposed that commissioners from the two kingdoms should meet at London, to devise a plan of union, which should be mutually advantageous to the two countries. This was accordingly done, in the month of April, 1706; and, after long negotiations, it was agreed, that the two kingdoms should be united into one under the British Parliament, with the addition of sixteen Scottish peers to the House of Lords, and of forty-five Scottish members to the House of Commons; that the Scotch should be entitled to all the privileges of the English in respect to trade, and be subject to the same excise and duties; that Scotland should receive £398,000 as a compensation or "equivalent" for the share of liability she assumed in the English debt of £20,000,000; and that the churches of England and Scotland respectively should be confirmed in all their rights and privileges, as a fundamental condition of the Union.

These arrangements were kept secret until October, 1706, when the Scottish Parliament met to consider and decide on the plan proposed. The moment the Articles were read in that body, and given to the public in print, they were met with a burst of indignant reprobation from every quarter. A federal union which should confer equal advantages for trade, was all that the Scotch in general had ever contemplated: an *incorporating* union, which should abolish their Parliament and extinguish their national existence, was what most Scotchmen had never dreamed of. Nor is it surprising, aside from all considerations of national honor, that such a union should have been regarded with jealousy and dread. "No past experience of history," says Hallam, "was favorable to the absorption of a lesser state (at least where the government partook so much of a republican form) in one of superior power and ancient rivalry. The representation of Scotland in the united Legislature, was too feeble to give any thing like security against the English prejudices and animosities, if they should continue or revive. The Church of Scotland was exposed to the most apparent perils, brought thus within the power of a Legislature so frequently influenced by one which held her, not as a sister, but rather as a bastard usurper of a sister's inheritance; and though her permanence was guaranteed by the treaty, yet it was hard to say how far the legal competence of Parliament might hereafter be deemed to extend, or, at least, how far she might be abridged of her privileges and impaired in her dignity."

It was with sentiments like these that, when the first article of the treaty was read, Lord Belhaven arose, and addressed the Parliament of Scotland in the following speech. It is obviously reported in a very imperfect manner, and was designed merely to open the discussion which was expected to follow, and not to enter at large into the argument. It was a simple burst of feeling, in which the great leader of the country party, who was equally distinguished for "the mighty sway of his talents and the resoluteness of his temper," poured out his emotions in view of that act of *parricide,* as he considered it, to which the Parliament was now called. He felt that no regard to consequences, no loss or advancement of trade, manufactures, or national wealth, ought to have the weight of a feather, when the honor and existence of his country were at stake. He felt that Scotland, if only united, was abundantly able to work out her own salvation. These two thoughts, therefore—National Honor and National Union—constitute the burden of his speech.[1]

SIR ROBERT WALPOLE

THE administration of Walpole was the longest which has occurred since the days of Queen Elizabeth. He was probably the most dexterous party leader which England ever had; "equally skilled to win popular favor, to govern the House of Commons, and to influence and be influenced by public opinion."

Descended from an ancient and respectable family, he was born at Houghton, in Norfolkshire, on the 26th day of August, 1676. Part of his boyhood was spent at Eton, and he was for two years a member of the University of Cambridge; but in neither of these places did he give any indications of superior talents. In early life he was remarkable for nothing but his high spirits and dislike of study. The only benefit he seems to have obtained from his early education, was a facility which he acquired at Eton of conversing in Latin. This became to him afterward an important instrument of power. George I could speak no English, and Walpole no German: so they compromised the matter when he was made Prime Minister; and all the communications between him and his master, involving the highest interests of the kingdom, were carried on in "very bad Latin."

The first impulse given to the mind of Walpole arose from his being elected a member of Parliament at the age of twenty-four. A vein was now struck which laid open the master principle of his character. It was a spirit of intense ambition. From this moment he laid aside all his sluggishness and love of ease; he threw himself at once into the arena of political strife; and the whole cast of his mind and feelings, as well as the character of the times, went to secure his early ascendency. He had naturally great force and penetration of intellect; a clear judgment; a dauntless spirit; a thorough knowledge of human nature, especially on its weak side; infinite dexterity in carrying on or counteracting political intrigues; a self-possession which never forsook him in the most trying circumstances; and a perfectly unscrupulous freedom in the adoption of every means that seemed necessary to the accomplishment of his designs. The only acquired knowledge which he brought with him into public life was a thorough acquaintance with finance. It was precisely the knowledge that was needed at that juncture; and it laid the foundation, at no distant period, of the long and almost despotic sway which he exercised over English affairs.

On taking his seat in Parliament in 1700, he joined himself to the Whig party, and in the year 1708 was brought into office as Secretary at War. Thrown out soon after by a change of ministry, which arose from the silly prosecution of Sacheverell, he was restored to office in 1714, when the Whigs came into power under George I. From this time, for nearly thirty years, he was an active member of the government, during twenty of which he was Prime Minister. To this office he was called, by general consent, in 1721, on the explosion of the South Sea project, which filled the whole island with consternation and ruin. He had opposed the scheme and predicted its failure from the outset, though he had the sagacity to profit largely by speculating in the stock; and now that his predictions were fulfilled, every eye was turned to Walpole, as the only one fitted, by his financial skill, to repair the shattered credit of the country. He was made First Lord of the Treasury, and Chancellor of the Exchequer, on the second of April, 1721.

Walpole had now reached the summit of his ambition; and if he had only been just and liberal to his political associates, he might, perhaps, even in that faithless and intriguing age, have gone on to enjoy an undisputed supremacy. But his ambition was domineering and exclusive. He was jealous of every man in his own party, whose growing influence or force of character seemed likely to raise him above the station of a humble dependent. In about two years he quarreled with Carteret, one of the most gifted men of the age, who came in with him as Secretary of State, simply because he would allow of no colleague, but was resolved to rule at the council board as sole master. Within two years more, he endeavored to put Pulteney out of the way by a specious offer of the peerage; and thus made the most eloquent speaker in the House, before the time of Chatham, his enemy for life. Chesterfield was turned out from his station as Lord Steward of the Household, with circumstances of personal insult, because he was against the Excise Bill, which Walpole himself soon after abandoned. Others of the nobility, with a number of military officers, among whom was Lord Chatham, were treated with the same indignity. Thus he alienated from him, by degrees, nearly all the talent of the Whig party.

The Opposition which he had to encounter was, therefore, composed of singularly discordant materials. To his natural opponents, the Jacobites and Tories, was added a large body of disaffected Whigs, who took the name of "Patriots." Bolingbroke, after the pardon of his treasons by George I, and his return to England in 1725, though not restored to his seat in the House of Lords, and therefore unable to share in public debate, was the acknowledged leader of the Tories and Jacobites; and, by a coalition which he soon after made with Pulteney, became for nearly ten years the real head of the Opposition. He was qualified for this station by extraordinary abilities and matured experience. He was a veteran in the arts of popular delusion. Such was the ascendency of his genius over the strongest minds, that he could unite Wyndham and Pulteney in the same measures; and from his station behind the scenes, could move the machinery of Opposition with the greater coolness because he had no share in public measures. Men were thus brought into one body, under the strictest party discipline, who could never have acted together for a moment on any other subject. They comprised a large part of the talent of the kingdom; and were engaged for years in the struggle to put Walpole down, animated, in most instances, not only by an intense desire for office, but by personal resentment and a spirit of revenge.

It was certainly a proof of consummate ability in Walpole that he was able to stand for a single year against such an Opposition. That he sustained himself, to a considerable extent, by the systematic bribery of the leading members of Parliament, there can be no doubt. Nor is he to be tried by the standard of the present day on that subject. Charles II commenced the system; it was continued under his successor; and when William III was placed on the throne by the Revolution of 1688, he found it impossible to carry on the government without resorting to the same means. "It was not, therefore," as remarked by Cooke in his History of Party, "the minister who corrupted the age; his crime was that he pandered to the prevailing depravity." But bribery alone could never have given Walpole so complete an ascendency. A ministerial majority, even when part of its members are bribed, demand of their leader at least plausible reasons for the vote they give. Against such an Opposition as he had to encounter, nothing but extraordinary talents, and a thorough knowledge of affairs, could have maintained him for a single month at the head of the government. And it is a remarkable fact, as to the leading measures for which he was so vehemently assailed, his Excise Bill, Wood's Patent, a Standing Army, Septennial Parliaments, the Hanover Treaty, and the Spanish Convention, that the verdict of posterity has been decidedly in his favor. Even Lord Chatham, who in early life was drawn under the influence of the Opposition leaders by their extraordinary talents and specious pretensions to patriotism, publicly declared, at a later period, that he had changed his views of the principal measures of Walpole.

But while posterity have thus decided for Walpole on the main questions in debate between him and the Opposition, they have been far from awarding to him the honors of a great statesman. He undoubtedly rendered a most important service to his country by the skill and firmness with which he defeated the machinations of the Jacobites, and held the house of Brunswick on the throne. It was not without reason that Queen Caroline, on her dying bed, commended, not Walpole to the favor of the King, but the King to the protection and support of Walpole. Still, it is apparent, from the whole tenor of his conduct, that in this, as in every other case, he was governed by the absorbing passion of his life, the love of office.

"He understood," says Lord Campbell, "the *material* interests of the country, and, so far as was consistent with the retention of power, he was desirous of pursuing them." We have here the key to every measure of his administration—*"the retention of power!"* It was this that dictated his favorite maxim, *ne quieta moveas,* because he felt that change, however useful, might weaken his hold on office. Hence his scandalous treatment of the Dissenters, whom he deluded for years with solemn promises of deliverance from the galling yoke of the Test Act, and thus held them as firm supporters of his ministry in the most trying seasons; but when driven at last to say, *"When* will the time come?" he answered, as he always meant, "Never!" He was afraid of the High Church party; and he chose rather to break his word, than to venture on what he acknowledged to be a simple act of justice. It was so in every thing. He would run no personal risk to secure the most certain and valuable improvements. He would do nothing to provide against remote dangers, if it cost any great and immediate sacrifice. He therefore did nothing for the advancement of English institutions. He was the minister of the Present, not of the Future. His conduct in respect to the Spanish war furnishes a complete exhibition of his character, and has covered his memory with indelible disgrace. He knew it to be unnecessary and unjust—"the most unprovoked and unjustifiable war," as a great writer has observed, "in the English annals." Any other minister, rather than be forced into it by the popular clamor, would have instantly resigned. But in the words of Lord Mahon, who was disposed, in general, to judge favorably of Walpole, "He still clung unworthily to his darling office; thus proving that a love of power, and not a love of peace (as has been pretended), was his ruling principle. It was a sin against light. No man had a clearer view of the impending mischief and misery of the Spanish war. On the very day of the Declaration, when joyful peals were heard from every steeple of the city, the minister muttered, 'They may ring the bells now; before long they will be *wringing* their hands.' Yet of this mischief and misery he could stoop to be the instrument!"

The selfish and temporizing policy of Walpole, on this occasion, proved his ruin. The war, which he never intended should take place, and for which he had, therefore, made no preparation, proved disastrous to the English; and the Opposition had the art to turn the popular odium with double violence upon the minister, for the failure of a measure which they had themselves forced upon him. The circumstances attending his fall from power will be detailed hereafter, in connection with his speech on a motion for his removal from office. He resigned all his employments on the 11th of February, 1742, and died about three years after, just as he was entering his sixty-ninth year.

The age of Walpole was an age rather of keen debate than impassioned eloquence. If we except Lord Chatham, whose greatest efforts belong to a later period, we shall find but little in the leading orators of the day that was lofty or imposing. They were emphatically business speakers, eagerly intent upon their object but destitute of any principles or feelings, which could raise them above the level of the most selfish minds, engaged in a desperate struggle for office and power. We find, therefore, in their speeches, no large views, no generous and elevated sentiments, none of those appeals to the higher instincts of our nature, which are the crowning excellence of our English oratory. Any thing of this kind would have been laughed down by Walpole as sheer affectation. Even patriotism, which is too often a limited and selfish virtue, he regarded as mere pretense. "Patriots," says he, "spring up like mushrooms! I could raise fifty of them within the twenty-four hours. I have raised many of them in a single night. It is but refusing to gratify an unreasonable or an insolent demand, and up starts a *patriot!*" The reasonings of that day were brief and pointed; with no attempts at philosophy; with but little breadth of illustration; with scarcely any disposition to discuss a subject in its principles. Parliamentary speaking was literally "a keen encounter of the wits," in which the ball of debate was tossed to and fro between men of high talent, who perfectly understood each other's motives, and showed infinite dexterity in twisting facts and arguments to serve a purpose. It was the maxim of the day that every thing was fair in politics.—The best speeches abounded in wit and sarcasm, in sly insinuations or cutting invective, all thrown off with a light, bold, confident air, in racy English, and without any apparent effort. The language of debate approached as near to that of actual conversation, as the nature of the topics, and the flow of continuous discourse, would permit. It was direct and idiomatic, the language of men who had lived in the society of Addison and Swift, and who endeavored to unite the ease and simplicity of the one with the pungency and force of the other. It is a style of speaking which has always been a favorite one in the British Senate; and notwithstanding the examples of a loftier strain of eloquence in that body since the days of Chatham, it is still (though connected with more thorough discussion) the style which is cultivated by a majority of speakers down to the present day in both houses of Parliament.[1]

WILLIAM PULTENEY

WILLIAM PULTENEY, first Earl of Bath, was born in 1682. He was elected a member of Parliament in early life, and applied himself to the diligent study of the temper of the House, and the best mode of speaking in so mixed and discordant an assembly. He made no attempts to dazzle by any elaborate display of eloquence; for it was his maxim that "that are few real orators who commence with set speeches." His powers were slowly developed. He took part in almost every important debate, more (at first) for his own improvement than with any expectation of materially changing the vote. He thus gradually rose into one of the most dexterous and effective speakers of the British Senate.

His speeches, unfortunately, have been worse reported, in respect to the peculiar characteristics of his eloquence, than those of any of his contemporaries. The following one, however, though shorter than might be wished, is undoubtedly a fair specimen of the bold, direct, and confident, though not overbearing manner, in which he ordinarily addressed himself to the judgment and feelings of the House. The language is uncommonly easy, pointed, and vigorous. The sentences flow lightly off in a clear and varied sequence, without the slightest appearance of stateliness or mannerism. It is the exact style for that conversational mode of discussion which is best adapted to the purposes of debate.

Walpole, when displaced by the exertions of Pulteney in 1742, had the satisfaction of dragging down his adversary along with him. He saw that the Opposition must go to pieces the moment they were left to themselves; that a new administration could never be framed out of such discordant materials;

and that whoever should undertake it would be ruined in the attempt. He therefore induced the King to lay that duty upon Pulteney. The result was just what he expected. The King insisted on retaining a large proportion of Walpole's friends. Comparatively few offices remained for others, and both Whigs and Tories were disappointed and enraged. Pulteney shrunk from taking office himself, under these circumstances. He professed great disinterestedness; he had no desire for power; he would merely accept a peerage, which all parties regarded as the reward of his perfidy. He was created Earl of Bath; and the name of *Patriot,* as Horace Walpole tells us, became a term of derision and contempt throughout all the kingdom. When the newly-created earls met for the first time in the House of Lords, Walpole walked up to Pulteney, and said to him, with a mixture of pleasantry and bitterness, for which he was always distinguished, "Here we are, my Lord, the two most insignificant fellows in England." Pulteney died on the 8th of June, 1764.[1]

LORD CHESTERFIELD

PHILIP DORMER STANHOPE, fourth Earl of Chesterfield, was born in 1694. He was equally distinguished for his love of polite literature, the grace of his manners, the pungency of his wit, and the elegance of his literary productions. In later times he has been most known by his Letters to his son. These, though admirable models of the epistolary style, are disfigured by a profligacy of sentiment which has cast a just odium on his character; while the stress they lay upon mere accomplishments has created a very natural suspicion, among those who have seen him only in that correspondence, as to the strength and soundness of his judgment. He was unquestionably, however, a man of great acuteness and force of intellect. As an orator, Horace Walpole gave him the preference over all the speakers of his day. This may have arisen, in part, from the peculiar dexterity with which he could play with a subject that he did not choose to discuss—a kind of talent which Walpole would be very apt to appreciate. It often happens that weak and foolish measures can be exposed more effectually by wit than by reasoning. In this kind of attack Lord Chesterfield had uncommon power. His fancy supplied him with a wide range of materials, which he brought forward with great ingenuity, presenting a succession of unexpected combinations, that flashed upon the mind with all the liveliness and force of the keenest wit or the most poignant satire. The speech which follows is a specimen of his talent for this kind of speaking. "It will be read with avidity by those who relish the sprightly sallies of genius, or who are emulous of a style of eloquence which, though it may not always convince, will never fail to delight."

The speech relates to a bill for granting licenses to gin-shops, by which the ministry hoped to realize a very large annual income. This income they proposed to employ in carrying on the German war of George II, which arose out of his exclusive care for his Electorate of Hanover, and was generally odious throughout Great Britain. Lord Chesterfield made two speeches on this subject, which are here given together, with the omission of a few unimportant paragraphs. It has been hastily inferred, from a conversation reported by Boswell, that these speeches, as here given, were written by Johnson. Subsequent inquiry, however, seems to prove that this was not the fact; but, on the contrary, that Lord Chesterfield prepared them for publication himself.

Lord Chesterfield filled many offices of the highest importance under the reign of George II. In 1728 he was appointed ambassador to Holland and, by his adroitness and diplomatic skill, succeeded in delivering Hanover from the calamities of war which hung over it. As a reward for his services, he was made Knight of the Garter and Lord Steward of the Royal Household. At a later period he was appointed Lord Lieutenant of Ireland. This difficult office he discharged with great dexterity and self-command, holding in check the various factions of that country with consummate skill. On his return to England in 1746, he was called to the office of Secretary of State; but, having become wearied of public employments, he soon resigned, and devoted the remainder of his life to the pursuits of literature and the society of his friends. He now carried on the publication of a series of papers in imitation of the Spectator, entitled the World, in which some of the best specimens may be found of his light, animated, and easy style of writing. Toward the close of his life he became deaf, and suffered from numerous bodily infirmities, which filled his latter days with gloom and despondency. He bore the most emphatic testimony to the folly and disappointment of the course he had led, and died in 1773, at the age of seventy-nine.[1]

LORD CHATHAM

THE name of Chatham is the representative, in our language, of whatever is bold and commanding in eloquence. Yet his speeches are so imperfectly reported that it is not so much from them as from the testimony of his contemporaries that we have gained our conceptions of his transcendent powers as an orator. We measure his greatness, as we do the height of some inaccessible cliff, by the shadow it casts behind. Hence it will be proper to dwell more at large on the events of his political life, and especially to collect the evidence which has come down to us by tradition, of his astonishing sway over the British Senate.

William Pitt, first Earl of Chatham, was descended from a family of high respectability in Cornwall, and was born at London, on the 15th of November, 1708. At Eton, where he was placed from boyhood, he was distinguished for the quickness of his parts and for his habits of unwearied application, though liable, much of his time, to severe suffering from a hereditary gout. Here he acquired that love of the classics which he carried with him throughout life, and which operated so powerfully in forming his character as an orator. He also formed at Eton those habits of easy and animated conversation for which he was celebrated in after life. Cut off by disease from the active sports of the school, he and Lord Lyttleton, who was a greater invalid than himself, found their chief enjoyment during the intervals of study in the lively interchange of thought. By the keenness of their wit and the brilliancy of their imaginations, they drew off their companions, Fox, Hanbury Williams, Fielding, and others, from the exercises of the playground, to gather around them as eager listeners; and gained that quickness of thought, that dexterity of reply, that ready self-possession under a sudden turn of argument or the sharpness of retort, which are indispensable to success in public debate. Almost every great orator has been distinguished for his conversational powers.

At the age of eighteen, Mr. Pitt was removed to the University of Oxford. Here, in connection with his other studies, he entered on that severe course of rhetorical training which he often referred to in after life as forming so large a part of his early discipline. He took up the practice of writing out translations from the ancient orators and historians, on the broadest scale. Demosthenes was his model; and we are told that he rendered a large part of his orations again and again into English, as the best means of acquiring a forcible and expressive style. The practice was highly recommended by Cicero, from his own experience. It aids the young orator far more effectually in catching the spirit of his model than any course of mere reading, however fervent or repeated. It is, likewise, the severest test of his command of language. To clothe the thoughts of another in a dress which is at once "close and easy" (an excellent, though quaint description of a good translation) is a task of extreme difficulty. As a means of acquiring copiousness of diction and an exact choice of words, Mr. Pitt also read and re-read the sermons of Dr. Barrow, till he knew many of them by heart. With the same view, he performed a task to which, perhaps, no other student in oratory has ever submitted. He went *twice* through the folio Dictionary of Bailey (the best before that of Johnson), examining each word attentively, dwelling on its peculiar import and modes of construction, and thus endeavoring to bring the whole range of our language completely under his control. At this time, also, he began those exercises in elocution by which he is known to have obtained his extraordinary powers of delivery. Though gifted by nature with a commanding voice and person, he spared no effort to add every thing that art could confer for his improvement as an orator. His success was commensurate with his zeal. Garrick himself was not a greater actor, in that higher sense of the term in which Demosthenes declared *action* to be the first, and second, and third thing in oratory. The labor which he bestowed on these exercises was surprisingly great. Probably no man of genius since the days of Cicero has ever submitted to an equal amount of drudgery.

Leaving the University a little before the regular time of graduation, Mr. Pitt traveled on the Continent, particularly in France and Italy. During this tour, he enriched his mind with a great variety of historical and literary information, making everything subservient, however, to the one great object of preparing for public life. "He thus acquired," says Lord Chesterfield, "a vast amount of premature and useful knowledge." On his return to England, he applied a large part of his slender patrimony to the purchase of a commission in the army, and became a Cornet of the Blues. This made him dependent on Sir Robert Walpole, who was then Prime Minister; but, with his characteristic boldness and disregard of consequences, he took his stand, about this time, in the ranks of Opposition. Walpole, by his jealously, had made almost every man of talents in the Whig party his personal enemy. His long continuance in office, against the wishes of the people, was considered a kind of tyranny; and young men like Pitt, Lyttleton, &c., who came fresh from college, with an ardent love of liberty inspired by the study of the classics, were naturally drawn to the standard of Pulteney, Carteret, and the other leading "Patriots" who declaimed so vehemently against a corrupt and oppressive government. The Prince of Wales, in consequence of a quarrel with his father, had now come out as head of the Opposition. A rival court was established at Leicester House, within the very precincts of St. James's Palace, which drew together such an assemblage of wits, scholars, and orators as had never before met in the British empire. Jacobites, Tories, and Patriots were here united. The insidious, intriguing, but highly-gifted Carteret; the courtly Chesterfield; the impetuous Argyle; Pulteney, with a keenness of wit, and a familiarity with the classics which made him as brilliant in conversation as he was powerful in debate; Sir John Barnard, with his strong sense and penetrating judgment; Sir William Wyndham, with his dignified sentiments and lofty bearing; and "the all-accomplished Bolingbroke, who conversed in language as elegant as that he wrote, and whose lightest table-talk, if transferred to paper, would, in its style and matter, have borne the test of the severest criticism"—these, together with the most distinguished literary men of the age, formed the court of Frederick, and became the intimate associates of Mr. Pitt. On a mind so ardent and aspiring, so well prepared to profit by mingling in such society, so gifted with the talent of transferring to itself the kindred excellence of other minds, the company of such men must have acted with extraordinary power; and it is probable that all his rhetorical studies had less effect in making him the orator that he was, than his intimacy with the great leaders of the Opposition at the court of the Prince of Wales.

Mr. Pitt became a member of Parliament in 1735, at the age of twenty-six. For nearly a year he remained silent, studying the temper of the House, and waiting for a favorable opportunity to come forward. Such an opportunity was presented by the marriage of the Prince of Wales, in April, 1736. It was an event of the highest interest and joy to the nation; but such was the King's animosity against his son, that he would not suffer the address of congratulation to be moved, as usual, by the ministers of the Crown. The motion was brought forward by Mr. Pulteney; and it shows the high estimate put upon Mr. Pitt, that, when he had not as yet opened his lips in Parliament, he should be selected to second the motion, in preference to some of the most able and experienced members of the House. His speech was received with the highest applause, and shows that Mr. Pitt's imposing manner and fine command of language gave him from the first that sort of fascination for his audience which he seemed always to exert over a popular assembly. The speech, which will be found below, if understood literally, is only a series of elegant and high-sounding compliments. If, however, as seems plainly the case, there runs throughout it a deeper meaning; if the glowing panegyric on "the *filial virtue*" of the Prince, and "the *tender* paternal delight" of the King, was intended to reflect on George II for his harsh treatment of his son—and it can hardly be otherwise—we can not enough admire the dexterity of Mr. Pitt in so managing his subject, as to give his compliments all the effect of the keenest irony, while yet he left no pretense for taking notice of their application as improper or disrespectful. Certain it is that the whole speech was wormwood and gall to the King. It awakened in his mind a personal hatred of Mr. Pitt, which, aggravated as it was by subsequent attacks of a more direct nature, excluded him for years from the service of the Crown, until he was forced upon a reluctant monarch by the demands of the people.

Sir Robert Walpole, as might be supposed, listened to the eloquence of his youthful opponent with anxiety and alarm; and is said to have exclaimed, after hearing the speech, "We must, at all events, muzzle that terrible Cornet of Horse." Whether he attempted to bribe him by offers of promotion in the army (as was reported at the time), it is impossible now to say; but finding him unalterably attached to the Prince and the Opposition, he struck the blow without giving him time to make another speech, and deprived him of his commission within less than eighteen days. Such a mode of punishing a political opponent has rarely been resorted to, under free governments, in the case of military and naval officers. It only rendered the Court more odious, while it created a general sympathy in favor of Mr. Pitt, and turned the attention of the public with new zest and interest to his speeches in Parliament. Lord Lyttleton, at the same time, addressed him in the following lines, which were eagerly circulated throughout the country, and set him forth as already leader of the Opposition.

> Long had thy virtues marked thee out for fame,
> Far, far superior to a Cornet's name;
> This generous Walpole saw, and grieved to find
> So mean a post disgrace the human mind,
> The servile standard from the free-born hand
> He took, and bade thee *lead the Patriot Band.*

As a compensation to Mr. Pitt for the loss of his commission, the Prince appointed him Groom of the Bed-chamber at Leicester House.

Thus, at the age of twenty-seven, Mr. Pitt was made, by the force of his genius and the influence of concurrent circumstances, one of the most prominent members of Parliament and an object of the liveliest interest to the great body, especially the middling classes, of the English nation. These classes were now rising into an importance never before known. They regarded Sir Robert Walpole, sustained as he was in power by the will of the sovereign and the bribery of Parliament, as their natural enemy. Mr. Pitt shared in all their feelings. He was the exponent of their principles. He was, in *truth,* "the Great Commoner." As to many of the measures for which Walpole was hated by the people and opposed by Mr. Pitt, time has shown that he was in the right and they in the wrong. It has also shown, that nearly all the great leaders of the Opposition, the Pulteneys and the Carterets, were unprincipled men, who played on the generous sympathies of Pitt and Lyttleton and lashed the prejudices of the nation into rage against the minister, simply to obtain his place. Still the struggle of the people, though in many respects a blind one, was prompted by a genuine instinct of their nature, and was prophetic of an onward movement in English society. It was the Commons of England demanding their place in the Constitution; and happy it was that they had a leader like Mr. Pitt, to represent their principles and animate their exertions. To face at once the Crown and the Peerage demanded not only undaunted resolution, but something of that imperious spirit, that haughty self-assertion, which was so often complained of in the greatest of English orators. In him, however, it was not merely a sense of personal superiority, but a consciousness of the cause in which he was engaged. *He was set for the defense of the popular part of the Constitution.*

In proceeding to trace briefly the course of Mr. Pitt as a statesman, we shall divide his public life into distinct periods, and consider them separately with reference to his measures in Parliament.

The *first* period consists of nearly ten years, down to the close of 1744. During the whole of this time, he was an active member of the Opposition, being engaged for nearly seven years in unwearied efforts to put down Sir Robert Walpole, and when this was accomplished, in equally strenuous exertions for three years longer, to resist the headlong measures of his successor, Lord Carteret. This minister had rendered himself odious to the nation by encouraging the narrow views and sordid policy of the King, in respect to his Continental possessions. George II was born in Hanover, and he always consulted its interests at the expense of Great Britain; seeking to throw upon the national treasury the support of the Hanoverian troops during his wars on the Continent, and giving the Electorate, in various other ways, a marked preference over the rest of the empire. To these measures, and the minister who abetted them, Mr. Pitt opposed himself with all the energy of his fervid argumentation, and the force of his terrible invective. It was on this subject that he first came into collision, December 10th, 1742, with his great antagonist Murray, afterward Lord Mansfield. Mr. Oswald, a distinguished literary man who was present, thus describes the two combatants: "Murray spoke like a pleader, who could not divest himself of the appearance of having been employed by others. Pitt spoke like a gentleman—like a statesman who felt what he said, and possessed the strongest desire of conveying that feeling to others, for their own interest and that of their country. Murray gains your attention by the perspicuity of his statement and the elegance of his diction; Pitt commands your attention and respect by the nobleness and greatness of his sentiments, the strength and energy of his expressions, and the certainty of his always rising to a greater elevation both of thought and sentiment. For, this talent he possesses, beyond any speaker I ever heard, of never *falling* from the beginning to the end of his speech, either in thought or expression. And as in this session he has begun to speak like a man of business as well as an orator, he will in all probability be, or rather *is,* allowed to make as great an appearance as ever man did in that House."

Mr. Pitt incessantly carried on the attack upon Carteret, who, strong in the King's favor, was acting against the wishes of his associates in office. He exclaimed against him as "a *sole* minister, who had renounced the British nation, and seemed to have drunk of that potion described in poetic fictions, which made men forget their country." He described the King as "hemmed in by German officers, and *one* English minister without an English heart." It was probably about this time that he made his celebrated retort on Sir William Yonge, a man of great abilities but flagitious life, who had interrupted him while speaking by crying out "Question! Question!" Turning to the insolent intruder with a look of inexpressible disgust, he exclaimed, "Pardon me, Mr. Speaker, my agitation! When that gentleman calls for the *question,* I think I hear the knell of my country's ruin." Mr. Pitt soon gained a complete ascendency over the House. No man could cope with him; few ventured even to oppose him; and Carteret was given up by all as an object of merited reprobation. Under these circumstances, Mr. Pelham, who had now become head of the government, opened a negotiation for a union with Mr. Pitt and the dismissal of Carteret. The terms were easily arranged, and a memorial was at once presented to the King by Lord Hardwicke, supported by the rest of the ministry, demanding the removal of the obnoxious favorite. The King refused, wavered, temporized, and at last yielded. Mr. Pelham formed a new ministry in November, 1744, with the understanding that Mr. Pitt should be brought into office at the earliest moment that the King's prejudices would permit. During the same year, the Duchess of Marlborough died, leaving Mr. Pitt a legacy of £10,000, "on account of his merit in the noble defense of the laws of England, and to prevent the ruin of the country." This was a seasonable relief to one who never made any account of money, and whose circumstances, down to this time, were extremely limited. It may as well here be mentioned, that about twenty years after, he received a still more ample testimony of the same kind from Sir William Pynsent, who bequeathed him an estate of £2500 a year, together with £30,000 in ready money.

We now come to the *second* period of Mr. Pitt's political life, embracing the ten years of Mr. Pelham's ministry down to the year 1754. So strong was the hostility of the King to his old opponent that no persuasions could induce him to receive Mr. Pitt into his service. On the contrary, when pressed upon the subject, he took decided measures for getting rid of his new ministers. This led Mr. Pelham and his associates, who knew their strength, instantly to resign. The King was now powerless. The Earl of Bath (Pulteney), to whom he had committed the formation of a ministry, could get nobody to serve under him; the retired ministers looked with derision on his fruitless efforts; and some one remarked sarcastically, "that it was unsafe to walk the streets at night, for fear of being pressed for a cabinet counselor." The *Long* Administration came to an end in just forty-eight hours! The King was compelled to go back to Mr. Pelham, and to take Mr. Pitt along with him; he stipulated, however, that the man who was thus forced upon him should not, at least for a time, be brought into immediate contact with his person. He could not endure the mortification of meeting with him in private. Mr. Pitt, therefore, received provisionally the situation of Joint Treasurer of Ireland. He now resigned the office of Groom of the Chamber to the Prince of Wales, and entered heartily into the interests of the Pelham ministry. A contemporary represents him as "swaying the House of Commons, and uniting in himself the dignity of Wyndham, the wit of Pulteney, and the knowledge and judgment of Walpole." He was "right [conciliatory] toward the King, kind and respectful to the old corps, and resolute and contemptuous to the Tory Opposition." About a year after (May, 1746), on the death of Mr. Winnington, he was made Paymaster of the Forces, as originally agreed on.

In entering upon his new office, Mr. Pitt gave a striking exhibition of disinterestedness, which raised him in the public estimation to a still higher level as a man, than he had ever attained by his loftiest efforts as an orator. It was then the custom, that £100,000 should constantly lie as an advance in the hands of the Paymaster, who invested the money in public securities, and thus realized about £4000 a year for his private benefit. This was obviously a very dangerous practice; for if the funds were suddenly depressed, through a general panic or any great public calamity, the Paymaster might be unable to realize his investments, and would thus become a public defaulter. This actually happened during the rebellion of 1745, when the army, on whose fidelity depended the very existence of the government, was for a time left without pay. Mr. Pitt, therefore, on assuming the duties of Paymaster, placed all the funds at his control in the Bank of England, satisfied with the moderate compensation attached to his office.

He also gave another proof of his elevation above pecuniary motives, by refusing a certain percentage, which had always been attached to his office, on the enormous subsidies then paid to the Queen of Austria and the King of Sardinia. The latter, when he heard of this refusal, requested Mr. Pitt to accept, as a token of royal favor, what he had rejected as a perquisite of office. Mr. Pitt still refused. It was this total disregard of the ordinary means of becoming rich, that made Mr. Grattan say, "his character astonished a corrupt age." Politicians were indeed puzzled to understand his motives; for bribery in Parliament and corruption in office had become so universal, and the spirit of public men so sordid, that the cry of the horse-leech was heard in every quarter, "Give! Give!" Ambition itself had degenerated into a thirst for gold. Power and preferment were sought chiefly as the means of amassing wealth. Well might George II say, when he heard of Mr. Pitt's noble disinterestedness, "His conduct does honor to human nature!"

In joining the Pelham ministry, Mr. Pitt yielded more than might have been expected, to the King's wishes in regard to German subsidies and Continental alliances. For this he has been charged with inconsistency. He thought, however, that the case was materially changed. The war had advanced so far, that nothing remained but to fight it through, and this could be done only by German troops. In addition to this, the Electorate was now in danger; and though he had resisted Carteret's measures for aggrandizing Hanover at the expense of Great Britain, he could, without any change of principles, unite with Pelham to prevent her being wrested from the empire by the ambition of France. He saw, too, that the King grew more obstinate as he grew older, and that if the government was to be administered at all, it must be by those who were willing to make some concessions to the prejudices, and even to the weakness, of an aged monarch. That he was influenced in all this by no ambitious motives, that his desire to stand well with the King had no connection with a desire to stand highest in the state, it would certainly be unsafe to affirm. But his love of power had nothing in it that was mercenary or selfish. He did not seek it, like Newcastle, for patronage, or, like Pulteney and Fox, for money. He had lofty conceptions of the dignity to which England might be raised as the head of European politics; he felt himself equal to the achievement; and he panted for an opportunity to enter on a career of service which should realize his brightest visions of his country's glory. With these views, he supported Pelham and endeavored to conciliate the King, waiting with a prophetic spirit for the occasion which was soon to arrive.

Mr. Pelham died suddenly in March, 1754; and this leads us to the *third* period of Mr. Pitt's public life, embracing about three years, down to 1757. The death of Pelham threw every thing into confusion. "Now I shall have no more peace," said the old King, when he heard the news. The event verified his predictions. The Duke of Newcastle, brother of Mr. Pelham, demanded the office of Prime Minister, and was enabled, by his borough interest and family connections, to enforce his claim. The "lead" of the House of Commons was now to be disposed of, and there were only three men who had the slightest pretensions to the prize, viz., Pitt, Fox, and Murray, afterward Lord Mansfield. And yet Newcastle, out of a mean jealousy of their superior abilities, gave it to Sir Thomas Robinson, who was so poor a speaker that "when he played the orator," says Lord Waldegrave, "which he frequently attempted, it was so exceedingly ridiculous that even those who loved him could not always preserve a friendly composure of countenance." "Sir Thomas Robinson lead us?" said Pitt to Fox; "the Duke might as well send his jack-boot to lead us!" He was accordingly baited on every side, falling perpetually into blunders which provoked the stern animadversions of Pitt, or the more painful irony of Fox. Robinson was soon silenced, and Murray was next brought forward. Mr. Pitt did not resign; but after this second rejection he felt absolved from all obligations to Newcastle, and determined to make both him and Murray feel his power. An opportunity was soon presented, and he carried out his design with a dexterity and effect which awakened universal admiration. At the trial of a contested election [that of the Dalavals], when the debate had degenerated into mere buffoonery which kept the members in a continual roar, Mr. Pitt came down from the gallery where he was sitting, says Fox, who was present, and took the House to task for their conduct "in his highest tone." He inquired whether the dignity of the House stood on such sure foundations that they might venture to shake it thus. He intimated that the tendency of things was to degrade the House into a mere French Parliament, and exhorted the Whigs of all conditions to defend their attacked and expiring liberties, "unless," said he, "you are to degenerate into a little assembly, serving no other purpose than to register the arbitrary edicts of *one* too powerful *subject*" (laying, says Fox, a most remarkable emphasis on the words *one* and *subject*). The application to Newcastle was seen and felt by all. "It was the finest speech," adds Fox, "that was ever made, and it was observed that by his first two sentences he brought the House to a silence and attention that you might have heard a pin drop. I just now learn that the Duke of Newcastle was in the utmost fidget, and that it spoiled his stomach yesterday."[1] According to another who was present, "this thunderbolt, thrown in a sky so long clear, confounded the audience. Murray crouched silent and terrified." Nor without reason, for *his* turn came next. On the following day, November 27, 1754, Mr. Pitt made two other speeches, ostensibly against Jacobitism, but intended for Murray, who had just been raised from the office of Solicitor to that of Attorney General. "In both speeches," says Fox, "every word was *Murray,* yet so managed that neither he nor any body else could take public notice of it, or in any way reprehend him. I sat near Murray, who *suffered* for an hour." It was, perhaps, on this occasion, says Charles Butler in his Reminiscences, that Pitt used an expression which was once in every mouth. After Murray had "suffered" for a time, Pitt stopped, threw his eyes around, then fixing their whole power on Murray, exclaimed, "I must now address a few words to Mr. Attorney; they shall be few, but shall be daggers." Murray was agitated; the look was continued; the agitation increased. "Felix trembles!" exclaimed Pitt, in a tone of thunder; *"He shall hear me some other day!"* He sat down. Murray made no reply; and a languid debate showed the paralysis of the House.[2]

Newcastle found it impossible to go on without adding to his strength in debate. He therefore bought off Fox in April, 1755, by bringing him into the Cabinet, while Pitt was again rejected with insult. To this incongruous union Mr. Pitt alluded, a few months after, in terms which were much admired for the felicity of the image under which the allusion was conveyed. Newcastle, it is well known, was feeble and tame, while Fox was headlong and impetuous. An address, prepared by the ministry, was complained of as obscure and incongruous. Mr. Pitt took it up, saying, "There are parts of this address which do not seem to come from the same quarter with the rest. I can not unravel the mystery." Then, as if suddenly recollecting the two men thus brought together at the head of affairs, he exclaimed, clapping his hand to his forehead, "Now it strikes me! I remember at Lyons to have been carried to see the conflux of the Rhone and the Saone—the one a feeble, languid stream, and, though languid, of no great depth; the other a boisterous and impetuous torrent. But, different as they are, they *meet at last;* and long," he added, with the bitterest irony, "*long* may they continue united, to the *comfort* of each other, and to the *glory, honor,* and *security* of this nation!" In less than a week Mr. Pitt was dismissed from his office as Paymaster.

This was the signal for open war—Pitt against the entire ministry. Ample occasion for attack was furnished by the disasters which were continually occurring in the public service, and the dangers resulting therefrom—the loss of Minorca, the defeat of General Braddock, the capture of Calcutta by Sujah Dowlah, and the threatened invasion by the French. These topics afforded just ground for the terrible onset of Mr. Pitt. "During the whole session of 1755–6," says an eye-witness, "Mr. Pitt found occasion, in every debate, to confound the ministerial orators. His vehement invectives were awful to Murray, terrible to Hugh Campbell; and no malefactor under the stripes of the executioner, was ever more helpless and forlorn than Fox, shrewd and able in Parliament as he confessedly is. Doddington sheltered himself in silence." With all this vehemence, however, he was never betrayed into any thing coarse or unbecoming the dignity of his character. Horace Walpole, writing to Gerard Hamilton, says of his appearance on one of these occasions, "There was more humor, wit, vivacity, fine language, more boldness, in short more astonishing perfection than even you, who are used to him, can conceive." And again, "He surpassed himself, as I need not tell you he surpassed Cicero and Demosthenes. What a figure would they make, with their formal, labored, cabinet orations, by the side of his manly vivacity and dashing eloquence at *one o'clock in the morning,* after a sitting of eleven hours!" The effect on the ministerial ranks was soon apparent. Murray was the first to shrink. The ablest by far among the supporters of the ministry —much abler, indeed, as a reasoner, than his great opponent, and incomparably more learned in every thing pertaining to the science of government, he could stand up no longer before the devouring eloquence of Pitt. On the death of Chief-justice Ryder, which took place May 25th, 1756, he instantly demanded the place. Newcastle resisted, entreated, offered, in addition to the profits of the Attorney Generalship, a pension of £2000, and, at last, of £6000 a year. It was all in vain. Nothing could induce Murray to remain longer in the House. He was accordingly made Chief Justice, in November with the title of Lord Mansfield; and on the day he took his seat upon the bench, Newcastle *resigned as minister.*

Nothing now remained for the King but to transfer the government to Mr. Pitt. It was a humiliating necessity, but the condition of public affairs was dark and threatening, and no one else could be found of sufficient courage or capacity to undertake the task. Pitt had said to the Duke of Devonshire, "My Lord, I am sure that I can save this country, and that nobody else can." The people believed him. "The eyes of an afflicted and despairing nation," says Glover, who was far from partaking in their enthusiasm, "were now lifted up to a private gentleman of slender fortune, wanting the parade of birth or title, with no influence except marriage with Lord Temple's sister, and even confined to a narrow circle of friends and acquaintances. Yet, under these circumstances, Mr. Pitt was considered the savior of England." His triumph was the triumph of the popular part of the Constitution. It was the first instance in which the middling classes, the true Commons of Great Britain, were able to break down in Parliament that power which the great families of the aristocracy had so long possessed, of setting aside or sustaining the decisions of the Throne.

Mr. Pitt's entrance on the duties of Prime Minister in December, 1756, brings us to the *fourth* period of his political life, which embraces nearly five years, down to October, 1761.

For about four months, however, during his first ministry, his hands were in a great measure tied. Though supported by the unanimous voice of the people, the King regarded him with personal dislike; Newcastle and his other opponents were able to defeat him in Parliament; and in April, 1757, he received the royal mandate to retire. This raised a storm throughout the whole of England. The stocks fell. The Common Council of London met and passed resolutions of the strongest kind. The principal towns of the kingdom, Bath, Chester, Norwich, Salisbury, Worcester, Yarmouth, Newcastle, and many others, sent Mr. Pitt the freedom of their respective cities, as a token of their confidence and as a warning to the King. "For some weeks," says Horace Walpole, "it rained gold boxes!" The King, in the mean time, spent nearly three months in the vain attempt to form another administration. It was now perfectly ap parent, that nothing could be done without concessions on both sides. Mr. Pitt therefore consented, June 29th, 1757, to resume his office as Principal Secretary of State and Prime Minister, in conjunction with Newcastle as head of the Treasury, satisfied that he could more easily overrule and direct the Duke as a member of the Cabinet than as leader of the Opposition. The result verified his expectations. His second ministry now commenced, that splendid era which raised England at once, as if by magic, from the brink of ruin and degradation. The genius of one man completely penetrated and informed the mind of a whole people. "From the instant he took the reins, the panic, which had paralyzed every effort, disappeared. Instead of mourning over former disgrace and dreading future defeats, the nation assumed in a moment the air of confidence, and awaited with impatience the tidings of victory." In every thing he undertook,

> "He put so much of his soul into his act
> That his example had a magnet's force,
> And all were prompt to follow whom all loved."

To this wonderful power of throwing his spirit into other minds, Colonel Barré referred at a later period, in one of his speeches in Parliament: "He was possessed of the happy talent of transfusing his own zeal into the souls of all those who were to have a share in carrying his projects into execution; and it is a matter well known to many officers now in the House, that no man ever entered his closet who did not feel himself, if possible, *braver at his return* than when he went in." He knew, also, how to use fear, as well as affection, for the accomplishment of his designs. "It will be impossible to have so many ships prepared so soon," said Lord Anson, when a certain expedition was ordered. "If the ships are not ready," said Mr. Pitt, "I will impeach your Lordship in presence of the House." They were ready as directed. Newcastle, in the mean time, yielded with quiet submission to the supremacy of his genius. All the Duke wanted was the patronage, and this Mr. Pitt cheerfully gave up for the salvation of the country. Horace Walpole says, in his lively manner, "Mr. Pitt *does* every thing, and the Duke of Newcastle *gives* every thing. As long as they can agree in this partition, they may do what they will."[3]

One of the first steps taken by Mr. Pitt was to grant a large subsidy to Frederick the Great, of Prussia, for carrying on the war against the Empress of Austria. This was connected with a total change which had already taken place in the Continental policy of George II, and was intended to rescue Hanover from the hands of the French. Still, there were many who had a traditional regard for the Empress of Austria, in whose defense England had expended more than ten millions of pounds sterling. The grant was, therefore, strenuously opposed in the House, and Mr. Pitt was taunted with a desertion of his principles. In reply, he defended himself, and maintained the necessity of the grant with infinite dexterity. "It was," says Horace Walpole, "the most artful speech he ever made. He provoked, called for, defied objections—promised enormous expense—demanded never to be tried by events." By degrees he completely subdued the House, until a murmur of applause broke forth from every quarter. Seizing the favorable moment, he drew back with the utmost dignity, and placing himself in an attitude of defiance, exclaimed, in his loudest tone, "Is there an *Austrian* among you? Let him come forward and reveal himself!" The effect was irresistible. "Universal silence," says Walpole, "left him arbiter of his own terms." Another striking instance of Mr. Pitt's mastery over the House is said also to have occurred about this time. Having finished a speech, he walked out with a slow step, being severely afflicted with the gout. A silence ensued until the door was opened to let him pass into the lobby, when a member started up, saying, "Mr. Speaker, I rise to reply to the right honorable gentleman." Pitt, who had caught the words, turned back and fixed his eye on the orator, who instantly sat down. He then returned toward his seat, repeating, as he hobbled along, the lines of Virgil, in which the poet, conducting Æneas through the shades below, describes the terror which his presence inspired among the ghosts of the Greeks who had fought at Troy:

> Ast Danaum proceres, Agamemnoniæque phalanges,
> Ut vidêre VIRUM, fulgentiaque arma per umbras,
> Ingenti trepidare metu; pars vertere terga,
> Ceu quondam petiêre rates; pars tollere vocem
> Exiguam: *inceptus clamor frustratur hiantes.*[4]
>
> VIRGIL, *Æn.,* vi., 489.

Reaching his seat, he exclaimed, "Now let me hear what the honorable gentleman has to say to me!" One who was present, being asked whether the House was not convulsed with laughter at the ludicrous situation of the poor orator and the aptness of the lines, replied, "No, sir; we were all too much awed to laugh."

There was, however, very little debate after his administration had fairly commenced. All parties united in supporting his measures. It is, indeed, a remarkable fact, that the Parliamentary History, which professes to give a detailed report of all the debates in Parliament, contains not a single speech of Mr. Pitt, and only two or three by any other person, during the whole period of his ministry. The supplies which he demanded were, for that day, enormous—twelve millions and a half in one year, and nearly twenty millions the next—"a most incredible sum," says Walpole, respecting the former, "and yet already all subscribed for, and even more offered! Our unanimity is prodigious. You would as soon hear 'No' from an old maid as from the House of Commons." "Though Parliament has met," says Walpole again, in 1759, "no politics are come to town.

One may describe the House of Commons like the stocks: Debates, nothing done; Votes, under par; Patriots, no price; Oratory, books shut!"

England now entered into the war with all the energy of a new existence. Spread out in her colonies to the remotest parts of the globe, she resembled a strong man who had long been lying with palsied limbs, and the blood collected at the heart; when the stream of life, suddenly set free, rushes to the extremities, and he springs to his feet with an elastic bound to repel injury or punish aggression. In the year 1758, the contest was carried on at once in Europe, Asia, Africa, and America—wherever France had possessions to be attacked, or England to be defended. Notwithstanding some disasters at first, victory followed upon victory in rapid succession. Within little more than two years, all was changed. In Africa, France was stripped of every settlement she had on that continent. In India, defeated in two engagements at sea, and driven from every post on land, she gave up her long contest for the mastery of the East, and left the British to establish their government over a hundred and fifty millions of people. In America, all her rich possessions in the West Indies passed into the hands of Great Britain. Louisburg, Quebec, Ticonderoga, Crown Point, Oswego, Niagara, Fort Duquesne [now Pittsburgh], were taken; and the entire chain of posts with which France had hemmed in and threatened our early settlements fell before the united arms of the colonists and the English, and not an inch of territory was left her in the Western World. In Europe, Hanover was rescued; the French were defeated at Creveldt, and again at Minden with still greater injury and disgrace; the coasts of France were four times invaded with severe loss to the English, but still with a desperate determination to strike terror into the hearts of the enemy; Hâvre was bombarded; the port and fortifications of Cherbourg were demolished; Brest and the other principal sea-ports were blockaded; the Toulon fleet was captured or destroyed; and the brilliant victory of Admiral Hawke off Quiberon, annihilated the French navy for the remainder of the war.[5] At home, the only part of the empire which continued hostile to the government, the Highlanders of Scotland, who had been disarmed for their rebellions, and insulted by a law forbidding them to wear their national costume, were forever detached from the Stuarts, and drawn in grateful affection around the Throne by Mr. Pitt's happy act of confidence in putting arms into their hands and sending them to fight the battles of their country in every quarter of the globe. Finally, the commercial interests of the kingdom, always the most important to a great manufacturing people, prospered as never before; and "COMMERCE," in the words inscribed by the city of London on the statue which they erected to Mr. Pitt, "COMMERCE, for the *first* time, was united with, and made to flourish by, WAR!"

France was now effectually humbled. In 1761 she sought for peace, and Mr. Pitt declared to his friends, when entering on the negotiation, that "no Peace of Utrecht should again stain the annals of England." He therefore resisted every attempt of France to obtain a restoration of conquests, and was on the point of concluding a treaty upon terms commensurate with the triumphs of the English arms when the French succeeded in drawing Spain into the contest. After a season of long alienation, an understanding once more took place between the two branches of the house of Bourbon. The French minister instantly changed his tone. He came forward with a proposal that Spain should be invited to take part in the treaty, specifying certain claims of that country upon England which required adjustment. Mr. Pitt was indignant at this attempt of a prostrate enemy to draw a third party into the negotiation. He spurned the proposal. He declared that "he would not relax one syllable from his terms, until the Tower of London was taken by storm." He demanded of Spain a disavowal of the French minister's claims. This offended the Spanish court, and France accomplished her object. The celebrated Family Compact was entered into, which once more identified the two nations in all their interests; and Spain, by a subsequent stipulation, engaged to unite in the war with France, unless England should make peace on satisfactory terms before May, 1762. Mr. Pitt, whose means of secret intelligence were hardly inferior to those of Oliver Cromwell, was apprised of these arrangements (though studiously concealed) almost as soon as they were made. He saw that a war was inevitable, that he had just ground of war; and he resolved to strike the first blow—to seize the Spanish treasure-ships which were then on their way from America, to surprise Havana, which was wholly unprepared for defense, to wrest the Isthmus of Panama from Spain, and thus put the keys of her commerce between the two oceans forever into the hands of the English. But when he proposed these measures to the Cabinet, he was met, to his surprise, with an open and determined resistance. George II was dead. Lord Bute, the favorite of George III, was jealous of Mr. Pitt's ascendency. The King probably shared in the same feelings, and in the language of Grattan, "conspired to remove him, in order to be relieved from his superiority." An obsequious cabinet voted down Mr. Pitt's proposal. He instantly resigned; and Spain, as if to prove his sagacity and justify the measure he had urged, drove England into war within three months.

The King, however, in thus ending the most glorious ministry which England had ever seen, manifested a strong desire to conciliate Mr. Pitt. The very next day he sent a message to him through Lord Bute, declaring that he was "impatient" to bestow upon him some mark of the royal favor. Mr. Pitt was melted by these unexpected tokens of kindness. He replied in terms which have often been censured as unbecoming a man of spirit under a sense of injury—terms which would certainly be thought obsequious at the present day, but which were probably dictated by the sudden revulsion of his feelings and the courtly style which he always maintained in his intercourse with the sovereign.[6] On the day after his resignation, he accepted a pension of £3000 (being much less than was offered him), together with a peerage for his wife. Some, indeed, complained that, acting as he did for the people, he should have allowed the King to place him under any pecuniary obligations. "If he had gone into the city," said Walpole, "and told them he had a poor wife and children unprovided for, and opened a subscription, he would have got £500,000 instead of £3000 a year." He could never have done so until he had ceased to be William Pitt. Mr. Burke has truly said, "With regard to the pension and the title, it is a shame that any defense should be necessary. What eye can not distinguish, at the first glance, between this and the exceptionable case of titles and pensions? What Briton, with the smallest sense of honor or gratitude, but must blush for his country, if such a man had retired unrewarded from the public service, let the motives of that retirement be what they would? It was not *possible* that his sovereign should let his eminent services pass unrequited; and the quantum was rather regulated by the moderation of the great mind that received, than by the liberality of that which bestowed it."[7] It is hardly necessary to add that the tide of public favor, which had ebbed for a moment, soon returned to its ordinary channels. The city of London sent him an address in the warmest terms of commendation. On Lord Mayor's day, when he joined the young King and Queen in their procession to dine at Guildhall, the eyes of the multitude were turned from the royal equipage to the modest vehicle which contained Mr. Pitt and his brother-in-law, Lord Temple. The loudest acclamations were reserved for the Great Commoner. The crowd, says an eye-witness, clustered around his carriage at every step, "hung upon the wheels, hugged his footmen, and even kissed his horses." Such were the circumstances under which he retired from office, having resigned on the 5th of October, 1761.

We now come to the *fifth* and last period of Mr. Pitt's life, embracing about sixteen years, down to his decease in 1778. During the whole of this period, except for a brief season when he was called to form a new ministry, he acted with the Opposition. When a treaty of peace was concluded by Lord Bute, in 1762, he was confined to his bed by the gout; but his feelings were so excited by the concessions made to France, that he caused himself to be conveyed to the House in the midst of his acutest sufferings, and poured out his indignation for three hours and a half, exposing in the keenest terms the loss and dishonor brought upon the country by the conditions of peace. This was called his "Sitting Speech;" because, after having stood for a time supported by two friends, "he was so excessively ill," says the Parliamentary History, "and his pain became so exceedingly acute, that the House unanimously desired he might be permitted to deliver his sentiments *sitting*—a circumstance that was unprecedented."[8] But whether the peace was disgraceful or not, the ministry had no alternative. Lord Bute could not raise money to carry on the war. The merchants, who had urged upon Mr. Pitt double the amount he needed whenever he asked a loan, refused their assistance to a minister whom they could not trust.

Under these circumstances, Lord Bute was soon driven to extremities; and as a means of increasing the revenues, introduced a bill subjecting cider to an excise. An Excise Bill has always been odious to the English. It brings with it the right of search. It lays open the private dwelling, which every Englishman has been taught to regard as his "castle." "You give to the dipping-rod," said one, arguing against such a law, "what you deny to the scepter!" Mr. Pitt laid hold of this feeling and opposed the bill with his utmost strength. There is no report of his speech, but a single passage has come down to us, containing one of the finest bursts of his eloquence. "The poorest man in his cottage may bid defiance to all the forces of the Crown. It may be frail; its roof may shake; the wind may blow through it; the storm may enter it; but *the King of England can not enter it!* All his power dares not cross the threshold of that ruined tenement!" It was on this occasion, as stated in the Parliamentary History, that Mr. Pitt uttered a *bon mot* which was long remembered for the mirth it occasioned. Mr. George Grenville replied to Mr. Pitt, and, though he admitted that an excise was odious, contended that the tax was unavoidable. "The right honorable gentleman," said he, "complains of the hardship of the tax—why does he not tell us *where* we can lay another in its stead?" "Tell me," said he, repeating it with strong emphasis, "tell me where you can lay another tax! Tell me where!" Mr. Pitt, from his seat, broke out in a musical tone, quoting from a popular song of the day, *"Gentle shepherd, tell me where!"* The House burst into a fit of laughter, which continued for some minutes, and Mr. Grenville barely escaped the *sobriquet* of Gentle Shepherd for the rest of his life. After six divisions, the bill was passed, but it drove Lord Bute from power. He resigned a few weeks after, and in May, 1763, was succeeded by Mr. Grenville, whose mistakes as minister, in connection with the peculiar temperament of the King, opened a new era in the history of Great Britain.

It was the misfortune of George III, in the early part of his life, to be governed first by favorites and then by his own passions. He was naturally of a quick and obstinate temper. During the first twenty years of his reign (for he afterward corrected this error), he allowed his feelings as a man to mingle far too much with his duties as a sovereign. This led him into two steps, one of which agitated, and the other dismembered his empire—the persecution of John Wilkes, and the attempt to force taxation on the American colonies. It is now known that he sent a personal order to have Wilkes arrested under a general warrant, against the advice of Lord Mansfield, and insisted on all the subsequent violations of law which gave such notoriety and influence to that restless demagogue. And although he did not originate the plan of taxing America, the moment the *right* was questioned, he resolved to maintain the principle to the utmost extremity. This it was that forced the "Declaratory Act" on Lord Rockingham, and held Lord North so long to the war, as it now appears, against his own judgment and feelings. In respect to both these subjects, Mr. Pitt took from the first, an open and decided stand against the wishes of the King. He did it on the principle which governed his whole political life; which led him, nearly thirty years before, to oppose so violently the issue of search-warrants for seamen—the principle of resisting arbitrary power in every form of defending, at all hazards, the rights and liberties of the subject, "however mean, however remote." During the remainder of his life, all his speeches of any importance, with a single exception, related to one or the other of these topics. It was his constant aim, in his own emphatic language, *"to restore, to save, to confirm* the CONSTITUTION."

This attachment of Mr. Pitt to the popular part of the government gave rise to an attack (it is not known on what occasion) which called forth one of those keen and contemptuous retorts with which he so often put down his opponents. Mr. Moreton, Chief Justice of Chester, having occasion to mention "the King, Lords, and Commons," paused, and, turning toward Mr. Pitt, added, "or, as the right honorable member would call them, Commons, Lords, and King." Mr. Pitt, says Charles Butler in relating the story, rose (as he always did) with great deliberation, and called to *order*. "I have," he said, "heard frequently in this House doctrines which surprised me; but now my blood runs cold! I desire the words of the honorable member may be taken down." The clerk wrote down the words. "Bring them to me!" said Mr. Pitt, in his loudest voice. By this time Mr. Moreton was frightened out of his senses. "Sir," said he, addressing the Speaker, "I meant nothing! King, Lords, and Commons; Lords, King, and Commons; Commons, Lords, and King—*tria juncta in uno*. I meant nothing! Indeed, I meant nothing!" "I don't wish to push the matter further," said Mr. Pitt, in a tone but little above a whisper. Then, in a higher note, "The moment a man acknowledges his error, he ceases to be guilty. I have a great regard for the honorable gentleman, and, as an instance of that regard, I give him this advice"—a pause of some moments; then, assuming a look of unspeakable derision, he added, in a colloquial tone, "Whenever that gentleman *means* nothing, I recommend to him to *say* nothing!"

It has already been intimated that during the period now under review, Mr. Pitt was called, for a brief season, into the service of the Crown. George Grenville, who succeeded Lord Bute, after acting as minister about two years, and inflicting on his country the evils of the American Stamp Act, became personally obnoxious to the King, and was dismissed from office about the middle of 1765. The eyes of the whole country were now turned toward Mr. Pitt, and the King asked the terms upon which he would accept office. Mr. Pitt replied that he was ready to go to St. James's, if he could "carry the Constitution along with him." But upon entering into details, it was found impossible to reconcile his views with that court influence which still overruled the King. Lord Rockingham was then called upon to form a ministry; and Mr. Pitt has been censured by many, and especially by his biographer, Mr. Thackeray, for not joining heartily in the design, and lending the whole weight of his influence to establish, under his Lordship, another great Whig administration. This might, perhaps, have been an act of magnanimity. But, considering his recent splendid services, the known wishes of the people, and his acknowledged superiority over every other man in the empire, it could hardly be expected of Mr. Pitt that he should make himself a stepping-stone for the ambition of another. Lord Rockingham, though a man of high integrity and generous sentiments, had not that force of character, that eloquence in debate, that controlling influence over the minds of others which could alone reanimate the Whig party and restore their principles and their policy under a Tory King. Mr. Pitt did not oppose the new ministers; but he declared, at the opening of Parliament, that he could not give them his confidence. "Pardon me, gentlemen," said he, bowing to the ministry, *"confidence is a plant of slow growth in an aged bosom!"* The event justified his delay and hesitation. "The Cabinet," says Cooke, in his History of Party, "was formed from the rear-guard of the Whigs—men who were timorous and suspicious of their own principles; who were bound in the chains of aristocratic expediency and personal interest, and who dared not to loose them, because they knew not the power of their principles or their ultimate tendency." The Rockingham administration performed one important service—they repealed the Stamp Act. But they held together only a year, and were dissolved on the 30th of July, 1766.

Mr. Pitt was now called upon to frame a ministry. It was plainly impossible for him to succeed; and no one but a man of his sanguine temperament would have thought of making the attempt. The Rockingham Whigs, forming the wealthy and aristocratic section of the party, might of course be expected to oppose. Lord Temple, who had hitherto adhered to Mr. Pitt in every emergency, now deserted him, and joined his brother, George Grenville, in justifying American taxation. Lord Camden and a few others, the pioneers of Whiggism as it now exists, supported Mr. Pitt, and carried with them the suffrages of the people. But the Tories were favorites at Court. They filled all the important stations of the household; they had the readiest access to the royal presence; and, though Mr. Pitt might, at first, undoubtedly rely on the King for support, he could hardly expect to enjoy it long without gratifying his wishes in the selection of the great officers of state. Under these circumstances, the moment Mr. Pitt discovered his real situation, he ought to have relinquished the attempt to form a ministry. But he was led on step by step. His proud spirit had never been accustomed to draw back. He at last formed one on coalition principles. He drew around him as many of his own friends as possible, and filled up the remaining places with Tories, hoping to keep the peace at the council-board by his personal influence and authority. He had put down Newcastle by uniting with him, and he was confident of doing the same with his new competitors. But he made one mistake at the outset, which, in connection with his subsequent illness, proved the ruin of his ministry. It related to the "lead" of the House of Commons. *His* voice was the only one that could rule the stormy discussions of that body, and compose the elements of strife which were thickening around him. And yet he withdrew from the House, and gave the lead to Charles Townsend. Never was a choice more unfortunate. Townsend was, indeed, brilliant, but he was rash and unstable; eaten up with the desire to please everybody; utterly devoid of firmness and self-command; and, therefore, the last man in the world for giving a lead and direction to the measures of the House. But Mr. Pitt's health was gone. He felt wholly inadequate, under his frequent attacks of the gout, to take the burden of debate; he therefore named himself Lord Privy Seal, and passed into the Upper House with the title of Lord Chatham. As might be expected, his motives in thus accepting the peerage were, for a time, misunderstood. He was supposed to have renounced his principles, and become a creature of the Court. The city of London, where he had ruled with absolute sway as the Great Commoner, refused him their support or congratulations as Lord Chatham. The press teemed with invectives; and the people, who considered him as having betrayed their cause, loaded him with maledictions. Such treatment, in connection with his sufferings from disease, naturally tended to agitate his feelings and sour his temper. He was sometimes betrayed into rash conduct and passionate language. His biographer has, indeed truly, said that, "highly as Lord Chatham was loved and respected by his own family, and great as were his talents and virtues, he possessed not the art of cementing political friendships. A consciousness of his superior abilities, strengthened by the brilliant successes of his former administration, and the unbounded popularity he enjoyed, imparted an austerity to his manners which distressed and offended his colleagues."

Such were the circumstances under which Lord Chatham formed his third ministry. It would long since have passed into oblivion had not Mr. Burke handed it down to posterity in one of the most striking pictures (though abounding in grotesque imagery) which we have in our literature. "He made an administration," says Mr. Burke in his speech on American Taxation, "so checkered and speckled; he put together a piece of joinery so crossly indented and whimsically dovetailed; a cabinet so variously inlaid; such a piece of diversified mosaic; such a tesselated pavement without cement, here a bit of black stone, and there a bit of white; patriots and courtiers, King's friends and Republicans, that it was indeed a very curious show, but utterly unsafe to touch and unsure to stand on. The colleagues whom he assorted at the same boards stared at each other, and were obliged to ask, 'Sir, your name?' 'Sir, you have the advantage of me.' 'Mr. Such-a-one, I beg a thousand pardons.' I venture to say it did so happen, that persons had a single office divided between them who had never spoke to each other in their lives until they found themselves (they knew not how) pigging together, heads and points, in the same truckle-bed."[9] . . . If ever he fell into a fit of the gout, or if any other cause withdrew him from public cares, principles directly the contrary were sure to predominate. When he had executed his plan, he had not an inch of ground to stand on. When he had accomplished his scheme of administration, *he was no longer a minister.*"

Such was literally the fact. Only a few weeks after his final arrangements were made, he was seized with a paroxysm of the gout at Bath, which threatened his immediate dissolution. Having partially recovered, he set out on his return for London, in February, 1767. But he was violently attacked on the road, and was compelled to retire to his country seat at Hayes, where he lay in extreme suffering, with a mind so agitated and diseased that all access to him was denied for many months. It was during this period that Charles Townsend, in one of his rash and boastful moods, committed himself to Mr.

Grenville in favor of taxing the colonies, and was induced to lay those duties on tea, glass, &c., which revived the contest, and led to the American Revolution. It is, indeed, a singular circumstance, that such a bill should have passed under an administration bearing the name of Chatham. But he had ceased to be minister except in name. Some months before, he had sent a verbal message to the King (for he was unable to write) that "such was the ill state of his health, that his majesty must not expect from him any further advice or assistance in any arrangement whatever." When Grafton became minister, he sent in his formal resignation by the hands of Lord Camden. It is striking to observe how soon great men are forgotten when they fall from power, and withdraw, in the decay of their faculties, from the notice of the public. Lord Chatham's former resignation was an era in Europe. The news of it awakened the liveliest emotions throughout the civilized world. The time of his second resignation was hardly known in London. His sun appeared to have sunk at mid-day amid clouds and gloom. Little did any one imagine, that it was again to break forth with a purer splendor, and to fill the whole horizon around with the radiance of its setting beams.[10]

After an entire seclusion from the world for nearly three years, Lord Chatham, to the surprise of all, made his appearance in Parliament with his health greatly improved, and in full possession of his gigantic powers. He was still so infirm, however, that he went on crutches and was swathed in flannels when he entered the House of Lords at the opening of the session, January 9, 1770. In commenting on the address, he came out at once in a loftier strain of eloquence than ever in reply to Lord Mansfield on the case of John Wilkes.[11] This speech gave a decisive turn to political affairs. A leader had now appeared to array the Whigs against the Duke of Grafton. Lord Camden, who as Chancellor had continued in the Cabinet though hostile to the measures which prevailed, came down from the wool-sack at the close of Lord Chatham's speech, and declared against the minister. "I have," said he, "hung down my head in council, and disapproved by my looks those steps which I knew my avowed opposition could not prevent. I will do so no longer. I now proclaim to the world that I entirely coincide in the opinion expressed by my noble friend—whose presence again reanimates us—respecting this unconstitutional vote of the House of Commons." He was of course dismissed; and united with Lord Chatham, Lord Rockingham, and the rest of the Whigs, to oppose the Grafton ministry. They succeeded in nineteen days: the Duke resigned on the twenty-eighth of the same month. But the Whigs did not profit by their victory. The hostility of the King excluded them from power, and Lord North was placed at the head of affairs. An attempt was now made to put down Lord Chatham by personal insult. He was taunted before the House, March 14, 1770, with having received a pension from the Crown, and having unjustifiably recommended pensions for others. He rose upon his antagonist, as he always did on such occasions, and turned his defense into an attack. He at once took up the case of Lord Camden, whom he had brought in as Chancellor three years before, with a pension of fifteen hundred pounds. "I could not," said he, "expect such a man to quit the Chief-justiceship of the Common Pleas, which he held for life, and put himself in the power of those who were not to be trusted, to be dismissed from the Chancery at any moment, without making some slight provision for such an event. The public has not been deceived by his conduct. My suspicions have been justified. His integrity has made him once more a poor and a private man; *he was dismissed for the vote he gave in favor of the right of election in the people.*" Here an attempt was made to overwhelm him with clamor. Some Lords called out, "To the bar! to the bar!" and Lord Marchmont moved that his words be taken down. Lord Chatham seconded the motion; and went on to say, "I neither deny, retract, nor explain these words. I do *reaffirm* the fact, and I desire to meet the sense of the House. I appeal to the honor of every Lord in this House whether he has not the same conviction." Lord Rockingham, Lord Temple, and many others, rose, and, upon their honor, affirmed the same. The ministry were now desirous to drop the subject; but Lord Marchmont, encouraged by Lord Mansfield, persisted, and moved that nothing had appeared to justify the assertion. Lord Chatham again declared, "My words remain unretracted, unexplained, and reaffirmed. I desire to know whether I am condemned or acquitted, and whether I may still presume to hold my head as high as the noble Lord who moved to have my words taken down." To this no answer was given. It was easy for the ministry to pass what vote they pleased, but they found that every attempt to disgrace such a man only recoiled on themselves. His glowing defense of the people's rights regained him the popularity he had lost by his accession to the peerage. The city of London addressed him in terms of grateful acknowledgment, thanking him for "the zeal he had shown in support of those most valuable privileges, the right of election and the right of petition." The people looked up to him again as their best and truest friend; and though promoted to an earldom, they felt, in the language of his grandson, Lord Mahon, "that his elevation over them was like that of Rochester Castle over his own shores of Chatham—that he was raised above them only for their protection and defense."

After this session, Lord Chatham was unable to attend upon Parliament except occasionally and at distant intervals. He spent his time chiefly on his estate at Burton Pynsent, superintending the education of his children and mingling in their amusements with the liveliest pleasure, notwithstanding his many infirmities. He sought to interest them not only in their books, but in rural employments and rural scenery. He delighted in landscape gardening, and, in speaking of its fine arrangements for future effect, called it, with his usual felicity of expression, "the prophetic eye of Taste." "When his health would permit," says the tutor of his son, "he never suffered a day to pass without giving instruction of some sort to his children, and seldom without reading the Bible with them." He seems, indeed, to have studied the Scriptures with great care and attention from early life. He read them not only for the guidance of his faith, but for improvement in oratory. "Not content," says Lord Lyttleton, "to correct and instruct his imagination by the works of men, he borrowed his noblest images from the language of inspiration." His practice, in this respect, was imitated by Burke, Junius, and other distinguished writers of the day. At no period in later times, has secular eloquence gathered so many of her images and allusions from the pages of the Bible.

Thus withdrawn from the cares and labors of public life,

there was only one subject that could ever induce him to appear in Parliament. It was the contest with America. He knew more of this country than any man in England except Burke. During the war in which he wrested Canada from the French, he was brought into the most intimate communication with the leading men of the colonies. He knew their spirit and the resources of the country. Two of the smallest states (Massachusetts and Connecticut) had, in answer to his call, raised *twelve thousand* men for that war in a single year. Feelings of personal attachment united, therefore, with a sense of justice, to make him the champion of America. Feeble and decrepit as he was, he forgot his age and sufferings. He stood forth, in presence of the whole empire, to arraign, as a breach of the Constitution, every attempt to tax a people who had no representatives in Parliament. It was the era of his sublimest efforts in oratory. With no private ends or party purposes to accomplish, with a consciousness of the exalted services he had rendered to his country, he spoke "as one having authority," and denounced the war with a prophetic sense of the shame and disaster attending such a conflict. His voice of warning was lost, indeed, upon the ministry and on the great body of the nation, who welcomed a relief from their burdens at the expense of America. But it rang throughout every town and hamlet of the colonies, and when he proclaimed in the ears of Parliament, "I rejoice that America has resisted," millions of hearts on the other side of the Atlantic swelled with a prouder determination to resist even to the end.[12]

But while he thus acted as the champion of America, he never for a moment yielded to the thought of her separation from the mother country. When the Duke of Richmond, therefore, brought forward his motion, in April, 1778, advising the King to withdraw his fleets and armies, and to effect a conciliation with America involving her independence, Lord Chatham heard of his design "with unspeakable concern," and resolved to go once more to the House of Lords for the purpose of resisting the motion. The effort cost him his life. A detailed account of the scene presented on that occasion will be given hereafter, in connection with his speech. At the close, he sunk into the arms of his attendants, apparently in a dying state. He revived a little when conveyed to his dwelling; and, after lingering for a few days, died on the 11th of May, 1778, in the seventieth year of his age.

Lord Chatham has been generally regarded as the most powerful orator of modern times. He certainly ruled the British Senate as no other man has ever ruled over a great deliberative assembly. There have been stronger minds in that body, abler reasoners, profounder statesmen, but no man has ever controlled it with such absolute sway by the force of his eloquence. He did things which no human being but himself would ever have attempted. He carried through triumphantly what would have covered any other man with ridicule and disgrace.

His success, no doubt, was owing, in part to his extraordinary personal advantages. Few men have ever received from the hand of Nature so many of the outward qualifications of an orator. In his best days, before he was crippled by the gout, his figure was tall and erect, his attitude imposing, his gestures energetic even to vehemence, yet tempered with dignity and grace.[13] Such was the power of his eye, that he very often cowed down an antagonist in the midst of his speech and threw him into utter confusion by a single glance of scorn or contempt. Whenever he rose to speak, his countenance glowed with animation and was lighted up with all the varied emotions of his soul, so that Cowper describes him, in one of his bursts of patriotic feeling,

"With all his country beaming in his face."

"His voice," says a contemporary, "was both full and clear. His lowest whisper was distinctly heard; his middle notes were sweet and beautifully varied; and, when he elevated his voice to its highest pitch, the House was completely filled with the volume of sound. The effect was awful, except when he wished to cheer or animate; then he had spirit-stirring notes which were perfectly irresistible." The prevailing character of his delivery was majesty and force. "The crutch in his hand became a weapon of oratory."[14]

Much, however, as he owed to these personal advantages, it was his character as a man which gave him his surprising ascendency over the minds of his countrymen. There was a fascination for all hearts in his lofty bearing; his generous sentiments; his comprehensive policy; his grand conceptions of the height to which England might be raised as arbiter of Europe; his preference of her honor over all inferior *material* interests. There was a fascination, too, for the hearts of all who loved freedom, in that intense spirit of liberty which was the animating principle of his life. From the day when he opposed Sir Charles Wager's bill for breaking open private houses to press seamen, declaring that he would *shoot* any man, even an officer of justice, who should thus enter his dwelling, he stood forth, to the end of his days, the Defender of the People's Rights. It was no vain ostentation of liberal principles, no idle pretense to gain influence or office. The nation saw it, and while Pulteney's defection brought disgrace on the name of "Patriot," the character of Pitt stood higher than ever in the public estimation. His political integrity, no less than his eloquence, formed "an era in the Senate;" and that comparative elevation of principle which we now find among English politicians dates back for its commencement to his noble example. It was his glory as a statesman, not that he was always in the right, or even consistent with himself upon minor points, but that, in an age of shameless profligacy, when political principle was universally laughed at, and every one, in the words of Walpole, "had his price," he stood forth to "stem the torrent of a downward age." He could truly say to an opponent, as the great Athenian orator did to Æschines, 'Εγὼ δή σοι λέγω, ὅτι τῶν πολιτευομένων παρὰ τοῖς Ἕλλησι διαφθαρέντων ἁπάντων, ἀρξαμένων ἀπὸ σοῦ, πρότερον μὲν ὑπὸ Φιλίππου, νῦν δ' ὑπ' 'Αλεξάνδρου, ἔμ' οὔτε καιρὸς οὔτε φιλανθρωπία λόγων οὔτ' ἐπαγγελιῶν μέγεθος οὔτ' ἐλπὶς οὔτε φόβος, οὔτε χάρις, οὔτ' ἄλλ' οὐδὲν ἐπῆρεν οὐδὲ προηγάγετο, ὧν ἔκρινα δικαίων καὶ συμφερόντων τῇ πατρίδι, οὐδὲν προδοῦναι: "When all our statesmen, beginning with yourself, were corrupted by bribes or office, no convenience of opportunity, or insinuation of address, or magnificence of promises—or hope, or fear, or favor—could induce me to give up for a moment what I considered the rights and interests of my country." Even his enemies were forced to pay homage to his noble assertion of his principles—his courage, his frankness, his perfect sincerity. Eloquent as he was, he impressed every hearer with the conviction that there was in him something higher than all eloquence. "Every one felt," says a contemporary, "that the man was infinitely greater than the orator." Even Franklin lost his coolness when speaking of Lord Chatham. "I have sometimes," said he, "seen eloquence without wisdom, and often wisdom without eloquence; but in him I have seen them united in the highest possible degree."

The range of his powers as a speaker was uncommonly wide. He was equally qualified to conciliate and subdue. When he saw fit, no man could be more plausible and ingratiating; no one had ever a more winning address, or was more adroit in obviating objections and allaying prejudice. When he changed his tone, and chose rather to subdue, he had the sharpest and most massy weapons at command—wit, humor, irony, overwhelming ridicule and contempt. His *forte* was the terrible; and he employed with equal ease the indirect mode of attack with which he so often tortured Lord Mansfield, and the open, withering invective with which he trampled down Lord Suffolk. His burst of astonishment and horror at the proposal of the latter to let loose the Indians on the settlers of America is without a parallel in our language for severity and force. In all such conflicts, the energy of his will and his boundless self-confidence secured him the victory. Never did that "erect countenance" sink before the eye of an antagonist. Never was he known to hesitate or falter. He had a feeling of superiority over every one around him, which acted on his mind with the force of an inspiration. He *knew* he was right! He *knew* he could save England, and that no one else could do it! Such a spirit, in great crises, is the unfailing instrument of command both to the general and the orator. We may call it arrogance; but even arrogance here operates upon most minds with the potency of a charm; and when united to a vigor of genius and a firmness of purpose like his, men of the strongest intellect fall down before it, and admire—perhaps hate—what they can not resist.

The leading characteristic of eloquence is *force;* and force in the orator depends mainly on the action of strongly excited feeling on a powerful intellect. The intellect of Chatham was of the highest order, and was peculiarly fitted for the broad and rapid combinations of oratory. It was at once comprehensive, acute, and vigorous; enabling him to embrace the largest range of thought; to see at a glance what most men labor out by slow degrees; and to grasp his subject with a vigor, and hold on to it with a firmness, which have rarely, if ever, been equaled. But his intellect never acted alone. It was impossible for him to speak on any subject in a dry or abstract manner; all the operations of his mind were pervaded and governed by intense feeling. This gave rise to certain characteristics of his eloquence which may here be mentioned.

First, he did not, like many in modern times, divide a speech into distinct compartments, one designed to convince the understanding, and another to move the passions and the will. They were too closely united in his own mind to allow of such a separation. All went together, conviction and persuasion, intellect and feeling, like chain-shot.

Secondly, the rapidity and abruptness with which he often flashed his thoughts upon the mind arose from the same source. Deep emotion strikes directly at its object. It struggles to get free from all secondary ideas—all mere accessories. Hence the simplicity, and even bareness of thought, which we usually find in the great passages of Chatham and Demosthenes. The whole turns often on a single phrase, a word, an allusion. They put forward a few great objects, sharply defined, and standing boldly out in the glowing atmosphere of emotion. They pour their burning thoughts instantaneously upon the mind, as a person might catch the rays of the sun in a concave mirror, and turn them on their object with a sudden and consuming power.

Thirdly, his mode of reasoning, or, rather, of dispensing with the forms of argument, resulted from the same cause. It is not the fact, though sometimes said, that Lord Chatham never reasoned. In most of his early speeches, and in some of his later ones, especially those on the right of taxing America, we find many examples of argument: brief, indeed, but remarkably clear and stringent. It is true, however, that he endeavored, as far as possible, to escape from the trammels of formal reasoning. When the mind is all aglow with a subject, and sees its conclusions with the vividness and certainty of intuitive truths, it is impatient of the slow process of logical deduction. It seeks rather to reach the point by a bold and rapid progress, throwing away the intermediate steps, and putting the subject *at once* under such aspects and relations as to carry its own evidence along with it. Demosthenes was remarkable for thus crushing together proof and statement in a single mass. When, for example, he called on his judges, μὴ τὸν ἀντίδικον σύμβουλον ποιήσασθαι περὶ τοῦ πῶς ἀκούειν ὑμᾶς ἐμοῦ δεῖ, 'not to make his enemy their counselor as to the manner in which they should hear his reply,' there is an argument involved in the very ideas brought together—in the juxtaposition of the words ἀντίδικον and σύμβουλον —an argument the more forcible because not drawn out in a regular form. It was so with Lord Chatham. The strength of his feelings bore him directly forward to the *results* of argument. He affirmed them earnestly, positively; not as mere assertions, but on the ground of their intrinsic evidence and certainty. John Foster has finely remarked, that "Lord Chatham struck on the results of reasoning as a cannon-shot strikes the mark, without your seeing its course through the air." Perhaps a *bomb-shell* would have furnished even a better illustration. It explodes when it strikes, and thus becomes the most powerful of *arguments*.

Fourthly, this ardor of feeling, in connection with his keen penetration of mind, made him often indulge in political prophecy. His predictions were, in many instances, surprisingly verified. We have already seen it in the case of Admiral Hawke's victory, and in his quick foresight of a war with Spain in 1762. Eight years after, in the midst of a profound peace, he declared to the House of Lords that the inveterate enemies of England were, at the moment he spoke, striking "a blow of hostility" at her possessions in some quarter of the globe. News arrived at the end of four months that the Spanish governor of Buenos Ayres was, at that very time, in the act of seizing the Falkland Islands and expelling the English. When this prediction was afterward referred to in Parliament, he remarked, "I will tell these young ministers the true secret of intelligence. It is sagacity—sagacity to compare causes and effects; to judge of the present state of things and discern the future by a careful review of the past. Oliver Cromwell, who astonished mankind by his intelligence, did not derive it from spies in the cabinet of every prince in Europe; he drew it from the cabinet of his own sagacious mind." As he advanced in years, his tone of admonition, especially on American affairs, became more and more lofty and oracular. He spoke as no other man ever spoke in a great deliberative assembly—as one who felt that the time of his departure was at hand; who, withdrawn from the ordinary concerns of life, in the words of his great eulogist, "came *occasionally* into our system to *counsel and decide,"*

Fifthly, his great preponderance of feeling made him, in the strictest sense of the term, an extemporaneous speaker. His mind was, indeed, richly furnished with thought upon every subject which came up for debate, and the matter he brought forward was always thoroughly matured and strikingly appropriate; but he seems never to have studied its arrangement, much less to have bestowed any care on the language, imagery, or illustrations. Every thing fell into its place at the moment. He poured out his thoughts and feelings just as they arose in his mind; and hence, on one occasion, when dispatches had been received which could not safely be made public, he said to one of his colleagues, "I must not speak to day; I shall let out the secret." It is also worthy of remark that nearly all these great passages, which came with such startling power upon the House, arose out of some unexpected turn of the debate, some incident or expression which called forth, at the moment, these sudden bursts of eloquence. In his attack on Lord Suffolk, he caught a single glance at "the tapestry which adorned the walls" around him, and one flash of his genius gave us the most magnificent passage in our eloquence. His highest power lay in these sudden bursts of passion. To call them *hits,* with Lord Brougham, is beneath their dignity and force. "They form," as his Lordship justly observes, "the grand charm of Lord Chatham's oratory; they were the distinguishing excellence of his great predecessor, and gave him at will to wield the fierce democratie of Athens and to fulmine over Greece."

To this intense emotion, thus actuating all his powers, Lord Chatham united a vigorous and lofty imagination, which formed his crowning excellence as an orator. It is this faculty which exalts *force* into the truest and most sublime eloquence. In this respect he approached more nearly than any speaker of modern times to the great master of Athenian art. It was here, chiefly, that he surpassed Mr. Fox, who was not at all his inferior in ardor of feeling or robust vigor of intellect. Mr. Burke had even more imagination, but it was wild and irregular. It was too often on the wing, circling around the subject, as if to display the grace of its movements or the beauty of its plumage. The imagination of Lord Chatham struck directly at its object. It "flew an eagle flight, forth and right on." It never became his master. Nor do we ever find it degenerating into *fancy,* in the limited sense of that term: it was never *fanciful.* It was, in fact, so perfectly blended with the other powers of his mind—so simple, so true to nature even in its loftiest flights—that we rarely think of it as imagination at all.

The style and language of Lord Chatham are not to be judged of by the early speeches in this volume, down to 1743. Reporters at that day made little or no attempt to give the exact words of a speaker. They sought only to convey his sentiments, though they might occasionally be led, in writing out his speeches, to catch some of his marked peculiarities of thought or expression. In 1766, his speech against the American Stamp Act was reported, with a considerable degree of verbal accuracy, by Sir Robert Dean, aided by Lord Charlemont. Much, however, was obviously omitted; and passages having an admirable felicity of expression were strangely intermingled with tame and broken sentences, showing how imperfectly they had succeeded in giving the precise language of the speaker. Five speeches (to be mentioned hereafter) were written out from notes taken on the spot by Sir Philip Francis and Mr. Hugh Boyd. One of them is said to have been revised by Lord Chatham himself. These are the best specimens we possess of his style and diction, and it would be difficult, in the whole range of our literature, to find more perfect models for the study and imitation of the young orator. The words are admirably chosen. The sentences are not rounded or balanced periods, but are made up of short clauses, which flash themselves upon the mind with all the vividness of distinct ideas, and yet are closely connected together as tending to the same point, and uniting to form larger masses of thought. Nothing can be more easy, varied, and natural than the style of these speeches. There is no mannerism about them. They contain some of the most vehement passages in English oratory; and yet there is no appearance of effort, no straining after effect. They have this infallible mark of genius—they make every one feel that if placcd in like circumstances, he would have said exactly the same things in the same manner. "Upon the whole," in the words of Mr. Grattan, "there was in this man something that could create, subvert, or reform; an understanding, a spirit, and an eloquence to summon mankind to society, or to break the bonds of slavery asunder, and rule the wildness of free minds with unbounded authority; something that could establish or overwhelm empire, and strike a blow in the world that should resound through its history."[15]

LORD MANSFIELD

WILLIAM MURRAY, first Earl of Mansfield, was born at Scone Castle, near Perth in Scotland, on the 2d of March, 1705. He was the fourth son of Lord Stormont, head of an ancient but decayed family which had been reduced to comparatively poverty by a long course of extravagance. The title having been conferred by James I, Lord Stormont, like his predecessors, remained true to the cause of the Stuarts. His second son, Lord Dunbar, was private secretary to the Pretender.

William was sent to London for his education at a very early age; and hence Johnson used sportively to maintain that his success in after life ought not to be put to the credit of his country, since it was well known that "much might be made of a Scotchman if he was *caught young*." Not a little, however, had been done for William before he left the grammar school of Perth. Though but fourteen years old, he could read quite freely in the Latin classics; he knew a large part of Sallust and Horace by heart; and was able not only to write Latin correctly, but to speak it with accuracy and ease. It is not surprising, therefore, considering his native quickness of mind, that within a year after he joined Westminster school he gained its highest distinction: that of being chosen one of the King's scholars. He soon stood as "dux," or leader of the school; and at the end of four years, after a rigorous examination, was put first on the list of those who were to be sent to Oxford, on the foundation at Christ Church. His choice had for some time been firmly fixed upon the law as a profession, and nothing could so gratify his feelings or advance his interests as to enter the University. But the straitened circumstances of his father seemed to forbid the thought, and he was on the point of giving up his most ardent wishes in despair when a casual conversation with a young friend opened the way for his being placed at Oxford with an honorable provision for his support. Lord Foley, father of the friend referred to, having heard of his superior abilities and his strong attachment to the law, generously offered to assist him with the requisite means, to be repaid only in the event of his succeeding in after life.

During his residence at Oxford, he gave himself to study with that fervor and diligence for which he was always distinguished, quickened by a sense of the responsibilities he had incurred and by a fixed resolve to place himself at the head of his profession. He made every thing subservient to a preparation for the bar; and while, in the spirit of that university, he studied Aristotle with delight as the great master of reasoning and thought, he devoted his most earnest efforts to improvement in oratory. He read every thing that had been written on the principles of the art; he made himself familiar with all the great masters of eloquence in Greece and Rome, and spent much of his time in translating their finest productions as the best means of improving his style. Cicero was his favorite author; and he declared, in after life, that there was not one of his orations which he had not, while at Oxford, translated into English, and, after an interval, according to the best of his ability, re-translated into Latin.

Having taken his degree at the age of twenty-two, he entered on the study of the law at Lincoln's Inn in 1737. His labors were now conducted on the broadest scale. While law had the precedence, he carried on the practice of oratory with the utmost zeal. To aid him in extemporaneous speaking, he joined a debating society, where the most abstruse legal points were fully discussed. For these exercises, he prepared himself beforehand with such copiousness and accuracy that the notes he used proved highly valuable in after life, both at the bar and on the bench. He found time, also, to pursue his historical studies to such an extent that Lord Campbell speaks of his familiarity with modern history as "astounding and even *appalling,* for it produces a painful consciousness of inferiority, and creates remorse for time misspent." When called to the bar in 1730, "he had made himself acquainted not only with international law, but with the codes of all the most civilized nations, ancient and modern; he was an elegant classical scholar; he was thoroughly imbued with the literature of his own country; he had profoundly studied our mixed constitution; he had a sincere desire to be of service to his country; and he was animated by a noble aspiration after honorable fame."

When he first came to London as a boy in Westminster school, he was introduced by his countryman, Lord Marchmont, to Mr. Pope, then at the height of his unrivaled popularity. The poet took a lively interest in the young Scotchman, attracted not only by the quickness of his parts and the fineness of his manners and person, but by "the silvery tones of his voice," for which he continued to be distinguished to the end of life. Mr. Pope entered with the warmest concern into all his employments, and assisted especially in his rhetorical studies during his preparation for the bar. One day, says his biographer, he was surprised by a friend, who suddenly entered the room, in "the act of practicing before a glass, while Pope sat by to aid him in the character of an instructor!" Their friendship continued throughout life; and in a new edition of the Dunciad Mr. Pope introduced his name, with that of other distinguished men, complaining that law and politics should have drawn them off from the more congenial pursuits of literature.

"Whate'er the talents and howe'er designed,
We hang one jingling padlock on the mind.
A poet the first day he dips his quill;
And what the last? a very poet still.
Pity the charm works only in our wall,
Lost—too soon lost—in yonder *House* or *Hall:*
There truant Wyndham ev'ry muse gave o'er;
There Talbot sank, and was a wit no more;
How sweet an Ovid, MURRAY, *was our boast!*
How many Martials were in Pulteney lost!"

Some years elapsed after Mr. Murray's call to the bar before he had any business of importance; and then, after a few successful cases, it poured in upon him to absolute repletion.

"From a few hundred pounds a year," said he, "I found myself in the receipt of thousands." Retainers came in from every quarter; and one, of a thousand guineas, was sent by Sarah, Duchess of Marlborough, with that ostentatious munificence which she sometimes affected. Nine hundred and ninety-five guineas were returned by Mr. Murray, with the significant remark that "a retaining fee was never more nor less than five guineas." He found her a very troublesome client. Not unfrequently she made her appearance at his chambers after midnight, crowding the street with her splendid equipage and her attendants with torches; and on one occasion when he was absent, his clerk, giving an account of her visit the next morning, said, "I could not make out, sir, who she was, for she would not tell me her name; but she *swore* so dreadfully that she must have been a lady of quality!"

Soon after the fall of Sir Robert Walpole in 1742, Mr. Murray was appointed Solicitor General, and elected a member of Parliament through the influence of the Duke of Newcastle. His powerful talents were needed for the support of the new administration, which was suffering under the vehement attacks of Mr. Pitt. Here commenced that long series of conflicts which divided for life the two most accomplished orators of the age. It could not be otherwise, for never were two men more completely the antipodes of each other. Pitt was a Whig; Murray was a High Tory. Pitt was ardent, open, and impetuous; Murray was cool, reserved, and circumspect. The intellect of Pitt was bold and commanding; that of Murray was subtle, penetrating, and refined. Pitt sought power; Murray, office and emolument. Two such men could not but differ, and differing as they did for life, it was natural that the one should distrust or despise, and the other fear, perhaps hate. In native talent, it would be difficult to say which had the advantage; but the mind of Murray was more perfectly trained, and his memory enriched with larger stores of knowledge. "In closeness of argument," says an able writer, "in happiness of illustration, in copiousness and grace of diction, the oratory of Murray was unsurpassed: and, indeed, in all the qualities which conspire to form an able *debater,* he is allowed to have been Pitt's superior. When measures were attacked, no one was better capable of defending them; when reasoning was the weapon employed, none handled it with such effect; but against declamatory invective, his very temperament incapacitated him for contending with so much advantage. He was like an accomplished fencer, invulnerable to the thrusts of a small sword, but not equally able to ward off the downright stroke of a bludgeon."

In 1754 Mr. Murray was appointed Attorney General, and soon after made leader of the House of Commons under the Duke of Newcastle. "At the beginning of the session," says Horace Walpole, "Murray was awed by Pitt; but, finding himself supported by Fox, he surmounted his fears, and convinced the House, and Pitt too, of his superior abilities. Pitt could only attack, Murray only defend. Fox, the boldest and ablest champion, was still more forward to worry; but the keenness of his saber was blunted by the difficulty with which he drew it from the scabbard—I mean, the hesitation and ungracefulness of his delivery took off from the force of his arguments. Murray, the brightest genius of the three, had too much and too little of the lawyer; he refined too much and could wrangle too little for a popular assembly." We have seen already, in the life of Lord Chatham, what difficulties Murray had to encounter that session in sustaining the ministry of Newcastle, and the crushing force with which he was overwhelmed by his opponent. In 1756 he resolved to endure it no longer, and on the death of Sir Dudley Ryder he demanded the office of Chief Justice of the King's Bench. Newcastle refused, remonstrated, supplicated. "The writ for creating Murray," he declared, "would be the death-warrant of his own administration." He resisted for several months, offering the most tempting bribes, including a pension of £6000 a year, if he would only remain in the House until the new session was opened, and the address voted in reply to the King's speech. Murray declared, in the most peremptory terms, that he would not remain "a month or a day even to support the address;" that "he never again would enter that assembly." Turning with indignation to Newcastle, he exclaimed, "What merit have I, that you should lay on this country, for which so little is done with spirit, the additional burden of £6000 a year;" and concluded with declaring his unalterable determination, if he was not made Chief Justice, to serve no longer as Attorney General. This brought Newcastle to a decision. On the 8th of November, 1756, Murray was sworn in as Chief Justice, and created a peer with the title of Baron Mansfield. At a later period he was raised to the earldom.

In entering on his new career, he was called upon to take public leave of his associates of Lincoln's Inn. On that occasion he was addressed in an elegant speech by the Honorable Charles Yorke. The reader will be interested in Mr. Murray's reply, as showing with what admirable dignity and grace he could receive the compliments bestowed upon him, and turn them aside in favor of another.

> I am too sensible, sir, of my being undeserving of the praises which you have so elegantly bestowed upon me, to suffer commendations so delicate as yours to insinuate themselves into my mind; but I have pleasure in that kind of partiality which is the occasion of them. To deserve such praises is a worthy object of ambition, and from such a tongue flattery itself is pleasing.
>
> If I have had, in any measure, success in my profession, it is owing to the great man who has presided in our highest courts of judicature the whole time I attended the bar.[1] It was impossible to attend to him, to sit under him every day, without catching some beams from his light. The disciples of Socrates, whom I will take the liberty to call the great lawyer of antiquity, since the first principles of all law are derived from his philosophy, owe their reputation to their having been the reporters of the sayings of their master. If we can arrogate nothing to ourselves, we can boast the school we were brought up in; the scholar may glory in his master, and we may challenge past ages to show us his equal. My Lord Bacon had the same extent of thought, and the same strength of language and expression, but his life had a stain. My Lord Clarendon had the same ability, and the same zeal for the Constitution of his country, but the civil war prevented his laying *deep* the foundations of law, and the avocations of politics interrupted the business of the chancellor. My Lord Somers came the nearest to his character, but his time was short, and envy and faction sullied the luster of his glory. It is the peculiar felicity of the

great man I am speaking of to have presided very near twenty years, and to have shone with a splendor that has risen superior to faction and that has subdued envy.

I did not intend to have said, I should not have said so much on this occasion, but that in this situation, with all that hear me, what I say must carry the weight of testimony rather than appear the voice of panegyric.

For you, sir, you have given great pledges to your country; and large as the expectations of the public are concerning you, I dare say you will answer them.

For the society, I shall always think myself honored by every mark of their esteem, affection, and friendship; and shall desire the continuance of it no longer than while I remain zealous for the Constitution of this country and a friend to the interests of virtue.

Lord Mansfield now entered on that high career of usefulness which has made his name known and honored throughout the civilized world. Few men have ever been so well qualified for that exalted station. He had pre-eminently a legal intellect, great clearness of thought, accuracy of discrimination, soundness of judgment, and strength of reasoning, united to a scientific knowledge of jurisprudence, a large experience in all the intricacies of practice, unusual courtesy and ease in the dispatch of business, and extraordinary powers of application. He came to the bench, not like most lawyers, trusting to his previous knowledge and the aid afforded by counsel in forming his decisions, but as one who had just entered on the real employment of his life. "On the day of his inauguration as Chief Justice, instead of thinking that he had won the prize, he considered himself as only starting in the race."

How he discharged the duties of his high station, it belongs especially to men of his own profession to determine. One fact, however, may stand in the place of many authorities. Out of the thousands of cases which he decided in the Court of King's Bench, there were only *two* in which his associates of that court did not unanimously agree with him in opinion. Yet they were, as all the world knows, men of the highest ability and the most perfect independence of mind. Junius, indeed, assailed him with malignant bitterness, but it is the universal decision of the bar that his charges were false as they were malignant. Against this attack we may set off the opinion of Chief Justice Story. "England and America, and the civilized world, lie under the deepest obligations to him. Wherever commerce shall extend its social influences; wherever justice shall be administered by enlightened and liberal rules; wherever contracts shall be expounded upon the eternal principles of right and wrong; wherever moral delicacy and judicial refinement shall be infused into the municipal code, at once to persuade men to be honest and to keep them so; wherever the intercourse of mankind shall aim at something more elevated than that groveling spirit of barter, in which meanness, and avarice, and fraud strive for the mastery over ignorance, credulity, and folly, the name of Lord Mansfield will be held in reverence by the good and the wise, by the honest merchant, the enlightened lawyer, the just statesman, and the conscientious judge. The proudest monument of his fame is in the volumes of Burrow, and Cowper, and Douglas, which we may fondly hope will endure as long as the language in which they are written shall continue to instruct mankind. His judgments should not be merely referred to and read on the spur of particular occasions, but should be studied as models of juridical reasoning and eloquence."

As a speaker in the House of Lords, the success of Lord Mansfield was greater than in the House of Commons. The calmness and dignity of the assembly were better suited to his habits of thought. Here, after a few years, he had again to encounter his great antagonist, who was raised to the same dignity in 1766. As Chatham was the advocate of the people's rights, Mansfield was the champion of the King's prerogative. He defended the Stamp Act, and maintained the right of Parliament to tax the Americans as being virtually represented in the House of Commons. A speech on that subject, corrected by himself, is given below. Lord Campbell, notwithstanding his strong predilections as a Whig, does not hesitate to pronounce it unanswerable. His speech in favor of taking away the protection extended to the servants of peers is the most finished of his productions, and will also be found in this volume. To these will be added his argument in the case of the Chamberlain of London *vs.* Allan Evans, which has often been spoken of as the most perfect specimen of juridical reasoning in our language. His address from the bench, when surrounded by a mob, during the trial of the outlawry of Wilkes, will also form part of the extracts.

After discharging his duties as Chief Justice nearly thirty-two years, he resigned his office on the 4th of June, 1788. His faculties were still unimpaired, though his strength was gone; and he continued in their unclouded exercise nearly five years longer, when he died, after an illness of ten days, on the 20th of March, 1793, in the eighty-ninth year of his age.

"The countenance of Lord Mansfield," says a friend and contemporary, "was uncommonly beautiful, and none could ever behold it, even in advanced years, without reverence. Nature had given him an eye of fire; and his voice, till it was affected by the years which passed over him, was perhaps unrivaled in the sweetness and variety of its tones. There was a similitude between his action and that of Mr. Garrick. In speaking from the bench, there was sometimes a confusion in his periods and a tendency to involve his sentences in parentheses; yet, such was the charm of his voice and action, and such the general beauty, propriety, and force of his expressions, that while he spoke, all these defects passed unnoticed."

The eloquence of Lord Mansfield, especially in his best speeches in the House of Lords, was that of a judge rather than an advocate or a party leader. He had the air of addressing the House of Lords, according to the theory of that body, as one who spoke *upon honor*. He sought not to drive, but to lead; not to overwhelm the mind by appeals to the passions, but to aid and direct its inquiries; so that his hearers had the satisfaction of seeming, at least, to form their own conclusions. He was peculiarly happy in his statement of a case. "It was worth more," said Mr. Burke, "than any other man's argument." Omitting all that was unnecessary, he seized, with surprising tact, on the strong points of a subject; he held them steadily before the mind; and, as new views opened, he led forward his hearers, step by step, toward the desired result, with almost the certainty of intuitive evidence. "It was extremely difficult," said Lord Ashburton, "to answer him when he was wrong, and impossible when he was in the right." His manner was persuasive, with enough of force and animation to secure the closest attention. His illustrations were always apposite, and sometimes striking and beautiful. His language, in his best speeches, was select and graceful, and his whole style of speaking approached as near as possible to that dignified conversation which has always been considered appropriate to the House of Lords.[2]

JUNIUS

THE letters of Junius[1] have taken a permanent place in the eloquence of our language. Though often false in statement and malignant in spirit, they will never cease to be read as specimens of powerful composition: for the union of brilliancy and force, there is nothing superior to them in our literature. Nor is it for his style alone that Junius deserves to be studied. He shows great rhetorical skill in his mode of developing a subject. There is an arrangement of a given mass of thought which serves to throw it upon the mind with the greatest possible effect. There is another arrangement which defeats its object, and renders the impression feeble or indistinct. Demosthenes was, of all men, most perfectly master of the one; the majority of extemporaneous speakers are equally good examples of the other.

Junius had evidently studied this subject with great care; and it is for the sake of urging it upon the young orator that some of the ablest of his productions will now be given. Happily, the selection is easy. There are ten or twelve of his letters which stand far above the rest for strength of thought and elegance of diction. These will be found below, with the exception of his Letters to Lord Mansfield, which, though highly finished in respect to style, are now universally condemned for their errors, both in law and fact, and their unmerited abuse of the greatest of English jurists. In regard to his treatment of others, it is hardly necessary to say that the statements of Junius are to be taken with great allowance. He was an unscrupulous political partisan, and though much that he said of the Duke of Grafton and the other objects of his vengeance was strictly true, they were by no means so weak or profligate as he here represents them. We might as well take Pope's Satires for a faithful exhibition of men and manners in the days of George II.

It is, therefore, only as an orator—for such he undoubtedly was in public life, and such he truly is in these letters—that we are now to consider him. In this character his writings are worthy of the closest study, especially in respect to the quality alluded to above. Each of these letters was the result of severe and protracted labor. We should have known it, if he had not himself avowed the fact, for we see every where the marks of elaborate forecast and revision, and we learn, from his private correspondence with Woodfall, that he expended on their composition an amount of anxiety and effort which hardly any other writer, especially one so proud, would have been willing to acknowledge. Yet it is certain that by far the greater part of all this toil was bestowed, not upon the language, but on the selection and arrangement of his ideas. His mind, in early life, had clearly been subjected to the severest logical training. Composition, with him, was the creation of a *system* of thought, in which every thing is made subordinate to a just order and sequence of ideas. One thought grows out of another in regular succession. His reasonings often take the form of a syllogism, though usually with the omission of one of the terms; and we never find him betrayed into that careless diffusion of style so common with those who are ignorant of the principles of logic. In this respect, the writings of Junius will amply repay the closest study and analysis. Let the young orator enter completely into the scope and design of the author. Let him watch the undercurrent of his thoughts and feelings. Let him observe how perfectly every thing coincides to produce the desired impression—the statement of principles and the reference to facts, the shadings of thought and the colorings of imagery. Let him take one of the more striking passages, and remark the dexterous *preparation* by which each of its several parts is so shaped that the leading thoughts come forward to the best advantage: clear in all their relations, standing boldly out, unencumbered by secondary ideas, and thus fitted to strike the mind with full and undivided force. Such a study of Junius will prepare the young reader to enter into the logic of thought. It will lead to the formation of a severe intellectual taste, which is the best guard against the dangers of hasty composition and the still greater dangers of extemporaneous speaking. Such speaking cannot be dispensed with. On the contrary, it is becoming more and more essential to the success of public men in every department of life. It is, therefore, of the highest importance for the student in oratory to be familiar with models which shall preserve the purity of his style and aid him in the formation of those intellectual habits without which there can be neither clearness, nor force, nor continuity of thought in extemporaneous speaking. One of our most eloquent advocates, the late William Wirt, whose early training was of a different kind, remarked, in an address delivered not long before his death, that here lay the chief deficiency of our public speakers—that the want of severe intellectual discipline was the great want of American orators.

There is also another lesson to be learned from Junius, viz., *the art of throwing away unnecessary ideas.* A large proportion of the thoughts which rise to the mind in first considering a subject are not really essential to its clear and full development. No one ever felt this more strongly than Junius. He had studied in the school of the classics; he had caught the spirit of the Grecian oratory; and he knew that the first element of its power was a rigid scrutiny of the ideas to be brought forward and a stern rejection of every form of thought, however plausible or attractive, which was not clearly indispensable to the attainment of his object. He learned, too, in the same school, another lesson of equal importance in relation to the ideas selected for use. He saw how much could be done to abridge their statement, and set aside the necessity of qualifying terms and clauses, by such an arrangement of the leading thoughts that each should throw light upon the other, and all unite in one full, determinate impression. Our language is, indeed, poorly fitted for such purposes. It is a weak and imperfect instrument compared with others, whose varied inflections and numerous illative particles afford the readiest means of graceful transition, and of binding ideas together in close-compacted masses. Such as it is, however, Junius has used it to the utmost advantage. In his best passages, there is a fine compression of thought, arising from the skillful disposition of his materials, which it is far more easy to admire than to imitate. Not an idea is excluded which could promote his object. It is all there, but in the narrowest compass. The stroke is a single one, because nothing more is needed; and it takes its full effect, because there is nothing in the way to weaken the force of the blow. He has thus given us some of the best specimens in our language of that "rich economy of cxpression," which was so much studied by the great writers of antiquity.

There is only one more characteristic of Junius which will here be noticed. It is the wonderful power he possessed of *insinuating* ideas into the mind without giving them a formal or direct expression. Voltaire is the only writer who ever enjoyed this power in an equal degree, and he used it chiefly in his hours of gayety and sport. Junius used it for the most serious purposes of his life. He made it the instrument of torturing his victims. It is a curious inquiry why this species of indirect attack is so peculiarly painful to persons of education and refinement. The question is not why they suffer more than others from contempt and ridicule, but why sarcasm, irony, and the other forms of attack by *insinuation* have such extraordinary power to distress their feelings. Perhaps the reason is that such persons are peculiarly qualified to understand and appreciate these forms of ingenious derision. The ignorant and vulgar have no power to comprehend them, and are therefore beyond their reach. But it is otherwise with men of cultivated minds. It is impossible for such men not to admire the efforts of genius; and when they find these efforts turned against themselves, and see all the force of a subtle intellect employed in thus dexterously insinuating suspicion or covering them with ridicule, whatever may be their consciousness of innocence, they can not but feel deeply. Coarse invective and reproachful language would be a relief to the mind. Any one can cry "fool," "liar," or "scoundrel." But to sketch a picture in which real traits of character are so ingeniously distorted that every one will recognize the likeness and apply the name, requires no ordinary force of genius, and it is not wonderful that men of the firmest spirit shrink from such an assailant. We have seen how Lord Mansfield "suffered" under inflictions of this kind from Lord Chatham, till he could endure them no longer, and abruptly fled the contest. In addition to this, he who is thus assailed knows that the talent which he feels so keenly will be perfectly understood by others, and that attacks of this kind diffuse their influence, like a subtle poison, throughout the whole republic of letters. They will be read, he is aware, not only by that large class who dwell with malicious delight on the pages of detraction, but by multitudes whose good opinion he prizes most highly—in whose minds all that is dear to him in reputation will be mingled with images of ridicule and contempt, which can not fail to be remembered for their ingenuity, how much soever they may be condemned for their spirit. For these and perhaps other reasons, this covert mode of attack has always been the most potent engine of wounding the feelings and destroying character. Junius had not only the requisite talent and bitterness to wield this engine with terrible effect, but he stood on a vantage ground in using it such as no other writer ever enjoyed. He had means of secret information, which men have labored in vain to trace out or conceive of. His searching eye penetrated equally into the retired circles of domestic life, the cabinets of ministers, and the closet of the King.[2] Persons of the highest rank and most callous feelings were filled with alarm when they found their darkest intrigues laid open, their most hidden motives detected, their duplicity and tergiversation exposed to view, and even their private vices blazoned before the eyes of the public. Nor did Junius, on these points, very scrupulously confine himself to the truth. He gave currency to some of the basest slanders of the day, which he could not but know were unfounded, in order to blacken the character of his opponents. He stood, in the meantime, unassailable himself, wrapped, like Æneas at the court of Dido, in the cloud around him, affording no opportunity for others to retort his accusations, to examine his past conduct, or to scan his present motives. With all these advantages, he toiled as few men ever toiled, to gain that exquisite finish of style, that perfect union of elegance and strength, which could alone express the refined bitterness of his feelings. He seemed to exult in gathering up the blunted weapons of attack thrown aside by others and giving them a keener edge and a finer polish. "Ample justice," says he to one whom he assailed, "has been done by abler pens than mine to the separate merits of your life and character. Let it be my humble office to collect the scattered sweets, *till their united virtue tortures the sense.*" In the success of these labors he felt the proud consciousness that he was speaking to other generations besides his own, and declared concerning one of his victims, "I would pursue him through life, and try the last exertion of my abilities to *preserve the perishable infamy of his name, and make it immortal.*"[3]

This reliance of Junius on his extraordinary powers of composition naturally leads us to consider his style. We might pronounce it perfect, if it were only free from a slight appearance of labor, and were as easy and idiomatic as it is strong, pointed, and brilliant. But it seems hardly possible to unite all these qualities in the highest degree. Where strength and compactness are carried to their utmost limit, there will almost of necessity be something rigid and unbending. A man in plate armor can not move with the freedom and lightness of an athlete. But Junius, on the whole, has been wonderfully successful in overcoming these difficulties. His sentences have generally an easy flow, with a dignified and varied rhythmus, and a harmonious cadence. Clear in their construction, they grow in strength as they advance, and come off at the close always with liveliness, and often with a sudden, stinging force. He is peculiarly happy in the *choice of words.* It has been said of Shakspeare, that one might as well attempt to push a brick out of its place in a well-constructed wall, as to alter a single expression. In his finest passages, the same is true of Junius. He gives you the exact word, he brings out the most delicate shadings of thought, he throws it upon the mind with elastic force, and you say, "What is written is written!" There are, indeed, instances of bad grammar and inaccurate expression, but these may be ascribed, in most cases, to the difficulty and danger of his correcting the press. Still, there is reason to believe that he was not an author by profession. Certain words and forms of construction seem plainly to show that he had never been trained to the minuter points of authorship. And, perhaps, for this very reason, he was a better writer. He could think of nothing but how to express his ideas with the utmost vividness and force. Hence he gave them a frank and fearless utterance, which, modified by a taste like his, has imparted to his best passages a perfection of style which is never reached by mere mechanical labor. Among other things, Junius understood better than most writers where the true strength of language lies, viz., in the nouns and verbs. He is, therefore, sparing in the use of qualifying expressions.[4] He relies mainly for effect on the frame-work of thought. In the filling out of his ideas, where qualifying terms must of course be employed, he rarely uses intensives. His adverbs and adjectives are nearly all descriptive, and are designed to shade or to color the leading thoughts with increased exactness and thus set them before the mind in bolder relief or with more graphic effect. He employs contrast also, with much success, to heighten the impression. No one has shown greater skill in crushing discordant thoughts together in a single mass, and giving them, by their juxtaposition, a new and startling force. Hardly any one but Demosthenes has made so happy a use of antithesis. His only fault is, that he now and then allows it to run away with his judgment, and to sink into epigram. The *imagery* of Junius is uncommonly brilliant. It was the source of much of his power. He showed admirable dexterity in working his bold and burning metaphors into the very texture of his style. He was also equally happy in the use of plainer images, drawn from the ordinary concerns of life, and intended not so much to adorn as to illustrate and enforce. A few instances of each will show his wide and easy command of figurative language. In warning his countrymen against a readiness to be satisfied with some temporary gain at the expense of great and permanent interests, he says, "In the shipwreck of the state, trifles float and are preserved, while every thing solid and valuable sinks to the bottom and is lost forever." Speaking of the numerous writers in favor of the ministry, he says, "They pile up reluctant quarto upon solid folio, as if their labors, because they are gigantic, could contend with truth and heaven."[5] Again, "The very sunshine you live in is a prelude to your dissolution: when you are ripe, you shall be plucked." Exhorting the King no longer to give importance to Wilkes by making him the object of royal persecution, he says, "The gentle breath of peace would leave him on the surface neglected and unremoved. It is only the tempest that lifts him from his place." And again, in a higher strain, "The rays of royal indignation collected upon him, served only to illuminate and could not consume." The last instance of this kind which will now be cited has been already referred to on a preceeding page, as perhaps suggested by a classical allusion of Lord Chatham. If so, it is a beautiful example of the way in which one man of genius often improves upon another. Many have pronounced it the finest metaphor in our language. Speaking of the King's sacrifice of honor in not instantly resenting the seizure of the Falkland Islands, he says, "A clear, unblemished character comprehends not only the integrity that will not offer, but the spirit that will not submit to an injury; and whether it belongs to an individual or to a community, it is the foundation of peace, of independence, and of safety. Private credit is wealth; public honor is security. *The feather that adorns the royal bird supports his flight. Strip him of his plumage, and you fix him to the earth."* Such are some of the characteristics of the style of Junius, which made Mr. Mathias, author of the Pursuits of Literature, rank him among the English classics, in the place assigned to Livy and Tacitus among the ancients.

Reference has already been made to the violent passions of Junius and his want of candor toward most of his opponents. Still it will be seen, from the following sentiments contained in a private letter, that in his cooler moments he had just and elevated views concerning the design of political discussions. He is speaking of an argument he had just stated in favor of rotten boroughs, and goes on to say, "The man who fairly and completely answers this argument, shall have my thanks and my applause. My heart is already with him. I am ready to be converted. I admire his morality, and would gladly subscribe to the articles of his faith. Grateful as I am to the Good Being, whose bounty has imparted to me this reasoning intellect, whatever it is, I hold myself proportionably indebted to him, whose enlightened understanding communicates another ray of knowledge to mine. But neither should I think the most exalted faculties of the human mind a gift worthy of the divinity, nor any assistance in the improvement of them a subject of gratitude to my fellow-creatures, if I were not satisfied that *really to inform the understanding, corrects and enlarges the heart.*" "Si sic omnia!" Would that all were thus! Happy were it for the character of Junius as a man, if he had always been guided as a writer by such views and feelings!

Who was Junius? Volumes have been written to answer this question, and it remains still undecided. At the end of eighty years of inquiry and discussion, after the claims of nearly twenty persons have been examined and set aside, only two names remain before the public as candidates for this distinction.[6] They are Sir Philip Francis, and Lord George Sackville, afterward Lord George Germain. In favor and against each of these, there is circumstantial evidence of considerable weight. Neither of them has left any specimens of style which are equal in elegance and force to the more finished productions of Junius. Lord George Sackville, however, is far inferior in this respect. He was never a practical writer; and it seems impossible to believe that the mind which expressed itself in the compositions he has left us could ever have been raised, by any excitement of emotion or fervor of effort, into a capacity to produce the Letters of Junius. Sir Philip Francis was confessedly a far more able writer. He had studied composition from early life. He was diligent in his attendance on Parliament, and he reported some of Lord Chatham's speeches with uncommon elegance and force. If we must choose between the two—if there is no other name to be brought forward, and this seems hardly possible—the weight of evidence is certainly in his favor. Mr. Macaulay has summed it up with his usual ability in the following terms:

"Was he the author of the Letters of Junius? Our own firm belief is that he was. The external evidence is, we think, such as would support a verdict in a peculiar handwriting of Francis, slightly disguised. As to the position, pursuits, and connections of Junius, the following are the most important facts which can be considered as clearly proved: First, that he was acquainted with the technical forms of the Secretary of State's office; secondly, that he was intimately acquainted with the business of the War office; thirdly, that he, during the year 1770, attended debates in the House of Lords, and took notes of speeches, particularly of the speeches of Lord Chatham; fourthly, that he bitterly resented the appointment of Mr. Chamier to the place of deputy Secretary at War; fifthly, that he was bound by some strong tie to the first Lord Holland. Now Francis passed some years in the Secretary of State's office. He was subsequently chief clerk of the War office. He repeatedly mentioned that he had himself, in 1770, heard speeches of Lord Chatham, and some of those speeches were actually printed from his notes. He resigned his clerkship at the War office from resentment at the appointment of Mr. Chamier. It was by Lord Holland that he was first introduced into the public service. Now, here are five marks, all of which ought to be found in Junius. They are all five found in Francis. We do not believe that more than two of them can be found in any other person whatever. If this argument does not settle the question, there is an end of all reasoning on circumstantial evidence.

"The internal evidence seems to us to point the same way. The style of Francis bears a strong resemblance to that of Junius; nor are we disposed to admit what is generally taken for granted, that the acknowledged compositions of Francis are very decidedly inferior to the anonymous letters. The argument from inferiority, at all events, is one which may be urged with at least equal force against every claimant that has ever been mentioned, with the single exception of Burke, who certainly was not Junius. And what conclusion, after all, can be drawn from mere inferiority? Every writer must produce his best work; and the interval between his best work and his second best work may be very wide indeed. Nobody will say that the best letters of Junius are more decidedly superior to the acknowledged works of Francis than three or four of Corneille's tragedies to the rest; than three or four of Ben Jonson's comedies to the rest; than the Pilgrim's Progress to the other works of Bunyan; than Don Quixote to the other works of Cervantes. Nay, it is certain that the Man in the Mask, whoever he may have been, was a most unequal writer. To go no farther than the Letters which bear the signature of Junius—the Letter to the King and the Letters to Horne Tooke have little in common except the asperity; and asperity was an ingredient seldom wanting either in the writings or in the speeches of Francis.

"Indeed, one of the strongest reasons for believing that Francis was Junius is the moral resemblance between the two men. It is not difficult, from the letters which, under various signatures, are known to have been written by Junius and from his dealings with Woodfall and others, to form a tolerably correct notion of his character. He was clearly a man not destitute of real patriotism and magnanimity—a man whose vices were not of a sordid kind. But he must also have been a man in the highest degree arrogant and insolent—a man prone to malevolence, and prone to the error of mistaking his malevolence for public virtue. 'Doest thou well to be angry?' was the question asked in old time of the Hebrew prophet. And he answered, 'I do well.' This was evidently the temper of Junius, and to this cause we attribute the savage cruelty which disgraces several of his Letters. No man is so merciless as he who, under a strong self-delusion, confounds his antipathies with his duties. It may be added, that Junius, though allied with the democratic party by common enmities, was the very opposite of a democratic politician. While attacking individuals with a ferocity which perpetually violated all the laws of literary warfare, he regarded the most defective parts of old constitutions with a respect amounting to pedantry—pleaded the cause of Old Sarum with fervor, and contemptuously told the capitalists of Manchester and Leeds that, if they wanted votes, they might buy land and become freeholders of Lancashire and Yorkshire. All this, we believe, might stand, with scarcely any change, for a character of Philip Francis."[7]

But, whatever may be thought of the origin of these Letters, it is not difficult to understand the political relations of the writer and the feelings by which he was actuated. A few remarks on this subject will close the present sketch.

The author of these letters, as we learn from Woodfall, had been for some years an active political partisan. He had written largely for the public prints under various signatures, and with great ability. A crisis now arrived which induced him to come forward under a new name, and urged him by still higher motives to the utmost exertion of his powers. Lord Chatham's "checkered and dovetailed" cabinet had fallen to pieces, and the Duke of Grafton, as Junius expressed it, became "minister by accident," at the close of 1767. He immediately endeavored to strengthen himself on every side. He yielded to the wishes of the King by making Lord North Chancellor of the Exchequer, and by raising Mr. Jenkinson, the organ of Lord Bute, to higher office and influence. Thus he gave a decided ascendency to the Tories. On the other hand, he endeavored to conciliate Lord Rockingham and the Duke of Bedford by very liberal proposals. But these gentlemen differing as to the lead of the House the Bedford interest prevailed: Lord Weymouth, a member of that family, was made Secretary of the Home Department, while Lord Rockingham was sent back to the ranks of Opposition under a sense of wrong and insult. Six months, down almost to the middle of 1768, were spent in these negotiations and arrangements.

These things wrought powerfully on the mind of Junius, who was a Grenville or Rockingham Whig. But in addition to this, he had strong private animosities. He not only saw with alarm and abhorrence the triumph of Tory principles, but he cherished the keenest personal resentment toward the King and most of his ministers. Those, especially, who had deserted their former Whig associates, he regarded as traitors to the cause of liberty. He therefore now determined to give full scope to his feelings and to take up a system of attack far more galling to his opponents than had ever yet been adapted. One thing was favorable to such a design. Parliament was to expire within a few months; and every blow now struck would give double alarm and distress to the government, while it served also to inflame the minds of the people and rouse them to a more determined resistance in the approaching elections. Accordingly, at the close of the Christmas holidays, when the business of the session really commences, he addressed his first Letter to the printer of the Public Advertiser, under date of January 21, 1769. It was elaborated with great care, but its most striking peculiarity was the daring spirit of personal attack by which it was characterized. Junius, for the first time, broke through the barriers thrown around the monarch by the maxim, "the King can do no wrong." He assailed him like any other man, though in more courtly and guarded language. Assuming an air of great respect for his motives, he threw out the most subtle insinuations, mingled with the keenest irony, as to his "love of low intrigue," and "the treacherous amusement of double and triple negotiations." It was plainly his intention not only to distress, but to terrify. He represented the people as driven to the verge of desperation. He hinted at the possible consequences. He spoke of the crisis as one "from which a reasonable man can expect no remedy but *poison,* no relief but *death.*" He attacked the ministry in more direct terms, commenting with great severity on the character of those who filled the principal departments of state, and declaring, "We need look no farther for the cause of every mischief which befalls us." "It is not a casual concurrence of calamitous circumstances—it is the pernicious hand of government alone, that can make a whole people desperate." All this was done with a dignity, force, and elegance entirely without parallel in the columns of a newspaper. The attention of the public was strongly arrested. The poet Gray, in his correspondence, speaks of the absorbing power of this letter over his mind when he took it up casually for the first time at a country inn where he had stopped for refreshment on a journey. He was unable to lay it down, or even to think of the food before him, until he had read it over and over again with the most painful interest. The same profound sensation was awakened in the higher political circles throughout the kingdom.

Still it may be doubted whether the writer, at this time, had formed any definite plan of continuing these Letters. Very possibly, except for a circumstance now to be mentioned, he might have stopped here, and the name of Junius have been known only in our literature by this single specimen of eloquent vituperation. But he was instantly attacked. As if for the very purpose of compelling him to go on, and of giving notoriety to his efforts, Sir William Draper, Knight of the Bath, came out under his *own signature,* charging him with "maliciously traducing the best characters of the kingdom," and going on particularly to defend the Commander in Chief, the Marquess of Granby, against the severe imputations of this Letter. Junius himself could not have asked, or conceived of, any thing more perfectly suited to make him conspicuous in the eyes of the public. Sir William had the character of being an elegant scholar, and had gained high distinction as an officer in the army by the capture of Manilla, the capital of the Philippine Islands, in 1762. It was no light thing for such a man to throw himself into the lists without any personal provocation, and challenge a combat with this unknown champion. It was the highest possible testimony to his powers. Junius saw his advantage. He perfectly understood his antagonist—an open-hearted and incautious man, vain of his literary attainments, and uncommonly sensitive to ridicule and contempt. He seized at once on the weak points of Sir William's letter. He turned the argument against him. He overwhelmed him with derision. He showed infinite dexterity in wresting every weapon from his hands, and in turning all his praises of the Marquess, and apologies for his failings, into new instruments of attack. "It is *you,* Sir William, who make your friend appear awkward and ridiculous, by giving him a *laced suit of tawdry qualifications* which Nature never intended him to wear!" "It is you who have taken pains to represent your friend *in the character of a drunken landlord,* who deals out his promises as liberally as his liquor, and will suffer no man to leave his table either sorrowful or sober!" He then turned upon Sir William himself. He glanced at some of the leading transactions of his life. He goaded him with the most humiliating insinuations and interrogatories. He hinted at the motives which the public would impute to him, in thus coming out from his retirement at Clifton; and concluded by asking in a tone of lofty contempt, "And do you now, after a retreat not very like that of Scipio, presume to intrude yourself, unthought of, uncalled for, upon the patience of the public?" Never was an assailant so instantaneously put on the defensive. Instead of silencing the "traducer," and making him the object of public indignation, he was himself dragged to the confessional, or rather placed at a culprit at the bar of the public. His feelings at this sudden change seem much to have resembled those of a traveler in the forests of Africa when he finds himself, without a moment's warning, wrapped in the folds of a boa constrictor darting from above, and crushed beneath its weight. He exclaimed piteously against this "uncandid Junius," his "abominable scandals," his delight in putting men to "the rack," and "mangling their carcasses with a hatchet." He quoted Virgil, and made a feeling allusion to Æsop's Fables: "You bite against a file; cease, viper!" Junius replied in three Letters, two of which will be found below. He tells Sir William that an "academical education had given him an unlimited command over the most beautiful figures of speech." "Masks, hatchets, racks, and vipers dance through your letters in all the mazes of metaphorical confusion. These are the gloomy companions of a disturbed imagination; the melancholy madness of poetry, without the inspiration." As the correspondence went on, Sir William did, indeed, clear himself of the imputations thrown out by Junius affecting his personal honesty, but he was so shocked and confounded by the overmastering power of his antagonist that he soon gave up the contest. Some months after, when he saw these Letters collected and republished in a volume, he again came forward to complain of their injustice. *"Hæret lateri lethalis arundo,"*[8] was the savage exclamation of Junius when he saw the writhings of his prostrate foe. Such was the first encounter of Junius before the public. The whole nation looked on with astonishment, and from this hour his name was known as familiarly in every part of the kingdom as that of Chatham or Johnson. It was a name of terror to the King, and his ministers, and of pride and exultation to thousands throughout the empire—not only of those who sympathized in his malignant feelings, but those who, like Burke, condemned his spirit, and yet considered him engaged in a just cause and hailed him as a defender of the invaded rights of the people.

Junius now resumed his attack on the ministry with still greater boldness and virulence. After assailing the Duke of Grafton repeatedly on individual points, he came out in two Letters, under date of May 30th and July 8th, 1769, with a general review of his Grace's life and conduct. These are among his most finished productions, and will be given below. On the 19th of September, he attacked the Duke of Bedford, whose interests had been preferred to those of Lord Rockingham in the ministerial arrangements mentioned above. This Letter has even more force than the two preceding ones, and will also be found in this collection. Three months after, December 19th, 1769, appeared his celebrated Letter to the King, the longest and most elaborate of all his performances. The reader will agree with Mr. Burke in saying, "it contains many *bold truths* by which a wise prince might profit." Lord Chatham now made his appearance on the stage, after an illness of three years, and at the opening of Parliament, January 9th, 1770, took up the cause with more than his accustomed boldness and eloquence. Without partaking of the bitter spirit of Junius, he maintained his principles on all the great questions of the day in their fullest extent. He at once declared in the face of the country, "A breach has been made in the Constitution—the battlements are dismantled—the citadel is open to the first invader—the walls totter—the Constitution is not tenable. What remains, then, but for us to stand foremost in the breach, to repair it, or perish in it?" The result has already been stated in connection with that and his other speech on this subject, p. 114–18. At the end of *nineteen* days, January 28th, 1770, the Duke of Grafton was driven from power! About a fortnight after, Junius addressed his fallen adversary in a Letter of great force which closes the extracts from his writings in this volume. Lord North's ministry now commenced. Junius continued his labors with various ability, but with little success, nearly two years longer, until in the month of January, 1772, the King remarked to a friend in confidence, "Junius is known, and will write no more." Such proved to be the fact. His last performance was dated January 21st, 1772, three years to a day from his first great Letter to the printer of the Public Advertiser. Within a few months Sir Philip Francis was appointed to one of the highest stations of profit and trust in India, at a distance of fifteen thousand miles from the seat of English politics![9]

EDMUND BURKE

EDMUND BURKE was the son of a respectable barrister in Dublin, and was born in that city on the first day of January, 1730. Being of a delicate and consumptive habit, he was unable to share in the ordinary sports of childhood, and was thus led to find his earliest enjoyment in reading and thought.

When eleven years old, he was sent to a school at Ballitore, about thirty miles from Dublin, under the care of a Quaker named Shackleton, who was distinguished not only for the accuracy of his scholarship, but for his extraordinary power of drawing forth the talents of his pupils and giving a right direction to their moral principles. Mr. Burke uniformly spoke of his instructor in after life with the warmest affection, and rarely failed, during forty years, whenever he went to Ireland, to pay him a visit. He once alluded to him in the House of Commons, in the following terms: "I was educated," said he, "as a Protestant of the Church of England, by a Dissenter who was an honor to his sect, though that sect has ever been considered as one of the purest. Under his eye, I read the Bible, morning, noon, and night; and have ever since been a happier and better man for such reading." Under these influences, the development of his intellect and of his better feelings was steady and rapid. He formed those habits of industry and perseverance which were the most striking traits in his character, and which led him to say in after life, "*Nitor in adversum* is the motto for a man like me." He learned that simplicity and frankness, that bold assertion of moral principle, that reverence for the Word of God, and the habit of going freely to its pages for imagery and illustration, by which he was equally distinguished as a man and an orator. At this period, too, he began to exhibit his extraordinary powers of memory. In every task or exercise dependent on this faculty, he easily outstripped all his competitors; it is not improbable that he gained, under his early Quaker discipline, those habits of systematic thought, and that admirable arrangement of all his acquired knowledge, which made his memory one vast storehouse of facts, principles, and illustrations, ready for use at a moment's call. At this early period, too, the imaginative cast of his mind was strongly developed. He delighted above all things in works of fancy. The old romances, such as Palmerin of England and Don Belianis of Greece, were his favorite study, and we can hardly doubt, considering the peculiar susceptibility of his mind, that such reading had a powerful influence in producing that gorgeousness of style which characterized so many of his productions in after life.

Quitting school at the end of three years, he became a member of Trinity College, Dublin, in 1744. Here he remained six years, engaged chiefly in a course of study of his own, though not to the neglect of his regular college duties. It was said by Goldsmith, perhaps to excuse his own indolence, that Burke's scholarship at college was low. This could not have been the case; for in his third year he was elected Scholar of the House, which, his biographer assures us, "confers distinction in the classics throughout life." Still, he gave no peculiar promise of his future eminence. Leland, the translator of Demosthenes, who was then a fellow, used to say, that "he was known as a young man of superior but unpretending talents, and more anxious to acquire knowledge than to display it." That his college life was one of severe study is evident from the extent and accuracy of his knowledge when he left the University. A few things have come down to us, as to his course of reading. He had mastered most of the great writers of antiquity. Demosthenes was his favorite orator, though he was led in after life, by the bent of his genius, to form himself on the model of Cicero, whom he more resembled in magnificence and copiousness of thought. He delighted in Plutarch. He read most of the great poets of antiquity and was peculiarly fond of Virgil, Horace, and Lucretius, a large part of whose writings he committed to memory.[1] In English he read the essays of

Lord Bacon again and again with increasing admiration, and pronounced them "the greatest works of that great man." Shakspeare was his daily study. But his highest reverence was reserved for Milton, "whose richness of language, boundless learning, and scriptural grandeur of conception," were the first and last themes of his applause. The philosophical tendency of his mind began now to display itself with great distinctness, and became, from this period, the master principle of his genius. "Rerum cognoscere *causas,*" seems ever to have been his delight, and soon became the object of all his studies and reflections. He had an exquisite sensibility to the beauties of nature, of art, and of elegant composition, but he could never rest here. "Whence this enjoyment?" "On what principle does it depend?" "How might it be carried to a still higher point?"—these are questions which seem almost from boyhood to have occurred instinctively to his mind. His attempts at philosophical criticism commenced in college and led to his producing one of the most beautiful works of this kind to be found in any language. In like manner, history to him, even at this early period, was not a mere chronicle of events, a picture of battles and sieges, or of life and manners: to make it *history,* it must bind events together by the causes which produced them. The science of politics and government was in his mind the science of man: not a system of arbitrary regulations, or a thing of policy and intrigue, but founded on a knowledge of those principles, feelings, and even prejudices, which unite a people together in one community—"ties," as he beautifully expresses it, "which, though light as air, are strong as links of iron." Such were the habits of thought to which his mind was tending even from his college days, and they made him pre-eminently the great philosophical orator of our language.[3]

Being intended by his father for the bar, Mr. Burke was sent to London at the age of twenty to pursue his studies at the Middle Temple. But he was never interested in the law. He saw enough of it to convince him that it is "one of the first and noblest of human sciences—a science which does more to quicken and invigorate the understanding than all other kinds of learning put together." Still, it was too dry and technical for a mind like his; and he felt that, "except in persons very happily born, it was not apt to open and liberalize the mind in the same proportion." He therefore soon gave himself up, with all the warmth of his early attachment, to the pursuits of literature and philosophy. His diligence in study was now carried to its highest point. He devoted every moment to severe labor, spending his evenings, however, in conversation with the ablest men engaged in the same employments, and thus varying, perhaps increasing, the demand for mental exertion. Few men ever studied to greater effect. He early acquired a power which belongs peculiarly to superior minds—that of *thinking* at all times and in every place and not merely at stated seasons in the retirement of the closet. His mind seems never to have floated on the current of passing events. He was always *working out trains of thought*. His reading, though wide and multifarious, appears from the first to have been perfectly digested. His views on every subject were formed into a complete system, and his habits of daily discussing with others whatever he was revolving in his own mind not only quickened his powers, but made him guarded in statement and led him to contemplate every subject under a great variety of aspects. His exuberant fancy, which in most men would have been a fatal impediment to any attempt at speculation, was in him the ready servant of the intellect, supplying boundless stores of thought and illustration for every inquiry. Such were his habits of study from this period, during nearly fifty years, down to the time of his death. Once only, as he stated to a friend, did his mind ever appear to flag. At the age of forty-five, he felt weary of this incessant struggle of thought. He resolved to pause and rest satisfied with the knowledge he had gained. But a week's experience taught him the misery of being idle, and he resumed his labors with the noble determination of the Greek philosopher, γηράσκειν διδασκόμενος, to grow old in learning. Gifted as he was with pre-eminent genius, it is not surprising that diligence like this, which would have raised even moderate abilities into talents of a high order, should have made him from early life an object of admiration to his friends and have laid the foundation of that richness and amplitude of thought in which he far surpassed every modern orator.

Being on a journey to Scotland in 1753, Mr. Burke learned that the office of Professor of Logic had become vacant in the University of Glasgow and would be awarded to the successful competitor at a public disputation. He at once offered himself as a candidate. Farther inquiries, however, showed that private arrangements in the city and University precluded all possibility of his being elected. He therefore withdrew from the contest, and the name of Mr. James Clow has come down to posterity as the man who succeeded when Edmund Burke failed.

Soon after his return from Scotland, the literary world was much excited by the publication of Lord Bolingbroke's philosophical works. Unwilling to incur the odium of so atrocious an attack on morals and religion, his Lordship had left his manuscripts, with a small legacy, in the hands of Mallet, to be published immediately after his death. This gave rise to Johnson's remark that "Bolingbroke was a scoundrel and a coward—a scoundrel, for charging a blunderbuss against religion and morality; and a coward, because he had not resolution to fire it himself, but left half a crown to a beggarly Scotchman to draw the trigger." Mr. Burke took this occasion to make his first appearance before the public. He wrote a pamphlet of one hundred and six pages, under the title of a Vindication of Natural Society, which came out in the spring of 1756 and had all the appearance of being a posthumous work of Bolingbroke. His object was to expose his Lordship's mode of reasoning by running it out into its legitimate consequences. He therefore applied it to civil society. He undertook, in the person of Bolingbroke, and with the closest imitation of his impetuous and overbearing eloquence, to expose the crimes and wretchedness which have prevailed under every form of government and thus to show that society is itself an evil, and the savage state the only one favorable to virtue and happiness. In this pamphlet he gave the most perfect specimen which the world has ever seen of the art of imitating the style and manner of another. He went beyond the mere choice of words, the structure of sentences, and the cast of imagery, into the deepest recesses of thought; and so completely had he imbued himself with the spirit of Bolingbroke that he brought out precisely what every one sees his Lordship *ought* to have said on his own principles, and might be expected to say if he dared to express his sentiments. The work, therefore, can hardly be called ironical, for irony takes care to make its object known by pressing things, at times, into open extravagance. But such was the closeness of the imitation that Chesterfield and Warburton were for a while deceived, and even Mallet felt called upon to deny its authenticity. If he had made it professedly ironical, it would undoubtedly have taken better with the public. Every one would have enjoyed its keenness, had it come in the form of satire. But, as it was, some were vexed to find they had mistaken the author's meaning, and others regarded it only as "a clever imitation." Thus it happened to Mr. Burke in his first appearance before the public, as in some cases of greater importance in after life, that the very ability with which he executed his task was for a time the reason of its being less highly appreciated. If his Vindication of Natural Society was at first a failure, his speech on the Nabob of Arcot's debts was so little understood at the time of delivery and heard with so much impatience by the House of Commons that Mr. Pitt and Lord Grenville considered it as needing no reply!

At the close of the same year, 1756, Mr. Burke published his celebrated treatise on the Sublime and Beautiful. This was the first attempt in our language to discuss the subject with philosophical accuracy and precision. Addison had, indeed, written a series of papers on the Pleasures of the Imagination; but his object was rather to exemplify and illustrate, than to trace those pleasures to any specific source. Mr. Burke boldly propounded a theory designed to account, upon a few simple principles, for all the diversified enjoyments of taste. His treatise shows great ingenuity, surprising accuracy of observation, and an exquisite sense of the sublime and beautiful, both in the works of nature and art. Like all his writings, it abounds in rich trains of thought, and observations of great value in themselves, whatever we may think of this theory. It contains, also, many things which are purely fanciful, as when he traces the pleasures of taste to states of the bodily system, and maintains that the sublime is connected with "an unnatural *tension* and certain violent motions of the nerves," while beauty acts "by *relaxing* the solids of the whole body!" These are some of the things which he learned to laugh at himself, in after life. His theory, as a whole, is rather defective than erroneous. It is one of those hasty generalizations which we are always to expect in the first stages of a new science. The work, however, was an extraordinary production for a youth of twenty-six, and in style and manner was regarded by Johnson as "a model of philosophical criticism." With some few blemishes, such as we always look for in the writings of Burke, it has a clearness of statement, a purity of language, an ease and variety in the structure of sentences, and an admirable richness of imagery which place it in the foremost rank of our elegant literature.

Such a work, from one who had been hitherto unknown to the public, excited a general and lively interest. Its author was everywhere greeted with applause. His acquaintance was sought by the most distinguished literary men and friends of learning, such as Pulteney, Earl of Bath; Markham, soon after Archbishop of York; Lord Lyttleton; Soame Jenyns; Johnson; and many others. In such society, his remarkable talents for conversation secured his success. Everyone was struck with the activity of his mind, the singular extent and variety of his knowledge, his glowing power of thought, and the force and beauty of his language. Even Johnson, whose acknowledged supremacy made him in most cases

> "Bear, like the Turk, no brother near the throne,"

was soon conciliated or subdued by the conversational powers of Burke. It was a striking spectacle to see one so proud and stubborn, who had for years been accustomed to give forth his *dicta* with the authority of an oracle, submit to contradiction from a youth of twenty-seven. But, though Johnson differed from Burke on politics and occasionally on other subjects, he always did him justice. He spoke of him from the first in terms of the highest respect. "Burke," said he, "is an extraordinary man. His stream of talk is perpetual, and he does not talk from any desire of distinction, but because his mind is full." "He is the *only* man," said he, at a later period when Burke was at the zenith of his reputation, "whose common conversation corresponds with the general fame which he has in the world. Take him up where you please, he is ready to meet you." "No man of sense," he said, "could meet Burke by accident under a gateway to avoid a shower without being convinced that he was the first man in England." A striking confirmation of this remark occurred some years after, when Mr. Burke was passing through Litchfield, the birth-place of Johnson. Wishing to see the Cathedral during the change of horses, he stepped into the building and was met by one of the clergy of the place, who kindly offered to point out the principal objects of curiosity. "A conversation ensued; but, in a few moments, the clergyman's pride of local information was completely subdued by the copious and minute knowledge displayed by the stranger. Whatever topic the objects before them suggested, whether the theme was architecture or antiquities, some obscure passage in ecclesiastical history, or some question respecting the life of a saint, he touched it as with a sun-beam. His information appeared universal; his mind, clear intellect, without one particle of ignorance. A few minutes after their separation, the clergyman was met hurrying through the street. 'I have had,' said he, 'quite an adventure. I have been conversing for this half hour past with a man of the most extraordinary powers of mind and extent of information which it has ever been my fortune to meet with; and I am now going to the inn, to ascertain, if possible, who this stranger is.' "

In 1757, Mr. Burke married a daughter of Dr. Nugent, of Bath, and took up literature as a profession. The colonies upon the American coast being now an object of public interest, he prepared, during this year (perhaps in conjunction with his two brothers), a work in two octavo volumes, entitled an Account of the European Settlements of America. These labors, thus casually undertaken, had great influence in shaping his subsequent course as a statesman. He became deeply interested in the early history of the British colonies, and was led naturally, by his habits of thought, to trace the character of their institutions to the spirit of their ancestors and to follow out that spirit in the enterprise, perseverance, and indomitable love of liberty which animated the whole body of the people. He saw, too, the boundless resources of the country and the irrepressible strength to which it must soon attain. Thus was he prepared, when the troubles came on ten years after, and when there was hardly a man in England except Lord Chatham who had the least conception of the force and resolution of the colonies, to come forward with those rich stores of knowledge and those fine trains of reasoning, conceived in the truest spirit of philosophy, which astonished and delighted, though they failed to convince, the Parliament of Great Britain.

In the next year, 1758, Mr. Burke projected the Annual Register, a work of great utility which has been continued for nearly a century down to the present time. The plan was admirable, presenting for each year a succinct statement of the debates in Parliament, a historical sketch of the principal occurrences in every part of the world connected with European politics, and a view of the progress of literature and science, with brief notices of the most important works published during the year. Such an undertaking required all the resources and self-reliance of a man like Burke and would never have been commenced except by one of his extraordinary vigor and enterprise. It was entirely successful. So great was the demand that some of the early volumes were reprinted five or six times. At first, Mr. Burke prepared the entire volume for the year, containing five or six hundred pages, with hardly any assistance. He finally confined himself to the debates and the historical sketches, which for quite a number of years were written by himself, and afterward by others under his direction and superintendence. No employment could have been suited more perfectly to train him for his subsequent duties as a statesman. His attendance on the debates in Parliament made him familiar with the rules of business. Questions were continually arising in respect to trade, finance, the relations of other countries, or the past history of his own, which, to one of his ardent and inquisitive mind, would furnish unnumbered topics for study and reflection. His views were enlarged by the nature of his task, so as to embrace the entire range of European politics. His disposition to philosophize was hemmed in and directed by the great facts in politics and history with which he had constantly to deal. The result was that he became, in the strictest sense of the term, a *practical* statesman, whose philosophy was that of a man in the concrete and as he exists in society; so that no one had ever a greater contempt of abstract principles, or was more completely governed in his reasonings by the lessons of time and experience. Rarely has any work been of so much benefit, at once to its author and the public, as the Annual Register in its earlier volumes.

Mr. Burke's first entrance on political life was in 1761. Lord Halifax, being appointed Lord Lieutenant of Ireland, took with him William Gerard Hamilton (commonly called *single-speech* Hamilton) as Principal Secretary of State.[3] Hamilton, from the nature of his office, was the acting minister for Ireland and needed the assistance of some able adviser who was well acquainted with the country. He therefore induced Mr. Burke to accompany him in this character under the title of private secretary. Halifax was highly successful in his administration, showing great dexterity in disarming or neutralizing the various factions into which Ireland was divided. How far he was indebted for this success to the counsels of Mr. Burke it is impossible to say, since the principal secretary would, of course, have the credit of every suggestion which came from that quarter. One thing, however, is certain; Hamilton perfectly understood the value of Mr. Burke's services. He obtained for him a pension of £300 on the Irish establishment; and after the secretaryship expired, and both had returned to England, in 1763, he actually endeavored to make this pension the means of attaching Mr. Burke to him for life as a coadjutor and humble dependent. "It was," said Mr. Burke, in a letter on the subject, "an insolent and intolerable demand, amounting to no less than a claim of *servitude* during the whole course of my life, without leaving me at any time a power either of getting forward with honor or of retiring with tranquillity." Such a demand was of course met with an indignant refusal. Mr. Burke's nice sense of honor made him propose, without the least reason or propriety, to surrender the pension which his services had richly merited. Hamilton had the meanness to accept it; and whether he pocketed the money himself, or gave it to some miserable dependent, he deserves a title more stinging and contemptuous even than the one he bears.

About two years after, in the month of July, 1765, Mr. Burke entered permanently on the duties of public life. The administration of Lord Rockingham was now formed; and the new minister, being desirous to avail himself of Mr. Burke's splendid abilities, invited him to become his confidential adviser, with a seat in Parliament and the office of private secretary. The arrangement was gratifying in a high degree to the friends of Rockingham. "The British dominions," says one who knew perfectly the character of the political men of the time, "did not furnish a more able and fit person for that important and confidential situation; the only man since the days of Cicero who united the graces of speaking and writing with irresistible force and elegance." Mr. Burke, on his part, though pleased with this unlooked-for token of confidence, had no very sanguine expectations of the success or permanency of the new ministry. Highly as he estimated Lord Rockingham himself, he knew the discordant materials of which the cabinet was composed. But there was a question at issue with which he was better acquainted than any man in the kingdom—American Taxation—and no opportunity of influencing the decision of such a question was to be lost or neglected. Accordingly, having taken his seat as member for Wendover, Mr. Burke came forward at the opening of the session, January, 1766, in a maiden speech of great compass and power, on the absorbing topic of the day, the Stamp Act. He was followed by Mr. Pitt (Lord Chatham), who commenced by saying that "the young member had proved a very able advocate. He had himself intended to enter at length into the details, but he had been anticipated with such ingenuity and eloquence that there was but little left for him to say. He congratulated him on his success, and his friends on the value of the acquisition they had made." Such an encomium, from the greatest of English orators, gave him at once a high reputation in the House and in the country. To a mind like Mr. Burke's, it afforded an ample recompense for all his labors. "Laudari a laudato viro,"[4] is perhaps the highest gratification of genius.

The ministry had determined to repeal the Stamp Act, but in doing so, to pass a declaration affirming the *right* of Parliament to lay taxes on America. This put them between two fires. The courtiers and landed interest resisted the repeal; Lord Chatham and Lord Camden condemned the declaration. "Everything on every side," to use the highly figurative language of Mr. Burke, "was full of traps and mines. Earth below shook; heaven above menaced; all the elements of ministerial safety were dissolved." The motion for repeal was made by General Conway; and Mr. Burke, who took a leading part in the debate, thus described the scene in one of his speeches at a later period. "I knew well enough the true state of things; but in my life, I never came with such spirits into this House. It was a time for a *man* to act in. We had a great battle to fight, but we had the means of fighting it. We did fight, that day, and conquer. . . . In that crisis, the whole trading interest of this empire, crammed in your lobbies with a trembling and anxious expectation, waited almost to a winter's return of light their fate from your resolution. When, at length, you had determined in their favor, and your doors, thrown open, showed them the figure of their deliverer [General Conway] in the well-earned triumph of his important victory, from the whole of that grave multitude there arose an involuntary burst of gratitude and transport. They jumped upon him like children on a long-absent father. All England, all America, joined in his applause. Nor did he seem insensible to the best of all earthly rewards. *'Hope elevated and joy brightened his crest.'*[5] I stood near him, and his face, to use the expression of the Scripture of the first martyr, 'his face was as if it had been the face of an angel.' I do not know how others feel; but if I had stood in that situation, I would never have exchanged it for all that kings in their profusion could bestow." Notwithstanding the generosity of Mr. Burke in thus transferring to another the honor of that victory, every one knows that he was himself the chief agent in providing "the means" of fighting the battle; and if Charles Townsend had not soon after thrown every thing into confusion by his rashness, posterity might have looked back to Edmund Burke, in his connection with Rockingham, as the great instrument of putting an end to the contest with America.

The King, much against his will, though pacified in some degree by the Declaration, signed the act for repeal, March 18th, 1766. But the fate of the ministry was sealed. Four months after, Lord Rockingham was dismissed.

Lord Chatham now followed with his third administration. Under this, Mr. Burke was offered a very important and lucrative office, that of one of the Lords of Trade. But, though "free to choose another connection as any man in the country," and even advised by Lord Rockingham to accept the offer, he had that delicate sense of honor which forbade him to share in the titles and emoluments of those who had united to remove his patron. The death of Charles Townsend thirteen months after, September 2d, 1767, put an end to this ministry, and that of the Duke of Grafton succeeded. Here commenced the ascendency of the Tories, which lasted about two years under the Duke of Grafton, and more than twelve years under Lord North, down to the close of the American war in 1782. During this whole period, Mr. Burke was the acknowledged leader of the Rockingham Whigs in the House, comprising the great body of the Opposition. He took part in every important debate, and, next to Chatham, who had now passed into the House of Lords, was universally regarded as the most eloquent speaker in Parliament.

The political career of Mr. Burke may be divided into three periods, corresponding to the three great subjects, America, India, and France, which successively occupied the anxieties and labors of his life. A brief notice of each of these periods is all that can be attempted in a sketch like this.

The *first* period, which is equal in length to both the others, consists of about sixteen years, extending from 1766, when he took his seat in Parliament, to the end of the American war in 1782. It was, on the whole, the happiest and most successful part of his life. Though he had many difficulties to encounter from his want of wealth, rank, and family connections, in addition to the strong prejudice under which he labored as an Irishman, he rose from year to year in the estimation of the House. Every one admired his talents; every one was delighted with his eloquence. The country cheered him on, as the great advocate of popular rights. His connection with Lord Rockingham secured him the support of a large proportion of the Whigs—a support which could not, indeed, have made him minister under a change of administration, but which enabled him to carry many important measures in their name and through their influence. It rendered him formidable, also, as leader of the Opposition, for those who are eager to gain office will rally under almost any one who has great powers of attack. In this respect, Mr. Burke stood for many years without a rival in the House of Commons. And, though inferior to Lord Chatham in that fire and condensed energy which are the highest characteristics of oratory, he far surpassed him in the patient examination of every subject in debate, the accuracy of his knowledge, the variety and force of his reasonings, and his views of policy, at once comprehensive and practical in the highest degree. Nor was his influence as a leader confined to the discussions of the House. No man, probably, in the whole history of English politics, ever did so much to instruct his friends in private on the questions in debate. His exuberant stores of information were open to every one. Mr. Fox declared toward the close of his life that he had learned more in conversation with Mr. Burke than from all the books he had ever read and all the other men with whom he had ever associated.

In 1771, Mr. Burke received the appointment of agent for the colony of New York, with a salary of about £700 a year. This office he held nearly four years, till the commencement of the American war. It gave him great advantages for obtaining a minute knowledge of the spirit and resources of the colonies, while, at the same time it lessened the influence of his speeches on American affairs by awakening the prejudice which is always felt against the arguments of a paid advocate.

Mr. Burke's first published speech was that on American Taxation, delivered April 19th, 1774. Often as he had dwelt on this topic in preceding years, no attempt had been made to give any regular report of his speeches. In the present instance, the evening was far advanced before he rose to address the House. The opening of the debate was dull, and many of the members had withdrawn into the adjoining apartments or places of refreshment. But the first few sentences of his stinging exordium awakened universal attention. The report of what was going on spread in every quarter; and the members came crowding back, till the hall was filled to the utmost, and resounded throughout the speech with the loudest expressions of applause. Highly as they had estimated Mr.

Burke's talents, the House were completely taken by surprise. Lord John Townsend exclaimed aloud, at the close of one of those powerful passages in which the speech abounds, "Heavens! what a man this is! Where could he acquire such transcendent powers!" The opening of his peroration, especially, came with great weight on the minds of all. "Let us embrace," said he, "some system or other before we end this session. Do you mean to tax America, and draw a productive revenue from thence? If you do, speak out; name, fix, ascertain this revenue; settle its quantity; define its objects; provide for its collection; and then fight, when you have something to fight for. If you murder, rob; if you kill, take possession; and do not appear in the character of madmen as well as assassins, violent, vindictive, bloody, and tyrannical, *without an object*."

The moment Mr. Burke closed, his friends crowded around his seat, and urged him to commit his speech to writing and give it immediately to the world as a protest against the headlong measures which threatened the dismemberment of the empire. He did so, and on five other occasions he repeated the task, thus leaving us *six* speeches as representatives of several hundreds, many of which are said to have been equal, if not superior, in eloquence to those which were thus preserved. One especially, delivered about four years after, on the employment of the Indians in the war, was spoken of by his friends as the most powerful appeal which he ever made. Colonel Barré, in the fervor of his excitement, declared that if it could be written out, he would nail it on every church door in the kingdom. Sir George Savile said, "He who did not hear that speech has failed to witness the greatest triumph of eloquence within my memory." Governor Johnstone said on the floor of the House, "It was fortunate for the noble Lords [North and Germaine] that spectators had been excluded during that debate, for if any had been present, they would have excited the people to tear the noble Lords in pieces in their way home."

Parliament being dissolved in the autumn of 1774, Mr. Burke was invited to offer himself as a candidate for Bristol, in connection with Mr. Henry Cruger, a merchant largely engaged in the American trade. The contest was a sharp one, requiring Mr. Burke and Mr. Cruger to appear daily on the hustings for nearly a month, ready to answer questions of every sort and to address the electors at a moment's call. Mr. Burke, of course, took the lead; and a laughable incident occurred on one of these occasions, showing the power with which he so often absorbed and bore away the minds of others in his glowing trains of thought. Mr. Cruger, being called upon to follow him after one of these harangues, was so lost in admiration that he could only cry out, with the genuine enthusiasm of the counting-house, "I say *ditto* to Mr. Burke; I say *ditto* to Mr. Burke!" It was undoubtedly the best speech that any man could have made under such circumstances.

The contest terminated in their favor, and Mr. Burke had the gratification of being declared a member from the second commercial city of the kingdom, November 3d, 1774. But at the moment of returning thanks, he offended a large part of his supporters by a manly assertion of his rights. It was a doctrine much insisted upon at Bristol that a representative was bound to act and vote according to the instructions of his constituents. To this doctrine Mr. Cruger gave a public assent at the close of the poll. Mr. Burke, in adverting to the subject, remarked, "My worthy colleague says his will ought to be subject to yours. If that be all, the thing is innocent. If government were a matter of *will* upon any side, yours, without question, ought to be superior. But government and legislation are matters of reason and judgment, and not of inclination; and what sort of reason is that in which determination precedes discussion, in which one set of men deliberate and another decide, and where those who form the conclusion are perhaps three hundred miles distant from those who hear the arguments?" These sentiments, as we shall see hereafter, lost him the vote of Bristol at the next general election.

America was the all-absorbing topic during the first session of the new Parliament. On the 20th of February, 1775, Lord North brought forward an artful scheme, professedly for the purpose of "conciliating the differences with America," but really intended to divide the colonies among themselves by exempting from taxation those who, through their General Assemblies, should "contribute their proportion to the common defense." Mr. Burke seized the opportunity thus presented and endeavored to turn the scheme into its true and proper shake—that of leaving all taxes levied within the colonies to be laid by their General Assemblies, and thus establishing the great principle of English liberty that *taxation and representation are inseparably conjoined.* This gave rise to his celebrated speech on Conciliation with America, delivered March 22d, 1775. It would seem hardly possible that in speaking so soon again on the same subject, he could avoid making this speech, to some extent, an echo of his former one. But never were two productions more entirely different. His "stand-point" in the first was *England.* His topics were the inconsistency and folly of the ministry in their "miserable circle of occasional arguments and temporary expedients" for raising a revenue in America. His object was to recall the House to the original principles of the English colonial system—that of *regulating* the trade of the colonies, and making it subservient to the interests of the mother country, while in other respects she left them "every characteristic mark of a free people in all their internal concerns." His "standpoint" in the second speech was *America.* His topics were her growing population, agriculture, commerce, and fisheries; the causes of her fierce spirit of liberty; the impossibility of repressing it by force; and the consequent necessity of some concession on the part of England. His object was (waiving all abstract questions about the right of taxation) to show that Parliament ought "to admit the people of the colonies into an interest in the Constitution," by giving them (like Ireland, Wales, Chester, and Durham) a share in the representation, and to do this by leaving internal taxation to the colonial Assemblies, since no one could think of an actual representation of America in Parliament at the distance of three thousand miles. The two speeches were equally diverse in their spirit. The first was in a strain of incessant attack, full of the keenest sarcasm, and shaped from beginning to end for the purpose of putting down the ministry. The second, like the plan it proposed, was conciliatory; temperate and respectful toward Lord North; designed to inform those who were ignorant of the real strength and feelings of America; instinct with the finest philosophy of man and of social institutions; and intended, if possible, to lead the House, *through* Lord North's scheme, into a final adjustment of the dispute on the true principles of English liberty. It is the most finished of Mr. Burke's speeches; and though it contains no passage of such vividness and force as the description of Hyder Ali in his speech on the Nabob of Arcot's debts, it will be read probably more than any of his other speeches for the richness of its style and the lasting character of the instruction it conveys. Twenty years after, Mr. Fox said, in applying its principles to the subject of parliamentary reform, "Let gentlemen read this speech by day and meditate on it by night; let them peruse it again and again, study it, imprint it on their minds, impress it on their hearts—they will there learn that *representation* is the sovereign remedy for every evil." Both of Mr. Burke's speeches on America, indeed, are full of materials for the orator and the statesman. After all that has been written on the origin of our Revolution, there is nowhere else to be found so admirable a summation of the causes which produce it. They both deserve to be studied with the utmost diligence by every American scholar.

The next speech which Mr. Burke wrote out for publication was that on Economical Reform, delivered February 11th, 1780. The subject is one which has no interest for the American reader, and the speech is therefore omitted in this collection. Like all his great efforts, it is distinguished by comprehensiveness of design and a minute knowledge of details. It has an exuberance of fancy and too much of that coarse humor in which Mr. Burke sometimes indulged. His proposal was to reduce the expenses of the government by abolishing a large number of those sinecure offices which gave such enormous patronage to the Crown. But he had the most formidable difficulties to encounter. Lord Talbot had previously attempted to reform a single class of expenses—those of the royal kitchen—but was foiled at the outset, as Mr. Burke tells us in his speech, "because the King's *turnspit* was a *member of Parliament!*" Against the present scheme were arrayed, not only every turnspit in the palace, but the keepers of the stag, buck, and fox hounds, in the shape of honorable members or lords in waiting, together with scores of others among the nobility and gentry who were living on offices now fallen into total disuse which once ministered to the pleasure or safety of the monarch. As might be expected, the plan, though highly approved of by the public, was voted down in the House, and Mr. Burke was left to console himself under his defeat with the popularity of his proposals and the praises bestowed on his eloquence.

Six years had now elapsed since Mr. Burke's election as member for Bristol; and he was suddenly called upon, by the dissolution of Parliament, September 1st, 1780, to appear again before his constituents, and solicit their favor. It was a difficult task. He had differed from them widely on several important subjects. Many had taken offense at the course he pursued, not only in respect to America, but to the opening of the Irish trade and other measures affecting the interests of Bristol. On some of these points he had explained and justified his conduct in three able pamphlets, to be found in his works, addressed to the Sheriffs of Bristol or to citizens of that place. Still, there was a violent hostility to his re-election. He had disobeyed the instructions of his constituents; he had, as they imagined, sacrificed some of their most important interests; he had wounded their pride by neglecting to visit them since the previous election. Hence, when he arrived in town to commence his canvass, he found himself met by the most formidable opposition. It was on this occasion that he came forward, September 6th, 1780, with his celebrated speech previous to the election at Bristol; "the best ever uttered on such an occasion, and perhaps never excelled by any thing he ever delivered elsewhere." Sir Samuel Romilly speaks of it as "perhaps the best piece of oratory in our language."—Works, i., 213. Being addressed to plain men, it has less fancy, less of studied ornament and classical allusion, than his speeches in Parliament. It is more business-like, simple, and direct. At the same time, it has all the higher qualities of Mr. Burke's mind: his thorough knowledge of human nature, his deep insight into political and social institutions, his enlarged views, his generous sentiments, his keen sensibility to the sufferings and wrongs of others, and his inflexible determination to do right at all hazards and under all circumstances. Its *manliness* is, after all, its most striking characteristic. He had the strongest motives to shuffle, to evade, to conciliate. But he met every thing full in the face. "I did not obey your instructions. No! I conformed to the instructions of truth and nature, and maintained your interests against your opinions with a constancy that became me. A representative worthy of you ought to be a person of stability. I am to look, indeed, to your opinions, but to such opinions as you and I *must* have five years hence. I was not to look to the flash of the day. I knew that you chose me, in my place, along with others, to be a pillar of the state and not a weathercock on the top of the edifice, exalted for my levity and versatility and of no use but to indicate the shiftings of every fashionable gale."

It was apparent at the close of his speech that although the main body of the Corporation and of the Dissenters were with him, together with much of the wealth and respectability of the city, there was no chance of his being re-elected. He therefore determined at once to decline the contest, and did so the 9th Sept., in a short speech containing one of those touching reflections, embalmed in the most beautiful imagery, which occur so often in the writings of Mr. Burke. One of his competitors, Mr. Coombe, overcome by the excitement and agitation of the canvass, had died the preceding night. Such an event was indeed "an awful lesson against being too much troubled about any of the objects of ordinary ambition." Well might Mr. Burke say, in taking leave, "The worthy gentleman who has been snatched from us at the moment of the election, and in the middle of the contest, while his desires were as warm and his hopes as eager as ours, has feelingly told us *what shadows we are, and what shadows we pursue!*"

Through the influence of Lord Rockingham, Mr. Burke was returned at once as member for Malton, and sat for this place during the remainder of his public life. "That humble borough," as Mr. Adolphus has remarked in his History of England, "gained by such a member an honor which the greatest commercial city might reasonably envy."

On the 27th of November, 1781, Mr. Burke, in animadverting on the King's speech, delivered one of his most eloquent philippics against the continuance of the American war. It was not, however, reported with any degree of fullness or accuracy, and is remembered only for the striking figure which it contained of "shearing the wolf." "The noble Lord tells us that we went to war for the maintenance of *rights:* the King's speech says, we will *go on* for the maintenance of our rights. Oh, invaluable rights, that have cost Great Britain thirteen provinces, four islands, a hundred thousand men, and seventy millions of money! Oh, inestimable rights, that have taken from us our rank among nations, our importance abroad, and our happiness at home; that have taken from us our trade, our manufactures, our commerce; that have reduced us from the most flourishing empire in the world to be one of the most miserable and abject powers on the face of the globe! All this we did because we had a *right* to tax America! Miserable and infatuated ministers! Wretched and undone country! Not to know that right signifies nothing without might—that the claim, without the power of enforcing it, is nugatory and idle! We had a right to tax America! Such is the reasoning by which the noble Lord justifies his conduct. Similar was the reasoning of him who was resolved to *shear the wolf!* What! shear a wolf? Have you considered the difficulty, the resistance, the danger? No! says the madman, I have considered nothing but the *right!* Man has a right of dominion over the inferior animals. A wolf has wool; animals that have wool are to be shorn; therefore I will shear the wolf!"

Well might Mr. Burke employ such language, for the news had reached London only two days before that Lord Cornwallis had capitulated at Yorktown, with the loss of his entire army. When the intelligence was carried to Lord North, he received it, says an eye-witness, "as he would have taken a ball into his breast!" He threw open his arms, exclaiming wildly, as he paced the room, "It is all over! it is all over!" And yet the war was to go on! Such was the inflexible determination of the King, who came forward the next day in his speech at the opening of Parliament with increased demands for "concurrence and assistance" to carry on the contest. Such obstinacy justified the remarks of Mr.

Burke and the still greater severity with which Mr. Fox, in the same debate, pointed directly at the King himself. "We have heard a speech," said he, "breathing vengeance, blood, misery, and rancor. It speaks exactly this language: 'Much has been lost; much blood, much treasure has been squandered; the burdens of my people are almost intolerable; but my passions are yet ungratified; my object of subjugation and revenge is yet unfulfilled; and therefore I am determined to persevere.' " And he did persevere. He compelled his ministers to persevere three months longer, during which the attack in the House of Commons was carried on with increased vehemence by Mr. Burke, Mr. Fox, and their associates, until, on the 27th of February, 1782, Lord North was voted down by a majority of 234 to 215. When the result was declared, there arose, says an eye-witness, a shout of triumph throughout the House which seemed to pierce the roof and then rolled away into the remotest parts of Westminster Hall. The King was conquered! At the close of March a new ministry was formed, with Lord Rockingham at its head, having a cabinet composed of five Rockingham and five Shelburne Whigs. As the two parties could not agree on the disposal of the great seal, Lord Thurlow, with all his violent Tory feelings, was retained as Lord Chancellor, much to the satisfaction of the King.

We now come to the *second* period of Mr. Burke's political life. It would naturally be supposed that he who had borne nearly all the labor of this protracted contest, and had for years been the acknowledged head of the Opposition, would now be rewarded with a seat in the cabinet and the leadership of the House. Had Lord North resigned three years before, such might perhaps have been the case; but the pupil had risen above the master. Mr. Fox was now actuated by the keenest desire for popularity and power, and at this juncture he enjoyed peculiar advantages for placing himself at the head of the Whig party. His manners were highly conciliating; he was universally popular among the middle classes; while, as the favorite son of Lord Holland, he had unbounded influence with many of the most powerful families of the kingdom among the nobility and gentry.

Though far inferior to Mr. Burke in richness of thought and copiousness of eloquence, he was a much more effective *debater*. He had made himself, by long practice, a perfect master of the science of attack and defense. When we add to this that he had a peculiar tact, beyond any of his contemporaries, for training and directing a political party, it is not surprising that he obtained the leadership of the House and was made Secretary of State, while Mr. Burke was appointed Paymaster-general of the Forces. Whatever pain it may have cost him, Burke submitted to this arrangement with that noble generosity of feeling which was one of the brightest traits in his character. His biographer has truly said, "A vain man would have resented this treatment; a weak man would have complained of it; an ambitious or selfish man would have taken advantage of the first opportunity to quit the connection and throw the weight of his name and talents into the opposite scale;" but Mr. Burke quietly yielded the precedence. He gave all the force of his transcendent abilities for the support and advancement of one who had crowded into his place. The whole history of politics affords hardly another instance of such a sacrifice, made in a spirit so truly noble and magnanimous. Nor did he ever separate himself, in action or feeling, from Mr. Fox, until the French Revolution put an end at once to their political connection and their private friendship.

Under the new ministry, measures of the highest importance were immediately brought forward and carried successfully through Parliament. In most of these measures Mr. Burke took the lead and responsibility far more than Mr. Fox. His plan of Economical Reform, which had previously been defeated, was now revived. Though narrowed in some of its provisions, it was strenuously resisted by the adherents of the Court, but ultimately passed by a large majority. Many useless offices were abolished in the royal household, with a saving of nearly a hundred thousand pounds a year. Provision was thus made for paying off the King's debts, which already amounted to £300,000, and a check was put to the recurrence of such exorbitant demands in future. His bill for regulating the duties of the Paymaster's department was considered an extraordinary specimen of tact and ingenuity in arranging the details of a most complicated business. Any material reform here had been regarded as hopeless. And so it would have proved, if he had not commenced with himself; if he had not swept away at once enormous perquisites attached to his own office, arising out of profits on contracts, &c., together with the use of nearly a million of the public money which made the situation of Paymaster the most lucrative one under the government. Considering his straitened circumstances, this was an extraordinary sacrifice. Lord Chatham alone had declined to use the public money and placed it on deposit in the bank. Mr. Burke did more. He stripped himself of all his perquisites. He abolished them forever, and thus made a saving to the public which a pension of ten thousand pounds a year would have poorly recompensed.

Lord Rockingham died suddenly on the first of July, 1782, at the end of thirteen weeks from the commencement of his administration. Lord Shelburne, without a word of consultation with his colleagues, instantly seized the reins. Mr. Fox and Mr. Burke, together with the Rockingham Whigs, considered themselves ill treated and at once resigned. The Shelburne administration, which will be spoken of more fully hereafter, lasted hardly eight months. It was overthrown February the 21st, 1783, by the famous coalition between Mr. Fox and Lord North, which, giving the nominal headship to the Duke of Portland, made Mr. Fox the real and responsible minister. To this ill-advised union with their former enemy, Mr. Burke acceded with reluctance, overcome, as his biographer declares, by "the persuasions of Mr. Fox, who was both eloquent and urgent with him on that occasion." Under the coalition ministry, he again became Paymaster of the Forces.

The great measure of this administration, on which its fate at last turned, was the celebrated East India Bill of Mr. Fox. As this measure originated with Mr. Burke, who was the animating spirit of every party to which he belonged, it will be proper to speak briefly on the subject in this place. More than ten years before, his attention was strongly drawn to the affairs of India. He studied the subject with his accustomed assiduity, and showed so intimate an acquaintance with its minutest details when the affairs of the East India Company came before the House in 1772 that Lord North, with a view, no doubt, to get rid of a troublesome opponent, sounded him on the question "whether he was willing to go out at the head of a commission for revising the whole interior administration of India." About four years after, his brother William went to that country, where he became agent for the Rajah of Tanjore and afterward Deputy Paymaster-general of India. Through him Mr. Burke obtained much minute information respecting the Company's concerns which could only have been collected by a person living on the spot. These studies were pursued with still greater diligence after he was appointed a member of the Select Committee to inquire into the concerns of the East India Company, and the result has been thus graphically described by Mr. Macaulay, who was qualified by a residence of some years on the banks of the Ganges to speak decisively on the subject: "Mr. Burke's knowledge of India was such as few, even of those Europeans who have passed many years in that country, have attained, and such as certainly was never attained by any public man who had not quitted Europe. He had studied the history, the laws, and the usages of the East with an industry such as is seldom found united to so much genius and so much sensibility. In every part of those huge bales of Indian information which repelled almost all other readers, his mind, at once philosophical and poetical, found something to instruct or to delight. His reason analyzed and digested those vast and shapeless masses; his imagination animated and colored them. He had in the highest degree that noble faculty whereby man is able to live in the past and the future, in the distant and the unreal. India and its inhabitants were not to him, as to most Englishmen, mere names and abstractions, but a real country and a real people. The burning sun; the strange vegetation of the palm and cocoa-nut tree; the rice-fields and the tank; the huge trees, older than the Mogul empire, under which the village crowds assemble; the thatched roof of the peasant's hut, and the rich tracery of the mosque, where the imaum prayed with his face toward Mecca; the drums, and banners, and gaudy idols; the devotee swinging in the air; the graceful maiden, with the pitcher on her head, descending the steps to the river side; the black faces, the long beards, the yellow streaks of seet; the turbans and the flowing robes; the spears and the silver maces; the elephants, with their canopies of state; the gorgeous palanquin of the prince, and the close litter of the lady—all these things were to him as the objects amid which his own life had been passed, as the objects which lay on the road between Beaconsfield and St. James's Street. All India was present to the eye of his mind, from the halls where suitors laid gold and perfumes at the feet of sovereigns to the wild moor where the gipsy-camp was pitched; from the bazaars, humming like bee-hives with the crowd of buyers and sellers, to the jungle where the lonely courier shakes his bunch of iron rings to scare away the hyenas. He had just as lively an idea of the insurrection at Benares as of Lord George Gordon's riots, and of the execution of Nuncomar as of the execution of Dr. Dodd. Oppression in Bengal was to him the same thing as oppression in the streets of London."[6]

And why should it not be? Under the government of India, as now administered, the crimes of Englishmen abroad are punished on the same principles as the crimes of Englishmen at home. If a hundredth part of the cruelty and extortion of which Burke complained were now found to exist among the Company's servants in India, all England would be moved with indignation, and nothing but the severest punishment could satisfy the demands of public justice. This change has been wrought mainly by the eloquence of Mr. Burke. The perpetrators of those crimes were indeed suffered to escape, for the nation had shared too largely in the profit to be fit executioners of the guilty. But every one felt that such enormities must cease, and the high ground taken by Mr. Burke was, perhaps, the only one which could have produced so entire a change of public sentiment. He was satisfied that the East India Company, from its very constitution, was unable to redress these evils; and he therefore proposed at once to set aside their charter and commit all their concerns, with the entire government of India, to Commissioners to be appointed by the House of Commons. Such, in substance, was the intent of Mr. Fox's East India Bill; and whatever ambitious designs that gentleman may have been charged with in bringing forward this measure, no one suspects Mr. Burke of having been actuated by any other motives but those of justice and humanity. On the question of going into a committee on the bill, December 1st, 1783, he delivered a speech of more than three hours in length which completely exhausted the subject. As a piece of lucid and powerful reasoning, entering into the minutest details and yet bringing every position to the test of general principles, it is incomparably superior to both of Mr. Fox's speeches in explanation and defense of his bill. This speech was committed to writing and published by Mr. Burke soon after its delivery. It will be found below, with the omission of some of the numerous details which were necessary to make out the argument but which have no longer any interest for the general reader. The bill, it is well known, passed the House of Commons by a large majority, but was defeated in the House of Lords by the direct interposition of the King. The details of this subject will be given hereafter in the sketch of Mr. Fox's life. Suffice it to say that the coalition ministry was dismissed on the 18th of December, 1783, and Mr. William Pitt placed at the head of affairs. Mr. Burke went into opposition with Mr. Fox, under a deep sense of wrong as to the means employed for driving them from office; and from this time, for nearly ten years, he was one of the most strenuous opponents of Mr. Pitt's administration.

On the 28th of February, 1785, Mr. Burke delivered the last of the six great speaches which he wrote out for publication. It was that on the Nabob of Arcot's debts. The theme was unpromising, and he rose to speak under every possible disadvantage. It was late at night, or rather early in the morning, and the House was so exhausted by the previous debate and so weary of the whole subject that they seemed almost to a man determined not to hear him. He proceeded, however, amid much noise and interruption, and poured out his feelings for nearly five hours with an ardor and impetuosity which he had never before equaled. In this speech we have the most surprising exhibition to be found in any of Mr. Burke's productions of the compass and variety of thought which he was able to crowd into a single effort. In rhetorical address, vivid painting, lofty declamation, bitter sarcasm, and withering invective, it surpasses all his former speeches. It has also more of the peculiar faults which belonged to his extemporaneous speaking. In some passages there is a violence of attack which seems almost savage and a coarseness of imagery, where he seeks to degrade, which he never allowed himself to use in any other of his printed productions.

Warren Hastings, whom he regarded as the responsible author of nearly all the calamities of India, landed in England about three months after, on the 16th of June, 1785. Within four days, Mr. Burke gave notice that *if no one else came forward* as his accuser, he should himself move for an inquiry into his conduct as Governor General of India, with a view to his impeachment before the House of Lords. In thus challenging the ministry to take up the prosecution, he acted wisely; for it is hardly possible for any one except those in power to command the necessary evidence in such a case or to use it with effect. Until within a brief period, the leading members of the administration had been nearly or quite as hostile to Mr. Hastings as Mr. Burke himself. Mr. Dundas, when chairman of a committee on Indian affairs, had moved a series of the severest resolutions against him, recommending, among other things, his immediate recall. But times were now changed. Mr. Pitt's East India Bill had virtually placed the government of India in the hands of Mr. Dundas, as head of the Board of Control. It was now the interest of the ministry to keep things quiet. They could not decently refuse an inquiry, but they had no wish to promote it. Mr. Pitt's policy was to gain credit by assuming the character of an umpire and to defeat the impeachment, if he saw fit, during the course of the introductory proceedings in the House.

To go forward under such circumstances required a degree of courage in Mr. Burke bordering upon rashness. It seemed almost certain that he must fail. Hastings was a personal favorite of the King. He had gained the confidence of the Board of Control, who were willing to overlook his past delinquencies in view of the stability he had given to the British empire in India. He had the warm support of the East India Company, which was saved from ruin and enriched with the spoils of kingdoms by his unscrupulous devotion to its interests. He was popular with the British residents in India, many of whom had gained immense fortunes under his administration at the expense of the natives and were therefore ready to testify in his favor. He had friends of the highest rank in England, and among them Lord Thurlow, the favorite Chancellor of George III, who had pledged all their influence for his elevation to the peerage, and even higher honors which it was supposed the King was ready to bestow. Intrenched as Mr. Hastings thus was on every side, what could seem more hopeless than Mr. Burke's attempt to obtain the evidence of his crimes? Accordingly, when he and Mr. Fox called for the requisite papers in February, 1786, they were met by the ministry with impediments at every step, showing the strong reluctance of Mr. Pitt and Mr. Dundas to go on with the inquiry. A stormy debate ensued which only increased the difficulty. Mr. Burke next brought forward (June, 1786) the Rohilla war as his first charge. Mr. Hastings' conduct in relation to this war had been pointedly condemned by Mr. Dundas himself in the resolutions mentioned above. It was a simple contract for blood, under which Mr. Hastings, in consideration of £400,000 received from Sujah Dowlah, *gave him a British army with which to subjugate, or rather destroy, the neighboring nation of the Rohillas,* who had never done the slightest injury to the British. Such were the facts, as admitted by all parties. The only defense was "state necessity!" The £400,000 were wanted to maintain the British conquests in India! It was, indeed, the price of blood. Nearly all the nation was exterminated. "More than a hundred thousand people fled from their homes to pestilential jungles, preferring famine and fever and the haunts of tigers to the tyranny of him to whom an English and a Christian government had for shameful lucre sold their substance and their blood and the honor of their wives and children!" And yet Mr. Dundas, admitting that "the Rohilla war was an unjustifiable measure," talked of *"state policy"* as the grand rule by which the sovereigns of powerful nations generally governed their public conduct, dwelt on "the essential services Mr. Hastings had rendered his country in the latter part of the war," and spoke of him as "The Savior of India!" Mr. Pitt *said nothing!* His friend, Mr. Wilberforce, did indeed support Mr. Burke's motion, declaring Mr. Hastings' contract with Sujah Dowlah "indefensible, and for an end inhuman and scandalous:" but the adherents of the minister understood how they were to vote, and absolved Mr. Hastings by a majority of 119 to 67.[7]

It is surprising that Mr. Burke and his friends did not instantly drop the prosecution. Hastings felt sure of the victory; and when Mr. Fox, supported by Sir Philip Francis, came forward ten days after with the charge of extortion in the case of Cheyte Sing, Rajah of Benares, the public universally expected a second acquittal, especially as the supporters of government in the House had received a note requesting them to be present, and to vote *against* Mr. Fox's motion. But, to the astonishment of all, the charge had hardly been made when Mr. Pitt rose and declared that he should vote *in favor* of the motion for inquiring into Mr. Hastings' conduct. A few independent men on the ministerial benches were so completely scandalized by this sudden change that they refused him their vote; but the great body remained true to the principles of party discipline, and the minister carried with him precisely the same number (119) for condemning Mr. Hastings which he had used ten days before to acquit him when charged with an offense incomparably more atrocious! Such a change must, of course, have been owing to some new light which had suddenly broke in upon the minds of Mr. Pitt and Mr. Dundas in the doubtful game of politics in which they were then engaged. It is thus alluded to by Mr. Macaulay in his elaborate sketch of the life and character of Hastings, first published in the Edinburgh Review: "It was asserted," he says, "by Mr. Hastings, that, early on the morning of that very day on which the debate took place, Dundas called on Pitt, woke him, and was closeted with him many hours. The result of this conference was a determination to give up the late Governor-general to the vengeance of the Opposition. . . . The friends of Mr. Hastings, most of whom, it is to be observed, generally supported the administration, affirmed that the motive of Pitt and Dundas was jealousy. Hastings was personally a favorite with the King. He was the idol of the East India Company. If he were absolved by the Commons, seated among the Lords, admitted to the Board of Control, closely allied with the strong-minded and imperious Thurlow, was it not almost certain that he would soon draw to himself the entire management of Indian affairs? Was it not possible that he might become a formidable rival in the cabinet? If the Commons impeached Hastings, all danger was at an end. The proceeding, however it might terminate, would probably last some years. In the mean time, the accused person would be excluded from honors and public employments, and could scarcely venture even to pay his service at court. Such were the motives attributed by a great part of the public to the young minister, whose ruling passion was generally believed to be avarice of power." From this time forth there was no more difficulty in the reception of charges. On the 7th of February, 1787, Mr. Sheridan delivered his brilliant speech on the cruelties practiced upon the Begums, or Princesses of Oude, and a Committee of Impeachment was soon after formed. This committee consisted of Burke, Fox, Sheridan, Windham, and Charles Grey, afterward Earl Grey, who acted as managers; together with fifteen others, who took no active part in the prosecution. The articles of impeachment were drawn up by Mr. Burke and delivered to the House on the 25th of April. After a brief discussion, they were adopted; and on the 10th of May, 1787, Mr. Burke, attended by the members of the House of Commons, went to the bar of the House of Lords, and there in form impeached Warren Hastings of high crimes and misdemeanor.

The trial commenced in Westminster Hall on the 13th of February, 1788. After two days spent in the preliminary ceremonies, Mr. Burke opened the case in a speech which lasted four days and was designed to give the members of the court a view of the character and condition of the people of India; the origin of the power exercised by the East India Company; the situation of the natives under the government of the English; the miseries they had endured through the agency of Mr. Hastings; and the motives by which he was influenced in his multiplied acts of cruelty and oppression. This speech has, perhaps, been truly characterized as the greatest intellectual effort ever made before the Parliament of Great Britain. A writer adverse to the impeachment has remarked, that "Mr. Burke astonished even those who were most intimately acquainted with him by the vast extent of his reading, the variety of his resources, the minuteness of his information, and the lucid order in which he arranged the whole for the support of his subject and to make a deep impression on the minds of his auditory." On the third day, when he described the cruelties inflicted upon the natives by Debi Sing, one of Mr. Hastings' agents, a convulsive shudder ran throughout the whole assembly. "In this part of his speech," says the reporter, "his descriptions were more vivid, more harrowing, more horrific, than human utterance, on either fact or fancy, perhaps ever formed before." Mr. Burke himself was so much overpowered at one time that he dropped his head upon his hands and was unable for some minutes to proceed; while "the bosoms of his auditors became convulsed with passion, and those of more delicate organs or a weaker frame swooned away." Even Mr. Hastings himself, who, not having ordered these inflictions, had always claimed that he was not involved in their guilt, was utterly overwhelmed. In describing the scene afterward, he said, "For half an hour I looked up at the orator in a revery of wonder, and actually felt myself to be the most culpable man on earth." "But at length," he added (in reference to the grounds just mentioned), "I recurred to my own bosom, and there found a consciousness that consoled me under all I heard and all I suffered."

Such a speech it was impossible for any reporter adequately to record, and Mr. Burke never wrote it out for publication. He left numerous papers, however, from which and the shorthand minutes a report was framed of this and his other speeches against Hastings, chiefly in his own language, though we can not suppose that in the vehement passages mentioned above we have the exact expressions, the vivid painting, or impassioned energy with which he electrified Westminster Hall and filled that vast assembly with mingled emotions of indignation and horror. The peroration of this speech, as delivered by Mr. Burke, will be given below.

The trial lasted one hundred and forty-seven days. If conducted in an ordinary court of justice, it would have been finished in less than three months; but in the House of Lords, being taken up only three or four hours at a time, in the intervals of other business, it extended through seven years. Mr. Burke made his closing speech in behalf of the managers on the 16th of June, 1794. It was in the darkest season of the French Revolution, a few days before the fall of Robespierre, when the British empire was agitated with conflicting passions, and fears were entertained by many of secret conspiracies to overthrow the government. To these things he referred at the close of his peroration, which has a grandeur and solemnity becoming the conclusion of such a trial.

"My Lords, I have done! The part of the Commons is concluded! With a trembling hand, we consign the product of these long, *long* labors to your charge. *Take it!* TAKE IT! It is a sacred trust! Never before was a cause of such magnitude submitted to any human tribunal!

"My Lords, at this awful close, in the name of the Commons and surrounded by them, I attest the retiring, I attest the advancing generations, between which, as a link in the chain of eternal order, we stand. We call this nation, we call the world, to witness that the Commons have shrunk from no labor; that we have been guilty of no prevarications; that we have made no compromise with crime; that we have not feared any odium whatsoever in the long warfare which we have carried on with the crimes, the vices, the exorbitant wealth, the enormous and overpowering influence, of Eastern corruption.

"A business which has so long occupied the councils and

tribunals of Great Britain cannot possibly be hurried over in the course of vulgar, trite, and transitory events. Nothing but some of those great revolutions that break the traditionary chain of human memory and alter the very face of nature itself, can possibly obscure it. My Lords, we are all elevated to a degree of importance by it. The meanest of us will, by means of it, become more or less *the concern of posterity*.

"My Lords, your House yet stands; it stands, a great edifice; but, let me say, it stands in the midst of ruins—in the midst of ruins that have been made by the greatest moral earthquake that ever convulsed and shattered this globe of ours. My Lords, it has pleased Providence to place us in such a state, that we appear every moment to be on the verge of some great mutation. There is one thing, and one thing only, that defies mutation—that which existed before the world itself. I mean *Justice;* that justice which, emanating from the Divinity, has a place in the breast of every one of us, given us for our guide with regard to ourselves and with regard to others, and which will stand after this globe is burned to ashes, our advocate or our accuser before the great Judge, when he comes to call upon us for the tenor of a well-spent life.

"My Lords, the Commons will share in every fate with your Lordships. There is nothing sinister which can happen to you, in which we are not involved. And if it should so happen that your Lordships, stripped of all the decorous distinctions of human society, should, by hands at once base and cruel, be led to those scaffolds and machines of murder upon which great kings and glorious queens have shed their blood amid the prelates, the nobles, the magistrates who supported their thrones, may you in those moments feel that consolation which I am persuaded they felt in the critical moments of their dreadful agony! . . .

"My Lords, if you must fall, may you so fall! But if you stand—and stand I trust you will, together with the fortunes of this ancient monarchy; together with the ancient laws and liberties of this great and illustrious kingdom—may you stand as unimpeached in honor as in power! May you stand, not as a substitute for virtue; may you stand, and long stand, the terror of tyrants; may you stand, the refuge of afflicted nations; may you stand, a sacred temple for the perpetual residence of inviolable *Justice!*"

Mr. Hastings, it is well known, was acquitted by the House of Lords. This, however, does not imply that the atrocities so eloquently described by Mr. Burke were found to be overstated. Far from it. They are now matters of undisputed history.[8] One difficulty lay in the mode of proof. In previous cases of impeachment, the High Court of Parliament had never been bound by those strict rules of evidence which prevail in the lower courts. Proof of every kind was admitted which goes to satisfy men in the ordinary concerns of life as to the truth or falsity of a charge. But it was now decided to adhere to the strict rules of legal evidence. The decision marks an advance in English justice. If these rules are wrong, they should be altered; but they should be one and the same in the highest and the lowest courts. The managers, however, were prepared for no such decision; and the moment it was made, the acquittal of Mr. Hastings became morally certain. Hundreds whom we know to be guilty are acquitted every year in our courts of justice for want of legal proof. Much of the proof relied upon by the managers was ruled out on the principles now adopted, and what every body believed to be true, and history has recorded as fact, the court could not receive in evidence. In addition to this, the cruelty and injustice in such cases must be chiefly exercised through intermediate agents, and it is often impossible to connect those agents by legal proof with the real author of the crimes. There was still another difficulty. These crimes, in most instances, as the court were made to believe, were the only possible means of upholding the Brish government in India. They were committed for the sake of raising money in crises of extreme danger, and often of sudden rebellion, when, without money to support his troops, Mr. Hastings and his government would have been swept out of India in a single month. These considerations were powerfully urged by Mr. Erskine in his defense of Stockdale for publishing a pamphlet in favor of Hastings. "It may and must be true that Mr. Hastings has repeatedly offended against the rights and privileges of Asiatic government if he was the faithful deputy of a power which could not maintain itself for an hour without trampling upon both. He may and must have offended against the laws of God and nature if he was the faithful viceroy of an empire wrested in blood from the people to whom God and nature had given it. He may and must have preserved that unjust dominion over timorous and abject nations by a terrifying, overbearing, insulting superiority if he was the faithful administrator of your government, which, having no root in consent or affection, no foundation in similarity of interests, no support from any one principle which cements men together in society, can be upheld only by alternate stratagem and force." Such were the considerations which turned the tide of popular sentiment in favor of Mr. Hastings, and made it impossible to convict him, though morally guilty, if not of all the crimes laid to his charge, at least of numerous and most flagrant acts of cruelty and oppression. But if Mr. Burke failed in the impeachment, he succeeded in the main object which he had in view, that of laying open to the indignant gaze of the public the enormities practiced under the British government in India. Nothing more was necessary to secure their correction; and his "long, long labors" in this cause became the means, though not so directly as he intended, of great and lasting benefits to a hundred and fifty millions of people.

In addition to these labors, and during their greatest urgency, Mr. Burke was drawn into a new conflict with Mr. Pitt of the most exciting nature. The King became deranged in October, 1788, and the "Regency Question" instantly arose to agitate and divide the empire. The Opposition took the ground that the Prince of Wales had the inherent right, as heir of the crown, to act as regent during his father's loss of reason. Mr. Pitt denied this right, affirming that it lay with Parliament alone to provide for such an exigency—that they might commit the custody of the King's person and the administration of the government to other hands if they saw fit, and might impose whatever restrictions they thought proper on the authority of the Prince of Wales if they declared him regent. The subject more naturally belongs to the measures of Mr. Fox and will be dwelt upon hereafter in the sketch of his life. It is necessary in this place only to say that Mr. Burke took up the question, which was debated nearly two months, with more than his ordinary zeal and strength of feeling. He thought the Prince of Wales was treated with harshness and injustice. He maintained his cause with consummate ability; and it is now known that he drew up the celebrated letter on the subject, addressed by the Prince to Mr. Pitt, which has been so much admired not only as a fine specimen of English composition but as showing "the true, transmigrating power of genius, which enabled him thus to pass his spirit into the station of royalty, and to assume the calm dignity, both of style and feeling, that became it."

It has been already remarked that the first period of Mr. Burke's political life was the happiest. He was on the ascendent scale of influence and usefulness. His faculties were fresh; his hopes were high; and whenever he rose to speak, he was cheered by the consciousness of being listened to with interest and respect. But after the defeat of Mr. Fox's East India Bill, all was changed. In common with Mr. Fox, he was loaded with unpopularity; and, being retired in his habits, he never attempted, like his great leader, to cast off the odium thus incurred by a familiar intercourse with his political opponents. On the contrary, he was often drawn into personal altercations with Mr. Pitt, in which he lost his temper and thus became doubly exposed to that cutting sarcasm or withering contempt with which the young minister knew how, better than any man of his age, to overwhelm an antagonist. A course of systematic insult was likewise adopted by certain members of the House for the purpose of putting him down. "Muzzling the lion" was the term applied to such treatment of the greatest genius of the age. When he arose to speak, he was usually assailed with coughing, ironical cheers, affected laughter, and other tokens of dislike. Such things, of course, he could not ordinarily notice; though he did in one instance stop to remark that "he could teach a pack of hounds to yelp with more melody and equal comprehension." George Selwyn used to tell a story with much effect of a country member who exclaimed, as Mr. Burke rose to speak with a paper in his hand, "I hope the gentleman does not mean to read that large bundle of papers and bore us with a speech into the bargain!" Mr. Burke was so much overcome, or rather suffocated with rage, that he was incapable of utterance, and rushed at once out of the House. "Never before," said Selwyn, "did I see the fable realized of a lion put to flight by the braying of an ass." Such treatment soured his mind, and as he advanced in years, he was sometimes betrayed into violent fits of passion before the House which were a source of grief to his friends and of increased insult from his enemies. Under all these discouragements, however, "Nitor in adversum" was still his motto. His public labors were such as no other man of the age could have performed. Besides his attendance on the House, he had nearly all the burden of carrying forward Mr. Hastings' impeachment, involving charges more complicated in their nature and embracing a wider range of proof than had ever been submitted to an English tribunal. Seven years were spent in this drudgery, and it shows the unconquerable spirit of Mr. Burke that he never once faltered, but brought his impeachment to a close with a dignity becoming his own character and the greatness of the interests involved.

In thus reaching forward to the end of Mr. Hastings' trial, we have already entered on the *third* period of Mr. Burke's political life. As America was the leading object of interest in the first and India in the second of these great divisions of his public labors, France and its portentous revolution occupied the third stage of his eventful career, and called forth, at the close of life, the most brilliant efforts of his genius. It is a striking fact that Mr. Burke was the only man in England who regarded the French Revolution of 1789, from its *very commencement,* with jealousy and alarm. Most of the nation hailed it with delight, and Mr. Pitt, no less than Mr. Fox, was carried away for a time in the general current of sympathy and admiration. But Mr. Burke, in writing to a friend only two months after the assembling of the States-General, expressed his fears of the result in the following terms: "Though I thought I saw something like this in progress for several years, it has something in it paradoxical and mysterious. The spirit it is impossible not to admire; but the Parisian ferocity has broken out in a shocking manner. It is true this *may* be no more than a sudden explosion; if so, no indication can be taken from it. But if it should be *character* rather than accident, the *people are not fit for liberty*." A few months confirmed his worst apprehensions. The levity, rashness, and presumption which had so long characterized the French nation gained a complete ascendency. The better class of men who shared in the early movement were at first set aside, and soon after driven away or murdered. The States-General, breaking up the original balance of the Constitution, resolved the three chambers into one, under the name of the National Assembly; and the Third Estate, or Commons, became not only the sole legislative, but the sole *governing* power of the country. The galleries of that assembly were filled with a Parisian mob which dictated to the representatives of the people the measures to be adopted. The sway of a ferocious populace became unrestrained. The King and Queen were dragged in triumph from Versailles to Paris, where they were virtually held as prisoners from the first, in fearful expectation of the fate which ultimately befell them. All this took place within little more than three months![9]

It may be said, however, that the Revolution was at last productive of important benefits to France, and some persons seem for this reason to have a vague impression that Mr. Burke did wrong in opposing it. There is no doubt that this utter disruption of society was the means of removing great and manifold abuses, just as the fire of London burned out the corruptions of centuries in the heart of that city. But no one hesitates, on this account, to condemn the spirit of the incendiary. It should also be remembered that these benefits were not the natural or direct results of the rash spirit of innovation opposed by Mr. Burke. On the contrary, they were never experienced until the nation had fled for protection against that spirit to one of the sternest forms of despotism. Nor can any one prove that the benefits in question could be purchased only at this terrible expense. Lafayette, at least, always maintained the contrary, and the writer has reason to know that, in recommending Mignet's History of the Revolution to a friend as worthy of confidence, he made a distinct exception on this point, censuring in the strongest terms a kind of fatalism which runs through the pages of that historian, who seems to have regarded the whole series of crimes and miseries which marked that frightful convulsion as the only possible means of doing away the evils of the old *régime*. But, even if this were so, who, at that early period, was to discover such a fact? And who is authorized, at the present day, to speak slightingly of Mr. Burke as rash and wanting in sagacity because, while his predictions were so many of them fulfilled to the very letter, an overruling Providence brought good out of evil in a way which no human forecast could anticipate? It should be remembered, too, that Mr. Burke never looked on the Revolution as an isolated fact, a mere struggle for power or for a new form of government involving the interests of the French people alone. Considered in this light, he would have left it to take its course; he would never probably have written a syllable on the subject. But an event of this kind could not fail to affect the whole system of European politics, as a fire, breaking out in the heart of a forest, endangers the habitations of all who dwell on its borders. Whatever he said and wrote respecting France was, therefore, primarily intended for England. "Urit proximus Ucalegon," was his own account of his reasons for coming forward. "Whenever our neighbor's house is on fire, it cannot be amiss for the engines to play a little on our own. Better be despised for too anxious apprehensions than ruined by too confident a security." There were many in Great Britain who not only justified the early excesses of the Revolution and exulted when they saw the King and Queen of France led to prison by a mob, but significantly pointed to a repetition of similar scenes upon English ground. Dr. Price, in a sermon before the Constitutional Society, said, in respect to the King of France, "led in triumph and surrendering himself to his subjects," "I am thankful that I have lived to see this period. I could almost say, 'Lord, now lettest thou thy servant depart in peace, for mine eyes have seen thy salvation.' " When clergymen went so far, men of the world very naturally went farther. Societies were soon formed in London and the other large towns of the kingdom, "with the avowed purpose of obtaining political reformation by other means than those which the Constitution pointed out as legitimate."[10] Some of them maintained a correspondence with the Jacobin clubs of Paris; and, at a somewhat later period, five thousand persons belonging to the united societies of London, Manchester, and other places, held the following language, in a public address to the French National Assembly: "We are of opinion that it is the duty of every true Briton to *assist,* to the utmost of our power, the defenders of the rights of man, and to swear inviolable friendship to a nation which proceeds on the plan you have adopted. Frenchmen, you are already free, and Britons are *preparing to become so.*"[11] It was under these circumstances, and while such a spirit was beginning to prevail in the country, that Mr. Burke came forward to guard the people of England against the infection of principles which tended to such results. Whatever may have been his errors at a later period, who will question whether he was right in warning his countrymen against every thing that could engender a spirit of insurrection? Without deciding whether the liberties of the people can ever be established on the Continent of Europe except by open rebellion, all will agree that nothing could be more disastrous to the cause of free principles than any attempts at reform in England by violence and bloodshed. The Revolution of 1688 has opened a new era on this subject. The progress of the English in throwing off the abuses which still belong to their political system will take place thereafter in a series of *peaceful* revolutions, like that of Parliamentary Reform in 1832. The right of petition among such a people has more force than the bayonet. When they are once united in a good cause, neither the crown nor the peerage can stand before them.

The first reference to the French Revolution on the floor of the House of Commons was made by Mr. Fox in a debate on the army estimates, February 5th, 1790. He spoke of it in terms of eulogy and of high expectation, applauding especially the *defection of the French soldiery* from their officers and government. "It is now known throughout all Europe," he said, "that a man, by becoming a soldier, does not cease to be a citizen." These last remarks were certainly unfortunate. Unqualified as they were, they might naturally be understood to recommend a similar course to British soldiers in the event of civil commotions. It was still more unfortunate that, when Colonel Phipps, who followed, reminded him of this, stating the entire difference between the situation of things in England and France, and pointing, as a better example, to the conduct of the English troops during the London riots of 1780, "who patiently submitted to insult, and, in defiance of provocation, maintained the laws of the realm, acting under the authority of the civil power," Mr. Fox did not instantly avail himself of the opportunity to explain his remarks, and guard them against such an application. On the contrary, *he remained silent!* In justice to Mr. Burke, this fact ought to be kept in view as we approach the period of his separation from Mr. Fox. The leader of the Whig party, if he expected the continued support of his adherents, was bound to free them from all imputations on a subject like this. Four days after, when the question came up again, Mr. Burke felt bound to express his feelings at large, in view of Mr. Fox's remarks. In the course of his speech, he said,

> Since the House was prorogued in the summer, much work has been done in France. The French have shown themselves the greatest architects of ruin that have hitherto existed in the world. In that very short space of time they have completely pulled down to the ground their monarchy, their Church, their nobility, their law, their revenue, their army, their navy, their commerce, their arts, and their manufactures. They have done their business for us as rivals in a way which twenty Ramillies and Blenheims could never have done.
>
> In the last age we were in danger of being entangled by the example of France in a net of relentless despotism. That no longer exists. Our present danger arises from the example of a people whose character knows no medium. It is, with regard to government, a danger from anarchy—a danger of being led, through admiration of successful fraud and violence, to imitation of the excesses of an irrational, unprincipal, proscribing, confiscating, plundering, ferocious, bloody, and tyrannical democracy. On the side of religion, the dan-

ger of their example is no longer in intolerance, but atheism —a foul, unnatural vice, foe to all the dignity and consolation of mankind, which seems in France, for a long time, to have been embodied into a faction, accredited and almost avowed. These are our present dangers from France.

But the very worst part of the example set is in the late assumption of citizenship by the army, and the whole of the arrangement of their military. I am sorry that my right honorable friend has dropped even a word expressive of exultation on that circumstance. I attribute this opinion of Mr. Fox entirely to his own zeal for the best of all causes—liberty. It is with pain inexpressible I am obliged to have even a shadow of a difference with my friend, whose authority would be always great with me and with all thinking people. My confidence in Mr. Fox is such and so ample as to be almost implicit. I am not ashamed to avow that degree of docility, for, when the choice is well made, it strengthens instead of oppressing our intellect. He who calls in the aid of an equal understanding doubles his own. He who profits of a superior understanding raises his power to a level with the height of the superior understanding he unites with. I have found the benefit of such a junction, and would not lightly depart from it. I wish almost on all occasions my sentiments were understood to be conveyed in Mr. Fox's words, and wish, among the greatest benefits I can wish the country, an eminent share of power to that right honorable gentleman, because I know that to his great and masterly understanding he has joined the greatest possible degree of that natural moderation which is the best corrective of power. He is of the most artless, candid, open, and benevolent disposition; disinterested in the extreme; of a temper mild and placable even to a fault, without one drop of gall in his whole constitution. The House must perceive, from my coming forward to mark an expression or two of my best friend, how anxious I am to keep the distemper of France from the least countenance in England, where some wicked persons have shown a strong disposition to recommend an imitation of the French spirit of reform.

I am so strongly opposed to any the least tendency toward the means of introducing a democracy like theirs, as well as to the end itself, that, much as it would afflict me if such a thing could be attempted, and that any friend of mine should concur in such measures, *I would abandon my best friends and join with my worst enemies to oppose either the means or the end.*[12]

Mr. Fox replied in kind and respectful language, but he did not explain or modify his expressions respecting the soldiery (referred to by Mr. Burke) in those full and explicit terms which the occasion seemed to require. He certainly looked for no reforms in England, except through the regular channels provided by the Constitution. He ought, therefore, to have accepted the distinction suggested by Colonel Phipps, and declared at once that whatever might be proper in France, the English soldiery ought not to turn upon their officers or resist the civil magistrate. Such a declaration would have been useful in the excited state of the public mind at that period and it seems to have been absolutely demanded by the shape which the question had assumed. Instead of this, he simply said, "He never would lend himself to support any cabal or scheme formed in order to introduce any *dangerous* innovation into our excellent Constitution"—language which was at least rather indefinite—and declared as to the soldiery that "when he described himself as exulting over the success of some of the late attempts in France, he certainly meant to pay a just tribute of applause to those who, feelingly alive to a sense of the oppressions under which their countrymen had groaned, disobeyed the despotic commands of their leaders and gallantly espoused the cause of their fellow-citizens in a struggle for the acquisition of that liberty the sweets of which we all enjoyed." He said also that while he lamented the scenes of bloodshed and curelty among the French, he thought these excesses should be "spoken of with some degree of compassion," and that he believed "their present state, unsettled as it was, to be preferable to their former condition." Such views were so entirely different from those of Mr. Burke that it was already apparent they could not act much longer in concert.

Mr. Sheridan now came forward to widen the breach. His remarks are given very differently by different reporters. One of them represents him as charging Mr. Burke with "deserting from the camp; with assaulting the principles of freedom itself; with defending despotism; with loving to obtrude himself as the libeler of liberty and the enemy of men laboring for the noblest objects of mankind." His language, as afterward given in the Parliamentary History, is less harsh; but, whatever may have been his exact expressions, they were such as induced Mr. Burke to rise at once and declare, in calm but indignant terms, that "such language ought to have been spared, were it only as a sacrifice to the ghost of *departed friendship*. The language itself was not new to him; it was but a repetition of what was to be perpetually heard at the reforming clubs and societies with which the honorable gentleman had lately become entangled, and for whose plaudits he had chosen to sacrifice his friends, though he might in time find that the value of such praise was not worth the price at which it was purchased. Henceforward *they were separated in politics forever.*"[13]

This debate has been given at greater length, because it was the immediate occasion of Mr. Burke's writing his work on the French Revolution, and more remotely of his separation from Mr. Fox and the Whig party. His breach with Mr. Sheridan put him on the defensive, and he at once determined to carry the question before the public. Accordingly, in the month of November, 1790, he published his "Reflections on the Revolution in France," in an octavo volume of four hundred pages. No political treatise in the English tongue has ever awakened so lively an interest or met with so widespread and rapid a circulation. Thirty thousand copies were sold in Great Britain alone, at a time when the reading public embraced hardly a third of its present number. Some of the principles of this work, whether true or false in regard to European society, can, of course, have no application to America, such as the necessity of an established Church and the benefits of a titled aristocracy, which last is beautifully described as "the Corinthian capital" of the state. It must also be admitted that in exposing the crimes of the revolutionists, Mr. Burke was betrayed into an error which his warmest admirers should be the first to acknowledge, since it arose from those generous sensibilities which are peculiarly liable to be misled. *All his sympathies were on one side.*

The horror he felt at the atrocities of the Revolution made him forget the wrongs by which it was occasioned. It led him to think too favorably of the immediate sufferers, to overlook and even palliate their vices or crimes. He felt only for princes and nobles, and forgot the body of the people, who had for ages been held down by Feudalism in ignorance, wretchedness, and degradation. The same feeling led him to defend institutions which, under other circumstances, he would have regarded only with abhorrence. This accounts for his arguing so strenuously in favor of monastic establishments which the whole history of Europe has shown to be cancers on the body politic. It accounts, also, for his maintaining that the old *régime* was "a despotism rather in appearance than in reality," an assertion which will awaken the reader's astonishment just in proportion as he is acquainted with the history of France and remembers the *lettres de cachet,* the *corvée,* the *gabelle,* and the thousand other instruments of tyranny which had held the nation for centuries under the most grinding oppression. These one-sided views were the result of a peculiarity of mind in Mr. Burke, which we have seen strikingly exemplified at a later period in Sir Walter Scott, that of looking with an excess of veneration upon every thing old. His prolific fancy covered all the early forms of society with romantic and venerable associations, so that abuses which would elsewhere have called forth his keenest reprobation seemed to him in old governments, if not positive benefits, at least evils to be touched with a trembling hand, like the weaknesses of an aged parent.

While we can not, for these reasons, give our sympathy or assent to every part of this volume, facts have shown that Mr. Burke was in the right far more than Mr. Fox as to the main point at issue, the character and prospects of the Revolution in France. Mr. Fox lived to see this, and when Lord Lauderdale once remarked in his presence that Burke was a splendid madman, Mr. Fox replied, "It is difficult to say whether he is mad or inspired, but whether the one or the other, every one must agree that he is a *prophet.*" Lord Brougham observed at a much later period, "All his predictions, except one momentary expression [relative to the martial spirit of the French], have been more than fulfilled." And down to the present day (for the Revolution is still in progress), what has been the result of the experiments which the French have been making in government for the last sixty years? They took refuge from their republic in a military despotism; they received back one branch of the Bourbons and exchanged it for another; they again tried a republic for a little more than three years; and they have now submitted to the usurpation of another Bonaparte, as weak in intellect and despicable in character as the former one was powerful and illustrious. In all this they have shown—and it was this, in reality, that Mr. Burke set out to inculcate—that a people who cast off the fear of God and are governed by impulse, not by fixed principle; who have extravagant hopes of regenerating society by a mere change of its outward forms; and have learned from a scoffing philosophy to despise those great original instincts of our nature and those finer sensibilities of the heart which are the ultimate security of social order, cannot, in the nature of things, be "fit for freedom." This was the real scope of Mr. Burke's "Reflections on the Revolution in France." He erred, indeed, in connecting these truths with church establishments and monarchical institutions, but the truths themselves were of imperishable value, not only for the age in which he wrote, but for all coming ages in that long struggle on which the world has entered for the establishment of free institutions.

In a literary view, there can be but one opinion of this work. Though desultory in its character and sometimes careless or prolix in style, it contains more richness of thought, splendor of imagination, and beauty of diction than any volume of the same size in our language. Robert Hall has truly said, "Mr. Burke's imperial fancy has laid all nature under tribute, and has collected riches from every scene of the creation and every walk of art. His eulogium on the Queen of France is a masterpiece of pathetic composition, so select in its images, so fraught with tenderness, and so rich with colors 'dipt in heaven,' that he who can read it without rapture may have merit as a reasoner, but must resign all pretensions to taste and sensibility." At the present day, however, when the topics discussed are no longer of any practical importance, it is a book, like Milton's Paradise Lost, to be *once* resolutely gone through with by every literary man, and then read and re-read *for life* in select passages, which will awaken an ever-growing admiration of Mr. Burke for his compass of thought, his keen sagacity, his profound wisdom, his generous sentiments, his truth to nature and the best feelings of the heart. It is, indeed, the great peculiarity of his writings that every reflecting man learns to estimate them more highly as he advances in knowledge and in years.

We now come to the most painful event of Mr. Burke's life, except the loss of his son—his separation from Mr. Fox. After the emphatic declaration he had made before the House that "he would abandon his best friends and join with his worst enemies" to oppose French principles, we should naturally expect that the Whigs would treat him with great tenderness and forbearance if they did not mean to drive him from their ranks, and especially would not goad him on the subject and provoke a quarrel by bringing it up unnecessarily in debate. But such was the warmth and frankness of Mr. Fox that whatever was upon his mind was on his tongue; and as he was conscious of having only the kindest feelings toward Mr. Burke and was slow to take offense himself, he seems never once to have dreamed that any liberties he might use could lead, by any possibility, to a breach between him and his old friend. He therefore expressed his dissent from the principles of Mr. Burke's work in the strongest terms; and during a debate on the formation of a government for Canada he made a pointed allusion to certain well-known passages of the volume, speaking in a sarcastic manner of "those titles of honor the extinction of which some gentlemen so much deplored," and of "that *spirit of chivalry* which had fallen into disgrace in a neighboring country." In a debate a few evenings after, he went out of his way to praise the new Constitution of France, declaring, with a direct reference to Mr. Burke's strictures on that instrument, "I for one admire the new Constitution, considered altogether, *as the most glorious fabric ever raised by human integrity since the creation of man!*" Mr. Burke instantly rose with visible emotion to give vent to his feelings, but his Whig friends interposed to prevent him; the cry of "Question, question" became general throughout the House; and as it was then three o'clock in the morning, Mr. Burke at last gave way and reserved himself for another occasion.

Great efforts were now made by the Whigs to prevent Mr. Burke from coming out in reply, but he felt himself pledged to the House and country; it would look like cowardice, he said, to shrink from a contest which was thus provoked. Still he spoke kindly and with honor of Mr. Fox, and, at a private interview between them, "talked over the plan of all he intended to say, opened the different branches of his argument, and explained the limitations which he meant to impose upon himself."[14] They then walked together to the House, and Mr. Fox took occasion almost immediately to say, that "he was extremely sorry to differ from any of his friends, but that he should never be backward in declaring his opinion and that he did not wish to recede from any thing he had formerly said." This was generally considered as a direct challenge, if not a defiance of Mr. Burke, who was desirous instantly to reply; but, finding that the House preferred to adjourn the questions over the holidays, which were then commencing, he again postponed his remarks.

When the recess was over and the Canada Bill came up (May 6th, 1791), Mr. Burke opened the debate. But the moment he touched on the French Revolution, in reply to Mr. Fox, he was called to order by a friend of the latter, and Mr. Fox himself immediately interposed in a strain of the bitterest irony, remarking "that his right honorable friend could hardly be said to be out of order. It seemed this was a day of privilege, when any gentleman might stand up, select his mark, and abuse any government he pleased. Although nobody had said a word on the subject of the French Revolution (*sic!*), his friend had risen up and abused that event. Every gentleman had a right that day to abuse the government of every country, whether ancient or modern, as much as he pleased, and in as gross terms as he thought proper, with his right honorable friend." A very extraordinary scene ensued. Mr. Burke attempted to explain and to discuss the question of order, but was continually interrupted from his own side of the House. Seven times were his remarks broken in upon by renewed calls of "order." Mr. Fox repeated his irony about "the gentleman's right to discuss the Constitution of France;" and when Mr. Pitt defended his old opponent, affirming that Mr. Burke, in examining the government proposed for Canada, had a right to draw his illustrations from that of France, Mr. Fox took the floor, and, after a series of very severe remarks, said that Mr. Burke had once told the House, in a speech on American affairs that he did not know how to draw up a bill of indictment against a whole people, but "he had now learned to do it, and to crowd it with all the technicalities which disgraced our statute-book, such as 'false,' 'wicked,' 'by instigation of the devil,' &c.; that no book his friend could cite, no words he could deliver in debate, however ingenious or eloquent, could induce him to change or abandon his opinions; he differed on that subject with his right honorable friend, *toto cœlo*."[15] Mr. Burke now rose and made an extended reply, commencing in "a grave and governed tone of voice." Among other things, he remarked that "his friend had treated him in every sentence with uncommon harshness," and "had endeavored to crush him at once by declaring a censure upon his whole life and opinions." "It was certainly an indiscretion," he said, "at any period, and especially at his time of life, to provoke enemies, or to give his friends occasion to desert him; yet if his firm and steady adherence to the British Constitution placed him in this dilemma, he would risk all; and as public duty and public prudence taught him, with his last words he would exclaim, 'Fly from the French Constitution.' " [Mr. Fox here whispered that "there was no loss of friends."] Mr. Burke replied, emphatically, "Yes, there *is* a loss of friends! I know the price of my conduct. I have done my duty at the price of my freind. *Our friendship is at an end!*" Mr. Fox rose in the utmost agitation, showing that he had never once suspected the extremities to which he was driving Mr. Burke. "For some minutes he could not proceed. Tears trickled down his cheeks, and he strove in vain to give utterance to his feelings." When at last he was able to speak, he adverted, in the most tender and generous terms, to their early friendship and his obligations to Mr. Burke, and expressed his hope "that, notwithstanding what had happened, his friend would think on past times, and, however any imprudent words or intemperance of his might have offended him, it would show that it had not been, at least, intentionally his fault." Unfortunately, however, when he came to reassert and defend his own views, he did it with some very pointed allusions to the former opinions of his friend as inconsistent with his present ones. This grated so harshly on Mr. Burke's feelings, that he remarked, in entering on his reply, that "the tenderness which had been displayed in the beginning and conclusion of Mr. Fox's speech had been quite obliterated by what had occurred in the middle." The breach was irreparable. They never met again except in public; and even on his death-bed, Mr. Burke declined an interview which Mr. Fox solicited in the kindest terms, declaring that "it had cost him the most heartfelt pain to obey the stern voice of duty in rending asunder a long friendship; that his principles continued the same and *could be enforced only by the general persuasion of his sincerity*." This last consideration appears to have governed him chiefly in breaking away from his old friend. It was not the irritability of his temper, as represented by Mr. Fox's adherents, nor was it mere wounded feeling, which time would easily have assuaged; it was a sense of duty (though carried, certainly, to an extreme), which impelled him, with all the force of a religious sentiment, to bear public testimony against one whose opinions he thought dangerous to the state; like the aged apostle, who is said to have hurried from one of the city baths when he saw Cerinthus enter it, declaring that he would not remain for a moment under the same roof with a man who inculcated such fatal errors.

From this time Mr. Burke began to act with Mr. Pitt, and, though he never took office under his old opponent, his son, whom he had long been training for public life, had an important station assigned him in the government of Ireland.

There is no page in the history of our English statesmen more full of tenderness and melancholy than that which records the disappointment of Mr. Burke in regard to this son. He was an only child, on whom all his parents' hopes were centered. In the prospect of a speedy retirement from public life, it was the last fond wish of the father that his son should take his place, especially as he was one who "had within him" (and would carry into the service of his country) "a salient, living spring of generous and manly action." *"He,"* as the father thought, "would have supplied every deficiency, and symmetrized every disproportion" in his own political life. No doubt he overrated his son's abilities, for he considered them greater than his own; but there is the best evidence that Richard Burke had not only a heart full of tenderness and generosity, but a finely-balanced mind, much knowledge, great firmness and decision, united to strict integrity and high moral principle. Without his father's suspecting it, his constitution had given way before his appointment to Ireland. He was sinking into consumption, and his physicians detained him from his post; not daring, however, to apprise Mr. Burke of the danger, for they knew that like the patriarch of old, "his life was bound up in the lad's life," and were convinced that a knowledge of the truth would prove fatal to him sooner than to his son. He was, therefore, kept in ignorance until a week before the closing scene and from that time until all was over, "he slept not, he scarcely tasted food, or ceased from the most affecting lamentations." The last moments of young Burke present one of those striking cases in which nature seems to rally all her powers at the approach of dissolution, as the taper often burns brightest in the act of going out. His parents were waiting his departure in an adjoining room (for they were unable to bear the sight), when he rose from his bed, dressed himself completely, and leaning on his nurse, entered the apartment where they were sitting. "Speak to me, my dear father," said he, as he saw them bowed to the earth under the poignancy of their grief. "I am in no terror; I feel myself better and in spirits; yet my heart flutters, I know not why! Pray talk to me—of religion—of morality—of indifferent subjects." Then turning, he exclaimed, "What noise is that? Does it rain? Oh no, it is the rustling of the wind in the trees;" and broke out at once, with a clear, sweet voice, in that beautiful passage (the favorite lines of his father) from the Morning Hymn in Milton:

> His praise, ye winds, that from four quarters blow,
> Breathe soft or loud; and wave your tops, ye pines,
> With every plant in sign of worship wave!

He began again, and again repeated them with the same tenderness and fervor, bowing his head as in the act of worship, and then "sunk into the arms of his parents as in a profound and sweet sleep." It would be too painful to dwell on the scenes that followed, until the father laid all that remained to him of his child beneath the Beaconsfield church, adjoining his estate. From that hour he never looked, if he could avoid it, toward that church! Eighteen months after, when he had somewhat recovered his composure, he thus adverted to his loss in his celebrated "Letter to a Noble Lord:" "The storm has gone over me, and I lie like one of those old oaks which the late hurricane has scattered around me. I am stripped of all my honors; I am torn up by the roots and lie prostrate on the earth! There, and prostrate there, I most unfeignedly recognize the divine justice and in some degree submit to it." *"I am alone! I have none to meet my enemies in the gate!"*

The "Letter" referred to was called forth by an ungenerous attack from the Duke of Bedford, a young man who had just entered upon life. At the age of sixty-five, after devoting more than thirty years to the service of his country, Mr. Burke found himself oppressed with debts arising chiefly from his kindness and liberality to indigent men of genius who sought his aid. This fact being known, a pension of £3700 a year was granted him in October, 1795, by the express order of the King, without the slightest solicitation of Mr. Burke or his friends. The Duke of Bedford, who had become infected with French principles in politics and religion, made a very offensive allusion to this grant in a debate soon after and has immortalized his name (the only way he could ever have done it) by the castigation which he thus provoked. Of this "Letter" Mr. Mathias says, in his "Pursuits of Literature," "I perceive in it genius, ability, dignity, imagination; sights more than youthful poets when they dreamed; and sometimes the philosophy of Plato and the wit of Lucan."

Within less than a year, Mr. Burke commenced his last work, being "Thoughts on the Prospect of a Regicide Peace," which came out in three successive letters in 1796–7. His object was to animate his countrymen to a zealous prosecution of the contest with France, and he now brought out with astonishing ingenuity and eloquence those extreme principles respecting a war with the French Republic which constituted the chief error of his life. In his "Reflections" he dwelt mainly on the rashness of the French in their experiments upon government, as a warning to his own countrymen against repeating the error. He now took the ground of shutting France out from the society of nations! "This pretended republic is founded in crimes and exists by wrong and robbery; and wrong and robbery, far from giving a title to any thing, is a war with mankind." *War,* therefore, to the utmost and to the end, was the only measure to be pursued with the French Republic! "To be at peace with robbery," said he, "is to be an accomplice with it!" It seems wonderful how a man like Burke could have fallen into this confusion of ideas between the crimes of individuals against the community in which they live, and the acts of an organized government, however wrongly constituted and however cruel or oppressive in the treatment of those within its borders. If the Republic robbed England or her subjects, there was just ground of war. But if the *internal* policy of a government—its crimes (however great) against those who live under it—can justify an attack from surrounding nations, what government in Europe could escape? or what would Europe itself be but a field of blood? The principle of Mr. Burke was that on which Austria and Prussia sent the Duke of Brunswick, in 1792, to invade France. And what was the consequence? Prostrate as she was—broken down so completely in her military spirit and resources that Mr. Burke seemed justified in his famous sarcasm, "Gallos quoque in bellis floruisse audivimus," we have *heard* that the French were *once* distinguished in war—France, in a little more than a month, chased every foreign soldier from her borders; the Republican leaders learned the art of composing every dissension by turning the passions of the people into a rage for foreign conquest, until seven hundred and fifty thousand men stood ready to carry their principles throughout Europe by fire and sword; and, what was worse than all, the sympathy of the friends of freedom in every country on the Continent was turned against their own governments and given for a time with the warmest zeal and confidence to this republic of blood. Still, Mr. Burke adhered to his principle. His only inference from the disasters of the allies was that they had used means which were shamefully inadequate to the occasion, that all they had done or attempted was only like "pelting a volcano with pebble stones," and that the whole of Europe ought to combine in one grand confederacy to "let loose the ministers of vengeance in famine, fever, plagues, and death upon a guilty race, to whose frame, and to all whose habit, order, peace, religion, and virtue were alien and abhorrent."

It is remarkable that this was the only subject on which Mr. Burke was ever betrayed into extreme opinions. Though many have thought otherwise from looking exclusively at this period of his life, his whole history shows that he was pre-eminently a man of cautious and moderate views. Lord Brougham has truly said, "It would be difficult to find any statesman of any age whose opinions were more habitually marked by moderation, by a constant regard to the dictates of an enlarged reason, by a fixed determination to be practical at the time he was giving scope to the most extensive general views, by a cautious and prudent abstinence from all extremes. He brought this spirit of moderation into public affairs with him, and if we except the very end of his life, when he had ceased to live much in public, it stuck by him to the last." And why did it now desert him? Because, apparently, the dangers of the French Revolution, magnified by his powerful imagination, turned his caution into terror; and all experience shows that nothing is so rash, so headlong, so cruel even, as extreme terror when it takes full possession of a vigorous and determined intellect. Even our virtues in such cases go to swell our excesses, and we thus see how a man of Mr. Burke's justice, humanity, and love of genuine freedom could become the advocate of war upon principles which would make it eternal, and be led to justify that doctrine of *intervention* which absolute governments have ever since been using to arrest the progress of liberal institutions in the world.

Before he had finished his "Regicide Peace," Mr. Burke found his health rapidly declining, and in February, 1797, he removed to Bath to try the effect of its waters. But his constitution was gone; and after remaining there two months, confined almost entirely to his bed, he made a last effort to return to Beaconsfield, that his bones might there rest with those of his son. "It will be so far, at least," said he, "on my way to the tomb, and I may as well travel it alive as dead!" During the short period that remained to him of life, he gave directions with the utmost calmness about the disposal of his papers; he bore his sufferings with placid resignation, hoping for divine mercy through the intercession of the Redeemer, which, in his own words, he "had long sought with unfeigned humiliation, and to which he looked with trembling hope." He died on the 9th of July, 1797, in the sixty-eighth year of his age, and was interred, according to his own directions, in the same grave with his son. It was the wish of his friends, and even proposed by Mr. Fox in the House of Commons, that he should be buried in Westminster Abbey, but the plan was abandoned when the provisions of his will were made known.

Pains have been taken in this memoir to bring out the most striking qualities of Mr. Burke's mind in connection with the principal events of his life and thus to avoid the necessity of an extended summation at the close. He was what the Germans would call a "many-sided man," so that any general analysis of his character must of necessity be imperfect. We can form a correct estimate of most orators from three or four of their best speeches, but fully to know Mr. Burke one must take into view all that he ever spoke, all that he ever wrote.

As an orator he derived little or no advantage from his personal qualifications. He was tall, but not robust; his gait and gesture were awkward; his countenance, though intellectual, was destitute of softness, and rarely relaxed into a smile; and as he always wore spectacles, his eye gave him no command over an audience. "His enunciation," says Wraxall, "was vehement and rapid; and his Irish accent, which was as strong as if he had never quitted the banks of the Shannon, diminished to the ear the effect of his eloquence on the mind."

The variety and extent of his powers in debate was greater than that of any other orator in ancient or modern times. No one ever poured forth such a flood of thought—so many original combinations of inventive genius; so much knowledge of man and the working of political systems; so many just remarks on the relation of government to the manners, the spirit, and even the prejudices of a people; so many wise maxims as to a change in constitutions and laws; so many beautiful effusions of lofty and generous sentiment; such exuberant stores of illustration, ornament, and apt allusion; all intermingled with the liveliest sallies of wit or the boldest flights of a sublime imagination. In actual debate, as a contemporary informs us, he passed more rapidly from one exercise of his powers to another than in his printed productions. During the same evening, sometimes in the space of a few moments, he would be pathetic and humorous, acrimonious and conciliating, now giving vent to his indignant feelings in lofty declamation, and again, almost in the same breath, convulsing his audience by the most laughable exhibitions of ridicule or burlesque. In respect to the versatility of Mr. Burke as an orator, Dr. Parr says, "Who among men of eloquence and learning was ever more profoundly versed in every branch of science? Who is there that can transfer so happily the results of laborious research to the most familiar and popular topics? Who is there that possesses so extensive yet so accurate an acquaintance with every transaction recent or remote? Who is there that can deviate from his subject for the purposes of delight with such engaging ease, and insensibly conduct his hearers or readers from the severity of reasoning to the festivity of wit? Who is there that can melt them, if the occasion requires, with such resistless power to grief or pity? Who is there that combines the charm of inimitable grace and urbanity with such magnificent and boundless expansion?"

A prominent feature in the character of Mr. Burke, which prepared him for this wide exercise of his powers, was *intellectual independence*. He leaned on no other man's understanding, however great. In the true sense of the term, he never borrowed an idea or an image. Like food in a healthy system, every thing from without was perfectly assimilated; it entered by a new combination into the very structure of his thoughts, as when the blood, freshly formed, goes out to the extremities under the strong pulsations of the heart. On most subjects, at the present day, this is all we can expect of *originality;* the thoughts and feelings which a man expresses must be *truly his own*.

In the structure of his mind he had a strong resemblance to

Bacon, nor was he greatly his inferior in the leading attributes of his intellect. In imagination he went far beyond him. He united more perfectly than any other man the discordant qualities of the philosopher and the poet, and this union was equally the source of some of his greatest excellencies and faults as an orator.

The first thing that strikes us in a survey of his understanding is its remarkable *comprehensiveness*. He had an amplitude of mind, a power and compass of intellectual vision, beyond that of most men that ever lived. He looked on a subject like a man standing upon an eminence, taking a large and rounded view of it on every side, contemplating each of its parts under a vast variety of relations, and those relations often extremely complex or remote. To this wide grasp of original thought he added every variety of information gathered from abroad. There was no subject on which he had not read, no system relating to the interests of man as a social being which he had not thoroughly explored. All these treasures of acquired knowledge he brought home to amplify and adorn the products of his own genius, as the ancient Romans collected every thing that was beautiful in the spoils of conquered nations, to give new splendor to the seat of empire.

To this largeness of view he added a surprising *subtlety of intellect*. So quick and delicate were his perceptions that he saw his way clearly through the most complicated relations, following out the finest thread of thought without once letting go his hold or becoming lost or perplexed in the intricacies of the subject. This subtlety, however, did not usually take the form of mere logical acuteness in the detection of fallacies. He was not remarkable for his dexterity as a disputant. He loved rather to build up than to pull down; he dwelt not so much on the differences of things as on some hidden agreement between them when apparently most dissimilar. The association of *resemblance* was one of the most active principles of his nature. While it filled his mind with all the imagery of the poet, it gave an impulse and direction to his researches as a philosopher. It led him, as his favorite employment, to trace out analogies, correspondencies, or contrasts (which last, as Brown remarks, are the necessary result of a quick sense of resemblance); thus filling up his originally comprehensive mind with a beautiful series of associated thoughts, showing often the identity of things which appeared the most unlike, and binding together in one system what might seem the most unconnected or contradictory phenomena. To this he added another principle of association, still more characteristic of the philosopher, that of *cause and effect*. "Why?" "Whence?" "By what means?" "For what end?" "With what results?" these questions from childhood were continually pressing upon his mind. To answer them in respect to *man* in all his multiplied relations as the creature of society, to trace out the working of political institutions, to establish the principles of wise legislation, to lay open the sources of national security and advancement, was the great object of his life, and he here found the widest scope for that extraordinary subtlety of intellect of which we are now speaking. In these two principles of association, we see the origin of Mr. Burke's inexhaustible richness of thought. We see, also, how it was that in his mode of viewing a subject there was never any thing ordinary or commonplace. If the topic was a trite one, the manner of presenting it was peculiarly his own. As in the kaleidoscope, the same object takes a thousand new shapes and colors under a change of light, so in his mind the most hackneyed theme was transformed and illuminated by the radiance of his genius, or placed in new relations which gave it all the freshness of original thought.

This amplitude and subtlety of intellect, in connection with his peculiar habits of association, prepared the way for another characteristic of Mr. Burke, his remarkable *power of generalization*. Without this he might have been one of the greatest of poets, but not a philosopher or a scientific statesman. "To generalize," says Sir James Mackintosh, "is to philosophize; and comprehension of mind, joined to the habit of careful and patient observation, forms the true genius of philosophy." But it was not in his case a mere "habit," it was a kind of instinct of his nature which led him to gather all the results of his thinking, as by an elective affinity, around their appropriate centers, and, knowing that truths are valuable just in proportion as they have a wider reach, to rise from particulars to generals, and so to shape his statements as to give them the weight and authority of universal propositions. His philosophy, however, was not that of abstract truth; it was confined to things in the *concrete,* and chiefly to man, society, and government. He was no metaphysician; he had, in fact, a dislike, amounting to weakness, of all abstract reasonings in politics, affirming, on one occasion, as to certain statements touching the rights of man, that just "in proportion as thy were metaphysically true, they were morally and politically false!" He was, as he himself said, "a philosopher in *action;"* his generalizations embraced the great facts of human society and political institutions as affected by all the interests and passions, the prejudices and frailties of a being like man. The impression he made was owing, in a great degree, to the remoteness of the ideas which he brought together, the startling novelty and yet justness of his combinations, the heightening power of contrast, and the striking manner in which he connected truths of imperishable value with the individual case before him. It is here that we find the true character and office of Mr. Burke. He was the *man of principles;* one of the greatest teachers of "civil prudence" that the world has ever seen. A collection of maxims might be made from his writings infinitely superior to those of Rochefoucauld: equally true to nature and adapted, at the same time, not to produce selfishness and distrust, but to call into action all that is generous, and noble, and elevated in the heart of man. His high moral sentiment and strong sense of religion added greatly to the force of these maxims; and, as a result of these fine generalizations Mr. Burke has this peculiarity, which distinguishes him from every other writer, that he is almost equally instructive whether he is right or wrong as to the particular point in debate. He may fail to make out his case; opposing considerations may induce us to decide against him; and yet every argument he uses is full of instruction: it contains great truths, which, if they do not turn the scale here, may do it elsewhere; so that he whose mind is filled with the maxims of Burke has within him not only one of the finest incentives of genius, but a fountain of the richest thought which may flow forth through a thousand channels in all the efforts of his own intellect to whatever subject those efforts may be directed.

With these qualities and habits of mind, the oratory of Mr. Burke was of necessity *didactic*. His speeches were *lectures*, and, though often impassioned, enlivened at one time with wit, and rising at another into sublimity or pathos, they usually became wearisome to the House from their minuteness and subtlety, as

"He went on refining,
And thought of convincing while they thought of dining."

We see, then, in the philosophical habits of his mind (admirable as the results were in most respects), why he spoke so often to empty benches, while Fox, by seizing on the strong points of the case, by throwing away intermediate thoughts, and striking at the heart of the subject, never failed to carry the House with him in breathless attention.

His *method* was admirable, in respect at least to his published speeches. No man ever bestowed more care on the arrangement of his thoughts. The exceptions to this remark are apparent, not real. There is now and then a slight irregularity in his mode of transition which seems purposely thrown in to avoid an air of sameness, and the subordinate heads sometimes spread out so widely that their connection with the main topic is not always obvious. But there is reigning throughout the whole a massive unity of design like that of a great cathedral, whatever may be the intricacy of its details.

In his *reasonings* (for he was one of the greatest masters of reason in our language, though some have strangely thought him deficient in this respect) Mr. Burke did not usually adopt the outward forms of logic. He has left us, indeed, some beautiful specimens of dialectical ability, but his arguments, in most instances, consisted of the amplest enumeration and the clearest display of all the facts and principles, the analogies, relations, or tendencies which were applicable to the case, and were adapted to settle it on the immutable basis of the nature and constitution of things. Here again he appeared, of necessity, more as a teacher than a logician, and hence many were led to underrate his argumentative powers. The exuberance of his fancy was likewise prejudicial to him in this respect. Men are apt to doubt the solidity of a structure which is covered all over with flowers. As to this peculiarity of his eloquence, Mr. Fox truly said, "It injures his reputation; it casts a veil over his wisdom. Reduce his language, withdraw his images, and you will find that he is more wise than eloquent; you will have your full weight of metal though you melt down the chasing."

In respect to Mr. Burke's *imagery,* however, it may be proper to remark that a large part of it is not liable to any censure of this kind; many of his figures are so finely wrought into the texture of his style that we hardly think of them as figures at all. His great fault in other cases is that of giving them too bold a relief, or dwelling on them too long, so that the primary idea is lost sight of in the image. Sometimes the prurience of his fancy makes him low and even filthy. He is like a man depicting the scenes of nature, who is not content to give us those features of the landscape that delight the eye, but fills out his canvas with objects which are coarse, disgusting, or noisome. Hence no writer in any language has such extremes of imagery as Mr. Burke, from his picture of the Queen of France, "glittering like the morning star, full of life, and splendor, and joy," or of friendship, as "the soft green of the soul, on which the eye loves to repose," to Lord Chatham's administration "pigging together in the same truckle-bed," and Mr. Dundas with his East India bills "exposed like the imperial sow of augury, lying in the mud with the prodigies of her fertility about her, as evidences of her delicate amours."

His *language,* though copious, was not verbose. Every word had its peculiar force and application. His chief fault was that of overloading his sentences with secondary thoughts which weakened the blow by dividing it. His style is, at times, more careless and inaccurate than might be expected in so great a writer. But his mind was on higher things. His idea of a truly fine sentence, as once stated to a friend, is worthy of being remembered. It consists, said he, in a union of thought, feeling, and imagery—of a striking truth and a corresponding sentiment, rendered doubly striking by the force and beauty of figurative language. There are more sentences of this kind in the pages of Mr. Burke than of any other writer.

In conclusion, we may say, without paradox, since oratory is only one branch of the quality we are now considering, that while Mr. Burke was inferior as an orator to Lord Chatham and Mr. Fox, he has been surpassed by no one in the richness and splendor of his eloquence; and that he has left us something greater and better than all eloquence in his countless lessons of moral and civil wisdom.[16]

HENRY GRATTAN

HENRY GRATTAN was born at Dublin on the third day of July, 1746. His father was an eminent barrister, and acted for many years as recorder of that city, which he also represented for a time in the Parliament of Ireland.

In the year 1763, young Grattan entered Trinity College, Dublin, where he was distinguished for the brilliancy of his imagination and the impetuosity of his feelings. Having graduated in 1767, with an honorable reputation, he repaired to London and became a member of the Middle Temple. His mind, however, was at first too exclusively occupied with literary pursuits to allow of his devoting much time to the study of the law. Politics next engaged his attention. The eloquence of Lord Chatham drew him as an eager listener to the debates in Parliament and acted with such fascination upon his mind as seemed completely to form his destiny. Every thing was forgotten in the one great object of cultivating his powers as a public speaker. To emulate and express, though in the peculiar forms of his own genius, the lofty conceptions of the great English orator was from this time the object of his continual study and most fervent aspirations.

In 1772 he returned to Ireland, where he was admitted to the bar, and in 1775 he became a member of the Irish Parliament under the auspices of Lord Charlemont. He, of course, joined the ranks of Opposition and united at once with Mr. Flood and the leading patriots of the day in their endeavors to extort from the English minister the grant of free trade for Ireland. The peculiar circumstances of the country favored their design. The corps of Irish Volunteers had sprung into existence upon the alarm of invasion from France and was marshaled throughout the country to the number of nearly fifty thousand for the defense of the island. With a semblance of some connection with the government, it was really an army unauthorized by the laws and commanded by officers of their own choosing. Such a force could obviously be turned, at any moment, against the English; and, seizing on the advantage thus gained, Mr. Grattan, in 1779, made a motion, which was afterward changed into a direct resolution, that "nothing but a free trade could save the country from ruin." It was passed with enthusiasm by the great body of the House, and the nation, with arms in their hands, echoed the resolution as the watch-word of their liberties. Lord North and his government were at once terrified into submission. They had tampered with the subject, exciting hopes and expectations only to disappoint them, until a rebellion in Ireland was about to be added to a rebellion in America. In the emphatic words of Mr. Burke, "a sudden light broke in upon us all. It broke in, not through well-contrived and well-disposed windows, but through flaws and breaches—through the yawning chasms of our ruin." Every thing they asked was freely granted, and Ireland, as the English minister imagined, was propitiated.

But Mr. Grattan had already fixed his eye on a higher object—the complete independence of the Irish Parliament. By an act of the sixth year of George the First, it was declared that Ireland was a subordinate and dependent kingdom, that the Kings, Lords, and Commons of England had power to make laws to bind Ireland, that the Irish House of Lords had no jurisdiction, and that all proceedings before that court were void. This arbitrary act Mr. Grattan now determined to set aside. He availed himself of the enthusiasm which pervaded the nation and, reminding them that the concessions just made might be recalled at any moment if England continued to bind Ireland by her enactments, he urged them to a Declaration of Right, denying the claim of the British Parliament to make laws for Ireland. His friends endeavored to dissuade him from bringing the subject before the Irish Parliament, but the voice of the nation was with him, and on the 19th of April, 1780, he made his memorable motion for a Declaration of Irish Right. His speech on that occasion, which is the first in this selection, "was the most splendid piece of eloquence that had ever been heard in Ireland." As a specimen of condensed and fervent argumentation, it indicates a high order of talent; while in brilliancy of style, pungency of application, and impassioned vehemence of spirit, it has rarely, if ever, been surpassed. The conclusion, especially, is one of the most magnificent passages in our eloquence.

Mr. Grattan's motion did not then pass, but he was hailed throughout Ireland as the destined deliverer of his country. No Irishman had ever enjoyed such unbounded popularity. He animated his countrymen with the hope of ultimate success; he inspired them with his own imaginative and romantic spirit, and awakened among them a feeling of nationality such as had never before existed. He taught them to cherish Irish affections, Irish manners, Irish art, Irish literature; and endeavored, in short, to make them a distinct people from the English in every respect but one, that of being governed by the same sovereign. Nothing could be more gratifying to the enthusiastic spirit of that ardent and impulsive race, and though it was impossible that such a plan should succeed, he certainly stamped his own character, in no ordinary degree, on the mind of the nation. That peculiar kind of eloquence, especially, which prevails among his countrymen, though springing, undoubtedly, from the peculiarities of national temperament, was rendered doubly popular by the brilliant success of Mr. Grattan, who presents the most perfect exhibition of the highly-colored and impassioned style of speaking in which the Irish delight, with but few of its faults, or, rather, for the most part, with faults in the opposite direction.

With this ascendency over the minds of the people, Mr. Grattan spent nearly two years in preparing for the next decisive step. The Volunteers held their famous meeting at Dungannon in February, 1782, and passed unanimously a resolution drawn up by Mr. Grattan, that "a claim of any body of men, other than the King, Lords, and Commons of Ireland, to make laws to bind this kingdom, is unconstitutional, illegal, and a grievance." This resolution was virtually a declaration of war in case the act of Parliament complained of was not repealed. It was adopted throughout the country, not merely by shouting thousands at mass meetings, but by armed regiments of citizens and owners of the soil and by grand juries at judicial assizes. The administration of Lord North was now tottering to its fall. The avowed friends of Ireland, Lord Rockingham, Lord Shelburne, and Mr. Fox, took his place in March, 1782; and Mr. Grattan determined at once to try the sincerity of their feelings. He therefore gave notice that, on the 16th of the ensuing April, he should repeat his motion in the Irish House of Commons for a Declaration of Irish Right. It was a trying moment for the new Whig administration. To concede at such a time, when the Irish stood with arms in their hands, was to lay England at their feet. Mr. Fox, therefore, seconded by Burke, Sheridan, Sir Philip Francis, Colonel Barré, and other distinguished Irishmen, pleaded for delay. Lord Charlemont brought the message to the bedside of Mr. Grattan, who was confined by a severe illness, and received for reply, "*No time! No time!* The Irish leaders are pledged to the people; they can not postpone the question; it is *public property*." When the day arrived, Mr. Grattan, to the surprise of all who knew his debilitated state, made his appearance in the House and delivered a speech, the second one in these extracts, which won universal admiration for its boldness, sublimity, and compass of thought. Lord Charlemont remarked afterward, in speaking of this effort and of Mr. Grattan's weakness of health when he came forward, that "if ever spirit could be said to act independent of body, it was on that occasion." It was in vain for the friends of the minister to resist. The resolutions were carried almost by acclamation. Mr. Fox, when he heard the result, decided instantly to yield, declaring that he would rather see Ireland wholly separated from the crown of England than held in subjection by force. He, therefore, soon after brought in a bill for repealing the act of the sixth of George First.

As an expression of their gratitude for these services, the Parliament of Ireland voted the sum of £100,000 to purchase Mr. Grattan an estate. His feelings led him, at first, to decline the grant; but, as his patrimony was inadequate to his support in the new position he occupied, he was induced by the interposition of his friends to accept one *half* the amount.

Mr. Flood had been greatly chagrined at the ascendency gained by Mr. Grattan, and he now endeavored to depreciate his efforts by contending that the "simple repeal" of the act of the sixth of George First was of no real avail; that the English Parliament must pass a distinct act, *renouncing* all claim to make law for Ireland. Every one now sees that the pretense was a ridiculous one, but he succeeded in confusing and agitating the minds of the people on this point until he robbed Mr. Grattan, to a considerable extent, of the honor of his victory. He came out, at last, into open hostility, stigmatizing him as "a *mendicant* patriot, subsisting on the public accounts—who, bought by his country for a sum of money, had sold his country for prompt payment." Mr. Grattan instantly replied in a withering piece of invective, to be found below, depicting the character and political life of his opponent and ingeniously darkening every shade that rested on his reputation.

As most of the extracts in this selection are taken from the early speeches of Mr. Grattan, it will be unnecessary any farther to trace his history. Suffice it to say, that, although he lost his popularity at times through the influence of circumstances or the arts of his enemies, he devoted himself throughout life to the defense of his country's interests. He was vehemently opposed to the union with England, but his countrymen were so much divided that it was impossible for any one to prevent it. At a later period (1805), he became a member of the Parliament of Great Britain, where he uniformly maintained those principles of toleration and popular government which he had supported in Ireland. He was an ardent champion of Catholic Emancipation, and may be said to have died in the cause. He had undertaken, in 1820, to present the Catholic Petition, and support it in Parliament, notwithstanding the remonstrances of his medical attendants, who declared it would be at the hazard of his life. "I should be happy," said he, "to die in the discharge of my duty." Exhausted by the journey, he did die almost immediately after his arrival in London, May 14th, 1820, at the age of seventy, and was buried, with the highest honors of the nation, in Westminster Abbey. His character was irreproachable; and Sir James Mackintosh remarked, in speaking of his death in the House of

Commons, "He was as eminent in his observance of all the duties of private life as he was heroic in the discharge of his public ones." "I never knew a man," said Wilberforce, "whose patriotism and love for his country seemed so completely to extinguish all private interests and to induce him to look invariably and exclusively to the public good."

The personal appearance and delivery of Mr. Grattan are brought vividly before us in one of the lively sketches of Charles Phillips. "He was short in stature and unprepossessing in appearance. His arms were disproportionately long. His walk was a stride. With a person swinging like a pendulum and an abstracted air, he seemed always in thought, and each thought provoked an attendant gesticulation. How strange it is that a mind so replete with grace, and symmetry, and power, and splendor, should have been allotted such a dwelling for its residence! Yet so it was; and so, also, was it one of his highest attributes that his genius, by its 'excessive light,' blinded his hearers to his physical imperfections. It was the victory of mind over matter." "The chief difficulty in this great speaker's way was the first five minutes. During his exordium laughter was imminent. He bent his body almost to the ground, swung his arms over his head, up, and down, and around him, and added to the grotesqueness of his manner a hesitating tone and drawling emphasis. Still, there was an earnestness about him that at first besought, and, as he warmed, enforced, nay, commanded attention."

The speeches of Mr. Grattan afford unequivocal proof, not only of a powerful intellect, but of high and original genius. There was nothing commonplace in his thoughts, his images, or his sentiments. Every thing came fresh from his mind, with the vividness of a new creation. His most striking characteristic was condensation and rapidity of thought. "Semper instans sibi," pressing continually upon himself, he never dwelt upon an idea, however important; he rarely presented it under more than one aspect; he hardly ever stopped to fill out the intermediate steps of his argument. His forte was reasoning, but it was "logic on fire," and he seemed ever to delight in flashing his ideas on the mind with a sudden, startling abruptness. Hence, a distinguished writer has spoken of his eloquence as a "combination of *cloud, whirlwind,* and *flame*"—a striking representation of the occasional obscurity and the rapid force and brilliancy of his style. But his incessant effort to be strong made him sometimes unnatural. He seems to be continually straining after effect. He wanted that calmness and self-possession which mark the highest order of minds, and show their consciousness of great strength. When he had mastered his subject, his subject mastered him. His great efforts have too much the air of harangues. They sound more like the battle speeches of Tacitus than the orations of Demosthenes.

His style was elaborated with great care. It abounds in metaphors which are always striking and often grand. It is full of antithesis and epigrammatic turns which give it uncommon point and brilliancy but have too often an appearance of labor and affectation. His language is select. His periods are easy and fluent—made up of short clauses, with but few or brief qualifications, all uniting in the expression of some one leading thought. His rhythmus is often uncommonly fine. In the peroration of his great speech of April 19th, 1780, we have one of the best specimens in our language of that admirable adaptation of the sound to the sense which distinguished the ancient orators.

Though Mr. Grattan is not a safe model in every respect, there are certain purposes for which his speeches may be studied with great advantage. Nothing can be better suited to break up a dull monotony of style—to give raciness and point—to teach a young speaker the value of that terse and expressive language which is, to the orator especially, the finest instrument of thought.[1]

RICHARD BRINSLEY SHERIDAN

RICHARD BRINSLEY SHERIDAN was born at Dublin in September, 1751. His father, Thomas Sheridan, author of the first attempt at a Pronouncing Dictionary of our language, was a distinguished teacher of elocution and during most of his life was connected with the stage. This fact very naturally turned the attention of young Sheridan, even from his boyhood, to theatrical composition, and, being driven to strenuous exertion in consequence of an early marriage, he became a dramatic writer at the age of twenty-four. His first production was *The Rivals,* which, by the liveliness of its plot and the exquisite humor of its dialogue, placed him at once in the first rank of comic writers. His next work was the opera of *The Duenna,* which was performed seventy-five times during the season in which it was first produced, and yielded him a very large profit. In the year 1776, in conjunction with two friends, he purchased Garrick's half of the Drury Lane Theater; and becoming proprietor of the other half at the end of two years, he gave his father the appointment of manager. He now produced his *School for Scandal,* which has been regarded by many as the best comedy in our language. This was followed by *The Critic,* which was equally admirable as a farce, and here ended, in 1779, his "legitimate offerings on the shrine of the Dramatic Muse." He still, however, retained his proprietorship in Drury Lane, which would have furnished an ample support for any one but a person of his expensive and reckless habits.

Mr. Sheridan had cherished from early life a very lively interest in politics; and now that his thirst for dramatic fame was satiated, his ambition rose higher and led him to seek for new distinction in the fields of oratory. He had already made the acquaintance of Lord John Townsend, Mr. Windham, and other distinguished members of the Whig party and was desirous of forming a political connection with Mr. Fox. To promote this object, Townsend made a dinner-party early in 1780, at which he brought them together. Speaking of the subject afterward, he said, "I told Fox that all the notions he might have conceived of Sheridan's talents and genius from the 'Rivals,' &c., would fall infinitely short of the admiration of his astonishing powers which I was sure he would entertain at the first interview. Fox told me, after breaking up from dinner, that he had always thought Hare, after my uncle, Charles Townsend, the wittiest man he had ever met with, but that Sheridan surpassed them both, infinitely." Sheridan, on his side, formed the strongest attachment for Mr. Fox as a man and a political leader and was soon after placed on terms of equal intimacy with Mr. Burke. He was admitted to Brooks's Club-house, the head-quarters of the Whigs[1] and soon after became a member for Stafford at an expense of £2000.

Mr. Sheridan's maiden speech was delivered on the 20th of November, 1780. The House listened to him with marked attention, but his appearance did not entirely satisfy the expectations of his friends. Woodfall, the reporter, used to relate that Sheridan came up to him in the gallery when the speech was ended, and asked him, with much anxiety, what he thought of his first attempt. "I am sorry to say," replied Woodfall, "that I don't think this is your line—you had better have stuck to your former pursuits." Sheridan rested his head on his hand for some minutes and then exclaimed, with vehemence, "It is *in* me, and it shall *come out of me!*" He now devoted himself with the utmost assiduity, quickened by a sense of shame, to the cultivation of his powers as a speaker; and having great ingenuity, ready wit, perfect self-possession, and a boldness amounting almost to effrontery, he made himself at last a most dexterous and effective debater.

During the short administration of the Marquess of Rockingham, in 1782, Mr. Sheridan came into office as Under Secretary of State, but on the decease of Rockingham, he resigned in common with Fox, Burke, and others, when Lord Shelburne was made prime minister in preference to Mr. Fox. Mr. William Pitt now came into the ministry, at the age of twenty-three, as Chancellor of the Exchequer, and undertook, soon after, to put down Mr. Sheridan by a contemptuous allusion to his theatrical pursuits. "No man," said he "admires more than I do the abilities of that right honorable gentleman —the elegant sallies of his thought, the gay effusions of his fancy, his dramatic turns, and his epigrammatic point. If they were reserved for the *proper* stage, they would no doubt receive the plaudits of the audience; it would be the fortune of the right honorable gentleman, "sui plausu gaudere theatri."[2] Mr. Sheridan replied to this insolent language, with admirable adroitness, in the following words: "On the particular sort of personality which the right honorable gentleman has thought proper to make use of, I need not comment. The propriety, the taste, and the *gentlemanly* point of it must be obvious to this House. But let me assure the right honorable gentleman that I do now, and will at any time he chooses to repeat this sort of allusion, meet it with the most perfect good humor. Nay, I will say more. Flattered and encouraged by the right honorable gentleman's panegyric on my talents, if I ever engage again in the composition he alludes to, I may be tempted to an act of presumption and attempt an improvement on one of Ben Jonson's best characters, that of the Angry Boy, in the *Alchymist.*" The effect was irresistible. The House was convulsed with laughter; and Mr. Pitt came very near having the title of the Angry Boy fastened on him for the remainder of his life.

When the administration of Lord Shelburne gave way to the Coalition Ministry of Mr. Fox and Lord North, in 1783, Sheridan was again brought into office as Secretary of the Treasury. The defeat of Mr. Fox's East India Bill threw him out of power at the close of the same year, and from that time, for more than twenty-two years, he was a strenuous and active opponent of Mr. Pitt.

In the year 1787, Mr. Burke, who had devoted ten years to the investigation of English atrocities in India, called forth the entire strength of the Whig party for the impeachment of

Warren Hastings. To Mr. Sheridan he assigned the management of the charge relating to the Begums or princesses of Oude. It was a subject peculiarly suited to his genius; and, aided by an intimate knowledge of the facts which was supplied him by the researches of Burke, he brought forward the charge in the House of Commons, on the 7th of February, 1787. His speech on this occasion was so imperfectly reported that it may be said to be wholly lost. It was, however, according to the representation of all who heard it, an astonishing exhibition of eloquence. The whole assembly, at the conclusion, broke forth into expressions of tumultuous applause. Men of all parties vied with each other in their encomiums, and Mr. Pitt concluded his remarks by saying that "an abler speech was perhaps *never delivered.*" A motion was made to adjourn, that the House might have time to recover their calmness and "collect their reason," after the excitement they had undergone, and Mr. Stanhope, in seconding the motion, declared that he had come to the House prepossessed in favor of Mr. Hastings, but that nothing less than a miracle could now prevent him from voting for his impeachment. Twenty years after, Mr. Fox and Mr. Windham, two of the severest judges in England, spoke of this speech with undiminished admiration. The former declared it to be the best speech ever made in the House of Commons. The latter said that "the speech deserved all its fame, and was, in spite of some faults of taste, such as were seldom wanting in the literary or in the parliamentary performances of Sheridan, the greatest that had been delivered within the memory of man."[3]

When the Commons voted to impeach Mr. Hastings, Sheridan was chosen one of the managers, and had assigned to him the charge relating to the Begums of Oude. He was thus called upon to reproduce, as far as possible, his splendid oration of the preceding year, in presence of an assembly still more dignified and august and under circumstances calculated to inflame all his ambition as an orator and a man. The expectation of the public was wrought up to the highest pitch. During the four days on which he spoke, the hall was crowded to suffocation; and such was the eagerness to obtain seats, that fifty guineas were in some instances paid for a single ticket.

These circumstances, undoubtedly, operated to the injury of Mr. Sheridan. They aggravated those "faults of taste" which were spoken of by Mr. Windham. They led him into many extravangances of language and sentiment, and though all who heard it agreed in pronouncing it a speech of astonishing power, it must have been far inferior in true eloquence to his great original effort in the House of Commons. His success in these two speeches was celebrated by Byron in the following lines, which are, however, much more applicable to Burke than to Sheridan:

> When the loud cry of trampled Hindostan
> Arose to Heaven, in her appeal to man,
> His was the thunder—his the avenging rod—
> The wrath—the delegated voice of God,
> Which shook the nations through his lips, and blazed,
> Till vanquished senates trembled as they praised.

Contrary to what might have been expected, Mr. Sheridan never attempted, in after life, that lofty strain of eloquence which gained him such rapturous applause on this occasion. "Good sense and wit were the great weapons of his oratory—shrewdness in detecting the weak points of an adversary and infinite powers of raillery in exposing them." This is exactly the kind of speaking which has always been most popular in the House of Commons. It made Mr. Sheridan much more formidable to Mr. Pitt, during his long and difficult administration, than many in the Opposition ranks of far greater information and reasoning abilities. Notwithstanding his habitual indolence and the round of conviviality in which he was constantly engaged, Sheridan contrived to pick up enough knowledge of the leading topics in debate to make him a severe critic on the measures of Mr. Pitt. If authorities or research were necessary, he would frankly say to his friends who desired his aid, "You know I am an ignoramus—here I am—instruct me, and I'll do my best." And such was the quickness and penetration of his intellect that he was able, with surprising facility, to make himself master of the information thus collected for his use and to pour it out with a freshness and vivacity which were so much the greater because his mind was left free and unencumbered by the effort to obtain it. A curious instance is mentioned of his boldness on such occasions when his materials happened to fail him. In 1794, when he came to reply to the argument of Mr. Hastings' counsel on the Begum charge, his friend, Mr. Michael Angelo Taylor, undertook to read for him any papers which it might be necessary to bring forward in the course of his speech. One morning, when a certain paper was called for, Mr. Taylor asked him for the bag containing his documents. Sheridan replied, in a whisper, that he *had neither bag nor papers*—that they must contrive, by dexterity and boldness, to get on without them. The Lord Chancellor, in a few moments, called again for the minutes of evidence. Taylor pretended to send for the bag, and Sheridan proceeded with the utmost confidence, as if nothing had happened. Within a few minutes the "*papers*" were again demanded when Mr. Fox ran up to Taylor and inquired anxiously for the bag. "The man *has* no bag," says Taylor, in a whisper, to the utter discomfiture of Mr. Fox. Sheridan, in the mean time, went on—taking the facts for granted—in his boldest strain. When stopped by the court and reproved for his negligence in not bringing forward the evidence, he assumed an indignant tone, and told the Chancellor that, "as a manager of the impeachment in behalf of the Commons, he should conduct the case as he thought fit, that it was his most ardent desire to be perfectly correct in what he stated, and that, should he fall into error, the *printed minutes* of the evidence would correct him!"

With all this apparent negligence, however, the papers of Mr. Sheridan, after his death, disclosed one remarkable fact, that his *wit* was most of it studied out beforehand. His commonplace book was found to be full of humorous thoughts and sportive turns, put down usually in a crude state just as they occurred to his mind and afterward wrought into form for future use. To this collection we may trace a large part of those playful allusions, keen retorts, sly insinuations, and brilliant sallies—the jest, the frolic, and the fun—which flash out upon us in his speeches in a manner so easy, natural, and yet unexpected that no one could suspect them of being any thing but the spontaneous suggestions of the moment. His biographer has truly said that in this respect, "It was the fate of Mr. Sheridan throughout life—and in a great degree, perhaps his policy—to gain credit for excessive indolence and carelessness, while few persons with so much natural brilliancy of talents ever employed more art and circumspection in their display."

Mr. Sheridan usually took part in every important debate in Parliament, and gained much applause, in 1803, by a speech of uncommon eloquence in which he endeavored to unite all parties for the defense of the country when threatened with invasion by France. In the course of this speech, he turned the ridicule of the House upon Mr. Addington, the prime minister, in a way which was not soon forgotten. Mr. Addington was one of those "respectable" half-way men with whom it is difficult to find fault and yet whom nobody confides in or loves. He was the son of an eminent physician, and there was something in his air and manner which savored of the profession and had given him, to a limited extent, the appellation of "The Doctor." Mr. Sheridan, in the course of his speech, adverting to the personal dislike of many to Mr. Addington, quoted the lines of Martial:

> Non amo te, Sabine, nec possum dicere quare:
> Hoc tantum possum dicere, non amo te;

and added the English parody:

> I do not like you, *Doctor* Fell;
> The reason why I can not tell;
> But this, I'm sure, I know full well,
> I do not like you, *Doctor* Fell.

His waggish emphasis on the word doctor, and his subsequent repetition of it in the course of his speech, called forth peals of laughter; and thenceforth the minister was generally known by the name of the *Doctor*.[4] The Opposition papers took up the title, and twisted and tortured it into every form of attack, till Mr. Addington was borne down and driven from office by mere ridicule—a weapon which is often more fatal than argument to men of moderate abilities in high political stations.

Mr. Sheridan had always lived beyond his means and was utterly ruined in 1809 by the burning of the Drury Lane Theater, which comprised all his property. He was also betrayed by his convivial habits into gross intemperance. Wine being no longer of sufficient strength to quicken his faculties for conversation or debate, stronger liquors were substituted. A person sitting one evening in a coffee-house, near St. Stephen's Chapel, saw, to his surprise, a gentleman with papers before him, after taking tea, pour the contents of a decanter of brandy into a tumbler and drink it off without dilution. He then gathered up his papers and went out. Shortly after, the spectator, on entering the gallery of the House of Commons, heard the brandy-drinker, to his astonishment, deliver a long and brilliant speech. It was Mr. Sheridan! The natural consequences of such a life were not slow in overtaking him: he soon became bankrupt in character and health as well as in fortune. The relief which he occasionally obtained from his friends served only to protract his misery. He was harassed with writs and executions at the moment when he was sinking under disease, and a sheriff's officer, but for the intervention of his physician, would have carried him in his blanket to prison. A powerful writer in the Morning Post now called the attention of the public to his wretched condition. "Oh! delay not to draw aside the curtain within which that proud spirit hides its sufferings. Prefer ministering in the chambers of sickness to mustering at 'the splendid sorrows which adorn the hearse'—I say, *life* and *succor* against Westminster Abbey and a funeral!" Men of all ranks were roused. His chamber was crowded with sympathizing friends, but it was too late. He died on the 7th of July, 1816, at the age of sixty-four, a melancholy example of brilliant talents sacrificed to a love of display and convivial indulgence. He was buried with great pomp in the only spot of the Poet's Corner which remained unoccupied. His pall was borne by royal and noble dukes, by earls and marquesses, and his funeral procession was composed of the most distinguished nobility and gentry of the kingdom.[5]

Wraxall, in his Posthumous Memoirs, vol. i., 36–8, gives the following description of Mr. Sheridan's person and manner of speaking in his best days, before intemperance had begun its ravages on his body or mind. "His countenance and features had in them something peculiarly pleasing, indicative at once of intellect, humor, and gayety. All these characteristics played about his lips when speaking, and operated with inconceivable attraction; for they anticipated, as it were, to the eye the effect produced by his oratory on the ear; thus opening for him a sure way to the heart or the understanding. Even the tones of his voice, which were singularly mellifluous, aided the general effect of his eloquence; nor was it accompanied by Burke's unpleasant Irish accent. Pitt's enunciation was unquestionably more imposing, dignified, and sonorous; Fox displayed more argument, as well as vehemence; Burke possessed more fancy and enthusiasm; but Sheridan won his way by a sort of fascination."

"He possessed a ductility and versatility of talents which no public man in our time has equaled, and these intellectual endowments were sustained by a suavity of temper that seemed to set at defiance all attempts to ruffle or discompose it. Playing with his irritable or angry antagonist, Sheridan exposed him by sallies of wit, or attacked him with classic elegance of satire, performing this arduous task in the face of a crowded assembly, without losing for an instant either his presence of mind, his facility of expression, or his good humor. He wounded deepest, indeed, when he smiled, and convulsed his hearers with laughter while the object of his ridicule or animadversion was twisting under the lash. Pitt and Dundas, who presented the fairest marks for his attack, found, by experience, that though they might repel, they could not confound, and still less could they silence or vanquish him. In every attempt that they made, by introducing personalities, or illiberal reflections on his private life and literary or dramatic occupations, to disconcert him, he turned their weapons on themselves. Nor did he, while thus chastising his adversary, alter a muscle of his own countenance; which, as well as his gestures, seemed to participate, and display the unalterable serenity of his intellectual formation. Rarely did he elevate his voice, and never except in subservience to the dictates of his judgment, with the view to produce a corresponding effect on his audience. Yet he was always heard, generally listened to with eagerness, and could obtain a hearing at almost any hour. Burke, who wanted Sheridan's nice tact and his amenity of manner, was continually coughed down, and on those occasions he lost his temper. Even Fox often tired the House by the repetitions which he introduced into his speeches. Sheridan never abused their patience. Whenever he rose, they anticipated a rich repast of wit without acrimony, seasoned by allusions and citations the most delicate, yet obvious in their application."[6]

CHARLES JAMES FOX

CHARLES JAMES FOX was born on the 24th of January, 1749, and was the second son of Henry Fox (the first Lord Holland) and Lady Georgiana Lennox, daughter of the second Duke of Richmond. The father, as heretofore mentioned, was the great antagonist of Lord Chatham. He was a man of amiable feelings but dissolute habits, poor (as the natural consequence) during most of his life, and governed in his politics by the master principle of the Walpole school—love of power for the sake of money. In 1757, he obtained the appointment of Paymaster of the Forces. This office, as then managed, afforded almost boundless opportunities for acquiring wealth, and so skillfully did he use his advantages that within eight years he amassed a fortune of several hundred thousand pounds. A part of this money he spent in erecting a magnificent house on his estate at Kingsgate, in the Isle of Thanet. "Upon a bleak promontory," says one of his contemporaries, "projecting into the German Ocean, he constructed a splendid villa worthy of Lucullus and adorned it with a colonnade in front of the building, such as Ictinus might have raised by order of Pericles." Here Charles spent a portion of his early years, and the estate fell to him, as a part of his patrimony, after his father's death.

Lord Holland's oldest son, Stephen, being affected with a nervous disease which impaired his faculties, Charles, who gave early proofs of extraordinary talent, became the chief object of pride and hope to the family. His father resolved to train him up for public life and to make him what he himself had always endeavored to be, *a leader in fashionable dissipation* and yet an *orator* and a *statesman.* He had lived in the days of Bolingbroke, and it would almost seem as if he intended to make that gifted but profligate adventurer the model of his favorite child. He began by treating him with extreme indulgence. His first maxim was, "Let nothing be done to break his spirit," and with this view he permitted no one either to contradict or to punish the boy. On the contrary, he encouraged him in the wildest whims and caprices. When about five years old, Charles was standing one day by his father as he wound up his watch, and said, "I have a great mind to break that watch." "No, Charles, that would be foolish." "But indeed I must do it—I *must*." "Nay," replied the father, "if you have so violent an inclination, I won't balk it," giving the watch to the boy, who instantly dashed it on the floor. Amid all this indulgence, however, his studies were not neglected; he showed surprising quickness in performing his tasks, and the same ready and retentive memory for which he was remarkable in after life. His father made him, from childhood, his companion and equal, encouraging him to converse freely at table and to enter into all the questions discussed by public men who visited the family. Charles usually acquitted himself to the admiration of all and was no doubt indebted to this early habit of thinking and speaking with freedom for that frankness and intrepidity, amounting often to rashness, which distinguished him as an orator. Lord Holland, in the mean time, was steadily aiming at the object he had in view. He wrought upon his son's pride; he inflamed him with that love of superiority which is usually the most powerful excitement of genius; he continually pointed him to public life, as the great theater of his labors and triumphs.

Under such influences, his progress at a private school of distinction, where he was sent from childhood, was uncommonly rapid; the severe discipline pursued having the effect at once to repress his irregularities and to turn his passion for superiority in the right direction. Here he laid the foundation of that intimate acquaintance with the classics, for which he was distinguished beyond most men of his age. He can hardly be said to have *studied* Latin or Greek after he was sixteen years old. So thoroughly was he grounded in these languages from boyhood that he read them throughout life much as he read English, and could turn to the great authors of antiquity at any moment, not as a mental effort, but for the recreation and delight he found in their pages. This was especially true of the Greek writers, which were then less studied in England than at present. He took up Demosthenes as he did the speeches of Lord Chatham and dwelt with the same zest on the Greek tragedians as on the plays of Shakespeare. As an instance of this, Mr. Trotter, who attended him at the close of life, mentions that Mr. Fox once entered the room, just as he was beginning to read the Alcestis of Euripides. "You will soon find something you like," said he; "tell me when you come to it." Mr. Fox, who had not opened the book for many years, watched the reader's countenance till he came to the description of Alcestis, after praying for her children, as she mourned so pathetically over her lot, when he broke out with a kind of triumph at the effect produced by the exquisite tenderness of the passage. In the wildest excesses of his life, the classics were still his companions; in the midst of public business, he corresponded with Gilbert Wakefield on the nicest questions of Greek criticism; he usually led to the subject in conversation with literary men; and we see in the Memoirs of the poet Campbell what delight he expressed at their first interview, in finding how perfectly they agreed on some disputed points in Virgil. As an orator, he was much indebted to his study of the Greek writers for the simplicity of his taste, his severe abstinence from every thing like mere ornament, the terseness of his style, the point and stringency of his reasonings, and the all-pervading cast of *intellect* which distinguishes his speeches, even in his most vehement bursts of impassioned feeling.

Charles was next sent to Eton, where he joined associates who were less advanced than himself in classical literature. This made him a leader in their studies and amusements. In every thing that called for eloquence, especially, whether in public meetings or private debate, or the contentions of the play-ground, he held an acknowledged pre-eminence. On such occasions, he always manifested those kind and generous feelings for which he was distinguished throughout life, espousing the cause of the weaker party and exerting all his powers of oratory in behalf of those who were injured or neglected through prejudice or partiality for others. Never content with mediocrity, he endeavored to surpass his companions in every thing he undertook; and his habits of self-indulgence unfortunately taking a new direction, he now became a leader in all the dissipation of the school. To complete the mischief, his father took him, at the age of fourteen, on a trip to the Spa in Germany, at that time the great center of gambling for Europe; and, incredible as it may seem, he there initiated him in all the mysteries of the gaming-table! At the end of three months, Charles returned to Eton with that fatal passion which so nearly proved his ruin for life and immediately introduced gambling among his companions to an extent never before heard of in a public school. Under his influence, one of the boys, it is said, contracted debts of honor to the amount of *ten thousand pounds* which he felt bound to pay when he arrived at manhood!

At the end of six years Charles was removed to Oxford, where he continued two years, still maintaining the highest rank as a scholar. Notwithstanding his love of pleasure, he must have devoted most of his time at the university to severe study; for his tutor, Dr. Newcombe, remarks, in a letter which Mr. Fox was fond of showing in after life, "Application like yours requires some intermission, and you are the only person with whom I have ever had connection, to whom I could say this." His studies were confined almost entirely to the classics and history; he paid but little attention to the mathematics, a neglect which he afterward lamented as injurious to his mental training; and perhaps for this reason he never felt the slightest interest, at this or any subsequent period, in those abstract inquiries which are designed to settle the foundations of moral and political science. Charles Butler having once mentioned to him that he had never read Smith's Wealth of Nations, "To tell you the truth," said Mr. Fox, "nor have I either. There is something in all these subjects which passes my comprehension; something so wide that I could never embrace them myself, nor find any one that did." This was one of the greatest defects in his character as a statesman. His tastes were too exclusively literary. With those habits of self-indulgence so unhappily created in childhood, he rarely did any thing but what he *liked*—he read poetry, eloquence, history, and elegant literature because he loved them, and he read but little else. He had never learned to grapple with difficulties, except in connection with a subject which deeply interested his feelings. To secure some favorite object, he would now and then submit to severe drudgery, but he soon reverted to his old habits; and, with powers which if rightly disciplined would have enabled him to enter more easily than almost any man of his age into the abstrusest inquiries, he never mastered the principles of his own profession; he was not, in the strict sense of the term, a *scientific* statesman. He could discuss the Greek meters with Porson; and when a friend once insisted that a certain line in the Iliad could not be genuine because it contained measures not used by Homer, he was able, from his early recollections of the poet, instantly to adduce nearly twenty examples of the same construction. But he had no such acquaintance with the foundations of jurisprudence or the laws of trade; at a period when the labors of Adam Smith were giving a new science to the world and establishing the principles of political economy, the true source of the wealth of nations, he was obliged to say, "it is a subject which passes my comprehension." His deficiency in this respect was indeed less seen, because, being in opposition nearly all his life, he was rarely called to propose measures of finance; his chief business was to break down and not to build up; yet he always felt the want of an early training in scientific investigation, correspondent to that he received in classical literature.

Mr. Fox left the University at the age of seventeen and entered at once upon manhood. The light restraints imposed during his education being now removed, he became sole master of his own actions, and the prodigal liberality of his father supplied him with unbounded means of indulgence. For two years he traveled on the Continent, making great proficiency in Italian and French literature, and plunging at the same time into all the extravagance and vice of the most corrupt capitals of Europe. His father had succeeded, even beyond his intentions, in making him a 'leader in fashionable dissipation,' and he now began to fear that he had thus defeated his main design, that of training him up to be an 'orator and a statesman.' He recalled him from the Continent and was compelled, in doing so (as afterward appeared from his banker's accounts), to pay *one hundred thousand pounds* of debt contracted in two years! To wean him from habits which he had himself engendered, Lord Holland now resorted to the extraordinary expedient of having his son returned as a member of Parliament from Midhurst, a borough under his control, in May, 1768, being a year and eight months before he was eligible by law!

Under this return, Mr. Fox took his seat in the House at the opening of Parliament in November, 1768. His deficiency in age was perhaps unknown; at all events, no one came forward to dispute his right. By education he was a Tory; he had distinguished himself when at Paris by some lively French verses reflecting severely on Lord Chatham; and in all his feelings, habits, and associations, he was opposed to the cause of popular liberty. He now came out a warm supporter of the Duke of Grafton, with whom his father was closely allied in politics, just after Junius's first attack on the administration of his Grace, and delivered his maiden speech, April 15th, 1769, in support of that flagrant outrage on the rights of the people, the seating of Colonel Luttrell as a member of the House in the place of John Wilkes. Horace Walpole speaks of him as distinguished for his "insolence" on this occasion, as well as "the infinite superiority of his parts." When Lord North came in as minister, in February, 1770, Mr. Fox, through the influence of his father, was appointed a junior Lord of the Admiralty, and three years after, one of the Lords of the Treasury. His time was now divided between politics and gambling, and he was equally devoted to both. In the House, he showed great, though irregular, power as an orator, and at the gaming-table he often lost from five to ten thousand pounds at a single sitting. Though he differed from Lord North on the Royal Marriage Bill and Toleration Act, he sustained his Lordship in all his political measures and even went at times beyond him—declaring that, for his part, he "paid no regard whatever to the voice of the people;" urging the imprisonment of Alderman Oliver and the Lord Mayor of London for the steps they took to guard the liberty of the press; and inveighing against Sergeant Glynn's motion respecting the rights of juries in cases of libel, the very rights which he himself afterward secured to them by an act of Parliament! To these views, derived from his father and confirmed by all his present associates, he might very possibly have adhered through life, except for a breach which now took place between him and Lord North: so much do political principles depend on party connections and private interest. But his Lordship found Mr. Fox too warm and independent in his zeal; he sometimes broke the ranks and took his place as a leader; and in one instance, when Woodfall was brought to the bar of the House for making too free a use of his press, Mr. Fox proposed an amendment to a motion made by his Lordship, and actually carried it against him, under which Woodfall was committed to Newgate—a measure never contemplated by the ministry and only calculated to injure them by its harshness. Such a violation of party discipline could not be overlooked, and it was decided at once to dismiss him. A day or two after (February 28th, 1774), as he was seated on the Treasury bench conversing with Lord North, the following note was handed him by the messenger of the House:

> "SIR,—His Majesty has thought proper to order a new commission of the Treasury to be made out, *in which I do not perceive your name.*
> (Signed) NORTH."

The cool contempt of this epistle shows the estimate in which he was held by the ministry, who plainly regarded him as a reckless gambler whose friendship or hatred, notwithstanding all his talents, could never be of the least importance to any party. There was too much reason for this opinion. His father, after expending an enormous sum in paying his debts (one statement makes it £140,000 in the year 1773 alone), died about this time, leaving him an ample fortune including his splendid estate in the Isle of Thanet; but the whole was almost immediately gone, sacrificed to the imperious passion which had taken such entire possession of his soul. Paris and London were equally witnesses to its power. The celebrated Madame Duffand, in a letter written at a somewhat later period, speaks of him and his companion, Colonel Fitzpatrick, as objects of curious speculation, but adds in another letter—"Je ne saurais m'interesser à eux: ce sont des têtes absolument dérangées et sans espérance de retour."[1] The whole world, in fact, regarded him in very much the same way as Lord North.

It is probable that nothing but a blow like this, showing him the contempt into which he had sunk, rousing all his pride, and driving him into the arms of new associates, whose talents commanded his respect and whose instructions molded his political principles, could ever have saved Mr. Fox from the ruin in which he was involved. As it was, years passed away before he gained a complete mastery over this terrible infatuation; and it may here be stated, by way of anticipation, that his friends, at a much later period (1793), finding him involved, from time to time, in the most painful embarrassments from this cause, united in a subscription with which they purchased him an annuity of £3000 a year which could not be alienated, and after this testimony of their regard he wholly abstained from gambling.

The period at which Mr. Fox now stood was peculiarly favorable to the formation of new and more correct political principles. Hitherto he had none that could be called his own; he had never, probably, reflected an hour on the subject; he had simply carried out those high aristocratic feelings with which he was taught from childhood to look down upon the body of the people. But a change in the policy of Lord North now made *America* the great object of political interest. Within a few weeks, the Boston Port Bill and its attendant measures were brought forward, designed to starve a town of twenty thousand inhabitants, with the adjoining province, into submission; the charter of that province was violently set aside; a British governor was empowered to send persons three thousand miles across the Atlantic to be tried in England for supposed offenses in America; and British troops were to be employed in carrying out these acts of violence and outrage. Mr. Fox was naturally one of the most humane of men; "He possessed," says Lord Erskine, "above all persons I ever knew, the most gentle and yet the most ardent spirit; he was tremblingly alive to every kind of private wrong or suffering; he had an indignant abhorrence of every species of cruelty, oppression, and injustice." With these feelings, quickened by the resentment which he naturally entertained against Lord North, it could not require much argument from Burke, Dunning, Barré, and the other leaders of the Opposition, into whose society he was now thrown, to make Mr. Fox enter with his whole soul into all their views of these violent, oppressive acts. He came out at once to resist them and was the first man in the House who took the ground of denying the *right* of Parliament to tax the colonies without their consent. He affirmed that on this subject, "Just as the House of Commons stands to the House of Lords, so stands America with Great Britain;" neither party having authority to overrule or compel the other. He declared, "There is not an American but must reject and *resist* the principle and right." He accused Lord North of the most flagrant treachery to his adherents in New England. "You boast," said he, "of having friends there; but, rather than not make the ruin of that devoted country complete, even *your friends are to be involved in one common famine!*" His Lordship soon found that he had raised up a most formidable antagonist where he had least expected. Mr. Fox now entered into debate, not occasionally, as before, when the whim struck him, but earnestly and systematically, on almost every question that came up; and his proficiency may be learned from a letter of Mr. Gibbon (who was then a member of the House and a supporter of the ministry), in which, speaking of a debate on the subject of America (February, 1775), he says: "The principal men both days were Fox and Wedderburne, on opposite sides: the latter displayed his usual talents; the former, taking the vast compass of the question before us, discovered powers for regular debate *which neither his friends hoped nor his enemies dreaded.*"—Misc. Works, ii., 21.

Mr. Fox's sentiments respecting the treatment of America, though springing perhaps at first from humane feelings alone, or opposition to Lord North, involved as their necessary result an entire change of his political principles. He was now brought, for the first time, to look at public measures not on the side of privilege or prerogative, but of the rights and interests of the people. From that moment, all the sympathies of his nature took a new direction, and he went on identifying himself more and more, to the end of life, with the popular part of the Constitution and the cause of free principles throughout the world. It was the test to which he brought every measure: it was his object, amid all the conflicts of party and personal interest, in his own expressive language, "to widen the basis of freedom—to infuse and circulate the spirit of liberty." As an orator, especially, he drew from this source the most inspiring strains of his eloquence. No English speaker, not even Lord Chatham himself, dwelt so often on this theme; no one had his generous sensibilities more completely roused; no one felt more strongly the need of a growing infusion of this spirit into the English government as the great means of its strength and renovation. He urges this in a beautiful passage in his speech on Parliamentary Reform, "because it gives a power of which nothing else in government is capable; because it incorporates every man with the state and arouses every thing that belongs to the soul as well as the body of man; because it makes every individual feel that he is fighting for himself and not for another; that it is his own cause, his own safety, his own concern, his own dignity on the face of the earth, and his own interest in that identical soil, which he has to maintain. In this principle we find the key to all the wonders which were achieved at Thermopylæ: the principle of liberty alone could create those sublime and irresistible emotions, and it is in vain to deny, from the striking illustration that our times have given, that the principle is eternal and that it belongs to the heart of man."

It was happy for Mr. Fox, in coming out so strongly against Lord North at the early age of twenty-five, that he enjoyed the friendship of some of the ablest men in the empire among the Whigs, on whom he could rely with confidence in forming his opinions and conducting his political inquiries. To Mr. Burke he could resort, in common with all the associates of that wonderful man, for every kind of knowledge on almost every subject; and he declared, at the time of their separation from each other in 1791 that "if he were to put all the political information which he had learned from books, all he had gained from science, and all which any knowledge of the world and its affairs had taught him, into one scale, and the improvement which he had derived from his right honorable friend's instruction and conversation were placed in the other, he should be at a loss to decide to which to give the preference." Mr. Dunning (afterward Lord Ashburton) was another leader among the Whigs, who, though less generally known as an orator from the imperfection of his voice and manner, was one of the keenest opponents in the House of those arbitrary acts into which George III drove the Duke of Grafton and Lord North, and it can hardly be doubted that he had great influence with Mr. Fox at this time (though they were separated at a later period) in weaning him from his early predilections for the royal prerogative and inspiring him with those sentiments which the Whigs expressed in their celebrated resolution (drawn up by Mr. Dunning himself) that *"the influence of the Crown has increased, is increasing, and* OUGHT TO BE DIMINISHED."[2]

The ambition of Mr. Fox was now directed to a single object, that of making himself *a powerful debater*. A debater, in the distinctive sense of the term, is described by a lively writer as "one who goes out in all weathers"—one who, instead of carrying with him to the House a set speech drawn up beforehand, has that knowledge of general principles, that acquaintance with each subject as it comes up, that ready use of all his faculties, which enables him to meet every question where he finds it, to grapple with his antagonist at a moment's warning, and to avail himself of every advantage which springs from a perfect command of all his powers and resources. These qualities are peculiarly necessary in the British House of Commons because the most important questions are generally decided at a single sitting; and there is no room for that pernicious custom so prevalent in the American Congress of making interminable speeches to constituents under a semblance of addressing the House. In addition to great native quickness and force of mind, long-continued practice is requisite to make a successful debater. Mr. Fox once remarked to a friend that he had literally gained his skill "at the expense of the House," for he had sometimes tasked himself, during an entire session, to speak on every question that came up, whether he was interested in it or not, as a means of exercising and training his faculties. He now found it necessary to be intimately acquainted with the history of the Constitution and the political relations of the country, and though he continued for some years to be a votary of pleasure, he had such wonderful activity of mind and force of memory that he soon gained an amount of information on these topics such as few men in the House possessed and was able to master every subject in debate with surprising facility and completeness. In all this he thought of but one thing—not language, not imagery, not even the best disposition and sequence of his ideas, but *argument:* how to put down his antagonist, how to make out his own case. His love of argument was, perhaps, the most striking trait in his character. Even in conversation (as noticed by a distinguished foreigner who was much in his society), he was not satisfied, like most men, to throw out a remark and leave it to make its own way, he must *prove* it, and subject the remarks of others to the same test, so that *discussion* formed the staple of all his thoughts and entered to a great extent into all his intercourse with others. With such habits and feelings, he rose, says Mr. Burke, "by slow degrees to be the most brilliant and accomplished debater the world ever saw." There was certainly nothing of envy or disparagement (though charged upon him with great bitterness by Dr. Parr) in Mr. Burke's selecting the term "debater" to express the distinctive character of Mr. Fox. The character is one which gives far more weight and authority to a speaker in Parliament than the most fervid oratory when unattended by the qualities mentioned above. It was not denied by Mr. Burke, but rather intimated by his use of the word "brilliant," that Mr. Fox did superinduce upon those qualities an ardor and an eloquence by which (as every one knows) he gave them their highest effect. It is emphatically true, also, notwithstanding Dr. Parr's complaint of the expression, that Mr. Fox did rise "by slow degrees" to his eminence as an orator, an eminence of so peculiar a kind that no human genius could ever have attained it in any other way, and it is equally true that whenever the name of Mr. Fox is mentioned, the first idea which strikes every mind is the one made thus prominent by Mr. Burke—we instantly think of him as "the most brilliant and accomplished *debater* the world ever saw." So much, indeed, was this the absorbing characteristic of his oratory that nearly all his faults lay in this direction. He had made himself so completely an intellectual gladiator that too often he thought of nothing but how to obtain the victory.

Notwithstanding the irregularities of his private life, to which Mr. Fox still unfortunately clung, he gradually rose as a speaker in Parliament, until at the end of Lord North's administration he was the acknowledged leader of the Whig party in the House. In many respects, he was peculiarly qualified for such a station. He had a fine, genial spirit, characteristic of the family, which drew his political friends around him with all the warmth of a personal attachment. "He was a man," said Mr. Burke, soon after their separation from each other, "who was *made* to be loved." His feelings were generous, open, and manly; the gaming-table had not made him, as it does most men, callous or morose; he was remarkably unassuming in his manners, yet frank and ardent in urging his views; he was above every thing like trick or duplicity, and was governed by the impulses of a humane and magnanimous disposition. These things, in connection with his tact and boldness, qualified him pre-eminently to be the leader of a Whig Opposition; while his rash turn of mind, resulting from the errors of his early training, would operate less to his injury in such a situation, and his very slight regard for political consistency would as yet have no opportunity to be developed.

It was with these characteristics that, at the end of the long struggle which drove Lord North from power, Mr. Fox came into office as Secretary of State under Lord Rockingham, in March, 1782. This administration was terminated in thirteen weeks by the death of his Lordship, and Mr. Fox confidently expected to be made prime minister. But he had now to experience the natural consequences of his reckless spirit and disregard of character. The King would not for a moment entertain the idea of placing at the head of affairs a man who, besides his notorious dissipation, had beggared himself by gambling and was still the slave of this ruinous passion. Nor was he alone in his feelings. Reflecting men of the Whig party, who were out of the circle of Mr. Fox's immediate influence, had long been scandalized by the profligacy of his life. In 1779, Dr. Price, who went beyond him in his devotion to liberal principles, remarked with great severity on his conduct in a Fast Sermon which was widely circulated in print. "Can you imagine," said he, "that a spendthrift in his own concerns will make an economist in managing the concerns of others? that a wild gamester will take due care of the state of a kingdom? Treachery, vanity, and corruption must be the effects of dissipation, voluptuousness, and impiety. These sap the foundations of virtue; they render men necessitous and supple, ready at any time to fly to a court in order to repair a shattered fortune and procure supplies for prodigality." In addition to this, Mr. Fox had made himself personally obnoxious to George III by another exhibition of his rashness. He had treated him with great indignity in his speeches on the American war, pointing directly to his supposed feelings and determinations in a manner forbidden by the theory of the Constitution, and plainly implying that he was governed by passions unbecoming his station as a King and disgraceful to his character as a man. It is difficult to understand how Mr. Fox could allow himself in such language (whatever may have been his private convictions) if he hoped ever to be made minister, and it was certainly to be expected, for these reasons as well as those mentioned above, that the King would never place him at the head of the government while he could find any other man who was competent to fill the station. He accordingly made Lord Shelburne prime minister early in July, 1782, and Mr. Fox instantly resigned.

This step led to another which was the great misfortune of his life. Parties were so singularly balanced at the opening of the next Parliament in December, 1782, that neither the minister nor any of his opponents had the command of the House. According to an estimate made by Gibbon, Lord Shelburne had one hundred and forty adherents, Lord North one hundred and twenty, and Mr. Fox ninety, leaving a considerable number who were unattached. Early in February, 1783, a report crept abroad that a *coalition* was on the *tapis* between Mr. Fox and Lord North. The story was at first treated as an idle tale. A coalition of some kind was indeed expected, because the government could not be administered without an amalgamation of parties; but that Mr. Fox could ever unite with Lord North, after their bitter animosities and the glaring contrast of their principles on almost every question in politics, seemed utterly incredible. There was nothing of a personal nature to prevent an arrangement between Lord Shelburne and Lord North, but Mr. Fox had for years assailed his opponent in such language as seemed forever to cut them off from any intercourse as men or any union of their interests as politicians. He had denounced him as "the most infamous of mankind," as "the greatest criminal of the state, whose *blood* must expiate the calamities he had brought upon his country;"[3] and, as if with the express design of making it impossible for him to enter into such an alliance, he had, only eleven months before, said of Lord North and his whole ministry in the House of Commons: "From the moment I should make any terms with one of them, I would rest satisfied to be called the most *infamous* of mankind. I could not for an instant think of a *coalition* with men who, in every public and private transaction as ministers, have shown themselves void of every principle of honor and honesty: in the hands of such men I would not trust my honor even for a minute."[4] Still, rumors of a coalition became more and more prevalent, until, on the 17th of February, 1783, says Mr. Wilberforce, in relating the progress of events, "When I reached the House, I inquired, 'Are the intentions of Lord North and Fox sufficiently known to be condemned?' 'Yes,' said Henry Banks, 'and the more strongly the better.' " The debate was on Lord Shelburne's treaty of peace with America; and every eye was turned to the slightest movements of the ex-minister and his old antagonist, until, at a late hour of the evening, Lord North came down from the gallery where he had been sitting and *took his place by Mr. Fox.* His Lordship then arose and attacked the treaty with great dexterity and force as bringing disgrace upon the country by the concessions it made. Mr. Fox followed in the same strain, adding, in reference to himself and Lord North, that all causes of difference between them had ceased with the American war. The Coalition was now complete! The debate continued until nearly eight o'clock the next morning, when

Lord Shelburne was defeated by a majority of sixteen votes and was compelled soon after to resign.

Next came the Coalition Ministry. To this the King submitted with the utmost reluctance, after laboring in vain first to persuade Mr. Pitt to undertake the government and then to obtain, as a personal favor from Lord North, the exclusion of Mr. Fox. So strong were the feelings of his Majesty that he hesitated and delayed for *six weeks,* until, driven by repeated addresses from the House, he was compelled to yield; and this ill-fated combination came into power on the 2d of April, 1783, with the Duke of Portland as its head, and Mr. Fox and Lord North as principal secretaries of state. "The occurrence of this coalition," says Mr. Cooke, one of Mr. Fox's warmest admirers, "is greatly to be deplored, as an example to men who, without any of the power, may nevertheless feel inclined to imitate the errors of Fox. It is to be deplored as a blot on the character of a great man, as a precedent which strikes at the foundation of political morality, and as a weapon in the hands of those who would destroy all confidence in the honesty of public men."[5] The laxity of principle which it shows in Mr. Fox may be traced to the errors of his early education. It was the result of the pernicous habit in which he was trained of gratifying every desire without the least regard to consequences and the still more pernicious maxims taught him by his father—"that brilliant talents would atone for every kind of delinquency, and that, in politics especially, any thing would be pardoned to a man of great designs and splendid abilities." Certain it is that Mr. Fox could never understand why he was condemned so severely for his union with Lord North. As an opponent, he had spoken of him, indeed, in rash and bitter terms, but never with a malignant spirit, for nothing was farther from his disposition; and, knowing the character of the men, we can credit the statement of Mr. Gibbon, who was intimate with both, "that in their political contests these great antagonists had never felt any *personal* animosity; that their reconciliation was easy and sincere; and that their friendship had never been clouded by the shadow of suspicion and jealousy." Every one now feels that Mr. Fox uttered his real sentiments when he said, "It is not in my nature to bear malice or ill will; my friendships are perpetual; my enmities are not so: *amicitiæ sempiternæ, inimicitiæ placabiles.*" But he had thus far shown himself to the world only on the worst side of his character, and it is not surprising that most men considered him (what in fact he appeared to be on the face of the transaction) as a reckless politician, bent on the possession of power at whatever sacrifice of principle or consistency it might cost him. Even the warmest Whigs regarded him, to a great extent, in the same light. "From the moment this coalition was formed," says Bishop Watson, "I lost all confidence in public men." "The gazettes," says Sir Samuel Romilly in a letter to a friend, "have proclaimed to you the scandalous alliance between Fox and Lord North. It is not Fox alone, but his whole party; so much so that it is no exaggeration to say that of all the public characters of this devoted country (Mr. Pitt only excepted) there is not a man who has, or deserves, the nation's confidence."[6]

The great measure of the Coalition ministry was Mr. Fox's East India Bill. Perilous as the subject was to a new administration lying under the jealousy of the people and the hostility of the King, it could not be avoided, and Mr. Fox met it with a fearless resolution which at least demands our respect. The whole nation called for strong measures, and Mr. Fox gave them a measure stronger than any one of them had contemplated. He cut the knot which politicians had so long endeavored to untie. He annulled the charter of the East India Company and, after providing for the payment of their debts, he took all their concerns into the hands of the government at home, placing the civil and military affairs of India under the control of a board of seven commissioners and putting their commercial interests into the hands of a second board to be managed for the benefit of the shareholders. Never, since the Revolution of 1688, has any measure of the government produced such a ferment in the nation. Lawyers exclaimed against the bill as a violation of chartered rights; all the corporate bodies of the kingdom saw in it a precedent which might be fatal to themselves; the East India Company considered it as involving the ruin of their commercial interests; and politicians regarded it as a desperate effort of Mr. Fox, after forcing his way into office against the wishes of the King, to set himself above the King's reach and, by this vast accession of patronage, to establish his ministry for life. Mr. Fox had again to suffer the bitter consequences of his disregard of character. These objections were plausible, and some of the provisions of the bill were certainly *impolitic* for one situated like Mr. Fox. Yet Mr. Mill, in his British India, speaks of the alarm excited as one "for which the ground was extremely scanty and for which, notwithstanding the industry and art with which the advantage was improved by the opposite party, it is difficult (considering the usual apathy of the public on much more important occasions) entirely to account."[7] As to the principal charge, Lord Campbell observes in his Lives of the Chancellors, "No one at the present day believes that the framers of the famous East India Bill had the intention imputed to them of creating a power independent of the Crown."[8] And as to the other objections, it is obvious to remark that *any* effectual scheme of Indian reform would, of necessity, encroach on the charter of the Company, that such encroachments must in any case be liable to abuse as precedents, and that if (as all agreed was necessary) the government at home assumed the civil and military administration of India, a large increase of patronage *must* fall into the hands of ministers, which others could abuse as easily as Mr. Fox. But the difficulty was, *no one knew how far to trust him!* His conduct had given boundless scope for jealousy and suspicion. He had put into the hands of his enemies the means of utterly ruining his character, and it is undoubtedly true, as stated by a late writer, that he was at this period regarded by the great body of the nation "as selfish, vicious, and destitute of virtue—by thousands he was looked upon as a man with the purposes of a Catiline and the manners of a Lovelace."[9]

Under all these difficulties, Mr. Fox placed his reliance on his majority in the House and went forward with an unbroken spirit, trusting to time and especially to the character of the men whom he should name as commissioners, for the removal of this wide-spread opposition. He introduced his bill on the 18th of November, 1783, in a speech explaining its import and design; and at the end of twelve days, after one of the hardest-fought battles which ever took place in the House, he closed the debate with a speech of great ability (to be found below), in reply to his numerous opponents and especially to Mr. Dundas and Mr. Pitt. Believing (as almost every one now does) that Mr. Fox was far from being governed by the base motives ascribed to him—that, though ambitious in a high degree and hoping, no doubt, to strengthen his ministry by this measure, his bill was dictated by generous and humane feelings and was no more stringent than he felt the exigency of the case to demand—we can not but admire the dignity and manliness with which he stood his ground. He had every inducement when he met this unexpected opposition, to shrink back, to modify his plan, to compromise with the East India Company, and to establish his power by uniting his interests with theirs. Even those who distrust his motives will therefore do honor to his spirit and will be ready to say with Mr. Moore,[10] "We read his speech on the East India Bill with a sort of breathless anxiety, which no other political discourses, except those, perhaps, of Demosthenes, could produce. The importance of the stake which he risks—the boldness of his plan—the gallantry with which he flings himself into the struggle, and the frankness of personal feeling that breathes throughout, all throw around him an interest like that which encircles a hero of romance; nor could the most candid autobiography that ever was written exhibit the whole character of a man more transparently through it."

The bill passed the Commons by a vote of 217 to 103, but when it came up in the House of Lords it met with a new and more powerful resistance. Lord Temple, a near relative of Mr. Pitt, had obtained a private audience of the King and represented the subject in such a light that his Majesty commissioned him to say that "whoever voted for the India Bill were not only not his friends, but that he should consider them his *enemies.*" At its first reading, Lord Thurlow denounced it in the strongest terms; and turning to the Prince of Wales, who was present as a peer with the view to support the bill, he added, with a dark scowl as he looked him directly in the face, "I wish to see the Crown great and respectable, but if the present bill should pass, it will be no longer worthy of a man of honor to wear. The King may take the diadem from his own head and put it on the head of Mr. Fox." An instantaneous change took place among the peerage. The King's message through Lord Temple had been secretly but widely circulated among the Lords, especially those of the royal household, who had given their proxies to the ministry. These proxies were instantly withdrawn. Even Lord Stormont, a member of the cabinet who at first supported the bill, changed sides after two days; the Prince of Wales felt unable to give Mr. Fox his vote; and the bill was rejected by a majority of ninety-five to seventy-six. The King hastened to town the moment he learned the decision of the Lords, and at twelve o'clock the next night, a messenger conveyed to Mr. Fox and Lord North his Majesty's orders "that they should deliver up the seals of their offices and send them by the under-secretaries, Mr. Frazer and Mr. Nepean, as a personal interview on the occasion would be disagreeable to him." The other ministers received their dismissal the next day in a note signed "Temple."

But the battle was not over. Mr. Fox had still an overwhelming majority in the House, and feeling that the interference of the King was an encroachment on the rights of the Commons, he resolved to carry his resistance to the utmost extremity. Accordingly, some days after, when Mr. Pitt came in as minister, he voted him down by so large a majority that a division was not even called for. Again and again he voted him down, demanding of him in each instance to resign in accordance with parliamentary usage, and bringing upon him at last a direct vote, "That after the expressed opinion of the House, the continuance of the present minister in office *is contrary to constitutional principles,* and injurious to the interests of his Majesty and the people." Earl Temple was terrified and threw up his office within a few days, but Mr. Pitt stood firm. The contest continued for three months, during which Mr. Fox delayed the supplies from time to time and distinctly intimated that he might *stop them entirely,* and prevent the passing of the Mutiny Bill, if Mr. Pitt did not resign.[11] But his impetuosity carried him too far. He was in this case, as in some others, his own worst enemy. The King's interference was certainly a breach of privilege, and under other circumstances the whole country would have rallied round Mr. Fox to resist it. But every one now saw that the real difficulty was his exclusion from office, and when he attempted to force his way back by threatening to suspend the operations of government, the nation turned against him more strongly than ever. They ascribed all that he did to mortified pride or disappointed ambition; they gave him no credit for those better feelings which mingled with these passions and which he seems to have considered (so easily do men deceive themselves) as the only motives that impelled him to the violent measures he pursued.[12] Addresses now poured in upon the King from every quarter, entreating him not to yield. At a public meeting in Westminster Hall, Mr. Fox, who was present with a view to explain his conduct, was put down by cries of "No Great Mogul!" "No India tyrant!" "No usurper!" "No turn-coat!" "No dictator!" The city of London, once so strongly in his favor, now turned against him. Sir Horace Mann relates that, going up to the King at this time with one of the addresses of the House against Mr. Pitt, he met the Lord Mayor of London and others who had just come down from presenting one in his favor, and on Sir Horace remarking, "I see I am among my friends," they replied, "We *were* your friends, but you have joined those who have set up a *Lord Protector!*" Such demonstrations of public feeling operated powerfully on the House. Mr. Fox's adherents gradually fell off until, on a division at the end of eleven weeks, March 8th, 1784, his majority had sunk from fifty-four to a *single vote!* A shout of triumph now broke forth from the ministerial benches. The contest in the House was ended, and the question was carried at once to the whole country by a dissolution of Parliament.

The elections which followed, in April, 1784, went against the friends of Mr. Fox in every part of the kingdom; more than a hundred and sixty having lost their places and become "Fox's Martyrs," in the sportive language of the day. In Westminster, which Mr. Fox and Sir Cecil Wray had represented in the preceding Parliament, the struggle was the most violent ever known—Wray in opposition to his old associate. At the end of eleven days Mr. Fox was in a minority of three hundred and eighteen and his defeat seemed inevitable, when relief came from a quarter never before heard of in a political canvass. Georgiana, Duchess of Devonshire, a woman of extraordinary beauty and the highest mental accomplishments, took the field in his behalf. She literally became the canvasser of Mr. Fox. She went from house to house soliciting votes; she sent her private carriage to bring mechanics and others of the lowest class to the polls; she appeared at the hustings herself in company with Mr. Fox; and on one occasion, when a young butcher turned the laugh upon her by offering his vote for a *kiss,* in the enthusiasm of the moment she took him at his word and paid him on the spot! With such an ally, Mr. Fox's fortunes soon began to mend, and at the termination of forty days, when the polls were closed, he had a majority over Sir Cecil Wray of two hundred and thirty-five votes. This triumph was celebrated by a splendid procession of Mr. Fox's friends, most of them bearing *fox tails,* which gave rise to one of Mr. Pitt's best sarcasms. Some one having expressed his wonder how the people could procure such an immense number of foxes' tails; "That is by no means surprising," said Pitt, "this has been a good sporting year and more *foxes* have been destroyed than in any former season. I think, upon an average, there has at least one Fox been run down in every borough of the kingdom!" The Prince of Wales showed the lively interest he had taken in the contest by joining the procession on horseback in his uniform of a colonel of the Tenth Dragoons. A few days after, he celebrated the victory in a fête at Carlton House, attended by more than six hundred persons, the gentlemen being dressed in the costume of Mr. Fox, "buff and blue," and some even of the ladies wearing the same colors with the "Fox laurel" on their heads, and the "Fox medal" suspended from their necks.

But Mr. Fox was not allowed to enjoy the fruits of his victory. Sir Cecil Wray demanded a *scrutiny* or revision of the poll, involving enormous expense and a delay, perhaps of years, in taking testimony as to disputed votes. All this time Mr. Fox was to be deprived of his seat—the object really aimed at in the whole transaction. The presiding officer lent himself to this design: he returned Lord Hood (the third candidate) as a member, and made a report to the House that he had granted a scrutiny in relation to Sir Cecil Wray and Mr. Fox. There was no precedent for a scrutiny in a case like this, where the poll had been continued down to the very day before the meeting of Parliament and the presiding officer was required by his writ to return *two* members for Westminster on the 18th of May, being the next day. If he could avoid this —if he was authorized (instead of doing the best he could) to reserve the question and enter on a scrutiny after the session had commenced—it is obvious that the entire representation of the country would be in the hands of the returning officers. Any one of them, from party views or corrupt motives, might deprive a member of his seat as long as he saw fit under the pretense (as in the present case) of satisfying his "conscience" by a protracted revision of the polls. The case came up early in the session, and Mr. Fox, being returned by a friend for the borough of Kirkwall in the Orkney Isles, was enabled to join in the debate. Under any other circumstances Mr. Pitt would never have allowed his passions to become interested in such an affair; even if he thought the scrutiny legal, he would have seen the necessity of putting an end at once to a precedent so obnoxious to abuse. But the conflict of the last session seems to have poisoned his mind and he showed none of that magnanimity which we should naturally expect in one who had achieved so splendid a victory at the recent elections. He assailed Mr. Fox in the language of taunt and ungenerous sarcasm, describing him as a man on whom a sentence of banishment had been passed by his country—as "driven by the impulse of patriotic indignation an exile from his native clime, to seek refuge on the stormy and desolate shores of the *Ultima Thule.*" Nothing could be more admirable than the firmness and elasticity of Mr. Fox's spirit under these depressing circumstances, stripped as he was of nearly all his former supporters in the House. He seemed, like the old Romans, to gather strength and courage from the difficulties that surrounded him. On the 8th of June, 1784, he discussed the subject of the Westminster scrutiny in one of the clearest and most fervid pieces of reasoning ever delivered in the House of Commons; adding at the same time some admonitions for Mr. Pitt and his other opponents which effectually secured him against uncivil treatment in all their subsequent contests. Although the vote went against him at that time by a majority of 117, the House and the country soon became satisfied that the whole proceeding was dishonorable and oppressive; and, at the end of nine months, Mr. Pitt had the mortification to see his majority, so firm on every other subject, turning against him upon this and, by a vote of 162 to 124, putting an end to the scrutiny and requiring an immediate return. Mr. Fox was accordingly returned the next day. The moment he took his seat as a member for Westminster, Mr. Fox moved that all the proceedings in regard to the scrutiny be expunged from the journals of the House. This motion was supported by Mr. Scott, afterward Lord Eldon, who on this occasion (the only one in his life) came out in opposition to Mr. Pitt; but the majority were unwilling to join him in so direct a vote of censure, and the motion was lost.[13] Mr. Fox recovered two thousand pounds damages from the presiding officer, the High Bailiff of Westminster, and a law was soon after passed providing against any farther abuses of this kind.

Mr. Fox was appointed one of the managers of the impeachment against Warren Hastings in 1786, and had assigned to him the second charge, relating to the oppressive treatment of Cheyte Sing, Rajah of Benares. This duty he performed in a manner which awakened general admiration and fully sustained the high character he had already gained as a parliamentary orator.

In the autumn of 1788, while traveling in Italy, Mr. Fox was unexpectedly presented with the prospect of being called again to the head of affairs. The King became suddenly deranged, and if the malady continued, the Prince of Wales would, of course, be Regent and Mr. Fox his prime minister. A messenger with this intelligence found him at Bologna and urged his immediate return, as the session of Parliament was soon to commence. He started at once and never quitted his chaise during the whole journey, traveling night and day until he reached London, on the 24th of November. At this time no definite anticipations could be formed in respect to the King's recovery. Parliament had voted a fortnight's recess to allow time for deciding on the proper steps to be taken, and the political world was full of intrigue and agitation. It was the great object of the Prince and his future ministers to come in untrammeled—to have his authority as Regent during his father's illness established on the same footing as if he had succeeded to the throne by the King's death. The existing ministry, on the other hand, who believed the King might speedily recover, were desirous to impose such restrictions on the Regency as would prevent Mr. Fox and his friends from intrenching themselves permanently in power. It is curious to observe how completely the two parties changed sides under this new aspect of their political interests. Mr. Fox became the defender of the prerogative and Mr. Pitt of the popular part of the Constitution. Before Mr. Fox returned from Italy, Lord Loughborough [Mr. Wedderburne] had devised a theory to meet the present case. He maintained that here (as in the case of natural death) "the administration of the government devolved to him [the Prince of Wales] of *right;*" that it belonged to Parliament "not to confer, but to declare the right;" and it is now known that he actually advised the Prince, in secret, to assume the royal authority at a meeting of the Privy Council and then to summon Parliament, in his *own* name, for the dispatch of business.[14] This theory, with one important modification, Mr. Fox took with him into the House. In a debate on the 10th of December, 1788, he maintained that during the incapacity of the King, the Prince "had as clear and express a right to assume the reins of government and exercise the power of sovereignty as in the case of his Majesty's having undergone a natural and perfect demise;" but he added (limiting the theory of Lord Loughborough) that "as to this right, the Prince himself was not to judge *when* he was entitled to exercise it, but the two Houses of Parliament, as the organs of the nation, were alone qualified to pronounce *when* the Prince ought to take possession of and exercise this right."[15] Mr. Pitt, the moment he heard this doctrine, exclaimed to a friend who sat by him in the House, "Now I'll *unwhig* that gentleman for the rest of his life!" He instantly rose and declared it to be "little less than treason against the Constitution: he pledged himself to prove that the Heir-apparent had no more right, in the case in question, to the exercise of the executive authority than any other subject in the kingdom, and that it belonged entirely to the two remaining branches of the Legislature, in behalf of the nation at large, to make such a provision for supplying the temporary deficiency as they might think proper." Mr. Fox, either seeing that he had been misunderstood or feeling that he had gone too far, explained himself, two days after, to have meant, that "from the moment the two Houses of Parliament *declared* the King unable to exercise the royal sovereignty, from *that* moment a right to exercise the royal authority attached to the Prince of Wales"—that "he must appeal to the court competent to decide whether it *belonged* to him or not or must wait till that court itself made such a declaration."[16] This was apparently taking still lower ground, but even this Mr. Pitt maintained was equally false and unfounded. "He denied that the Prince had any *right* whatever;" he declared it "subversive of the principles of the Constitution to admit that the Prince of Wales might set *himself* on the throne during the lifetime of his father; he denied that Parliament were mere judges in this emergency, affirming that they acted for the entire body of the people in a case not provided for in the Constitution;" and affirmed it to be "a question of greater magnitude and importance even than the present exigency, a question that involved in it the principles of the Constitution, the protection and security of our liberties, and the safety of the state." A Regency Bill was now framed by the Ministers, making the Prince of Wales Regent, but committing the King's person to the care of the Queen, with the right of appointing the officers of the royal household. It provided that the Prince should have no power over the personal property of the King and no authority either to create new peers or to grant any pension, place, or reversion to be held after the King's recovery, except offices made permanent by law. Nearly three months were spent in debating this subject, every possible delay being interposed by Mr. Pitt, who was now confident of the King's early recovery. Accordingly, about February 19th, his Majesty was declared by the physicians to be restored to a sound state of mind, and Mr. Fox's prospect of office became more remote than ever, the King and the people being equally imbittered against him as having again endeavored to establish himself in power by the use of violent and illegal means.[17] On the question so vehemently discussed at that time touching the rights of the Prince of Wales, there has been a diversity of opinion down to the present day. All agree in considering Lord Loughborough's theory as "a flimsy speculation;" but men have differed greatly as to Mr. Fox's doctrine. When the Regency question came up again in 1810, an able writer in favor of the Prince remarked in the Edinburgh Review: "Strict legal right, which could be asserted and made good in a court of judicature, he [the Prince] certainly had none. It was observed, with more truth than decorum by Mr. Pitt, that every individual of his father's subjects had as good a legal right to the Regency as his Royal Highness the Prince of Wales."[18] Lord Campbell, however, would seem to hold with Mr. Fox, when he says: "The next heir to the throne is *entitled,* during the continuance of this [the King's] disability, to carry on the executive government as Regent with the same authority as if the disabled Sovereign were naturally dead;"[19] unless, indeed, he uses the word "entitled" in a looser sense to describe not what is strictly a *legal right,* but what is most accordant with the analogies of the Constitution and the nature of a hereditary monarchy. If so, he agrees with Lord Brougham, who nevertheless regarded the restrictions imposed on the Prince Regent as wise and necessary. After stating what he considered the argument from analogy, he says in respect to this case: "There were reasons of a practical description which overbore these obvious considerations and reconciled men's minds to such an anomalous proceeding. It seemed necessary to provide for the safe custody of the King's person, and for such a sure restoration of his powers as should instantly replace the scepter in his hand the very moment that his capacity to hold it should return. His Vicegerent must plainly have no control over this operation, neither over the royal patient's custody, nor over the resumption of his office and the termination of his own. But it would not have been very easy to cut off all interference on the Regent's part in this most delicate matter, had he been invested with the full powers of the Crown. So, in like manner, the object being to preserve things as nearly as possible in their present state, if those full powers had been exercised uncontrolled, changes of a nature quite irreversible might have been effected while the monarch's faculties were asleep; and not only he would have awakened to a new order of things, but the affairs of the country would have been administered under that novel dispensation by one irreconcilably hostile to it, while its author, appointed in the course of nature once more to rule as his successor, would have been living and enjoying all the influence acquired by his accidental, anticipated, and temporary reign. These considerations, and the great unpopularity of the Heir-apparent and his political associates, the Coalition party, enabled Mr. Pitt to carry his proposition of a Regency with restricted powers, established by a bill to which the two remaining branches alone of the crippled Parliament had assented; instead of their addressing the Heir-apparent, declaring the temporary vacancy of the throne, and desiring him temporarily to fill it." When the same question came up again, in 1810, the Prince waived the claim of *right,* and yielded quietly to the restrictions enumerated above. These two precedents have settled the constitutional law and usage on this subject.

Mr. Fox's next conflict with his antagonist related to the Russian Armament, and here he carried the whole country with him in opposition to the warlike designs of the ministry. The courts of London and Berlin had demanded of the Empress of Russia, not only to desist from her war with Turkey, but to restore the numerous and important conquests she had made. Unwilling to provoke the resentment of these powerful and self-created arbiters, Catharine consented to yield every thing but a small station on the Black Sea called Ockzakow, with the dependent territory. Mr. Pitt, under a mistaken view of the importance of this fortress, peremptorily insisted on its surrender; the Empress, taking offense at this treatment, as peremptorily refused; and the British ministry made the most active preparations for war. When the subject came before Parliament, early in 1791, Mr. Fox put forth all his strength against this armament. Reflecting men throughout the country condemned Mr. Pitt for interfering in the contests of other nations; and, as the discussion went on in Parliament, ministers found their majority so much reduced that they promptly and wisely gave up the point in dispute. Mr. Fox gained greatly in the public estimation by his conduct on this occasion. He appeared in his true character, that of a friend of peace, and was justly considered as having saved the country, probably from a long and bloody war, certainly from much unnecessary expense contemplated by the ministry. While this question was under discussion, he sent a friend, Mr. Adair, to St. Petersburgh, as it was generally supposed with confidential communications for the Empress. Mr. Burke, after his breach with Mr. Fox, spoke of this mission as involving, if not treason, at least a breach of the Constitution fraught with the most dangerous consequences. It is not easy to understand the ground of this severe charge. Mr. Fox was not in the secrets of the government and could communicate nothing to the Empress which was not known to the world at large. He could only assure her that the English people were averse to war and might, perhaps, exhort her not to lower her terms (though this was never proved); but as the two nations were still at peace, his communications with Catharine were certainly less objectionable than Burke's correspondence with Dr. Franklin during the American war, which he once proposed to read in Parliament and which caused Lord New Haven to exclaim: "Do not my senses deceive me? Can a member of this Assembly not only avow his correspondence with a rebel, but dare to read it to us?"[20] There is one decisive fact which shows that Mr. Adair's mission could not have been regarded by the King and ministry as it was by Mr. Burke. He was afterward sent as Envoy to the courts of Vienna and Constantinople. "The confidence of the Sovereign," as Dr. Parr remarks, "completely and visibly refutes the accusations of Mr. Burke." After Mr. Pitt was thus beaten off from the Russian Armament, Mr. Fox and his friends opened upon him one of the severest attacks he ever experienced by proposing a vote of *censure,* on the ground that he had acted the part either of a bully or a coward—that he had disgraced the country by disarming if there was just cause of war, and by arming if there was not. Mr. Fox's speech on that occasion will be found in this volume; it was one of his most powerful and characteristic efforts.

Mr. Fox likewise distinguished himself at this period by his efforts to defend the rights of juries. The law of libel, as laid down by Lord Mansfield in the case of Woodfall, restricted the jury to the question of *fact,* "Was the accused guilty of publishing, and did he point his remarks at the government?" They were not allowed to inquire into his motives or the legality of what he said, and the real issue was therefore in the hands of the judges, who, being appointed by the Crown, were peculiarly liable to be swayed by court influences. This made the trial by jury in libel cases a mere nullity, and too often turned it into an instrument for crushing the liberty of the press. Mr. Burke took up the subject at the time of Woodfall's trial and prepared a bill giving juries the right to judge of the law as well as the fact, but it was rejected by a large majority. This bill, in all its leading features, Mr. Fox brought forward again in the year 1791, after the famous trial of the Dean of St. Asaph in which Mr. Erskine made his masterly argument on the rights of juries. "When a man," said Mr. Fox, in urging his bill, "is accused of murder, a crime consisting of law and fact, the jury every day find a verdict of guilty; and this also is the case in felony and every criminal indictment. *Libels are the only exception, the single anomaly.*" "All will admit that a *writing* may be an overt act of treason; but suppose in this case the Court of King's Bench should charge the jury; 'Consider only whether the criminal *published* the papers—do not inquire into the nature of it—do not examine whether it corresponds to the definition of treason'—would Englishmen endure that death should be inflicted by the decision of a jury thus trammeled and overruled?" Mr. Pitt generously seconded Mr. Fox in this effort, and as he raised Mr. Grenville to the House of Lords in 1790, he could give the bill a more powerful support in that body; but Lord Thurlow succeeded in defeating it that session. It was passed, however, in 1792, notwithstanding the pertinacious opposition of the law Lords, Thurlow, Kenyon, and Bathurst, and Mr. Fox had the satisfaction of thus performing one of the most important services ever rendered to the liberty of the press.

The progress of our narrative has led us forward insensibly into the midst of the French Revolution. Some one, speaking of this convulsion, remarked to Mr. Burke that it had shaken the whole world. "Yes," replied he, "and it has shaken the *heart of Mr. Fox* out of its place!" Certain it is that every thing Mr. Fox did or said on this subject, whether right or wrong, sprung directly from his heart, from the warm impulse of his humane and confiding nature. In fact, the leading statesmen of that day were all of them governed in the part they took far more by temperament and previous habits of thought than by any deep-laid schemes of policy. Mr. Burke was naturally cautious. His great principle in government was prescription. With him abstract right was nothing, circumstances were every thing, so that his first inquiry in politics was not what is true or proper in the nature of things, but what is practicable, what is expedient, what is wise and safe in the present posture of affairs. Hence, on the question of taxing America, he treated all discussions of the abstract right with utter contempt. "I do not enter into these metaphysical distinctions," said he, "I hate the sound of them." Mr. Fox, on the contrary, instantly put the question on the ground of *right;* all the sympathies of his nature were on the side of the colonies as injured and insulted. "There is not an American," said he, "but must reject and resist the principle and the right." With such feelings and habits of thought, it might have been foreseen from the beginning that Mr. Burke and Mr. Fox would be at utter variance respecting the French Revolution, carried on, as it was, upon the principle of the inherent "rights of man." The difficulty was greater because each of them, to a certain extent, had the truth on his side. The right of self-government in a people, as Mr. Fox truly said, does not depend on precedent or the concessions of rulers, but is founded in the nature of things. "It is not because they *have* been free, but because they have a *right* to be free, that men demand their freedom." Mr. Burke, on the other hand, was equally correct in maintaining that the question of resistance is far from being a question of mere abstract right. *Circumstances,* to a great extent, enter as an essential element into the decision of that question. No one is weak enough to suppose that any nation, however oppressed, can be justified in a rebellion which it is plainly impossible to carry through, or that self-government would be any thing but a curse to a people who are destitute of moral and political virtue. These are points, however, on which it is usually impossible to decide in the early stages of a revolution. A people sometimes *make* their destiny by the energy of their own will. The trials and privations through which they pass (as in the case of the seven United Provinces) prepare them for self-government. It was, therefore, natural for a man of Mr. Fox's sanguine temperament, especially with the example of America before him, to have confident hopes of the same auspicious results in France.

The first instance of popular violence that occurred was the attack on the Bastile (July 14th, 1789), and Mr. Fox, in referring to it in the House, quoted, very happily, from Cowper's Task (which had been recently published), the beautiful lines respecting that fortress:

> "Ye horrid towers, th' abode of broken hearts,
> Ye dungeons and ye cages of despair,
> That monarchs have supplied from age to age
> With music such as suits their sovereign ears:
> The sighs and groans of miserable men!
> There's not an English heart that would not leap
> To hear that ye were fall'n at last."

So far as this event was concerned, Mr. Burke's sympathies were entirely with Mr. Fox. He said it was impossible not to admire the spirit by which the attack was dictated; but the excesses which followed brought him out soon after as an opponent of the Revolution, while Mr. Fox, as might be expected from one of his ardent feelings, still clung to the cause he had espoused. He lamented those excesses as truly as Mr. Burke, but his hopeful spirit led him to believe they would speedily pass away. He ascribed them to the feelings naturally created by the preceding despotism, and thus insensibly became the apologist of the revolutionary leaders, as Mr. Burke was of the court and nobility.

The false position into which Mr. Fox was thus drawn was the great misfortune of his subsequent life. He had no feelings in common with the philosophizing assassins of France, and from the moment he learned their true character and saw the utter failure of their experiments, it is much to be regretted that he should in any way have been led to appear as their advocate. And yet it seemed impossible for one of his cast of mind to avoid it. When Austria and Russia invaded France (July, 1792) for the avowed purpose of putting back the Bourbons on the throne, he felt (as the whole world now feels) that it was not only the worst possible policy, but a flagrant violation of national right. He sympathized with the French. He rejoiced and proclaimed his joy in the House of Commons when they drove out the invaders and seized, in their turn, upon the Austrian Netherlands. So, too, on the questions in dispute between England and France, which soon after resulted in war, he condemned the course taken by his own government as harsh and insulting. He thus far sided with the French, declaring that the English ministry had provoked the war and were justly chargeable with the calamities it produced. And when the French, elated by their success in the Netherlands, poured forth their armies on the surrounding nations with the avowed design of carrying out the Revolution by fire and sword, Mr. Fox was even then led by his peculiar position to palliate what he had no wish to justify. He dwelt on the provocations they had received and showed great ingenuity in proving that the spirit of conquest and treachery which characterized the Republic was only the spirit of the Bourbons transfused into the new government—that *they* had taught the nation and trained it up for ages to be the plunderers of mankind. It is difficult to conceive, at the present day, how all this grated upon the ears of an immense majority of the English people. The world has learned many lessons from the French Revolution, and one of the most important is that which Mr. Fox was continually inculcating, that nations, however wrong may be their conduct, should be left to manage their internal concerns in their own way. But the doctrines of Mr. Burke had taken complete possession of the higher class of minds throughout the country. The French were a set of demons. They had murdered their king and cast off religion; it was, therefore, the duty of surrounding nations to put them out of the pale of civilized society—to treat them as robbers and pirates; and whatever violence might result from such treatment was to be charged on the revolutionary spirit of the French. That spirit was certainly bad enough and would very likely, under any circumstances, have produced war; but if Mr. Fox's advice had been followed, much of the enthusiasm with which the whole French nation rushed into the contest would have been prevented and the fire of the Revolution might possibly have burned out within their own borders, instead of involving all Europe in the conflagration. But the great body of the English people were unprepared for such views, and Mr. Fox was the last man from whom they could hear any thing of this kind even with patience. His early mistakes as to the Revolution had made him the most unpopular man in the kingdom, and it must be admitted that while he was right in the great object at which he aimed, the nature of the argument and the warmth of his feelings made him seem too often to be the advocate of the French, even in their worst excesses. It was hardly possible, indeed, to oppose the war without appearing to take part with the enemy. Even Mr. Wilberforce, when he made his motion against it in 1794, was very generally suspected of revolutionary principles. "When I first went to the levee," said he, "after moving my amendment, the King *cut* me." "Your friend Mr. Wilberforce," said Mr. Windham to Lady Spencer, "will be very happy any morning to hand your Ladyship to the guillotine!"

The name of Mr. Windham naturally suggests another event connected with Mr. Fox's views of the French Revolution. Nearly all his friends deserted him and became his most strenuous opponents. Mr. Burke led the way, as already stated in the sketch of his life. The Duke of Portland, Lord

Loughborough, Mr. Windham, and a large number of the leading Whigs, followed at a somewhat later period, leaving him with only a handful of supporters in the House to maintain the contest with Mr. Pitt. Any other man, in such circumstances, would have given up in despair, but Mr. Fox's spirit seemed always to rise in exact proportion to the pressure that was laid upon him. While he pleaded incessantly for peace with France, he maintained a desperate struggle for the rights of the English people during that memorable season of agitation and alarm from 1793 to 1797. His remedy for the disaffection which prevailed so extensively among the middling and lower classes was that of Lord Chatham: "Remove their grievances: that will restore them to peace and tranquillity." "It may be asked," said he, "what would I propose to do in times of agitation like the present? I will answer openly. If there is a tendency in the Dissenters to discontent, because they conceive themselves to be unjustly suspected and cruelly calumniated, what would I do? I would instantly repeal the Test and Corporation Acts and take from them, by such a step, all cause of complaint. If there are any persons tinctured with a republican spirit because they think that the representative government would be more perfect in a republic, I would endeavor to amend the representation of the Commons, and to show that the House, though not chosen by all, can have no other interest than to prove itself the representative of all. If there are men dissatisfied in Scotland, or Ireland, or elsewhere, by reason of disabilities and exemptions, of unjust prejudices, and of cruel restrictions, I would repeal the penal statutes, which are a disgrace to our law books. If *I* were to issue a proclamation [the King had just issued one against seditious writings], this should be my proclamation: 'If any man has a grievance, let him bring it to the bar of the Commons' House of Parliament with the firm persuasion of having it honestly investigated.' These are the subsidies that I would grant to government."

Such were, indeed, the *subsidia,* the support and strength in the hearts of his people, which the King of England needed. But George III and his counselors at that time looked only to restriction and force. A repeal of the Corporation and Test Acts was not to be thought of (though strenuously urged by Mr. Fox), because Dr. Price and Dr. Priestley, who were leading Dissenters, had been warm friends of the French Revolution. The King would hear nothing of any relief for the Roman Catholics; his coronation oath required him to keep them in perpetual bondage. As to parliamentary reform, Mr. Fox himself, at an earlier period, saw no plan which he thought free from objections; and hence Mr. Moore, and others of his friends, have been led hastily to represent him as a cold, if not a hypocritical advocate of this measure. But from a private letter (see article "Fox," in the Encyclopedia Britannica), it appears that his views at this time experienced a material change. "I think," said he, "we ought to go further toward agreeing with the democratic or popular party than at any former period." Accordingly, in May, 1797, he supported Mr. Grey's motion for reform in a speech (to be found below) of uncommon beauty and force. His great struggle, however, for the rights of the people was somewhat earlier, during the period which has been called (though with some exaggeration) the "Reign of Terror." Lord Loughborough and the other Whigs who seceded to Mr. Pitt had urged the ministry, with the proverbial zeal of new converts, into the most violent measures for putting down political discussion. The Habeas Corpus Act was suspended; the Traitorous Correspondence Bill made it high treason to hold intercourse with the French or supply them with any commodities; the Treasonable Practice Bill was designed to construe into treason a conspiracy to levy war, even without an *overt act* amounting thereto; and the Seditious Meetings' Bill forbade any assembly of more than fifty persons to be held for political purposes without the license of a magistrate. The two bills last mentioned were so hostile to the spirit of a free government that even Lord Thurlow opposed them in the most vehement manner. It was during the discussion of the latter that Mr. Fox made his famous declaration that "if the bill should pass into a law, contrary to the sense and opinion of a great majority of the nation, and if the law, after it was passed, should be executed according to the rigorous provisions of the act, *resistance would not be a question of duty, but of prudence.*"[21]

It was unfortunate for Mr. Fox that he was so often hurried into rash declarations of this kind. Threats are not usually the best mode of defending the cause of freedom. Nor is it true that men, under a representative government, have a right instantly to resist any law which the Legislature have regularly enacted, unless it be one diametrically opposed to the law of God. There is another remedy both in the judiciary and in the popular branch of the government. Mr. Fox's doctrine, that "a law, contrary to the *sense* and *opinion* of the great majority of the nation," may be rightfully resisted, is a species of "nullification" hitherto unknown in America. Another of his hasty expressions did him great injury about three years after. At a dinner of the Whig club in 1798, he gave as a toast, "The *Sovereignty* of the People of Great Britain." Exactly what he meant by this, it is difficult to say. He was a firm friend of the British Constitution, with its three estates of King, Lords, and Commons. He always declared himself to be against a republic, and he could not, therefore, have wished that the functions of sovereignty should be taken from the existing head of the government and conferred on the body of the people or their representatives in Parliament. If he only meant that the King and Lords ought to yield in all cases to the deliberate and well-ascertained wishes of the people (a doubtful doctrine, certainly, in a mixed government), he took a very unfortunate mode of expressing his views. It is not wonderful, at all events, that the King considered it as a personal insult and ordered his name to be struck from the list of Privy Counselors, a step never taken in any other case during his long reign, except in that of Lord George Germaine when convicted of a dereliction of duty, if not of cowardice, at the battle of Minden.

Mr. Pitt's ascendency in the House was now so complete that Mr. Fox had no motive to continue his attendance in Parliament. He therefore withdrew from public business for some years, devoting himself to literary pursuits and the society of his friends. At no time does his character appear in so amiable a point of view. He had gradually worn out his vices. His marriage with Mrs. Armstead, which was announced at a later period, exerted the happiest influence on his character. This was truly, as a friend remarked, the golden season of his life. He devoted much of his time to the study of the classics, and especially of the Greek tragedians. At this time, also, he commenced his work on the Revolution of 1688, which was published after his death.

From this retirement he was temporarily called forth by an occurrence which led to one of the noblest efforts of his eloquence. In December, 1799, Bonaparte was elected First Consul of France for ten years, and the day after his induction into office, he addressed a letter to the King of England in his own hand, making proposals of peace. Mr. Pitt, however, refused even to *treat* with him on the subject. Upon the third of February, 1800, the question came before the House on a motion for approving the course taken by the ministry, and Mr. Fox again appeared in his place. Mr. Pitt, who felt the difficulty of his situation, had prepared himself beforehand with the utmost care. In a speech of five hours long, he went back to the origin of the war, brought up minutely all the atrocities of the Revolution, dwelt on the instability of the successive governments which had marked its progress, commented with terrible severity on the character and crimes of Bonaparte during the preceding four years, and justified on these grounds his backwardness to recognize the new government or to rely on its offers of peace. When he concluded, at four o'clock in the morning, Mr. Fox, who was always most powerful in reply, instantly rose and answered him in a speech of nearly the same length, meeting him on all the main topics with a force of argument, a dexterity in wresting Mr. Pitt's weapons out of his hands and turning them against himself, a keenness of retort, a graphic power of description, and an impetuous flow of eloquence, to which we find no parallel in any of his published speeches. Both these great efforts will be found in this collection, with all the documents which are necessary to a full understanding of the argument. Respecting one topic dwelt upon in these speeches, namely, the *justice* of the war with France, it may be proper to add a few words explanatory of Mr. Fox's views, to be followed by similar statements, on a future page, as to the ground taken by Mr. Pitt.

Mr. Fox held that the grievances complained of by the

English, viz., the opening of the River Scheldt, the French Decree of Fraternity, and the countenance shown to disaffected Englishmen (points to be explained hereafter in notes to these speeches), ought to have been made the subject of full and candid negotiation. England was bound not only to state her wrongs, but to say explicitly what would satisfy her. But Mr. Pitt recalled the English embassador from Paris on the tenth of August, 1792 (when Louis XVI became virtually a prisoner), *before* the occurrence of any of these events. He suspended the functions of M. Chauvelin, the French embassador at London, from the same date. He began to arm immediately after the alleged grievances took place; and when called upon by the French for an explanation of this armament, he declined to acknowledge their agents as having any diplomatic character, so that the points in dispute could not be regularly discussed; and after the execution of Louis XVI, he not only refused to accredit any minister from France, but sent M. Chauvelin out of the kingdom. Mr. Fox maintained that England, under these circumstances, was the aggressor, though the formal declaration of war came from France. He who shuts up the channel of negotiation while disputes are pending is the author of the war which follows. No nation is bound to degrade herself by submitting to any clandestine modes of communication; she is entitled to that open, avowed, and honorable negotiation commonly employed by nations for the pacific adjustment of their disputes. Mr. Fox did not ask the ministry to treat with the new French government as having any existence *de jure*—he expressly waived this—but simply *de facto;* and as the English government had refused this, he held them responsible for the war. Such was his argument, and it was certainly one of great force. It may be true, as alleged by the friends of Mr. Pitt, that the French government were insincere in their offers and explanations; it is highly probable that the enthusiasm awakened by their triumph over their Austrian and Prussian invaders had filled the nation with a love of conquest which would ultimately have led to a war with England. For this very reason, however, the course marked out by Mr. Fox ought to have been studiously followed. But Mr. Pitt shared in the common delusion of the day. He felt certain that France, split up as she was into a thousand factions, could not long endure the contest. "It will be a very short war," said he to a friend, "and certainly ended in one or two campaigns." Mr. Wilberforce, who at this time enjoyed his confidence, while he would not admit that the English were strictly the assailants, says in his Journal, "I had but too much reason to know that the ministry had not taken due pains to prevent its breaking out." As might be expected, Mr. Wilberforce united with Mr. Fox in condemning the refusal of Mr. Pitt to negotiate with Bonaparte.

But Mr. Fox's ardent desires for peace, though disappointed at this time, were soon after gratified by the treaty of Amiens, at the close of 1801. It proved, however, to be a mere truce. War was declared by England May 18th, 1803. To this declaration Mr. Fox was strenuously opposed and made a speech against it, which Lord Brougham refers to as one of his greatest efforts. It does not so appear in any of the reports which have come down to us, and his Lordship perhaps confounded it with the speech of October, 1800, which he does not even mention.

Mr. Pitt, who had been again placed at the head of affairs, died in January, 1806; and Mr. Fox, at the end of twenty-two years, was called into the service of his country as Secretary of Foreign Affairs, on the 5th of February, 1806, through the instrumentality of Lord Grenville. His office was at that time the most important one under the government, and he may be considered as virtually minister. One of his first official acts was that of moving a resolution for an early abolition of the slave trade, which he had from the first united with Mr. Wilberforce in opposing. This resolution was carried by a vote of 114 against 15, and was followed up, the next session, by effectual measures for putting an end to this guilty traffic. He soon after entered on a negotiation for peace with France, which commenced in a somewhat singular manner. A Frenchman made his appearance at the Foreign Office, under the name of De la Grevilliere, and requested a private interview with Mr. Fox. He went on to say that "it was necessary for the tranquillity of all crowned heads to put to death the ruler of France, and that a house had been hired at Passy for this purpose." On hearing these words, Mr. Fox drove him at once from his presence and dispatched a communication to Talleyrand informing him of the facts. "I am not ashamed to confess to you who know me," said he, "that my confusion was extreme at finding myself led into conversation with an avowed assassin. I instantly ordered him to leave me. Our laws do not allow me to detain him, but I shall take care to have him landed at a seaport as remote as possible from France." A reply was sent from Bonaparte, saying, among other things, "I recognize here the principles, honor, and virtue of Mr. Fox. Thank him on my part." In connection with this reply, Talleyrand stated, that the Emperor was ready to negotiate for a peace, "on the basis of the treaty of Amiens." Communications were accordingly opened on the subject, but at this important crisis Mr. Fox's health began to fail him. He had been taken ill some months before in consequence of exposure at the funeral of Lord Nelson, and his physicians now insisted that he should abstain for a time from all public duties. In July the disease was found to be dropsy of the chest, and, after lingering for three months, he died at the house of the Duke of Devonshire, at Chiswick, on the 13th of September, 1806. He was buried with the highest honors of the nation in Westminster Abbey, his grave being directly adjoining the grave of Lord Chatham and close to that of his illustrious rival, William Pitt.[22]

Mr. Fox was the most completely *English* of all the orators in our language. Lord Chatham was formed on the classic model—the express union of force, majesty, and grace. He stood raised above his audience and launched the bolts of his eloquence like the Apollo Belvidere, with the proud consciousness of irresistible might. Mr. Fox stood on the floor of the House like a Norfolkshire farmer in the midst of his fellows: short, thick-set, with his broad shoulders and capacious chest, his bushy hair and eyebrows, and his dark countenance working with emotion, the very image of blunt honesty and strength.

His *understanding* was all English—plain, practical, of prodigious force—always directed to definite ends and objects, under the absolute control of sound common sense. He had that historical cast of mind by which the great English jurists and statesmen have been so generally distinguished. Facts were the staple of his thoughts; all the force of his intellect was exerted on the actual and the positive. He was the most practical speaker of the most practical nation on earth.

His *heart* was English. There is a depth and tenderness of feeling in the national character which is all the greater in a strong mind because custom requires it to be repressed. In private life no one was more guarded in this respect than Mr. Fox; he was the last man to be concerned in getting up a *scene*. But when he stood before an audience, he poured out his feelings with all the simplicity of a child. "I have seen his countenance," says Mr. Godwin, "lighten up with more than mortal ardor and goodness; I have been present when his voice was suffocated with tears." In all this, his powerful understanding went out the whole length of his emotions, so that there was nothing strained or unnatural in his most vehement bursts of passion. "His feeling," says Coleridge, "was all intellect, and his intellect was all feeling." Never was there a finer summing up; it shows us at a glance the whole secret of his power. To this he added the most perfect sincerity and artlessness of manner. His very faults conspired to heighten the conviction of his honesty. His broken sentences, the choking of his voice, his ungainly gestures, his sudden starts of passion, the absolute scream with which he delivered his vehement passages—all showed him to be deeply moved and in earnest, so that it may be doubted whether a more perfect delivery would not have weakened the impression he made.

Sir James Mackintosh has remarked, that "Fox was the most Demosthenean speaker since Demosthenes," while Lord Brougham says, in commenting on this passage, "There never was a greater mistake than the fancying a close resemblance between his eloquence and that of Demosthenes." When two such men differ a point like this, we may safely say that both are in the right and in the wrong. As to certain qualities, Fox was the very reverse of the great Athenian; as to others, they had much in common. In whatever relates to the forms of oratory—symmetry, dignity, grace, the working up of thought and language to their most perfect expression —Mr. Fox was not only inferior to Demosthenes, but wholly unlike him, having no rhetoric and no ideality; while, at the same time, in the structure of his understanding, the modes of its operation, the soul and spirit which breathes throughout his eloquence, there was a striking resemblance. This will appear as we dwell for a moment on his leading peculiarities.

(1) He had a luminous simplicity, which gave his speeches the most absolute unity of impression, however irregular might be their arrangement. No man ever kept the great points of his case more steadily and vividly before the minds of his audience.

(2) He took every thing in the concrete. If he discussed principles, it was always in direct connection with the subject before him. Usually, however, he did not even discuss a subject—he grappled with an antagonist. Nothing gives such life and interest to a speech, or so delights an audience, as a direct contest of man with man.

(3) He struck instantly at the heart of his subject. He was eager to meet his opponent at once on the real points at issue; and the moment of his greatest power was when he stated the argument against himself with more force than his adversary or any other man could give it, and then seized it with the hand of a giant, tore it in pieces, and trampled it under foot.

(4) His mode of enforcing a subject on the minds of his audience was to come back again and again to the strong points of his case. Mr. Pitt *amplified* when he wished to impress, Mr. Fox *repeated*. Demosthenes also repeated, but he had more adroitness in varying the mode of doing it. "Idem haud iisdem verbis."

(5) He had rarely any preconceived method or arrangement of his thoughts. This was one of his greatest faults, in which he differed most from the Athenian artist. If it had not

been for the unity of impression and feeling mentioned above, his strength would have been wasted in disconnected efforts.

(6) Reasoning was his forte and his passion. But he was not a regular reasoner. In his eagerness to press forward, he threw away every thing he could part with and compacted the rest into a single mass. Facts, principles, analogies, were all wrought together like the strands of a cable, and intermingled with wit, ridicule, or impassioned feeling. His arguments were usually personal in their nature, *ad hominem,* &c., and were brought home to his antagonist with stinging severity and force.

(7) He abounded in *hits*—those abrupt and startling turns of thought which rouse an audience, and give them more delight than the loftiest strains of eloquence.

(8) He was equally distinguished for his *side blows,* for keen and pungent remarks flashed out upon his antagonist in passing as he pressed on with his argument.

(9) He was often dramatic, personating the character of his opponents or others, and carrying on a dialogue between them, which added greatly to the liveliness and force of his oratory.

(10) He had astonishing dexterity in evading difficulties, and turning to his own advantage every thing that occurred in debate.

In nearly all these qualities he had a close resemblance to Demosthenes.

In his language, Mr. Fox studied simplicity, strength, and boldness. "Give me an elegant Latin and a homely Saxon word," said he, "and I will always choose the latter." Another of his sayings was this: "Did the speech read well when reported? If so, it was a bad one." These two remarks give us the secret of his style as an orator.

The life of Mr. Fox has this lesson for young men, that early habits of recklessness and vice can hardly fail to destroy the influence of the most splendid abilities and the most humane and generous dispositions. Though thirty-eight years in public life, he was in office only eighteen months.

WILLIAM PITT

WILLIAM PITT, the younger, was born at Hayes, in Kent, on the 28th of May, 1759, and was the second son of Lord Chatham and of Lady Hester Grenville, Countess of Temple. His constitution was so weak from infancy that he was never placed at a public school, but pursued his studies as he was able, from time to time, under a private tutor at his father's residence in the country. After eight years spent in this way, half of which time, however, was lost through ill health, he was sent at the age of fourteen to the University of Cambridge; and so great had been his proficiency, notwithstanding all his disadvantages that, according to his tutor, Dr. Prettyman, afterward Bishop of Lincoln, "in Latin authors he seldom met with difficulty; and it was no uncommon thing for him to read into English six or eight pages of Thucydides which he had not previously seen, without more than two or three mistakes, and sometimes without even one." His ardor of mind and love of study may be inferred from a letter written by his father at this time which gives a beautiful view of the familiarity and affection which always reigned in the intercourse of Lord Chatham with his children. "Though I indulge with inexpressible delight the thought of your returning health, I can not help being a little in pain lest you should make more haste than good speed to be well. You may, indeed, my sweet boy, better than any one practice this sage dictum [festina lentè] without any risk of being *thrown out* (as little James would say) in the chase of learning. All you want at present is *quiet;* with this, if your ardor to excel can be kept in till you are stronger, you will make noise enough.

How happy the task, my noble, amiable boy, to caution you only against pursuing too much all those liberal and praise-worthy things to which less happy natures are perpetually to be spurred and driven! I will not teaze you with too long a lecture in favor of inaction and a competent stupidity—your two best tutors and companions at present. You have time to spare: consider there is but the *Encyclopedia;* and when you have mastered all that, what will remain? You will want, like Alexander, another world to conquer! Your mamma joins me in every word, and we know how much your affectionate mind can sacrifice to our earnest and tender wishes. Vive, vale, is the increasing prayer of your truly loving father. CHATHAM."

But all these cautions were unavailing. His constitution was so frail, and his strength so much reduced by the illness referred to that during the first three years of his college life he was never able to keep his terms with regularity. It was not until the age of eighteen that he gained permanent health, and from that time onward few persons had greater powers of application to the most exhausting study or business. But though his early life at Cambridge seems to have been "one long disease," his quickness and accuracy of thought made up for every deficiency arising from bodily weakness. His whole soul from boyhood had been absorbed in one idea—that of becoming a distinguished orator; and when he heard, at the age of seven, that his father had been raised to the peerage, he instantly exclaimed, "Then I must take his place in the House of Commons." To this point all his efforts were now directed with a zeal and constancy which knew of no limits but the weakness of his frame and which seemed almost to triumph over the infirmities of nature. His studies at the University were continued nearly seven years, though with frequent intervals of residence under his father's roof, and the reader will be interested to know how the greatest of English orators trained his favorite son for the duties of public life.

Three things seem to have occupied his time and attention for many years, viz., the classics, mathematics, and the logic of Aristotle applied to the purposes of debate. His mode of translating the classics to his tutor was a peculiar one. He did not construe an author in the ordinary way, but after reading a passage of some length in the original, he turned it at once into regular English sentences, aiming to give the ideas with great exactness and to express himself, at the same time, with idiomatic accuracy and ease. Such a course was admirably adapted to the formation of an English style, distinguished at once for copiousness, force, and elegance. To this early training Mr. Pitt always ascribed his extraordinary command of language which enabled him to give every idea its most felicitous expression and to pour out an unbroken stream of thought, hour after hour, without once hesitating for a word, or recalling a phrase, or sinking for a moment into looseness or inaccuracy in the structure of his sentences. One of the great English metaphysicians was spoken of by Voltaire as "a reasoning machine," and the mind of Mr. Pitt might, in the same way, be described as a fountain ever flowing forth in clear, expressive, and commanding diction. In most persons, such a mode of translating would have a tendency to draw off the mind from the idiomatic forms of the original to those of our own language, but it was otherwise with him. "He was a nice observer," says Dr. Prettyman, "of the different styles of the authors read, and alive to all their various and characteristic excellences. The quickness of his comprehension did not prevent close and minute application. When alone, he dwelt for hours upon striking passages of an orator or historian, in noticing their turns of expression, marking their manner of arranging a narrative, or of explaining the avowed or secret motives of action. He was in the habit of copying any eloquent passage or any beautiful or forcible expression which occurred in his reading." The poets, in the mean time, had a large share of his attention; his memory was stored with their finest passages; and few men ever introduced a quotation in a more graceful manner, or with a closer adaptation to the circumstances of the case. "So anxious was he to be acquainted with every Greek poet that he read with me," says his tutor, "at his own request, the obscure and generally uninteresting work of Lycophron, and with an ease, at first sight, which if I had not witnessed it, I should have considered beyond the compass of the human intellect. The almost intuitive quickness with which he saw the meaning of the most difficult passages of the most difficult authors made an impression on my mind which time can never efface. I am persuaded that, if a play of Menander or Æschylus, or an ode of Pindar, had been suddenly found, he would have understood it as soon as any professed scholar." Dr. Prettyman adds, that there was scarcely a Greek or Latin classical writer of any eminence, the *whole of whose works* Mr. Pitt had not read to him in this thorough and discriminating manner before the age of twenty.

Mathematics, in the mean time, had its daily share of attention, being regularly intermingled with his classical studies. Here he was equally successful, showing surprising promptitude and acuteness in mastering the greatest difficulties, and especially in solving problems in algebra, trigonometry, &c.—an employment which, though many consider it as dull and useless, is better fitted than almost any mental exercise to give penetration, sagacity, and fixedness of thought, and to establish the habit of never leaving a subject until all its intricacies are fully explored. When we remember the high standard of mathematical study at Cambridge, we learn with surprise that, in addition to all his attainments in the classics, "he was master of *every thing* usually known by young men who obtain the highest academical honors, and felt a great desire to fathom still farther the depths of the pure mathematics." "When the connection of tutor and pupil was about to cease between us," says Dr. Prettyman, "from his entering on the study of the law, he expressed a hope that he should find leisure and opportunity to read Newton's Principia *again* with me after some summer circuit; and, in the later periods of his life, he frequently declared that no portion of his time had been more usefully employed than that which had been devoted to these studies, not merely from the new ideas and actual knowledge thus acquired, but also on account of the improvement which his mind and understanding had received from the habit of close attention and patient investigation."

In regard to dialectics, Dr. Prettyman gives us less information as to the course pursued; but Mr. Pitt being asked by a friend how he had acquired his uncommon talent for *reply,* answered at once that he owed it to the study of Aristotle's Logic in early life and the habit of applying its principles to all the discussions he met with in the works he read and the debates he witnessed. Dr. Prettyman thus describes a mode of studying the classics which opened to Mr. Pitt the widest scope for such an exercise of his powers: "It was a favorite employment with him to compare opposite speeches on the same subject and to examine how each speaker managed his own side of the argument or answered the reasoning of his opponent. This may properly be called a study peculiarly useful to the future lawyer or statesman. The authors whom he preferred for this purpose were Livy, Thucydides, and Sallust. Upon these occasions his observations were often committed to paper and furnished a topic for conversation at our next meeting." But he carried this practice still farther. He spent much of his time at London during the sessions of Parliament, and as he listened to the great speakers of the day, Burke, Fox, Sheridan, and others, he did so, not to throw his mind on the swelling tide of their eloquence, not even to analyze their qualities as orators and catch the excellences of each with a view to his own improvement, but to see how he could *refute* the arguments on the one side, or *strengthen* them on the other, as he differed or agreed with the speakers. It was this practice which enabled him to rise, at the end of a debate of ten or twleve hours extending over a vast variety of topics, and reply to the reasonings of every opponent with such admirable dexterity and force while he confirmed the positions of his friends, and gave a systematic thoroughness to the whole discussion such as few speakers in Parliament have ever been able to attain.

This severe training prepared Mr. Pitt to enter with ease and delight into the abstrusest questions in moral and political science. Locke on the Human Understanding was his favorite author upon the science of mind; he soon mastered Smith's Wealth of Nations, which was first published when he was a member of college; he gave great attention to an able course of lectures by Dr. Halifax on the Civil Law; and, in short, whatever subject he took up, he made it his chief endeavor to be deeply grounded in its *principles,* rather than extensively acquainted with mere details. "Multum haud multa" was his motto in pursuing these inquiries and, indeed, in most of his studies for life. The same maxim gave a direction to his reading in English literature. He had the finest parts of Shakspeare by heart. He read the best historians with great care. Middleton's Life of Cicero and the political and historical writings of Bolingbroke were his favorite models in point of style; he studied Barrow's sermons, by the advice of his father, for copiousness of diction, and was intimately acquainted with the sacred Scriptures, not only as a guide of his faith and practice, but, in the language of Spenser, as the true *"well* of English undefiled."

How far Lord Chatham contributed by direct instruction to form the mind and habits of his son, it is difficult now to say. That he inspired him with his own lofty and generous sentiments; that he set integrity, truth, and public spirit before him as the best means of success even in politics; that he warned him against that fashionable dissipation which has proved the ruin of half the young English nobility; that he made him feel intensely the importance of *character* to a British statesman; that, in short, he pursued a course directly opposite to that of Lord Holland with his favorite son, is obvious from what remains to us of his correspondence and from the results that appear in the early life of Mr. Pitt. But there is no evidence that he took any active part in his intellectual training. Dr. Prettyman says "the *only* wish ever expressed by his Lordship relative to Mr. Pitt's studies was that I would read Polybius with him;" and we should naturally conclude, from the character of Lord Chatham and the confidence he had in the talents and industry of his son, that having settled the general outline of his studies, he left his mind to its own free growth, subject only to those occasional influences which would, of course, be felt when they met in the intervals of collegiate study. Such, at least, is the only inference we can draw from the statements contained in the biographies of the father and the son, from all the letters between them which have come down to us; and especially from the course which Lord Chatham pursued with his favorite nephew, Lord Camelford, as shown in his correspondence afterward published. There must, therefore, have been an entire mistake in the statements of Coleridge on this subject. In a bitter, disparaging sketch of Mr. Pitt, written in early life, under the influence of hostile feelings, he says: "His father's rank, fame, political connections, and parental ambition were his *mold*—he was *cast* rather than *grew*. A palpable election, a conscious predestination controlled the free agency and transfigured the individuality of his mind, and that which he *might* have been was compelled into that which he *was* to be. From his early childhood, it was his father's custom to make him stand upon a chair and declaim before a large company, by which exercise, practiced so frequently, and continued for so many years, he acquired a premature and unnatural dexterity in the combination of words, which must, of necessity, have diverted his attention from present objects, obscured his impressions, and deadened his genuine feelings." This story of his declaiming from a chair is not alluded to either by Dr. Prettyman in his Life of Mr. Pitt, or by Mr. Thackeray in his Memoirs of Lord Chatham. That the boy sometimes *recited* the speeches of others in a circle of family friends is not improbable, for it was at that time a very common practice in England; but if Coleridge meant that Lord Chatham set a child, under fourteen years of age, to "declaim," or make speeches *of his own,* "before a large company," and that Mr. Pitt thus "acquired a premature and unnatural dexterity in the combination of words," productive of all the evils stated, it is what few men would believe, except from a desire to make out some favorite theory.[1] Mr. Coleridge's theory (for he could do nothing without one) was intended to *run down* Mr. Pitt as having "an education of words," which "destroys genius;" as "a being who had no feelings connected with man or nature, no spontaneous impulses, no unbiased and desultory studies, nothing that constitutes individualty of intellect, nothing that teaches brotherhood or affection." So much for theory; we may learn the *fact* from the testimony of his tutor and of his most intimate companions. Dr. Prettyman says: "Mr. Pitt now began [at the age of sixteen] to mix with other young men of his own age and station in life then resident in Cambridge, and no one was ever more admired and beloved by his acquaintances and friends. He was always the same person in company, abounding in playful and quick repartee." Mr. Wilberforce, who became his most intimate friend at the age of twenty, remarks: "He was the wittiest man I ever knew, and, what was quite peculiar to himself, had at all times his wit under entire control. Others appeared struck by the unwonted association of brilliant images; but every possible combination of ideas seemed always present to his mind, and he could at once produce whatever he desired. I was one of those who met to spend an evening in memory of Shakspeare, at the Boar's Head, East Cheap. Many professed wits were present, but Pitt was the most amusing of the party and the readiest and most apt in the required allusions. He entered with the same energy into all our different amusements."

The truth is, Mr. Pitt had by nature a mind of such peculiar and unyielding materials that Lord Chatham would have been wholly unable (whatever might be his wishes) to mold or fashion it after any preconceived model of his own. With some general resemblance in a few points, it has rarely happened in the case of two individuals so highly gifted and placed in such similar circumstances, that a son has been so entirely unlike a father in all the leading traits of his intellectual character. It may interest the reader to dwell for a moment on some of the differences between them, before we follow Mr. Pitt into the scenes of public life. Lord Chatham, with all his splendid abilities, was still pre-eminently a man of feeling and impulse, governed by the suggestions of an ardent imagination, hasty in his resolves, wanting in self-command, irregular and often changeable in his plans and purposes. Mr. Pitt, with all his burning energy, was equally the man of *intellect,* deficient in imagination, gifted with extraordinary powers of abstract reasoning, having all his faculties brought into complete subjection to his will; so wary and circumspect in the midst of his boldest schemes that Mr. Fox declared "he had never caught him tripping in a single instance" during a twenty years' contest; inflexible in his determinations, regular and symmetrical in the entire structure of his character. Both were lofty and assuming, but these qualities in Lord Chatham were connected with a love of display, with ceremonious manners notwithstanding the warmth of his affections, and a singular delight in the forms of office and state; while Mr. Pitt had the severe simplicity of one of the early Romans, with a coldness of address, as he advanced in life, which was repulsive to every one except his most intimate friends. Lord Chatham loved fame and was influenced more than he would have been willing to acknowledge by a desire for popularity and a regard to the opinion of others. Mr. Pitt loved power: he cared but little for office except as it gave him command over others. Without a particle of vanity, he had excessive pride; he despised popularity and looked with contempt on the vulgar, "among whom he included a large proportion of the peerage and commonalty of England." Mr. Pitt had less genius than his father, but greater strength of mind; and while the one swayed the feelings of his countrymen by the vehemence of his own, the other guided their wills and formed their purposes by the intense energy of his understanding.

Mr. Pitt lost his father in 1778, and being left in straitened circumstances, applied himself to the law as affording the most direct means of support and was called to the bar on the 12th of June, 1780. He rode the western circuit during that and the next year, having causes put occasionally into his hands which he managed with great skill and success, especially one which he argued before Judge Buller in a manner that awakened the admiration of the bar and another before Lord Mansfield, on granting the writ of *habeas corpus* to a man charged with murder, in which he received the warmest applause from that distinguished jurist. He was a favorite with his brethren of the circuit, one of whom remarks: "Among the lively men of his own time of life, Pitt was always the most animated and convivial in the many hours of leisure which occur to young men on circuit. He joined all the little excursions to Southampton, Weymouth, and such parties of amusement as were habitually formed. He was extremely popular. His name and reputation for high acquirements at the University commanded the attention of his seniors. His wit and good humor endeared him to the younger part of the bar. After he became minister he continued to ask his old circuit intimates to dine with him, and his manners remained unchanged."

In January, 1781, he was returned as member of Parliament from Appleby, a borough belonging to Sir James Lowther. He immediately joined the Opposition under Burke and Fox, at a time when Lord North, besides the revolt of the American colonies, was engaged in a war with France, Spain, and Holland. His maiden speech was delivered on the twenty-sixth of the next month and, being wholly unpremeditated, gave a surprising exhibition of the readiness and fertility of his mind. One of Mr. Burke's bills on Economical Reform was under debate, and when Lord Nugent rose to oppose it, Mr. Byng, a member from Middlesex, asked Mr. Pitt to come forward in reply. He partly assented, but afterward changed his mind and determined not to speak. Byng, who understood him otherwise, the moment Lord Nugent sat down, called out "Pitt, Pitt," and the cry at once became general throughout the House. At first he declined; but finding that the House were bent on hearing him, he rose with entire self-possession, took up the argument with all the dexterity and force of a practiced debater, and threw over the whole a glow, an elegance, a richness of thought and fervor of emotion which called forth a round of applause from every quarter of the House. Burke took him by the hand, declaring that he was "not merely a chip of the old block, but the old block itself." Fox carried him to Brookes' when the House adjourned and had him enrolled among the *élite* of the Whigs; and the nation felt that the mantle had fallen upon one who was already qualified to go forth in "the spirit and power" of his illustrious predecessor. He spoke but twice that session, and at the close of it, as some one was remarking "Pitt promises to be one of the first speakers that was ever heard in Parliament," Mr. Fox, who was passing at the moment, turned instantly round and replied, *"He is so al-*

ready." Thus, at the age of twenty-two, when most men are yet in the rudiments of political science and just commencing their first essays in oratory, he placed himself at a single bound in the foremost rank of English statesmen and orators at the proudest era of English eloquence. What is still more wonderful, he became, not by slow degrees like Mr. Fox, but, as it were, by "inspiration" (in the language of Lord Brougham), one of the most accomplished *debaters* in the British Parliament.

At the next session, commencing in November, 1781, Mr. Pitt entered into debate on the broadest scale and made the most strenuous exertions to put an end to the American war. The defeat of Cornwallis had rendered the contest absolutely hopeless, and he denounced it as one which "wasted the blood and treasure of the kingdom without even a rational object." But he avoided the error of Fox; he made no personal attack on the King. With that forecast which marked all his actions, in opposing the favorite measure of his sovereign he did nothing to wound his pride or to rouse his resentment. He put the responsibility on his ministers, where the Constitution rests it, and inveighed against them as men, "who, by their fatal system, had led the country, step by step, to the most calamitous and disgraceful situation to which a once flourishing and glorious empire could possibly be reduced—a situation which threatened the final *dissolution* of the state if not prevented by timely, wise, and vigorous efforts." A few days after, he again called forth a burst of admiration by one of those classical allusions, united to the keenest sarcasm, with which his early productions were so often adorned. In a speech on the army estimates, while commenting with great severity on a contradiction in the statements of Lord North and Lord George Germaine, he saw the two (who were seated near each other) conversing with great earnestness, while Welbore Ellis, Treasurer of the Navy, was interposing between them as if to impart some seasonable information. Stopping in the middle of a sentence and turning the eyes of the whole House upon the group, he said, in a significant tone, "I will *pause* until the Nestor of the Treasury Bench shall settle the difference between Agamemnon and Achilles." The suddenness of the stroke and the idea especially of making Lord George an *Achilles* after the part he acted at the battle of Minden, produced a roar of laughter throughout the House which was instantly followed by a tumult of applause. It was by such means that Mr. Pitt always took care to repress any disposition to treat his remarks with levity or disrespect.

At the end of a few weeks, Lord North was driven from office and the Rockingham administration came into power, March 28, 1782, with Mr. Fox and Lord Shelburne as principal secretaries of state. Various stations, and among them one of great emolument, the vice-treasurership of Ireland, were offered Mr. Pitt, but he declined them all, having resolved, with that lofty feeling which always marked his character, never to take office until he could come in at once as a member of the cabinet.

The Rockingham ministry was terminated by the death of its chief at the end of thirteen weeks. Lord Shelburne succeeded, and with him brought in Mr. Pitt as Chancellor of the Exchequer and leader of the House of Commons. Such an event had never beforc happened in the history of English politics. The conduct of the entire finances of the empire had hitherto been reserved for men of tried experience. Godolphin, Oxford, Walpole, Pelham, Grenville, Townsend, and North, had risen by slow degrees to this weighty and responsible office. Mr. Pitt alone received it at once without passing through any subordinate station, at the age of *twenty-three,* and the country hailed him with joy as worthy to take his father's place in the management of the highest concerns of the empire. Lord Shelburne now made peace (Novem. 30, 1782), on terms quite as favorable as could have been expected after the disgraceful results of Lord North's contest with America and France. But it was already obvious that his Lordship, though head of the government, was not master of the House of Commons. Mr. Fox, who had seceded when the new ministry came in, held the balance of power between them and Lord North: some union of parties was, therefore, indispensable, or the government could not go on, and Mr. Pitt was commissioned to negotiate with Mr. Fox for a return to power. Their interview was short. Fox instantly demanded whether, under the proposed arrangement, Lord Shelburne was still to remain prime minister. Pitt replied that nothing else had ever been contemplated. "I can not," said Fox, warmly, "ever consent to hold office under his Lordship." "And I certainly have not come here," replied Pitt, "to *betray* Lord Shelburne." They parted and never again met under a private roof. From the entire contrariety of their habits and feelings, they could never have acted except as political opponents. Fox now united with Lord North and voted down the ministry, as already mentioned, on the 17th of February, 1783. Four days after, Lord John Cavendish followed up the blow by moving a resolution involving a severe censure upon ministers for the terms on which they had concluded peace. The debate was a long one, and Mr. Fox reserved himself for the close of the evening, obviously intending to overwhelm his young antagonist and put an end to the discussion by the force and severity of his remarks.[2] The moment he sat down, Mr. Pitt rose, to the surprise of all, and grappled at once in argument with "the most accomplished debater the world ever saw." Though imperfectly reported, his speech contains passages which he never surpassed in his long and brilliant career of eloquence. Some of them will here be given, and the reader can not fail to admire the dignity with which he faces his opponent, the compact energy of his defense touching the concessions made in the treaty, and the lofty spirit of self-assertion with which he turns back the assault of Mr. Fox, and vindicates his conduct and his motives.

Sir, revering as I do the great abilities of the honorable gentleman who spoke last, I lament, in common with the House, when those abilities are misemployed, as on the present question, to inflame the imagination and mislead the judgment. I am told, sir, 'he does not envy me the triumph of my situation on this day,' a sort of language which becomes the *candor* of that honorable gentleman as ill as his *present* principles. The triumphs of party, sir, with which this self-appointed minister seems so highly elate, shall never seduce *me* into any inconsistency which the busiest suspicion shall presume to glance at. *I* will never engage in political enmities without a public cause! I will never forego such enmities without the public approbation; nor will *I* be *questioned* and *cast off* in the face of this House *by one virtuous and dissatisfied friend!*[3] These, sir, the sober and durable triumphs of reason over the weak and profligate inconsistencies of party violence; these, sir, the steady triumphs of virtue over success itself, shall be mine, not only in my present situation, but through every future condition of my life—triumphs which no length of time shall diminish, which no change of principle shall ever sully.

Having dwelt at large on the disgraces and dangers of the country at the close of the American war, Mr. Pitt now asks, "Could Lord Shelburne, thus surrounded with scenes of ruin, affect to *dictate* the terms of peace? Are these articles seriously compared with those of the peace of Paris in 1763?" This leads him to speak of the elevated position in which the country was at that time left by his father, and from this he passes to defend the concessions made by Lord Shelburne.

I feel, sir, at this instant, how much I have been animated in my childhood by the recital of England's victories. I was taught, sir, by one whose memory I shall ever revere, that at the close of a war far different, indeed, from this, she had dictated the terms of peace to submissive nations. This, in which I have something more than a common interest, was the memorable era of England's glory. But that era has passed; she is under the awful and mortifying necessity of employing a language which corresponds to her true condition: the visions of her power and pre-eminence are passed away.

We have acknowledged American independence. That, sir, was a needless form: the incapacity of the noble Lord North]; the events of war; and even a vote of this House, had already granted what it was impossible to withhold.

We have ceded Florida. We have obtained Providence and the Bahama Islands.

We have ceded an extent of fishery on the coast of Newfoundland. We have established an extensive right to the most valuable banks.

We have restored St. Lucia and given up Tobago. We have regained Grenada, Dominica, St. Kitts, Nevis, and

Montserrat, and have wrested Jamaica from her impending danger. In Africa we have ceded Goree, the grave of our countrymen; and we possess Senegambia, the best and most healthy settlement.

We have likewise permitted his most Christian Majesty to repair his harbor of Dunkirk. The humiliating clause for its destruction was inserted, sir, after *other* wars than the past; and the immense expense attending its repair will still render the indulgence of no value to the French.

In the East Indies, where alone we had power to dictate the terms of peace, we have restored what was useless to ourselves, and scarcely tenable in a continuance of the war.

But we have abandoned the American Loyalists to their implacable enemies. Little, sir, are those unhappy men befriended by such language in this House; nor shall we give much assistance to their cause, or add stability to the reciprocal confidence of the two states, if we already impute to Congress a violence and injustice which decency forbids us to suspect. Would a continuance of the war have been justified on the single principle of assisting these unfortunate men? or would a continuance of the war, if so justified, have procured them a more certain indemnity? Their hopes must have been rendered desperate, indeed, by any additional distresses of Britain; those hopes which are now revived by the timely aid of peace and reconciliation.

These are the ruinous conditions to which this country, engaged with four powerful states and exhausted in all its resources, thought fit to subscribe for the dissolution of that alliance and the immediate enjoyment of peace. Let us examine what is left with a manly and determined courage. Let us strengthen ourselves against inveterate enemies and reconciliate our ancient friends. *The misfortunes of individuals and of kingdoms, when laid open and examined with true wisdom, are more than half redressed;* and to this great object should be directed all the virtue and abilities of this House. Let us feel our calamities—let us bear them, too, like men!

But, sir, I fear I have too long engaged your attention to no real purpose, and that the public safety is this day risked, without a blush, by the malice and disappointment of faction. The honorable gentleman who spoke last [Mr. Fox] has declared, with that sort of consistency that marks his conduct, 'Because he is prevented from *prosecuting* the

> noble Lord in the blue ribbon [Lord North] to the satisfaction of public justice, he will heartily *embrace* him as his friend.' So readily does he reconcile extremes, and love the man whom he wishes to prosecute! With the same spirit, sir, I suppose he will cherish this peace, too—*because he abhors it!*

We have here another instance of that keen and polished sarcasm which Mr. Pitt had more perfectly at command than any orator in our language and which enabled him, as Charles Butler remarks, "to inflict a wound, even in a single member of a sentence, that could never be healed." From this passing notice of Mr. Fox, he turns to Lord Shelburne, for whom he had a personal attachment as a friend and adherent of his father, and bestows upon him the following splendid eulogium:

> This noble Earl, like every other person eminent for ability and acting in the first department of a great state, is undoubtedly an object of envy to some, as well as of admiration to others. The obloquy to which his capacity and situation have raised him has been created and circulated with equal meanness and address; but his merits are as much above my panegyric, as the arts to which he owes his defamation are beneath my attention. When, stripped of his power and emoluments, he once more descends to private life without the invidious appendages of place, men will see him through a different medium and perceive in him qualities which richly entitle him to their esteem. That official superiority which at present irritates their feelings, and that capacity of conferring good offices on those he prefers, which all men are fond of possessing, will not then be any obstacle to their making an impartial estimate of his character. But notwithstanding a sincere predilection for this nobleman, whom I am bound by every tie to treat with sentiments of deference and regard, I am far from wishing him retained in power against the public approbation; and if his removal can be innocently effected, if he can be compelled to resign without entailing all those mischiefs which seem to be involved in the resolution now moved, great as his zeal for his country is, powerful as his abilities are, and earnest and assiduous as his endeavors have been to rescue

the British empire from the difficulties that oppress her, I am persuaded he will retire, firm in the dignity of his own mind, conscious of his having contributed to the public advantage, and, if not attended with the fulsome plaudits of a mob, possessed of that substantial and permanent satisfaction which arises from the habitual approbation of an upright mind. I know him well; and dismiss him from the confidence of his sovereign and the business of the state when you please, to this transcendent consolation he has a title, which no accident can invalidate or affect. It is the glorious reward of doing well, of acting an honest and honorable part. By the difficulties he encountered on his accepting the reins of government, by the reduced state in which he found the nation, and by the perpetual turbulence of those who thought his elevation effected at their own expense, he has certainly earned it dearly; and with such a solid understanding, and so much goodness of heart as stamp his character, he is in no danger of losing it.

Mr. Pitt next took up the Coalition, which had not yet assumed any definite shape, and delighted the House with one of those sudden *hits* as to its going on to be consummated, which have always so peculiar a power in a large and promiscuous assembly.

I repeat it, sir, it is not this treaty, it is the Earl of Shelburne alone whom the movers of this question are desirous to wound. This is the object which has raised this storm of faction; this is the aim of the unnatural Coalition to which I have alluded. If, however, the baneful alliance is not already formed—if this ill-omened marriage is not already solemnized, I know *a just and lawful impediment*—and, in the name of the public safety, I HERE FORBID THE BANS!

Pausing for a moment during the applause which followed this bold image, he then addressed himself to Mr. Fox with a proud consciousness of integrity, glancing at the same time at the supposed motives of those, lately the bitterest enemies, who were now transformed into bosom friends.

My own share in the censure, pointed by the motion before the House against his Majesty's ministers, I will bear with fortitude, because my own heart tells me I have not acted wrong. To this monitor, which never did, and, I trust, never will deceive me, I shall confidently repair, as to an adequate asylum from all clamor which interested faction can raise. I was not very eager to come in, and shall have no great reluctance to go out, whenever the public are disposed to dismiss me from their service. It has been the great object of my short official existence to do the duties of my station with all the ability and address in my power, and with a fidelity and honor which should bear me up and give me confidence under every possible contingency or disappointment. I can say, with sincerity, I never had a wish which did not terminate in the dearest interests of the nation. I will, at the same time, imitate the honorable gentleman's candor, and confess that I too have my ambition. High situation and great influence are desirable objects to most men, and objects which I am not ashamed to pursue—which I am even solicitous to possess, whenever they can be acquired with honor and retained with dignity. On these conditions, I am not less ambitious to be great and powerful than it is natural for a young man, with such brilliant examples before him, to be. But even these objects I am not beneath relinquishing, the moment my duty to my country, my character, and my friends, renders such a sacrifice indispensable. Then I hope to retire, not disappointed, but triumphant; triumphant in the conviction that my talents, humble as they are, have been earnestly, zealously, and strenuously employed, to the best of my apprehension, in promoting the truest welfare of my country; and that, however I may stand chargeable with weakness of understanding or error of judgment, nothing can be imputed to me in my official capacity which bears the most distant connection with an interested, a corrupt, or a dishonest intention.

But it is not any part of my plan, when the time shall come that I quit my present station, to threaten the repose of my country, and erect, like the honorable gentleman, *a fortress and a refuge for disappointed ambition.* The self-created and self-appointed successors to the present administration have asserted, with much confidence, that this is likely to be the case. I can assure them, however, when they come from that side of the House to this, I will for one most cordially accept the exchange. The only desire I would indulge and cherish on the subject, is that the service of the public may be ably, disinterestedly, and faithfully performed. To those who feel for their country as I wish to do, and will strive to do, it matters little who are out or in; but it matters much that her affairs be conducted with wisdom, with firmness, with dignity, and with credit. Those intrusted to my care I shall resign, let me hope, into hands much better qualified to do them justice than mine. But I will not mimic the parade of the honorable gentleman in avowing an indiscriminate opposition to whoever may be appointed to succeed. I will march out with no warlike, no hostile, no menacing protestations; but hoping the new administration will have no other object in view than the real and substantial welfare of the community at large; that they will bring with them into office those truly public and patriotic principles which they formerly held, but which they abandoned in opposition; that they will save the state, and promote the great purposes of public good, with as much steadiness, integrity, and solid advantage as I am confident it must one day appear the Earl of Shelburne and his colleagues have done. I promise them, beforehand, my uniform and best support on every occasion where I can honestly and conscientiously assist them.

He had now carried the House to the utmost point of interest and expectation. Something more directly relating to himself was obviously yet to come; and it is not wonderful that the ablest of the eloquent men before him, when they saw the perilous height to which he had raised his audience, felt he could never descend to his own personal concerns without producing in the minds of his hearers a painful shock and revulsion of feeling. But no, his crowning triumph was yet to come.

Unused as I am to the factions and jarring clamors of this day's debate, I look up to the independent part of the House, and to the public at large, if not for that impartial approbation which my conduct deserves, at least for that acquittal from blame to which my innocence entitles me. My earliest impressions were in favor of the noblest and most disinterested modes of serving the public: these impressions are still dear, and will, I hope, remain forever dear to my heart: I will cherish them as a legacy infinitely more valuable than the greatest inheritance. On these principles alone I came into Parliament, and into place; and I now take the whole House to witness, that *I* have not been under the necessity of *contradicting one public declaration I have ever made.*[4]

I am, notwithstanding, at the disposal of this House, and with their decision, whatever it shall be, I will cheerfully comply. It is impossible to deprive me of those feelings which must always result from the sincerity of my best endeavors to fulfill with integrity every official engagement. You may take from me, sir, the privileges and emoluments of place, but you can not, and you shall not, take from me those habitual and warm regards for the prosperity of Great Britain, which constitute the honor, the happiness, the pride of my life, and which, I trust, death alone can extinguish. And, with this consolation, the loss of power, sir, and the loss of fortune, though I affect not to despise them, I hope I soon shall be able to forget.

Here he went on to quote the beautiful lines of Horace in respect to Fortune (Odes, book iii. Ode 29, line 53–6):

> Laudo manentem; si celeres quatit
> Pennas, resigno quæ dedit—

when the thought struck him that the next words, *"et mea virtute me involvo,"* would appear unbecoming if taken (as they might be) for a compliment to himself. Mr. Wraxall, who was present, describes him as instantly casting his eyes upon the floor, while a momentary silence elapsed which turned upon him the attention of the whole House. He drew his handkerchief from his pocket, passed it over his lips, and then, recovering as it were from his temporary embarrassment, he struck his hand with great force upon the table and finished the sentence in the most emphatic manner, omitting the words referred to:

> Laudo manentem; si celeres quatit
> Pennas, resigno quæ dedit, [*et mea*
> *Virtute me involvo*] probamque
> Pauperiem sine dote quæro.[5]

"The effect was electric, and the cheers with which his friends greeted him as he sat down were followed with that peculiar kind of buzz which is a higher testimony to oratorical merit than the noisier manifestations of applause."[6]

Lord North, in following Mr. Pitt that night, spoke of his eloquence as "amazing," and added, "It is no small presumption of my innocence that I could hear his thunder without being dismayed, and even listen to it with a mixture of astonishment and delight."[7] But the Coalition was too strong to be dissolved. The vote of censure was passed by a majority of seventeen, and the Earl of Shelburne resigned.

The King now sent for Mr. Pitt and urged him, in the most pressing terms, to accept the office of prime minister; but, with that strength of judgment which never deserted him in the most flattering or the most adverse circumstances, he steadfastly rejected the offer, satisfied that it would be impossible to resist the combined force of Lord North and Mr. Fox in the House. To gratify the King, however, while endeavoring to form a ministry to his mind, Mr. Pitt remained in office for six weeks, carrying on the government with a dignity of deportment and an ease and dexterity in the dispatch of business which excited the admiration of all and produced the frequent remark, "there is no need of a ministry while Mr. Pitt is here." In the mean time, the King, though urged by repeated addresses from the House, continued to shrink back from the Coalition, and it is now known that he seriously meditated a retirement to Hanover as the only means of relief from the painful situation to which he was reduced. It was Thurlow that deterred him from so hazardous a step. "Your Majesty may go to your Electoral dominions," said the Chancellor, bluntly; "nothing is easier; but you may not find it so easy to return when you grow tired of staying there. James II did the same; *your Majesty must not follow his example.*" He therefore advised the King to submit with patience, assuring him that the Coalition could not remain long in power without committing some error which would lay them open to successful attack. The King saw the wisdom of his advice. He permitted the Coalition ministry to be formed, April 2, 1783, but with an express reservation that he was to be understood as no way concerned in their measures.

Soon after the close of this session, Mr. Pitt visited France in company with Mr. Wilberforce and spent some months in studying the institutions of the country. He was treated with great distinction; and, as Mr. Wilberforce states, "it was hinted to him, through the intervention of Horace Walpole, that he would be an acceptable suitor for the daughter of the celebrated Necker, afterward Madame De Staël. Necker is said to have offered to endow her with a fortune of £14,000 a year." But he declined the proposal and remained unmarried to the end of life.[8] With all the diversity of his powers, there were two characters which Mr. Pitt would have been quite unable to sustain—to play the part of the lover or the husband would have been equally beyond his reach.

The measure foretold by Thurlow came earlier than was expected. During the first week of the next session (November 18th, 1783), Mr. Fox brought forward his *East India Bill.* In opposing this scheme, Mr. Pitt spoke the sentiments of most men in the kingdom. The firmest Whigs, like Lord Camden, the most strenuous enemies of oppression, like Wilberforce, united with the supporters of the Crown and the entire moneyed interest of the country to denounce it in the strongest terms. There were two features which exposed the bill to this general reprobation. First, it put the civil and military government of India in the hands of Commissioners, appointed, not, as usual in such cases, by the Crown, but by Parliament. Considering the manner in which Fox came into office, this was calculated to awaken the very worst suspicions. It looked like a direct defiance of the sovereign—like a determination on the part of the Coalitionists to make use betimes of their ascendency in Parliament and establish themselves so firmly in power through this immense increase of patronage that the King would be unable to remove them. As already stated in the memoir of Mr. Fox, few men at the present day believe he had any such scheme of desperate ambition. He was actuated, there is reason to think, by humane sentiment. He did not mean to have his plan crippled in its execution by the personal animosity of the King, and he therefore gave to Parliament the *first* appointment of the Commissioners for four years;

and while he expected, no doubt, to add greatly to the strength of his administration by these means, the idea of his aiming at an *imperium in imperio,* or "a perpetual dictatorship" over England, is now generally discarded. Still, the jealousy which prevailed was perfectly natural. Mr. Fox had made it for himself, and Mr. Pitt used it against him only as the best men in the kingdom believed it to be founded in truth. Secondly, the bill stripped the Company of all their commercial rights and placed their property in the hands of another board of Commissioners. This was a much more doubtful measure. "It was tantamount," as Lord Camden truly said, "to a commission of bankruptcy or a commission of lunacy against them; it pronounced them to be unable to proceed in their trade, either from want of property or from want of mental capacity." Nothing could justify it but the extremest necessity; and though Mr. Fox was convinced of that necessity, he ought, in prudence at least, to have delayed such a measure until the other part of his plan had been tried; until experience had shown that the abuses in India were incapable of redress by a change of its civil and military government—that the Company were fit only to be treated as bankrupts or lunatics. It is unnecessary to dwell on the means by which the East India Bill was defeated and the Coalition ministry driven from power. They have been detailed in the memoir of Mr. Fox. What share Mr. Pitt had in Lord Temple's communications with the King has never been made known; but the course taken was regarded by all concerned as an extreme measure on the part of the Crown to repel an extreme measure of Mr. Fox which endangered the rights of the King and the balance of the Constitution. The great body of the people gave it their sanction and rejoiced in a step which they would have resisted, in almost any other case, as an invasion of their rights.

Mr. Pitt now came in as Prime Minister at the age of *twenty-four* (December 22d, 1783), under circumstances wholly without precedent in the history of English politics. Against him was arrayed an overwhelming majority in the House, led on by the most eloquent men of the age, inflamed by a sense of injury and disappointed ambition. So hopeless did his prospect appear, that a motion for a new writ to fill his place for the borough of Appleby was received with a general shout of laughter. In the contest which followed and which turned the eyes of the whole empire on the House of Commons for nearly three months, the young minister's situation was not only trying beyond measure in a political point of view, but, as Wraxall observes, "appeared at times to be not wholly exempt from personal danger. Fox might be said, without exaggeration, to hold suspended over his head the severest marks of the indignation of the offended House. His removal from the King's presence and councils as an enemy of his country—his impeachment or his commitment to the Tower—any or all of these propositions might, nay, might *certainly* have been carried in moments of effervescence, when the passions of a popular assembly inflamed by such a conductor as Fox seemed to be ripe for any acts of violence."[9] Under these circumstances, Mr. Pitt displayed a presence of mind, a skill and boldness in repelling attack, a dexterity in turning the weapons of his adversaries against themselves, and making the violence of their assault the very means of their final discomfiture, which we can not even now contemplate, as remote spectators of the scene, without wonder and admiration. Mr. Fox's first step was to demand, rather than request of the King, that Parliament should not be *dissolved,* intimating, in his speech on the subject that it would not be safe to adopt such a measure "merely to suit the convenience of an ambitious young man." Mr. Pitt, who had wisely determined to fight the battle for a new Parliament *in* and *through* the present House, replied by a friend (for he had not yet been re-elected as a member) that he had no designs of this sort and "that if any idea of proroguing or dissolving Parliament should be entertained *any where,* Mr. Pitt would instantly resign." To make himself still more sure, Mr. Fox next moved a resolution, declaring "the payment of any public money for services, voted in the present session, after Parliament should be prorogued or dissolved (if such events should take place before an act should have passed appropriating the supplies for such services), to be a high crime and misdemeanor." To this Mr. Pitt made no objection, and the motion was carried by general consent. These things combined brought Mr. Pitt apparently to the feet of Mr. Fox. The majority were not to be broken down by a new election, and if they stopped the supplies, he had no longer the resource of proroguing Parliament and using the money on hand as absolutely *necessary* for continuing the government: he must resign, or bring the country at once into a state of anarchy. So certain did Mr. Fox consider the result that he said on the floor of the House, "To talk of the permanency of such an administration would be only *laughing at and insulting them;*" and at the close of the same speech, he spoke of "the *youth* of the Chancellor of the Exchequer, and the *weakness* incident to his early period of life, as the only possible excuse for his temerity!"

The Mutiny Bill had been already delayed by Mr. Fox for a month, and the same decisive step was soon after taken with the supplies. Mr. Pitt was thus distinctly warned of the inevitable consequences of his persisting in a refusal to resign, while he was insulted for many weeks by one resolution after another, passed by large majorities, reflecting in the severest terms on the means by which he had gained power and declaring that his ministry did not possess the confidence of the House or the country. As to the first point, he repelled with indignation the charge of having come into office by indirect or unworthy means. "I declare," said he, "that I came up no *back stairs*. When my Sovereign was pleased to send for me, in order to know whether I would accept of employment, I was compelled to go to the royal closet; *but I know of no secret influence!* My own integrity forms my protection against such a concealed agent, and whenever I discover it, the House may rest assured I will not remain one hour in the cabinet! I will neither have the *meanness* to act upon advice given by others, nor the *hypocrisy* to pretend, when the measures of an administration in which I occupy a place are censured, that they were not of my advising. If any *former* ministers are hurt by these charges, *to them be the sting!*[10] Little did I conceive that I should ever be accused within these walls as the abettor or the tool of secret influence! The nature and the singularity of the imputation only render it the more contemptible. This is the sole reply that I shall ever deign to make. The probity and rectitude of my private, as well as of my public principles, will ever constitute my sources of action. I never will be responsible for measures not my own, nor condescend to become the instrument of any secret advisers whatever. With respect to the questions put to me on the subject of a dissolution of Parliament, it does not become me to comment on the expressions composing the gracious answer of the sovereign, delivered by him from the Throne. Neither will I compromise the royal prerogative, nor bargain it away in the House of Commons!"

The King, whose residence was then at Windsor, waited with deep emotion for a daily account of the conflict going on in the House; and such was his anxiety during part of the time that *hourly* expresses were sent him with a report of the debates. It was, indeed, more his battle than that of the ministry. His correspondence shows that he had resolved to stake every thing on the firmness of Mr. Pitt. His honor as a sovereign forbade the thought of his receiving back Lord North and Mr. Fox, after the means they were using to force themselves again into power: if Mr. Pitt sunk in the conflict, it was the King's determination to sink with him. After a night of the greatest disaster, when the ministry had been five times beaten—twice on questions directly involving their continuance in office—his Majesty wrote to Mr. Pitt in the following terms: "As to myself, I am perfectly composed, as I have the self-satisfaction of feeling that I have done my duty. Though I think Mr. Pitt's day will be fully taken up in considering with the other ministers what measures are best to be adopted in the present crisis, yet, that no delay may arise from my absence, I shall dine in town and consequently be ready to see him in the evening, if he should think that would be of utility. At all events, I am ready to take any step that may be proposed to oppose this faction and to struggle to the last period of my life. But I can never submit to throw myself into its power. If they at the end succeed, *my line is a clear one, and to which I have fortitude enough to submit.*" These words, pointing directly to a withdrawal from England (with the case of James II in full view), if not to consequences even more fatal, must have wrought powerfully on the mind of Mr. Pitt. It was not merely his love of office or scorn of being beaten that nerved him with such energy for the conflict; it was sympathy and respect for his Sovereign and the hope of averting those terrible civil commotions which seemed inevitable if Mr. Fox, at the head of the Commons, drove the King, supported by the nobility, into the desperate measure contemplated.[11]

As the contest went on, Mr. Pitt having been beaten on an East India Bill which he introduced, Mr. Fox moved the same night for leave to bring in another of his own, which he declared to be the same as his former one in all its essential principles. He then turned to Mr. Pitt and demanded to know whether the King would dissolve Parliament to prevent the passing of such a bill. All eyes were turned to the treasury bench, and a scene ensued of the most exciting nature. "Mr. Pitt," says the Parliamentary History, *"sat still* —the members on all sides calling upon him in vain to rise."[12] Sir Grey Cooper then broke out into some very severe remarks and closed with saying that if the gentleman persisted in his silence, the House ought "to *come to a resolution*" on the subject. "On Mr. Pitt's sitting still, the cry was very loud of *Move, move!*" calling on Sir Grey to bring forward a resolution. Mr. Fox then made some very cutting observations on "the sulky silence of the gentleman," his treating the House with so little decency," &c., when "the House still called most vehemently on Mr. Pitt to rise." General Conway now came out with great warmth and attacked the character and motives of ministers in the bitterest terms, declaring that "the present ministry, originating in darkness and secrecy, maintained themselves by artifice. All their conduct was dark and intricate. They existed by *corruption,* and they were now about to dissolve Parliament, after sending their agents about the country to bribe men." Mr. Pitt now rose, not to answer the interrogatories put him, but with a call *to order*. As Conway was advanced in years, Pitt treated him with respect, but demanded that he should *"specify* the instances of corruption" charged, and told him that "what he could not prove, *he ought never to assert.*"

"No man," said he, in his loftiest tone, "shall draw me aside from the purpose which, on mature deliberation, I have formed. Individual members have no right to call upon me for replies to questions involving in them great public considerations. Nor is it incumbent on me to answer interrogatories put in the harsh language that has been used." Turning again to Conway, whose age ought to have taught him more moderation, he reproved his intemperance of language in a way which called forth a burst of applause from the House, by quoting the noble reply of Scipio to Fabius, "Si nullâ aliâ re, modestiâ certe et temperando linguam *adolescens senem* vicero!"[13]

Some of Mr. Fox's friends now became anxious for a *compromise*. Among them was Mr. Powys, who had been so scandalized by the Coalition and the East India Bill that he joined Mr. Pitt in opposing them, but went back to Fox the moment he was dismissed and Pitt was put in his place. He now urged a coalition between them as the only possible means of giving peace and harmony to the country. He proposed to remove the difficulty as to Lord North (whom Fox could not desert) by raising him to the Upper House. "I did not," said he, "approve of the coalition between the late secretary [Mr. Fox] and the noble Lord. The ambition of the former was certainly laudable in itself, though he was not very delicate in the means of its gratification; still the noble Lord must not be disgraced. He shines, indeed, no longer except with a borrowed light. He is a man of whom I can not say laudandus; but *ornandus, tollendus.*" His Lordship, with his accustomed suavity and wit, in alluding to Powys' observation about his shining with "a borrowed light," observed, that "a classical expression had been applied to him, though with the difference of a monosyllable—*non* laudandus—sed ornandus, tollendus." "I hope," continued he, "*tollendus* is not to be taken in the worst sense: it is not meant to *kill* me! It is only intended I should be *ornandus*—or, in vulgar English, *kicked upstairs!* But, sir, I have no inclination to be kicked upstairs. I should be very unwilling to stand in the way of any political agreement which might be beneficial to the country, but I will not go up to the House of

Peers. An acceptance of the peerage would place me in Agrippina's situation—

" 'Je vois mes honneurs croître, et tomber mon crédit.' "[14]

No one knew better than Lord North how to soften the asperity of debate by good-humored pleasantry or elegant allusion.

A large number of country gentlemen had now become so anxious for a coalition (which Fox himself proposed) that a meeting, attended by nearly seventy members of the House, was held at St. Alban's Tavern under the auspices of Powys and Mr. Grovesnor of Chester. On applying to the Duke of Portland as head of the Opposition, they received for answer that the only obstacle in the way was *"Mr. Pitt's being in office."* He was required to resign as preliminary to negotiation! The King, though with great reluctance, consented to receive some of the Opposition "as a respectable part of one [a ministry] on a broad basis," but insisted on "their giving up the idea of having the administration in *their own hands.*" In accordance with these views, Mr. Pitt refused to resign, and when afterward reproached by Mr. Powys on the subject, said, "The honorable gentleman has talked of the fortress which I occupy and has declared that *he* did not wish me to march out with a halter about my neck. Sir, the only fortress that I know of, or desire ever to defend, is the fortress of the Constitution. To preserve it, I will resist every attack and every seduction. With what regard, either to my own personal honor or to public principle, could I change my armor and meanly beg to be received as a volunteer under the forces of the enemy? But, sir, I have declared, again and again, only prove to me that there is but a reasonable hope—show me even but the most distant prospect—that that my resignation will at all contribute to restore peace to the country, and I will instantly resign. But, sir, I declare, at the same time, I *will not resign* as a preliminary to negotiation. I will not abandon this situation, in order to throw myself on the *mercy* of the right honorable gentleman. He calls me now a nominal minister—the mere puppet of secret influence. Sir, it is because I will not consent to become a merely nominal minister of his creation—it is because I disdain to become the puppet of that right honorable gentleman—that I will not resign. Neither shall his contemptuous expressions provoke me to resignation. My own honor and reputation I never will resign. That I am now standing on the rotten ground of secret influence I will not allow; nor yet will I quit my ground in order to put myself under the right honorable gentleman's *protection*—in order to accept of my nomination at his hands—to become a poor, self-condemned, helpless, and unprofitable minister in his train; a minister, perhaps, in some way serviceable to that right honorable gentleman, but totally unserviceable to my King and to my country. If I have, indeed, submitted to become the puppet and minion of the Crown, why should he condescend to receive me into his band?"

It was in this speech that Mr. Pitt, with reference to Fox's boasts of the great names that adorned the Opposition, broke forth into his splendid eulogium on Lord Camden. "Sir, I am not afraid to match the minority against the majority, either on the score of independence, of property, of long hereditary honors, of knowledge of the law and Constitution, of all that can give dignity to the peerage. Mr. Speaker, when I look round me, when I see near *whom* I am standing (Lord Camden was present at the debate), I am not afraid to place in the front of that battle—for at that battle the noble peer was not afraid to buckle on his armor and march forth, as if inspired with his youthful vigor, to the charge—I am not afraid to place foremost that noble and illustrious peer—venerable as he is for his years—venerable for his abilities—venerated throughout the country for his attachment to our glorious Constitution—high in honors—and possessing, as he does, in these tumultuous times, an equanimity and dignity of mind that render him infinitely superior to *the wretched party spirit* with which the world may fancy us to be infected!"

In concluding his speech, Mr. Pitt thus defied Mr. Fox to stop the supplies. "The right honorable gentleman tells you, sir, that he means not to stop the supplies again to-night, but that he shall only *postpone* them occasionally. He *has* stopped them once, because the King did not listen to the voice of his Commons. He now ceases to stop them, though the same cause does not cease to exist. Now, sir, what is all this but a mere bravado?—a bravado calculated to alarm the country, but totally ineffectual to the object. I grant, indeed, that if the money destined to pay the public creditors is voted, one great part of the mischief is avoided. But, sir, let not this House think it a small thing to stop the money for all *public services.* Let us not think that, while such prodigious sums of money flow into the public coffers without being suffered to flow out again, the circulation of wealth in the country will not be stopped, nor the public credit affected. It has been said, 'How is it possible that Parliament should trust public money in the hands of those in whom they have expressly declared that they can not confide?' What, sir, is there anything, then, in *my* character so flagitious? Am I, the Chief Minister of the Treasury, so suspected of alienating the public money to my own, or any other sinister purpose, that I am not to be trusted with the ordinary issues?" (A cry of No, no, from the Opposition.) "Why, then, sir," he exclaimed, seizing on the admission with instant effect, *"if they renounce the imputation, let them also renounce the argument!"*

It was not without reason that Mr. Fox had been desirous of a compromise; the whole country had begun to move *"for Pitt and the King."* Addresses in favor of the ministry now poured in from every part of the kingdom. London led the way, and sent a deputation to Mr. Pitt's residence, in Berkeley Square, preceded by the City Marshal and Sheriffs, to present him with the freedom of the city in a gold box of one hundred guineas in value, "as a mark of gratitude for, and approbation of, his zeal and assiduity in supporting the legal prerogatives of the Crown and the constitutional rights of the people." Mr. Fox's majority now began to diminish, until, on the 27th of February, it was reduced to *seven.* On the 8th of March he made his last great effort in a "Representation to the King," drawn up in powerful language, containing reasons for the removal of ministers. So great was the anxiety to be present at this debate that the gallery was filled to overflowing more than six hours before the House assembled.

The debate was opened by Mr. Fox's moving that this Representation be entered on the records of the House; it continued till midnight, and when the vote was taken he had only *one majority!* Tremendous cheers now broke forth from the Treasury benches: the Coalition was defeated; the Mutiny Bill was passed; parliament was soon after dissolved; and the nation was called upon to decide, at the hustings, between Fox and Pitt.[15]

The people ratified at the polls what they had declared in their addresses to the King and ministry. Never was there so complete a revolution in any House of Commons. More than a hundred and sixty of Mr. Fox's friends lost their seats; at the opening of the new Parliament, May 18th, 1784, it might truly be said, in the words of Lord Campbell, "No administration in England ever was in such a triumphant position as that of Mr. Pitt, when, after the opposition it had encountered, the nation, applauding the choice of the Crown, declared in its favor, and the Coalition leaders, with their immense talents, family interest, and former popularity, found difficulty to obtain seats in the House of Commons."[16] From this period for seventeen years, and, after a short interval, during three years more, Mr. Pitt swayed the destinies of England under circumstances, for the most part, more perilous and appalling than have fallen to the lot of any British statesman in modern times. As to his leading measures, men differ now almost as much as during the heat of the contest in the judgment they pronounce between him and his great opponent. But there is more candor in estimating the *motives* and *intentions* of both. Very few, at the present day, would call in question the honor, the integrity, or the sincere patriotism of William Pitt. All, too, have come to feel that, in deciding on the conduct of public men during the French Revolution, the question is not so much, 'Who was in the right,' as 'Who was least in the wrong.' Facts, also, are beginning to come out through the diaries of such men as Mr. Wilberforce, Lord Malmesbury, &c., who knew the secret history of the times, which put a new face upon many transactions, or on the motives in which they originated; but half a century must still elapse before the world will have the means of forming a full and impartial estimate of Mr. Pitt's administration. All that can here be attempted is a brief survey of his most important measures, commencing with those of the eight years previous to the war with France, and then touching lightly on the grounds and conduct of that fearful contest. Reference will occasionally be made to the opinions of Lord Campbell in his Lives of the Chancellors, not only because his judgments have been formed from the most recent information, but because his views, when favorable to Mr. Pitt, may be relied upon the more as coming from a strong political opponent.

The first measure of Mr. Pitt was a bill for the better government of India. It differed from that of Mr. Fox chiefly in the two particulars mentioned above: it left the commercial concerns of the Company in the hands of the Directors; and, instead of the seven Commissioners of Mr. Fox, it established a Board of Control appointed by the Crown, whose members come in and go out with the ministry and exercise the government of India in conjunction with the Directors. "The joint sway," says Lord Campbell, "of the Court of Directors and the Board of Control being substituted for the arbitrary rule of the "Seven Kings," our Eastern empire has been governed with wisdom, with success, and with glory."[17]

Early in 1785, Mr. Pitt brought forward a plan of Reform in Parliament. On this subject he had, from early life, entered with great warmth into the feelings of his father, and had twice before (in 1782 and 1783) moved similar resolutions, supported by able speeches, though without success. He now took it up as minister. His plan was to disfranchise thirty-six decayed boroughs (making due compensation to the owners) and transfer the representation, consisting of nearly a hundred members, to the counties and unrepresented large towns. He also proposed to extend the right of voting in populous places to the inhabitants in general. Mr. Fox strenuously resisted the proposed compensation, and the friends of reform being thus divided, Mr. Pitt was beaten by a majority of 248 to 174. As he never brought up the subject again, he has been accused by some of insincerity; but we learn his true feelings from a record in the diary of Mr. Wilberforce:

"At Pitt's all the day. It (reform) goes on well: sat up late chatting with Pitt, who has good hopes of the country—noble and patriotic heart! To town (next day)—House—Parliamentary Reform—*terribly disappointed and beat.*"[18] It is not surprising that, after being defeated three times, he should be in no haste to revive the subject again, especially as the King was strongly opposed to the measure; nor does it show any want of sincerity in his early efforts that he afterward changed his views as to the expediency of agitating the question. Even Lord Brougham, with all his disposition to censure Mr. Pitt, says "the alarms raised by the French Revolution and its cognate excitement among ourselves, justified a reconsideration of the opinions originally entertained on our parliamentary system and might induce an honest alteration of them."[19]

At this time, also, Mr. Pitt proposed two measures which the reader may recollect as denounced in bitter terms by Mr. Burke, in his speech on the Nabob of Arcot's Debts. Neither of them deserved these censures. The first related to fees in the public offices and, instead of being designed "to draw some resource out of the crumbs dropped from the trenchers of penury," was intended to abolish sinecures which, in some cases, yielded £16,000 a year. The bill was passed almost unanimously and proved highly useful. The other was intended to give Ireland the benefits of free trade. Every one now sees that Mr. Pitt's plan was wise and salutary. Lord Campbell speaks of "the propositions for commercial union with Ireland which do so much honor to the memory of Mr. Pitt, and not only show that he was disposed to govern that country with justice and liberality, but that, being the first disciple of Adam Smith who had been in power, he thoroughly understood and was resolved to carry into effect, the principles of free trade."[20] He was defeated, however, partly through the clamor raised by the English traders and manufacturers and partly by the unfounded jealousy of the Irish. Moore says, in his Life of Sheridan, "the acceptance of the terms then proffered by the minister might have averted much of the evil of which she [Ireland] was afterward the victim."[21]

In 1786, Mr. Pitt brought forward his celebrated plan for paying the national debt of £239,000,000, by means of a Sinking Fund. The suggestion came from Dr. Price, who offered three schemes to the ministry, and it has often been said that Mr. Pitt "chose the worst." True it is that on the other two the debt would have been paid sooner, but they were more complicated and required an annual outlay to begin with which Mr. Pitt clearly saw the country could never endure. He, therefore, chose the plan which, though less expeditious, was the only one he deemed practicable. It was founded on the fact that he had a *surplus* revenue of £900,000 a year. To this £100,000 might be added from taxes without burdening the country; and "this sum of one million a year, improved at compound interest by being regularly invested in public stocks, would, in twenty-eight years, amount to four millions a year at the supposed interest of five per cent., a sum which would pay off one hundred millions of three per cents." The scheme was professedly founded on the continuance of peace. While this remained, the surplus could be relied on without adding any new debt; and, as the nations of Europe seemed tired of war after the exhausting contest from which they had just escaped, Mr. Pitt not unnaturally hoped that England might enjoy so long a season of repose as to place her Sinking Fund on high and safe ground before the occurrence of another war. But unfortunately, within seven years there commenced the most terrible conflict in which the country was ever engaged. The surplus failed; and, though the form of a Sinking Fund was kept up, it became from this time a mere bubble—paying a debt with one hand while borrowing with the other. This was not the Sinking Fund devised by Dr. Price and Mr. Pitt. If the peace in Europe had been as lasting then as since the fall of Bonaparte, and the original plan had been faithfully carried out, the fund would probably by this time have extinguished a large part, if not the whole, of the public debt.

Mr. Pitt's Commercial Treaty with France, in 1787, was the first step on the part of England toward those enlarged principles of national intercourse which now so generally prevail. His armament against France, the same year, in behalf of Holland, was applauded by all; that against Spain, in 1790, was ultimately approved by Mr. Fox; that against Russia, in 1791, was promptly and wisely given up (as already stated) when the voice of the nation declared against it.

The ground taken by Mr. Pitt on the exciting question of the Regency has already been stated in the memoir of Mr. Fox; the measures he then proposed now form an acknowledged part of the constitutional law on this subject. His change of policy in regard to the impeachment of Mr. Hastings was mentioned in the memoir of Mr. Burke. Mr. Wilberforce always ascribed it to a growing conviction of Mr. Hastings' guilt; but the personal considerations referred to in the memoir are believed by most persons to have had a powerful influence with the ministry.

Mr. Pitt was a warm advocate of the immediate abolition of the slave trade, and in 1792 made the most eloquent speech on this subject ever delivered in the House of Commons. Lord Brougham speaks of him in the harshest terms for not making this a ministerial question and compelling his adherents to unite with him at once in a vote for suppressing the traffic. It may be doubted, however, whether a great moral question of this kind ought ever to be carried by mere force. Years of inquiry and argument are often necessary to make the removal, even of enormous abuses, either permanent or useful. The King and his whole family remained to the last strenuous opponents of the abolition of the slave trade. Most of the nobility, for a long time, had the same feelings, and nearly all the mercantile interest of the kingdom resisted it for many years with their utmost strength. Some of the ablest of Mr. Pitt's colleagues were vehemently opposed to what they regarded as a rash and impracticable scheme, while they professed a sincere desire for a gradual abolition of the traffic. It certainly does honor to Mr. Pitt that under these circumstances he never wavered or shrunk back. He gave Mr. Wilberforce all the influence of his personal and official character; he spoke and voted for immediate abolition. If he had gone farther and attempted what Lord Brougham condemns him so bitterly for not doing, he would probably have put an end at once to his ministry without the slightest advantage, and perhaps with serious detriment, to the cause he had espoused.

In 1791, it became the duty of Mr. Pitt to frame a new Constitution for Canada. He did it upon wise and liberal principles. He forever took away the question which led to the American war, that of taxing the colonies for the sake of revenue. The British Parliament now expressly relinquished the right of laying any taxes except for the regulation of trade (to which the Americans were always ready to submit); and, in order to guard this point more fully, Mr. Pitt provided that the proceeds even of these taxes should go to the provincial assemblies, and not to the government at home. It was much for George III to make such concessions.

The financial measures of Mr. Pitt, during the period under review, were highly successful. He took the government at the end of Lord North's wars with an unfunded debt of thirty millions sterling and a national income wholly unequal to the expense of even a moderate peace establishment. There were large claims to be provided for in favor of the American Loyalists; there was a system of enormous fraud in the collection of the public revenues to be searched out and collected; there were permanent arrangements to be made for commercial intercourse with America and some countries of Europe; and the vast concerns of India, all resting back on the treasury at home, were to be reduced to order and placed on a new foundation. In carrying out his plans, he had to fight his way at every step against the acutest and most eloquent men of England; and he did it under the disadvantage of having no common ground of argument on which to meet them, since they were ignorant of the principles of Adam Smith, while the popular maxims and prejudices of the day were all on their side. Within five years the debt was funded and reduced five millions of pounds, notwithstanding the expense of two armaments and other outlays to the amount of six millions. An entire and most beneficial change was made in the manner of collecting the customs and auditing the public accounts, requiring more than three thousand distinct resolutions of Parliament to carry the plan into effect.[22] Under this system, the public revenue went on gradually increasing, until early in 1792 he "felt justified in proposing a repeal of the most burdensome imposts and an addition of £400,000 to the annual million already appropriated as a Sinking Fund. In respect, then, to the first eight years of Mr. Pitt's administration, it was not, perhaps, too much for Mr. Gibbon to say that "in all his researches in ancient and modern history, he had nowhere met with a parallel—with one who at so early a period of life had so important a trust reposed in him, which he had discharged with so much credit to himself and advantage to the kingdom."

We now come to the course adopted by Mr. Pitt respecting the Revolution in France and a war with that country. This, as Lord Brougham remarks, "is the *main* charge against him." It is obvious that, whatever may have been his errors on this subject, he had every possible motive to desire the continuance of peace. On this depended all his plans of finance, and especially the success of his Sinking Fund, to which he looked as the proudest memorial of his greatness as a statesman. That he did ardently desire it, no one doubts, and so sanguine were his expectations that he remarked in the House of Commons, about the middle of 1792, "England had never a fairer prospect of a long continuance of peace. I think we may confidently reckon upon peace for *ten years.*" Mr. Burke had previously expressed similar views. England had no longer any thing to fear from her hereditary rival. "France," said he, "in a political light, is to be considered as *expunged* out of the system of Europe." At this moment (July 25th, 1792) Austria and Prussia invaded France for the avowed purpose of restoring Louis XVI to all his rights as an absolute monarch. It is unnecessary to say that this step kindled the fire which soon after wrapped the whole of Europe in one general conflagration. But it is now known that England had no privity or concern in this invasion. On the contrary, Mr. Pitt declined all communication with Austria on the subject and declared to Prussia his unalterable resolution to maintain neutrality and avoid all interference with the internal concerns of France. It is also known that, some months after, he endeavored to put a stop to the contest by "negotiating," in the words of Mr. Wilberforce, "with the principal European powers for the purpose of obtaining a joint representation to France, assuring her that if she would formally engage to keep within her own limits and not molest her neighbors, she should be suffered to settle her own internal government and constitution without interference."[23] This negotiation was broken off in the midst by the execution of Louis XVI, and Mr. Pitt thus failed in his efforts to arrest the war on the Continent.

When the French drove out the Austrians and Prussians, they seized, in turn, on the Austrian Netherlands, early in November, 1792. Here arose the first point of collision between England and France. The Republican rulers forced the passage of the River Scheldt from the Netherlands down to the sea. This river had been closed, under the provisions of the treaty of Westphalia, for a century and a half, out of regard to the rights of Holland, through which it flows, and England was bound by treaty to defend those rights. A second point of collision was the French Decree of Fraternity, passed November 19, 1792, by the National Assembly, declaring that the French "would grant *fraternity* and *assistance* to all those people who wish to procure liberty, and charged the executive power to send orders to their generals to give assistance to such people as have suffered, or are now suffering, in the cause of liberty." This was considered as a declaration of war against all the monarchies of Europe and a direct call upon their subjects to rise in rebellion. It was brought home to England by the fact that delegates from societies in London and elsewhere, consisting of many thousands, were received at the bar of the French National Convention nine days after the publication of this decree, where they declared their intention to "adopt the French form of government and establish a National Convention in Great Britain." The President of the Convention replied in very significant terms: "Royalty in Europe is either destroyed or on the point of perishing, and the Declaration of Rights placed by the side of thrones is a devouring fire which will consume them. The festival which you have celebrated in honor of the French Revolution is *the prelude to the festival of nations!*" There is no doubt that the French, at this time, expected a revolution in England.

These aggressions and insults would have justified the English government in demanding ample reparation. But there was a difficulty as to the mode of negotiating. When Louis XVI was made a prisoner of the Convention by the events of August 10th, 1792, his government ceased, and Mr. Pitt recalled the English embassador from Paris, and suspended the functions of M. Chauvelin, the French embassador at London. How, then, were the two countries to communicate? This soon after became a practical question. England began to arm, which she might reasonably do under existing circumstances. The French government instructed M. Chauvelin, who remained at London, to demand whether this armament was directed against France, tendering at the same time an explanation of the Decree of Fraternity as not aimed at England, and proposing to negotiate in relation to the Scheldt. What was Mr. Pitt now to do? No one would expect him instantly to recognize the National Convention as *de jure* the government of France. Mr. Fox proposed to treat with them as the government *de facto;* but this is a distinction which has sprung up chiefly since the French Revolution, and it is easy to see how strong a repugnance George III and most of the English must have felt to any recognition of the new government, while they held their King as a prisoner and were calling on the subjects of every other monarch in Europe to join with them in rebellion. Mr. Pitt took a middle course. He did not refuse to communicate with the French rulers, but he declined to receive the paper of M. Chauvelin as "an *official* communication." He did, however, reply "under a form neither regular nor official," telling him, "If France is really desirous of maintaining friendship and peace with England, she must show herself disposed to renounce her views of aggression and aggrandizement and confine herself within her own territory, without insulting other governments, without disturbing their tranquillity, without violating their rights." Within less than a month the King of France was beheaded. M. Chauvelin, whose functions had been suspended during the imprisonment of Louis, was now dismissed and sent out of the kingdom, and seven days after, France declared war against England. Such is an exact representation of the facts. It is certainly to be regretted that Mr. Pitt did not adopt the course recommended by Mr. Fox and thus take from France all pretense of putting him in the wrong. But in passing a sentence on his conduct we are not to be influenced by our knowledge of the result. He acted under the prevailing delusion that, even if war took place, it could not be severe or calamitous. "It must certainly be ended," said he to a friend, "in one or two campaigns." He acted as most men act who feel strong, in dealing with those whom they consider as weak. He acted, also, under the belief (which subsequent events proved correct) that the French were insincere in their disavowals, that they only wished to gain time. The French Minister of War is now understood to have said at this juncture, "We have three hundred thousand men in arms, and we must make them march as far away as their legs will carry them, or they will return and cut our throats." From the moment of their triumph in the Austrian Netherlands, the policy of the French government was war. On the other hand, George III and the great body of the English people were equally bent on fighting. "If a stop is not put to French principles," said he, "there will not be a king left in Europe in a few years."[24] The only stop then thought of was to shut out these principles by war and to put down the authors of them as enemies of the human race. "Had Mr. Pitt refused to go to war," says a late writer, who was by no means friendly to his measures, "he would have been driven from power by the united voice of king and people; his successor, whether Whig or Tory, would have been compelled to pursue the course of policy which was only reluctantly followed by that celebrated statesman."[25] The war, therefore, was not Mr. Pitt's war; it was equally the war of the English and of the French nation.

As to "French principles," which were an object of so much terror to the King, they had, no doubt, to some extent, gained a foothold among the middling and lower classes.

Paine's Rights of Man and other publications of a still more radical character were widely circulated, and it has since been stated on high authority that "the soldiers were every where tampered with." "You have a great estate," said one of these radical reformers to General Lambton; "we shall soon divide it among us." "You will presently spend it in liquor," replied the general, "and what will you do then?" "Why, then *we will divide again!*"

Between 1793 and 1795 very stringent measures were adopted for putting down this spirit. Acts of Parliament were passed, as already stated in the memoir of Mr. Fox, suspending the Habeas Corpus Act, imposing severe restrictions on the holding of political meetings, and giving a wider extent to the crime of treason. They were designed, however, only as temporary measures, and were limited to three years. Still, they brought great reproach on Mr. Pitt, though it now appears that they originated not with him, but with the followers of Mr. Burke, who had been recently brought into the ministry. Lord Campbell, speaking of this period, says, "Now began that system of policy for the repression of French principles which has caused the period in which it prevailed to be designated, in the language of exaggeration, 'the Reign of Terror.' I think the system was unwise, and that Lord Loughborough is chiefly answerable for it. I am afraid that, if he did not originate, he actively encouraged it, and that he, as the organ of the alarmist party, forced it upon the reluctant Prime Minister. Pitt had not only come forward in public life on the popular side, but I believe that his propensities continued liberal and that, if he could have fulfilled his wishes, he would have emancipated the Catholics—he would have abolished slavery—he would have established free trade—and he would have reformed the House of Commons. His regard for the liberty of the press he had evinced by carrying Fox's Libel Bill by the influence of government, notwithstanding the furious opposition of Lord Chancellor Thurlow. He was likewise particularly adverse to any stringent measures against reformers, being aware that, having himself very recently belonged to that body, he would appear rather in an invidious light as the persecutor of his former associates. But he found that he could not adhere to constitutional laws and constitutional practices without the disruption of his administration."[26] During this period, also, occurred those state trials, arising out of some wild attempts at parliamentary reform, in which Erskine was so much distinguished. Some reproach has fallen upon Mr. Pitt for allowing them to go on. It appears, however, from the statement of Lord Campbell, that "Lord Loughborough was the principal adviser of them. He had surrendered himself to the wildest apprehensions of Burke, he feared that any encouragement to parliamentary reform was tantamount to rebellion, and he believed that general bloodshed would be saved by the sacrifice of a few individuals. . . . When the plan was first proposed of arresting the members of the Corresponding Society and proceeding capitally against them, it is said that Pitt, who had studied the law, expressed some disapprobation of the notion of 'constructive treason,' but he did not like to rely upon the objection that the Duke of Richmond and himself had supported similar doctrines and no doubt in his heart he believed that, under the pretense of parliamentary reform, deeper designs were now carried on. The Attorney and Solicitor General, being consulted by the Chancellor, gave an opinion that the imputed conspiracy to change the form of government was a compassing of the King's death within the meaning of the statute of Edward III —and the King himself, upon this opinion, was eager for the prosecutions. So in an evil hour an order was made that they should be instituted, and warrants were signed for the arrest of the supposed traitors." "Happily, English juries," adds Lord Campbell, "and the returning sober sense of the English people, at last saved public liberty from the great peril to which it was then exposed. . . . To the credit of George III, when the whole subject was understood by him, he rejoiced in the acquittals and, laying all the blame on the Chancellor, he said, 'You have got us into the wrong box, my Lord, you have got us into the wrong box. Constructive treason won't do, my Lord, constructive treason won't do.' "[27]

Mr. Pitt saw, within three years from the commencement of the war, how idle it was to think of refusing to recognize the French Republic as forming part of the political system of Europe. She had extorted that recognition from all around her at the point of the bayonet and had nearly doubled her territory and dependencies at the expense of her neighbors. He therefore brought down a message from the King, acknowledging her government as established under the Directory in October, 1795, and in October, 1796, sent a plenipotentiary to Paris with proposals of peace. His terms were highly liberal. He offered to restore the conquests he had made from France, being all her rich colonies in the East and West Indies, receiving nothing in return, and only asking for Austria, as the ally of England, a similar restoration of the territory which had been wrested from her by the French. This the Directory refused and, after a short negotiation, ordered the English embassador to quit Paris in twenty-four hours.

The next year, 1797, was one of the darkest seasons that England had known for centuries. In April, Austria was compelled to sue for peace, leaving the English to carry on the contest single-handed; and at the moment when this intelligence arrived, a mutiny had broken out in the fleets both at the Nore and Spithead, more extensive and threatening than has ever occurred in the English navy; while Ireland was on the brink of rebellion and actually had deputies in France soliciting the aid of her troops. Never were the funds so low, even in the worst periods of the American war. These events were ushered in by the greatest calamity that can befall a commercial people, a drain of specie arising from the operation of the war which endangered the whole banking system of the country. Whether Mr. Pitt was to blame or not for the causes which produced this drain, it is certain that his daring resolution saved the country in this alarming crisis. He issued an order of the Privy Council, February 26th, 1797, requiring the Bank of England *to suspend specie payments.* He might have avoided the personal hazard thus incurred by throwing the responsibility on Parliament, which was then in session—the order, indeed, was generally considered as unconstitutional; but the case would not admit of delay: a single night's debate on such a question might have destroyed all credit throughout the kingdom. Parliament and the country justified the course he took, while the bankers in every part of the empire united to sustain him. The mutiny was quelled by a judicious union of firmness and concession; Ireland was held down for another year; and Great Britain, instead of being plunged into the gulf of national and individual bankruptcy as predicted by Mr. Fox, was placed on a vantage ground which enabled her to sustain the pressure of the war without injury to her financial system. It is not wonderful that the friends of Mr. Pitt were loud in their applause of "the pilot that weathered the storm."

About the middle of the same year, July, 1797, Mr. Pitt renewed his proposals of peace. He sent Lord Malmesbury to Lisle, offering, as in the former case, to restore all his conquests, and, as Austria was now out of the way, demanding nothing in return. There were at this juncture two parties in the Directory, one for peace and the other for war, and the negotiation changed its aspect, from time to time, during the two months of its continuance, as the one or the other obtained the mastery. It is a curious circumstance, showing the difficulties he had to encounter, that a similar division existed in his own cabinet; so that among the "astounding disclosures" made in Lord Malmesbury's diary, we find that it was necessary for his Lordship to send two sets of dispatches every time he communicated with his government, one of a more general nature to be read by Lord Loughborough and his associates, who were bent on defeating the negotiation, and the other for Mr. Pitt, Lord Grenville, and Mr. Dundas! The violent part of the Directory at last prevailed. War became the policy of the government, and Lord Malmesbury was dismissed. The French were to be deluded with new visions of conquest. Bonaparte was sent to subdue Egypt and thus open a pathway to India, and the whole of Hindostan, with its hundred and fifty millions of inhabitants, was to become a tributary of the Republic. Mr. Pitt laid the subject before Parliament, November 10th, 1797, in a masterly speech, which is given in this collection. Parliament, without one dissenting voice, approved of his conduct and united in the emphatic declaration, "We know that great exertions are wanted; we are ready to make them; and we are, at all events, determined to stand or fall by the laws, liberties, and religion of our country." The people came forward with that noble spirit and unanimity which has always distinguished the English in times of great peril and subscribed fifteen hundred thousand pounds, not as a loan, but as a voluntary gift for carrying on the war.

The Directory lasted a little more than four years and then yielded to the power of Bonaparte, who usurped the government and became First Consul in December, 1799. He immediately proposed a peace, and it was now Mr. Pitt's turn to reject the offer. Wounded by the insults which he had received in the two preceding negotiations, doubting whether the power of the First Consul would be at all more permanent than that of others who had gone before him, and convinced, at all events, that he could not be sincere in his offer, since the genius and interests of Bonaparte led only to war, Mr. Pitt declined to negotiate on the subject. It appeared afterward, as already stated, that Bonaparte did not wish for peace. When the question came before Parliament, February 3d, 1800, he delivered the third of his speeches contained in this volume. It is the most elaborate of all his efforts, and though worse reported than the other two so far as language is concerned (Mr. Canning, indeed, says that Mr. Pitt suffered more in this respect than any orator of his day), it can hardly be too much admired for its broad and luminous statements, the closeness of its reasonings, and the fervor of its appeals.

In 1800, Mr. Pitt accomplished his favorite plan of a legislative union of Ireland with Great Britain. But he was unable to effect it without a distinct intimation to the Roman Catholics that they should receive, as a reward for their acquiescence, the boon of emancipation which they had been so long seeking. He did this without the privity of the King, and knowing his scruples on the subject, but still with a firm belief that his Majesty, in attaining so great an object, would yield those scruples to the wishes of the most enlightened men in the kingdom. But the moment he disclosed his plan to his colleagues, Lord Loughborough, says Lord Campbell, "set secretly to work and composed a most elaborate and artful paper, showing forth the dangers likely to arise from Mr. Pitt's plan in a manner admirably calculated to make an impression on the royal mind." The King was thus fortified against the proposal before Mr. Pitt had time to present his reasons; and, adopting the course he had taken with the East India Bill of Mr. Fox, declared at the levee, with a view to have his words circulated, "that he should consider any person who voted for the measure proposed by his minister as *personally indisposed toward himself!*" Mr. Pitt justly considered this as a direct exclusion from the public service and so informed the cabinet, in February, 1801, having held the office of Prime Minister between sixteen and seventeen years. It was generally supposed at the time that he retired with a view to open a more easy way for negotiating a peace with France. He certainly desired peace, but the circumstances here stated were the true cause of his withdrawing from the government.

Mr. Addington (afterward Lord Sidmouth) succeeded him, and Mr. Pitt gave the new minister a cordial support. Mr. Wilberforce, in his diary, says, "Pitt has really behaved with a magnanimity unparalleled in a politician and is wishing to form for Addington the best and strongest possible administration." He approved of the peace, and again, when the rupture took place, he gave the declaration of war, May 18th, 1803, his warmest support. His speech on this occasion (which, through an accident in the gallery, was never reported) is said by Lord Brougham to have "excelled all his other performances in vehement and spirit-stirring declamation; and this may be the more easily believed when we know that Mr. Fox, in his reply, said, 'The orators of antiquity would have admired, probably would have envied it.' The last half hour is described as having been one unbroken torrent of the most majestic declamation."

Mr. Addington had a timidity and inertness which wholly unfitted him for carrying on the war. The people were clamorous for a change of ministers, and Mr. Pitt was again called to the head of affairs, May 12th, 1804. Lord Brougham has reproached him for accepting office without insisting upon Catholic emancipation; but his former step had thrown the King into a fit of derangement for nearly three weeks, a new agitation of the subject might have produced the same result, and, as it was now obvious that emancipation could never be granted during the life of George III, Mr. Pitt, surely, was not to exclude himself from office on a mere point of etiquette without the slightest advantage to the cause. He now formed his last great coalition against Bonaparte, but the battle of Austerlitz (December 2d, 1805) was a death blow to his hopes. Worn out with care and anxiety, his health had been declining for some months. On the 21st of January, 1806, the Bishop of Lincoln apprised him that his end was approaching. Mr. Pitt heard him with perfect composure, and after a few moments, rising as he spoke, and clasping his hands with the utmost fervor, he exclaimed, "I throw myself *entirely* (laying a strong emphasis on the last word) upon the mercy of God through the merits of Christ." He now arranged all his secular concerns with perfect calmness and died at a quarter past four, Thursday morning, the 23d of January, 1806, in the forty-seventh year of his age. He was buried near his father in Westminster Abbey, and his debts, amounting to £40,000, were paid by the public. Mr. Wilberforce, who knew him more intimately than any other man, has given this testimony to his character: "Mr. Pitt had his foibles, and of course they were not diminished by so long a continuance in office; but for a clear and comprehensive view of the most complicated subject in all its relations; for that fairness of mind which disposes a man to follow out, and, when overtaken, to recognize the truth; for magnanimity, which made him ready to change his measures when he thought the good of the country required it, though he knew he should be charged with inconsistency on account of the change; for willingness to give a fair hearing to all that could be urged against his own opinions, and to listen to the suggestions of men whose understandings he knew to be inferior to his own; for personal purity, disinterestedness, integrity, and love of country, I have never known his equal. His strictness in regard to truth was astonishing, considering the situation he so long filled."[28]

In person, Mr. Pitt was tall and slender; his features were somewhat harsh, but lighted up with intelligence by the flashes of his eye; his gesture was animated, but devoid of grace; his articulation was remarkably full and clear, filling the largest room with the volume of sound. His manner of entering the House was strikingly indicative of his absorption in the business before him. "From the instant he passed the doorway," says Wraxall, "he advanced up the floor with a quick and firm step, his head erect and thrown back, looking neither to the right nor the left, nor favoring with a nod or a glance any of the individuals seated on either side, among whom many who possessed £5000 a year would have been gratified even by so slight a mark of attention." Those who knew him best as a speaker expatiated with delight on "the perfection of his arrangement, the comprehensiveness of his reasonings, the power of his sarcasm, the magnificence of his declamation, the majestic tone of his voice, the legislative authority of his manner, and his felicitous observance of the temper of his audience." Mr. Canning has given the following sketch of his character, which will form an appropriate conclusion to this memoir.

"The character of this illustrious statesman early passed its ordeal. Scarcely had he attained the age at which reflection commences, when Europe with astonishment beheld him filling the first place in the councils of his country and managing the vast mass of its concerns with all the vigor and steadiness of the most matured wisdom. Dignity—strength—discretion—these were among the masterly qualities of his mind at its first dawn. He had been nurtured a statesman, and his knowledge was of that kind which always lay ready for practical application. Not dealing in the subtleties of abstract politics, but moving in the slow, steady procession of reason, his conceptions were reflective and his views correct. Habitually attentive to the concerns of government, he spared no pains to acquaint himself with whatever was connected, however minutely, with its prosperity. He was devoted to the state. Its interests engrossed all his study and engaged all his care. It was the element alone in which he seemed to live and move. He allowed himself but little recreation from his labors. His mind was always on its station, and its activity was unremitted.

"He did not hastily adopt a measure, nor hastily abandon it. The plan struck out by him for the preservation of Europe was the result of prophetic wisdom and profound policy. But, though defeated in many respects by the selfish ambition and short-sighted imbecility of foreign powers—whose rulers were too venal or too weak to follow the flight of that mind which would have taught them to outwing the storm—the policy involved in it has still a secret operation on the conduct of surrounding states. His plans were full of energy, and the principles which inspired them looked beyond the consequences of the hour.

"He knew nothing of that timid and wavering cast of mind which dares not abide by its own decision. He never suffered popular prejudice or party clamor to turn him aside from any measure which his deliberate judgment had adopted. He had a proud reliance on himself, and it was justified. Like the sturdy warrior leaning on his own battle-ax, conscious where his strength lay, he did not readily look beyond it.

"As a debater in the House of Commons, his speeches were logical and argumentative. If they did not often abound in the graces of metaphor, or sparkle with the brilliancy of wit, they were always animated, elegant, and classical. The strength of his oratory was intrinsic; it presented the rich and abundant resource of a clear discernment and a correct taste. His speeches are stamped with inimitable marks of originality. When replying to his opponents, his readiness was not more conspicuous than his energy. He was always prompt and always dignified. He could sometimes have recourse to the sportiveness of irony, but he did not often seek any other aid than was to be derived from an arranged and extensive knowledge of his subject. This qualified him fully to discuss the arguments of others and forcibly to defend his own. Thus armed, it was rarely in the power of his adversaries, mighty as they were, to beat him from the field. His eloquence, occasionally rapid, electric, and vehement, was always chaste, winning, and persuasive—not awing into acquiescence, but arguing into conviction. His understanding was bold and comprehensive. Nothing seemed too remote for its reach or too large for its grasp.

"Unallured by dissipation and unswayed by pleasure, he never sacrificed the national treasure to the one, or the national interest to the other. To his unswerving integrity the most authentic of all testimony is to be found in that unbounded public confidence which followed him throughout the whole of his political career.

"Absorbed as he was in the pursuits of public life, he did not neglect to prepare himself in silence for that higher destination, which is at once the incentive and reward of human virtue. His talents, superior and splendid as they were, never made him forgetful of that Eternal Wisdom from which they emanated. The faith and fortitude of his last moments were affecting and exemplary."

LORD ERSKINE

THOMAS ERSKINE, youngest son of the Earl of Buchan, was born at Edinburgh, on the 10th day of January, 1750. The family had once been eminent for rank and wealth; but their ample patrimony being gradually wasted, the income of their estates was at last reduced to two hundred pounds a year. To conceal their poverty, they removed to the capital from an old castle, which was all that was left of their wide domains, and "in a small and ill-furnished room in an upper *flat,* or story, of a lofty house in the old town of Edinburgh, first saw the light the Honorable Thomas Erskine, the future defender of Stockdale and Lord Chancellor of Great Britain."

Young Erskine displayed in very early life that quickness of intellect and joyous hilarity of spirits for which he was so remarkable throughout his professional career. He was kept for some years at the High School of Edinburgh and then removed to the University of St. Andrew's, where he spent less than a year. His early education was, therefore, extremely limited. He had but little knowledge of Latin and none of Greek.[1] In the rudiments of English literature, however, he was uncommonly well instructed for one of his age. He profited greatly by conversation with his mother, who was a woman of uncommon strength of mind, and owed much of the daring energy of his character to her example and instructions. Being accustomed, notwithstanding the poverty of the family, to associate from childhood with persons of high rank and breeding, he early acquired that freedom and nobleness of manner for which he was so much distinguished in after life. He was the favorite of all who knew him—of his masters, his school-mates, and the families in which he visited. Full of fun and frolic, with a lively fancy, ready wit, and unbounded self-reliance, he found his chief delight in society, and probably laid the foundation, at this early period, of those extraordinary powers of conversation to which he was greatly indebted for his subsequent success. He was one of the few who seem to have gained by being left chiefly to themselves in their early years. If he had less learning, he had more freedom and boldness; and when the time arrived for his entering into the conflicts of the bar, it is not surprising that, with high native talent, extraordinary capacity for application, and a self-confidence amounting to absolute egotism, he was able to put forth his powers, under the impulse of strong motive, with prodigious effect and to make himself, without any preparatory training, one of the most ready and eloquent speakers of the age.

He showed a great desire from boyhood to be fitted for one of the learned professions and had even then his dreams of distinction in eloquence; but the poverty of his father forbade the attempt. At the age of fourteen, he was placed as a midshipman in the navy and was commended to the particular care of his captain by Lord Mansfield, who took a lively interest in the Buchan family. He now spent four years in visiting various parts of the globe, particularly the West Indies and the coast of North America. He was often on shore; and it was probably on one of these occasions that he witnessed that meeting of an Indian chief with the governor of a British colony which he described so graphically in his defense of Stockdale and made the starting-point of one of the noblest bursts of eloquence in our language.

At the end of four years he returned to England; the ship was paid off, and he was cast without employment on the world. At this moment of deep perplexity his father died, leaving him but a scanty pittance for his support. After consulting with his friends, he saw no course but to try his fortune in the army, and accordingly he spent the whole of his little patrimony in purchasing an ensign's commission in the Royals, or First Regiment of Foot. The regiment remained for some years at home and was quartered, from time to time, in different provincial towns. Erskine, with his habitual buoyancy of spirits, mingled in the best society of the places where he was stationed and attracted great attention by the elegance of his manners and the brilliancy of his conversation. He at last became entangled with an affair of the heart, and was married in April, 1770, at the age of twenty, to a lady of respectable family, though without fortune—the daughter of Daniel Moore, Esq., member of Parliament for Marlow.

This rash step would to most persons have been the certain precursor of poverty and ruin; but in his case it was a fortunate one. It served to balance his mind, to check his natural volatility, to impress him with a sense of new obligations and higher duties. The regiment was ordered to Minorca, where he spent two years in almost uninterrupted leisure. In the society of his wife, he now entered on the systematic study of English literature, and probably no two years were ever better spent for the purposes of mental culture. As a preparation for his future efforts in oratory, they were invaluable. In addition to his reading in prose, he devoted himself with great ardor to the study of Milton and Shakspeare. A large part of the former he committed to memory, and became so familiar with the latter that "he could almost, like Porson, have held conversations on all subjects for days together in the phrases of the great English dramatist." Here he acquired that fine choice of words, that rich and varied imagery, that sense of harmony in the structure of his sentences, that boldness of thought and magnificence of expression, for which he was afterward so much distinguished. It may also be remarked that there are passages in both these writers which are the exact counterpart of the finest eloquence of the ancients. The speeches in the second book of the Paradise Lost have all the condensed energy and burning force of expression which belong to the great Athenian orator. The speech of Brutus, in Shakspeare's Julius Cæsar, has all the stern majesty of Roman eloquence. That of Anthony over the dead body of Cæsar is a matchless exhibition of the art and dexterity of insinuation which characterized the genius of the Greeks. It is not in regard to poetry alone that we may say of these great masters,

Hither, as to a fountain,
Other suns repair, and in their urns
Draw golden light.

In respect to eloquence, also, to use the words of Johnson, slightly varied, he who would excel in this noblest of arts must give his days and nights to the study of Milton and Shakspeare.

In the year 1772 the regiment returned to England, and the young ensign obtained a furlough of six months. Most of this time he spent in the best society of London; and Boswell speaks of Johnson and himself as dining, April 6, 1772, with "a young officer in the regimentals of the Scots Royals who talked with a vivacity, fluency, and precision which attracted particular attention." It was Erskine, who, with his characteristic boldness, entered at once into a literary discussion with Johnson, disputing his views on the comparative merits of Fielding and Richardson in a manner which rather gained him the favor of the great English moralist.

At the end of six years from his entering the army, when he had reached the rank of Lieutenant, the attention of Erskine was by mere accident directed to the bar. Being stationed, during the summer of 1774, in a country town where the Assizes were held, he rambled one day into court, and Lord Mansfield, who presided, having noticed his uniform, was led to inquire his name. Finding that it was the boy whom he had aided ten years before in going to sea, he invited him to a seat on the bench, briefly stating the principal points of the case and showing him other civilities which were peculiarly gratifying under such circumstances. Erskine listened with the liveliest interest. The counsel were considered skillful and eloquent; but it often occurred to him in the course of the argument on both sides, how much more clearly and forcibly he could have presented certain points and urged them on the minds of the jury. "And why not be a lawyer?" was the thought which instantly forced itself on his mind. "Why not carry out the early aspirations of boyhood?" Any one of a less sanguine temperament would have felt the attempt to be hopeless, burdened as he was with a young and growing family and wholly destitute of any means of subsistence except his commission, which must, of course, be relinquished if he entered on the study of the law. But Erskine's whole life was one of daring enterprise. The very difficulty of an undertaking seemed only to impel him forward with greater eagerness. Being invited to dinner by Lord Mansfield, who was delighted with his conversational powers, he brought out at the close of the evening the question which was already beating at his heart, "Is it impossible for me to become a lawyer?" Mansfield, who admired his talents and spirit, did his sanguine temperament. He consulted his mother, who had the same habit of looking on the bright side of things and who perfectly understood the force of his character, and found to his delight that she was almost as eager as he was to see him enter on the undertaking. He accordingly became a member of Lincoln's Inn, about the middle of 1775. His term of legal study might be materially abridged by his taking a degree at one of the universities, and to this he was entitled, as son of a nobleman, without passing an examination, if he kept his regular terms. He therefore became a member of Trinity College, Cambridge, early in 1776, paying no attention whatever to the studies of the place and contriving, at the same time, to keep his terms at Lincoln's Inn. He still retained his office in the army as a means of support, having obtained leave of absence for six months, and at the end of this time sold out his commission and husbanded his resources to the utmost. He lived in a small village just out of London; and Reynolds, the comic writer, says, in his "Life and Times," "The young student resided in small lodgings near my father's villa at Hampstead and openly avowed that he lived on cow-beef because he could not afford any of a superior quality; he dressed shabbily, and expressed the greatest gratitude to Mr. Harris for occasional free admissions to Covent Garden, and used boastingly to exclaim to my father, "Thank fortune, out of my own family, I don't know a Lord." In July, 1778, he was called to the bar, and according to all ordinary experience of the profession in London, he had reason to expect a delay of some years before his business would support his family.

But the early life of Erskine was full of singular adventure. Not long after his call to the bar, he was dining with a friend and happened to speak of a Captain Baillie, whose case at that time awakened great interest in the public mind. As Lieutenant Governor of Greenwich Hospital, Baillie had discovered enormous abuses in the management of the institution (which was used for political purposes) and had publicly charged them on Lord Sandwich, First Lord of the Admiralty. For this he was prosecuted on a charge of a libel, at the instance of Sandwich, who kept, however, behind the scenes to avoid any opportunity of bringing him before the court on the merits of the case. As the trial was soon to come on, Erskine remarked on this conduct at table with great severity, not knowing that Baillie *was present as one of the guests.* The captain was delighted with what he heard; and learning that his volunteer advocate was a young lawyer, as yet without business, who had himself been a sailor, declared to a friend that he should at least have one brief. Accordingly, Erskine's first retainer of a guinea was put into his hands the next day and it never occurred to him but that he was the only counsel in the case. As the trial approached, however, he found there were four distinguished advocates before him and he also found they had so little hope of success that they advised Baillie, at a consultation, to pay the costs, and in this way escape trial, as the prosecutors had kindly proposed. Erskine alone dissented. "My advice, gentlemen," said he, "may savor more of my former profession than my present, but I am against consenting." "You are the man for me," said Baillie, hugging the young advocate in his arms; "I will never give up."

The case came on before Lord Mansfield in the afternoon of November 23d, 1778. The senior counsel of Baillie consumed the time till late in the evening in showing cause why the rule should be dismissed; and no one expecting Erskine to come forward, the case was adjourned until the next day. The court was crowded in the morning, as the Solicitor General was expected to speak in support of the rule, and, just as Lord Mansfield was about to call upon him to proceed, Erskine rose, unknown to nearly every individual in the room except his Lordship, and said, in a mild but firm tone, "My

Lord, *I am likewise counsel for the author of this supposed libel,* . . . and when a British subject is brought before a court of justice only for having ventured to attack abuses which owe their continuance to the danger of attacking them, . . . I can not relinquish the privilege of doing justice to such merit; I will not give up even my share of the honor of repelling and exposing so odious a prosecution." The whole audience was hushed into a pin-fall silence, and he then went on to ask in regard to his client, *"Who is he? What was his duty? What has he written? To whom has he written? and what motive induced him to write?"* Taking these inquiries as the heads of his speech, he went on, in brief but eloquent terms, to show that Baillie, as Lieutenant Governor of the Hospital, was bound in duty to expose the abuses of the institution—that he had written nothing on the subject but what was undeniably true—that he had written it for the information of the Governors of the Hospital, who ought to be informed on such a subject—and that his only motive in writing had been the protection of those who had lost their limbs and periled their lives in fighting the battles of their country. In closing, he turned from Captain Baillie to the First Lord of the Admiralty, "Indeed, Lord Sandwich," said he, "has in my mind—" [Mansfield here reminded him that Lord Sandwich was not before the court, when Erskine, borne away by his feelings, instantly broke forth], "I know he is not formally before the court, but for that very reason *I will bring him before the court!* He has placed these men [the prosecutors] in the front of the battle, in hopes to escape under their shelter; but I will not join in the battle with them; *their* vices, though screwed up to the highest pitch of human depravity, are not of dignity enough to vindicate the combat with *me.* I will drag *him* to light, who is the dark mover behind this scene of iniquity. I assert, that the Earl of Sandwich has but one road to escape out of this business without pollution and disgrace, and *that is* by publicly disavowing the acts of the prosecutors and restoring Captain Baillie to his command. If he does this, then his offense will be no more than the too common one of having suffered his own personal interest to prevail over his public duty, in placing his voters in the hospital. But if, on the contrary, he continues to protect the prosecutors, in spite of the evidence of their guilt which has excited the abhorrence of the numerous audience that crowd this court; *if he keeps this injured man suspended, or dares to turn that suspension into a removal, I shall then not scruple to declare him an accomplice in their guilt, a shameless oppressor, a disgrace to his rank and a traitor to his trust. . . .* "FINE AND IMPRISONMENT! The man deserves a *palace* instead of a *prison* who prevents the palace, built by the public bounty of his country, from being converted into a dungeon and who sacrifices his own security to the interests of humanity and virtue." Considering all the circumstances of the case, it is not surprising that Lord Campbell should pronounce this "the most wonderful forensic effort which we have in our annals." It is hardly necessary to say that the decision was for the defendant; the rule was dismissed with costs.

Never did a single case so completely make the fortune of any individual. Erskine entered Westminster Hall that morning not only in extreme poverty, but with no reasonable prospect of an adequate subsistence for years. He left it a rich man. He received thirty retainers from attorneys who were present, it is said, while retiring from the hall. Not only was his ambition gratified, but the comfort and independence of those whose happiness he had staked on his success as a lawyer were secured for life. Some one asked him, at a later period, how he dared to face Lord Mansfield so boldly on a point where he was clearly out of order, when he beautifully replied, "I thought of my children as plucking me by the robe, and saying, 'Now, father, is the time to get us bread.'" His business went on rapidly increasing until he had an annual income of £12,000.

The next year he added to his reputation by a masterly defense of Admiral Keppel before a court-martial at Portsmouth. His experience in naval affairs recommended him for this service, and he performed it with unabated zeal for thirteen days which were spent in examining witnesses and arguing points of order, after which he wrote out the speech which the Admiral read to the court. This was followed by a unanimous verdict of acquittal; so strongly did Keppel feel the value of the young advocate's services that he addressed him a note in token of his gratitude containing a present of a thousand pounds, adding, "I shall ever rejoice in this commencement of a *friendship* which I hope daily to improve." Erskine, with the boyish hilarity which always marked his character, hastened to the villa of the Reynoldses and, displaying his bank-notes, exclaimed, "Voilà the non-suit of cow-beef, my good friends."

He came into the House five years after, in November, 1783, as a supporter of the Coalition ministry of Mr. Fox and Lord North. Nearly all the lawyers being on the other side, great reliance was placed on his services by the friends of the new government. But they were sorely disappointed. His habits were not suited to parliamentary debate. His understanding was eminently a legal one; he wanted the stimulus and encouragement of a listening court and jury, and was embarrassed by the presence of sneering opponents ready to treat him with personal indignity. His vanity now turned to his disadvantage and put him in the power of his antagonists. When he commenced his maiden speech, says Mr. Croly, in his Life of George IV., "Mr. Pitt, evidently intending to reply, sat with pen and paper in his hand, prepared to catch the arguments of his formidable adversary. He wrote a word or two. Erskine proceeded; but, with every additional sentence, Pitt's attention to the paper relaxed, his look became more careless and he obviously began to think the orator less and less worthy of his attention. At length, while every eye in the House was fixed upon him, with a contemptuous smile he dashed the pen through the paper and flung them on the floor. Erskine never recovered from this expression of disdain; his voice faltered, he struggled through the remainder of his speech and sank into his seat dispirited and shorn of his fame." Sheridan remarked to him at a later period, "I'll tell you how it happens, Erskine; you are *afraid* of Pitt, and that is the flabby part of your character." There was too much truth in the remark. Erskine could bear any thing but contempt. He recovered himself, however, at a later period of life and made quite a number of very able and eloquent speeches; in fact, he would have stood high as a parliamentary orator if he had not so completely outshone himself by the brilliancy of his efforts in Westminster Hall.

"As an advocate in the forum," says Lord Campbell, "I hold him to be without an equal in ancient or modern times." What is rare in one of so brilliant a genius, he had no less power with the court than with the jury. It was remarked of him, as of Scarlett, that "he had invented a machine by the secret use of which, in court, he could make the head of a judge nod assent to his propositions; whereas his rivals, who tried to pirate it, always made the same head move from side to side." He was certainly not a profound lawyer, as the result of original investigation; his short period of study rendered this impossible. But he had the power of availing himself more completely than almost any man that ever lived of the knowledge collected for his use by others. His speech on the Rights of Juries in the case of the Dean of St. Asaph, is universally admitted to show "a depth of learning which would have done honor to Selden or Hale;" and so completely had he thrown his mind into the case and made himself master of what black-letter lawyers spent months in searching out as the materials of his brief that he poured forth all this learning in his argument before the court with the freshness and precision of one who had spent his life in such researches. He always, indeed, grasped a cause so firmly that he never forgot a principle or a decision, an analogy or a fact which made for his client, while he showed infinite dexterity in avoiding the difficulties of his case and turning to his own advantage the unexpected disclosures which sometimes come out in the progress of a trial. Nothing could be more incorrect than the idea of some, that Erskine owed his success chiefly to the warmth and brilliancy of his genius. The dryest special pleader never managed a cause with greater caution. Even in his Indian Chief, in the case of Stockdale, a passage which verges more toward poetry than any thing in our eloquence, he was still, as a writer in the Edinburgh Review remarks, "*feeling his way* every step he took." His boldness was equal to his caution. In his defense of the liberty of the press and of the rights of the subject when assailed by the doctrine of constructive treason, he had some of the severest conflicts with the court which any advocate was ever called to maintain. When the jury, in the case of the Dean of St. Asaph, brought in their verdict, "Guilty of publishing *only,*" which would have the effect of clearing the defendant, Justice Buller, who presided, acting on the principle then held by the court, considered it beyond their province to make this addition and determined they should withdraw it. Erskine, on the other hand, seized upon the word the moment it was uttered and demanded to have it recorded. After some sparring between him and the court, he put the question to the foreman, "Is the word *only* to stand as a part of the verdict?" "Certainly," was the reply. "Then I insist it shall be recorded," says Erskine. "The verdict," says Buller, "must be misunderstood: let me understand the jury." "The jury," replied Erskine, "do understand their verdict." *Buller*. "Sir, I will not be interrupted." *Erskine*. "I stand here as an advocate for a brother citizen, and I desire the word *only* may be recorded." *Buller*. "SIT DOWN SIR. REMEMBER YOUR DUTY, OR I SHALL BE OBLIGED TO PROCEED IN ANOTHER MANNER." *Erskine*. "YOUR LORDSHIP MAY PROCEED IN WHAT MANNER YOU THINK FIT; I KNOW MY DUTY AS WELL AS YOUR LORDSHIP KNOWS YOURS. I SHALL NOT ALTER MY CONDUCT." The spirit of the judge sunk before the firmness of the advocate; no attempt was made to carry the threat into execution.

It was this mixture of boldness and caution, it was the keen sagacity and severe logic of Erskine, which laid the foundation of his unrivaled power over a jury. It was owing to these qualities that when he threw into his argument all the strength of his ardent feelings and all that beauty and richness of illustration which his glowing fancy supplied, no one ever suspected him of wishing to play upon their passions; the appeal was still so entirely to their intellect that the jury gave him their sympathies without hesitation or reserve. And if he seemed to digress for a moment from the line of his reasoning, as he sometimes did for the sake of relieving the minds of his auditors, he still showed the same sagacity in turning even this to the furtherance of his argument, for he always brought back with him from these excursions some weighty truth which he had gathered by the way and which served to give a new and startling force to the urgency of his appeal. To these qualities he added a good-humored cheerfulness in the most difficult cases which put him on the best terms with the court and jury. They wished him to succeed, even when they had made up their minds that he must fail. It is easy to see the advantage he thus gained. Sometimes, under his management, the worst cause seemed wholly to change its aspect; as in the case of Hadfield (given below), in which Kenyon, who presided, showed himself at first to be strongly prejudiced against the prisoner, but had his views so entirely changed that at the close of Erskine's argument, he took the extraordinary step of recommending to the Attorney General not to proceed in the case, but to allow an immediate acquittal. Only one trait more will be added to his character as an advocate. He was uniformly kind to the younger members of the profession. He was the last man on earth to injure or depress a rival. When Sir James Mackintosh made his celebrated defense in the case of Peltier—a case which he might naturally expect, from his superior age and devotion to a free press, would have been committed to his care—he showed no mean jealousy; he attended the trial and, before retiring to bed that night, addressed a note to the young advocate expressing his warmest admiration of the defense, as "one of the most splendid monuments of genius, learning, and eloquence."

Nine of Mr. Erskine's ablest arguments are given in this collection.[2] It is unnecessary here to dwell upon their merits or the circumstances out of which they sprung: these are detailed at large in the Introductions which precede the speeches. The writer would only urge upon the general student in oratory not to pass over, as belonging exclusively to the lawyer, the four great arguments of Erskine in the cases of Lord George Gordon, of the Dean of St. Asaph, of Hardy, and of Hadfield. The technical terms are briefly explained in notes, so that no embarrassment need arise from this cause. As specimens of acute and powerful reasoning, enlivened occasionally by glowing eloquence, they are among the finest efforts of genius in our language. Nothing can be more useful to our young orators of any profession than to make themselves perfectly acquainted with these admirable specimens of reasoning, whatever toil it may cost them. Such productions, as Johnson said of a similar class of writings, "are bark and steel to the mind."

Mr. Erskine, as already mentioned, came into Parliament in 1783, as the friend and supporter of Mr. Fox. He adhered to him in all his reverses and at last shared in his success. When Lord Grenville and Mr. Fox came into power in 1806, Erskine was appointed Lord Chancellor, thus verifying a prediction which he made twenty-seven years before, just after he was called to the bar, and which (for he was inclined to be superstitious) he probably ascribed to some supernatural agency. "Willie," said he to his friend William Adam, after a long silence, as they were riding together over a blasted heath between Lewes and Guilford, in 1779, "Willie, the time will come when I shall be Lord Chancellor, and the Star of the Thistle shall blaze on my bosom!" His dream was now accomplished. But the office of Lord Chancellor was one to which he was very little suited. All his practice had lain in another direction; he was wholly unacquainted with the laws of property, so essential to the decision of cases in chancery, and "the doctrines which prevail in the courts of equity," as Sir Samuel Romilly remarked, "were to him almost like the laws of a foreign country." He had always thrown contempt upon proceedings in these courts, and was sometimes taunted with his pathetic appeal to Lord Kenyon, when recommending that his client should apply to chancery for redress: "Would your Lordship send a *dog* you loved there?" Still, he endeavored to gain what information he could on the subject at his period of life, and said humorously to Romilly, who excelled in this knowledge of these proceedings, "You must make me a chancellor now, that *I may afterward make you one*." Though he added no honor to the office, he did not disgrace it. None of his decisions except one were ever called in question, and that was affirmed by the House of Lords. He presided with dignity, and when he retired from office, as he did at the end of thirteen months,

Sir Arthur Pigot addressed him in the name of the bar, expressing "their grateful sense of the kindness shown them while he presided."

The remainder of Erskine's life was saddened by poverty and unworthy of his early fame. The usages of the profession forbade his returning to the bar; the pension on which he retired was small; the property he had gained was wasted in speculations; and his early sense of character was unhappily lost, to some extent, in the general wreck of his fortunes. He died on a visit to Scotland, at Almondell, the residence of his sister-in-law, on the 17th of November, 1823, in the seventy-third year of his age.

The oratory of Erskine owed much of its impressiveness to his admirable delivery. He was of the medium height, with a slender but finely-turned figure, animated and graceful in gesture, with a voice somewhat shrill but beautifully modulated, a countenance beaming with emotion, and an eye of piercing keenness and power. "Juries," in the words of Lord Brougham, "have declared that they felt it impossible to remove their looks from him when he had riveted and, as it were, fascinated them by his first glance; and it used to be a common remark of men who observed his motions that they resembled those of a *blood-horse;* as light, as limber, as much betokening strength and speed, as free from all gross superfluity or encumbrance."

His style was chaste, forcible, and harmonious, a model of graceful variety, without the slightest mannerism or straining after effect. His rhythmus was beautiful; that of the passage containing his Indian Chief is surpassed by nothing of the kind in our language. His sentences were sometimes too long—a fault which arose from the closeness and continuity of his thought.

The exordium with which Erskine introduced a speech was always natural, ingenious, and highly appropriate; none of our orators have equaled him in this respect. The arrangement of the matter which followed was highly felicitous; and he had this peculiarity, which gave great unity and force to his arguments, that "he proposed," in the words of another, "a *great leading principle,* to which all his efforts were referable and subsidiary—which ran through the whole of his address, governing and elucidating every part. As the principle was a true one, whatever might be its application to that particular case, it gave to his whole speech an air of honesty and sincerity which it was difficult to resist."[3]

JOHN PHILPOT CURRAN

JOHN PHILPOT CURRAN was born at Newmarket, an obscure village in the northwest corner of the county of Cork, Ireland, on the 24th of July, 1750. The family was in low circumstances, his father being seneschal, or collector of rents, to a gentleman of small property in the neighborhood. He was a man, however, of vigorous intellect and acquirements above his station; while his wife was distinguished for that bold, irregular strength of mind, that exuberance of imagination and warmth of feeling, which were so strikingly manifested in the character of her favorite son.

The peculiar position of his father brought the boy, from early life, into contact with persons of every class, both high and low; and he thus gained that perfect knowledge of the mind and heart of his countrymen and that kindling sympathy with their feelings, which gave him more power over an Irish jury than any other man ever possessed. Though sent early to school, his chief delight was in society—in fun, frolic, mimicry, and wild adventure. The country fairs, which were frequent in his native village, were his especial delight; and, as he moved in the crowded streets among the cattle and pigs, the horse-dealers and frieze-dealers, the match-makers and the peddlers, he had his full share of the life, and sport, and contention of the scene. He was a regular attendant on dances and wakes, and dwelt with the deepest interest on the old traditions about the unfinished palace of Kanturk, in the neighborhood, or listened to the stories concerning the rapparees of King William's wars, or to "the strains of the piper as he blew the wild notes to which Alister M'Donnel marched to battle at Knocknanois, and the wilder ones in which the women mourned over his corse." Every thing conspired from his earliest years to give him freedom and versatility of mind, to call forth the keenest sagacity as to character and motives, to produce a quick sense of the ridiculous, to cherish that passionate strength of feeling which expressed itself equally in tears and laughter; to make him, at once, of *reality* and *imagination* "all compact."

When he was about fourteen years old, as he was rolling marbles one morning and playing his tricks in the ball-alley, he attracted the notice of an elderly gentleman who was passing by. It was the Rev. Mr. Boyse, a clergyman of the Church of England, who held the rectorship of the parish. The family of Curran were attendants on his ministry, and he had heard much of the brightness and promise of the boy. He invited him to his house and was so much pleased with his frank and hearty conversation that he offered at once to instruct him in the classics with a view to his entering Trinity College, Dublin. Young Curran was ready for any thing that could gratify his curiosity. He removed to the Rectory; he devoted himself to study, though with occasional outbreaks of his love of fun and frolic; he made such proficiency that, within three years, he fairly outran his patron's ability to teach him; he was then removed by Mr. Boyse to a school at Middleton, and supported partly at his expense; and was prepared for the University in 1769, at the age of nineteen.

Here he studied the classics especially, with great ardor, perfecting himself so fully both in the Latin and Greek languages that he could read them with ease and pleasure throughout life. His exertions were rewarded by honors and emoluments which very nearly provided for his support while in college, and he carried with him into life an enthusiasm for these studies which never subsided, amid all the multiplied cares of business and politics. For a long time he read Homer once every year; Mr. Phillips speaks of seeing him, late in life, on board a Holyhead packet in a storm, absorbed in the Æneid, while every one around was deadly sick; and in the last journey he ever took, Horace and Virgil were still, as in early life, his traveling companions. He was also distinguished at college for his love of metaphysical inquiries and subtle disquisition. He showed great ingenuity in the discussion of subjects; and his companions were so much struck with his dexterity and force on a certain occasion that they declared, with one consent, that "the bar, and the bar alone, was the proper profession for the talents of which he had that day given such striking proof." "He accepted the omen," says his son, "and never after repented of his decision."[1]

Having completed his college course and qualified himself for the degree of Master of Arts, in 1773, he removed to London and commenced the study of the law in the Middle Temple. Here he was supported in part by a wealthy friend, but his life in London was "a hard one." He spent his mornings, as he states, "in reading even to exhaustion," and the rest of the day in the more congenial pursuits of literature and especially in unremitted efforts to perfect himself as a speaker. His voice was bad and his articulation so hasty and confused that he went among his school-fellows by the name of "stuttering Jack Curran." His manner was awkward, his gesture constrained and meaningless, and his whole appearance calculated only to produce laughter, notwithstanding the evidence he gave of superior abilities. All these faults he overcame by severe and patient labor. Constantly on the watch against bad habits, he practiced daily before a glass, reciting passages from Shakspeare, Junius, and the best English orators. He frequented the debating societies, which then abounded in London; and though mortified at first by repeated failures, and ridiculed by one of his opponents as "Orator Mum," he surmounted every difficulty. "He turned his shrill and stumbling brogue," says one of his friends, "into a flexible, sustained, and finely-modulated voice; his action became free and forcible; he acquired perfect readiness in thinking on his legs;" he put down every opponent by the mingled force of his argument and wit, and was at last crowned with the universal applause of the society and invited by the president to an entertainment in their behalf. Well might one of his biographers say, "His oratorical training was as severe as any Greek ever underwent."

Mr. Curran married during his residence in London, with

but little accession to his fortune and, returning soon after to Ireland, commenced the practice of the law in Dublin, at the close of 1775. He soon rose into business, because he *could not do without it;* verifying the remark of Lord Eldon that some barristers succeed by great talents, some by high connections, some by miracle, but the great majority by *commencing without a shilling."* Within four years, he gained an established reputation and a lucrative practice; and at this time, 1779, he united with Mr. Yelverton, afterward Lord Avonmore, in forming a Society called "The Monks of the Order of St. Patrick," embracing a large part of the wit, literature, eloquence, and public virtue of the metropolis of Ireland. From the title familiarly given its members of the "Monks of the Screw," it has been supposed by many to have been chiefly a drinking-club. So far was this from being the case that, by an express regulation, every thing stronger than beer was excluded from the meeting. "It was a union," says one acquainted with its proceedings, "of strong minds, brought together like electric clouds by affinity and flashing as they joined. They met, and shone, and warmed—they had great passions and generous accomplishments, and, like all that was then good in Ireland, they were heaving for want of freedom." Nearly thirty years after, when the angry politics of the day had thrown Lord Avonmore and his friend into hostile parties so that they were no longer on speaking terms, Mr. Curran adverted to the meetings of this society in arguing a case before Lord Avonmore, as Chief Baron of the Exchequer, in a manner which was deeply interesting to those who witnessed it. After delicately alluding to his Lordship, as differing from the Chief Justice of England on a point of law and as having "derived his ideas from the purest fountains of Athens and Rome," Mr. Curran expressed his hope that such would be the decision of the court, embracing as it did members of the society referred to. "And this soothing hope," said he, "I draw from the dearest and tenderest recollections of my life—from the remembrance of those Attic nights and those refections of the gods which we have spent with those admired, and respected, and with beloved companions who have gone before us, over whose ashes the most precious tears of Ireland have been shed. [Here Lord Avonmore became so much affected that he could not refrain from tears.] Yes, my good Lord, I see you do not forget them. I see their sacred forms passing in sad review before your memory. I see your pained and softened fancy recalling those happy meetings, where the innocent enjoyment of social mirth became expanded into the nobler warmth of social virtue, and the horizon of the board became enlarged into the horizon of man—where the swelling heart conceived and communicated the pure and generous purpose—where my slenderer and younger taper imbibed its borrowed light from the more matured and redundant fountain of yours. Yes, my Lord, we can remember those nights without any other regret than that they can never more return; for,

> "We spent them not in toys, or lust, or wine,
> But search of deep philosophy,
> Wit, eloquence, and poesy,
> Arts which I loved—for they, my friend, were thine."
> —COWLEY.[2]

The space allowed to this sketch will not permit any minute detail of Mr. Curran's labors at the bar or in public life. Nor was there any thing in either which calls for an extended notice. He was a member of the Irish House of Commons from 1783 to 1797, and entered warmly into the cause of emancipation and reform; but he was never distinguished as a parliamentary orator. His education was forensic; his feelings and habits fitted him pre-eminently to act on the minds of a jury and for more than twenty years he had an unrivaled mastery over the Irish bar. His speeches at state trials arising out of the United Irish conspiracy were the most splendid efforts of his genius. He condemned insurrection; but he felt that the people had been goaded to madness by the oppression of the government and for nearly six years he tasked every effort of his being to save the victims of misguided and unsuccessful resistance. He did it at the hazard of his life. As he drove to town at this period from his residence in a neighboring village, he was in daily expectation of being shot at. The court-room was crowded with troops during some of the trials, with a view, it was believed, of intimidating the jury or the advocates of the prisoners. *"What's that?"* exclaimed Mr. Curran, as a clash of arms was heard from the soldiery at the close of one of his bold denunciations of the course pursued by the government. Some who stood near him seemed, from their looks and gestures, about to offer him personal violence, when he fixed his eye sternly upon them and added, *"You may assassinate, but you shall not intimidate me!"* "They were not mere clients for whom he pleaded," says his biographer, "they were friends for whose safety he would have coined his blood; they were patriots who had striven by means which he thought desperate or unsuited to himself for the freedom of their country. He came in the spirit of love and mercy, inspired by genius and commissioned by Heaven to walk on the waters with these patriots and lend them his hand when they were sinking. He pleaded for some who, nevertheless, were slaughtered; but was his pleading therefore in vain? Did he not convert many a shaken conscience, sustain many a frightened soul? Did he not keep the life of genius, if not of hope, in the country? Did he not help to terrify the government into the compromise which they so ill kept? He did all this, and more. His speeches will ever remain less as models of eloquence than as examples of patriotism and undying exhortations to justice and liberty."

In 1803 there was another attempt at insurrection which Mr. Curran regarded with very different emotions. It was that of Robert Emmett. Whatever we may think of the motives or the genius of this extraordinary young man, there can be but one opinion of the enterprise in which he was engaged. It was, from the first, rash and hopeless. He was just from college, with no character throughout the country to give him authority as a leader and no experience in the conduct of affairs, hasty in his judgments, obstinate to an extreme in his resolves, and fatally deceived by weak or false advisers. The moment he began to move, the ground sunk under him. "His attempt," as remarked by a friend of his principles, "had not the dignity of even partial success, and did a vast injury to the country." To Mr. Curran it was peculiarly afflictive, because it commenced with the murder of his old friend, Lord Chief Justice Kilwarden, in the streets of Dublin. In addition to this, Emmett had won the affections of Sarah Curran without the knowledge of her father; a correspondence between them was found among his papers; and Mr. Curran, thus brought under the suspicions of the government, was compelled to undergo the interrogatories of the Privy Council and had the pain of being laid under obligations to the generosity of the Attorney General, while his character was exposed to obloquy and the cause he had espoused subjected to the basest imputations from his political opponents. It is not, therefore, surprising that he refused to defend Emmett—defense was, indeed, impossible—or even to see him. Nor, perhaps, it is surprising that his feelings continued to be so much wounded at Sarah's clandestine engagement and its results as to make her home an unhappy one; so that she left his house, married without love, and carried her broken heart to an early grave in a foreign land.[3] To complete his wretchedness, Mr. Curran, through the villainy of a friend, was called to suffer the severest calamity which a husband can ever endure.

The remaining events of his life can be briefly told. On the accession of the Whigs to power, under Lord Grenville, in 1806, he was appointed Master of the Rolls. But the bench was not his place. He was but poorly fitted for its duties, and, though he discharged them with a moderate degree of ability, it was always with reluctance. To assuage the melancholy which now preyed upon him, he carried his former habits of convivality to a still greater extent. He surrounded himself with gay companions, especially at his dinner-table; "and when roused," says one of his biographers, "he used to run over jokes of every kind, good, bad, and indifferent. No epigram too delicate, no mimicry too broad, no pun too little, and no metaphor too bold for him. He wanted to be happy, and to make others so, and rattled away for mere enjoyment. These afternoon dinner sittings were seldom prolonged very late; but they made up in vehemence what they wanted in duration." But his health failed him, and in 1814 he resigned the Mastership of the Rolls. He now traveled, spending most of his time in England, but occasionally visiting Paris and other places on the Continent. In the spring of 1817, while dining with his friend, Thomas Moore, he had a slight attack of paralysis. His physician ordered him at once to the south of Europe, and, to arrange his affairs, he went over to Ireland for the last time. He returned to London and was attacked with apoplexy, of which he died after lingering a few days on the 14th of October, 1817.

Mr. Curran was short of stature, with a swarthy complexion and "an eye that glowed like a live coal." His countenance was singularly expressive; and, as he stood before a jury, he not only read their hearts with a searching glance, but he gave them back his own, in all the fluctuations of his feelings, from laughter to tears. His gesture was bold and impassioned; his articulation was uncommonly distinct and deliberate; the modulations of his voice were varied in a high degree and perfectly suited to the widest range of his eloquence.

His power lay in the variety and strength of his emotions. He delighted a jury by his wit; he turned the court-room into a scene of the broadest farce by his humor, mimicry, or fun; he made it "a place of tears," by a tenderness and pathos which subdued every heart; he poured out his invective like a stream of lava, and inflamed the minds of his countrymen almost to madness by the recital of their wrongs. His rich and powerful imagination furnished the materials for these appeals, and his instinctive knowledge of the heart taught him how to use them with unfailing success. He relied greatly for effect on his power of painting to the eye, and the actual condition of the country, for months during the insurrection and after it, furnished terrific pictures for his pencil. Speaking of the ignorance which prevailed in England as to the treatment of the Irish, he said, "If you wished to convey to the mind of an English matron the horrors of that period, when, in defiance of the remonstrances of the ever-to-be-lamented Abercromby, our poor people were surrendered to the brutality of the soldiery by the authority of the state, you would vainly attempt to give her a *general* picture of lust, and rapine, and murder, and conflagration. By endeavoring to comprehend every thing, you would convey nothing. When the father of poetry wishes to portray the movements of contending armies and an embattled field, he *exemplifies,* he does not describe. So should your story to her keep clear of generalities. You should take a cottage, and place the affrighted mother with her orphan daughters at the door, the paleness of death in her face and more than its agonies in her heart—her aching heart, her anxious ear struggling through the mist of closing day to catch the approaches of desolation and dishonor. The ruffian gang arrives—the feast of plunder begins—the cup of madness kindles in its circulation—the wandering glances of the ravisher become concentrated upon the shrinking and devoted victim. You need not dilate—you need not expatiate; the unpolluted matron to whom you tell the story of horror beseeches you not to proceed; she presses her child to her heart—she drowns it in her tears—her fancy catches more than an angel's tongue could describe; at a single view she takes in the whole miserable succession of force, of profanation, of despair, of death. So it is in the question before us."

The faults of Mr. Curran arose from the same source as his excellences. They lay chiefly on the side of *excess;* intense expressions, strained imagery, overwrought passion, and descriptions carried out into too great minuteness of circumstance. But he spoke for the people; the power he sought was *over the Irish mind;* and, in such a case, the cautious logic and the Attic taste of Erskine, just so far as they existed, would only have weakened the effect. There are but few parts of our country where Curran would be a safe model for the bar, but our mass meetings will be swayed most powerfully by an eloquence conceived in the spirit of the great Irish Orator.[4]

SIR JAMES MACKINTOSH

JAMES MACKINTOSH was the son of a captain in the British army, and was born at Aldourie, near Inverness, in Scotland, on the 24th of October, 1765. He was very early remarkable for his love of reading, making it his constant employment whether at home or abroad, and being accustomed, when a mere child, to take his book and dinner with him into the wild hills around his father's residence where he gave up the whole day in some secluded nook to his favorite employment.

At the age of ten, he was sent to a boarding-school at a small town called Fortrose, where he soon made such proficiency in his studies that "the name of *Jamie Mackintosh* was synonymous, all over the country side, with a prodigy of learning." He early assisted his instructor in teaching the younger boys and before he reached his thirteenth year, he showed a singular love of politics and extemporaneous speaking. "It was at this period," says his instructor, the Reverend Mr. Wood, "that Fox and North made such brilliant harangues on the American war. Jamie espoused the cause of liberty and called himself a *Whig;* and such was his influence among his school-fellows that he prevailed on some of the older ones, instead of playing at ball and such out-of-door recreations, to join him in the school-room during the hours of play and assist at debates, in what they called the *House of Commons,* on the political events of the day. When Jamie ascended the rostrum, he harangued until his *soprano* voice failed him. One day he was Fox, another Burke or some leading member of the Opposition; and when no one ventured to reply to his arguments, he would change sides for the present, personate North, and endeavor to combat what he conceived to be the strongest parts of his own speech. When I found out this singular amusement of the boys," adds Mr. Wood, "I had the curiosity to listen when Jamie was on his legs. I was greatly surprised and delighted with his eloquence in the character of Fox, against some supposed or real measure of the minister. His voice, though feeble, was musical, and his arguments so forcible that they would have done credit to many an adult."

At the age of fifteen he was placed at King's College, Aberdeen, and at once showed his predilection for those abstract inquiries in which he spent so large a part of his life. Though a mere boy, his favorite books were Priestley's Institutes of Natural and Revealed Religion, Beattie on Truth, and Warburton's Divine Legation which last delighted him, as he stated in after life, more than any book he ever read. He soon after made the acquaintance of Robert Hall, then a student at Aberdeen, who was deeply interested in the same pursuits, and though both were diligent in their classical studies, they gave their most strenuous and unwearied labors to a joint improvement in philosophy. They read together; they sat side by side at lecture; they were constant companions in their daily walks. In the classics, they united in reading much of Xenophon and Herodotus, and more of Plato; and so far did they carry it, says the biographer of Hall, that, "exciting the admiration of some and the envy of others, it was not unusual for their class-fellows to point at them and say, 'There go Plato and Herodotus!' But the arena in which they most frequently met was that of morals and metaphysics. After having sharpened their weapons by reading, they often repaired to the spacious sands on the sea-shore and, still more frequently, to the picturesque scenery on the banks of the Don above the old town, to discuss with eagerness the various subjects to which their attention had been directed. There was scarcely an important position in Berkeley's Minute Philosopher, in Butler's Analogy, or in Edwards on the Will, over which they had not thus debated with the utmost intensity. Night after night, nay, month after month, they met only to study or dispute, yet no unkindly feeling ensued. The process seemed rather, like blows in the welding of iron, to knit them more closely together." From this union of their studies and the discussions which ensued, Sir James afterward declared himself to have "learned more than from all the books he ever read;" while Mr. Hall expressed his opinion throughout life that Sir James "had an intellect more like that of Bacon than any person of modern times."

Having taken his degree of Bachelor of Arts at the age of nineteen, Mr. Mackintosh repaired to Edinburgh in 1784 and commenced the study of medicine. Here he was soon received as a member of the Speculative Society, an association for debate which then exerted a powerful influence over the University and was the means of training some of the most distinguished speakers which Scotland has ever produced. In this exciting atmosphere, his early passion for extemporaneous speaking, in connection with his subsequent habits of debate, gained the complete ascendency, so that, although his medical studies were not wholly neglected, a large part of his time was given to those miscellaneous subjects which would furnish topics for the Society and that desultory reading and speculation in which he always delighted.

After four years spent at Edinburgh, Mr. Mackintosh went to London in 1788, with a view to medical practice, but found no immediate prospect of business and but little encouragement for the future. His father died about this time, leaving him a very scanty patrimony; and, as he married soon after, without adding to his property, he was driven, like Burke in early life, to the public press for the means of support. He wrote from the first with uncommon force and elegance and was thus introduced to the acquaintance of some distinguished literary men, chiefly of the extreme Whig party. He was much in the society of Horne Tooke and found great delight in the rich, lively, and sarcastic conversation of that extraordinary man; while Tooke, though jealous and sparing of praise, was so struck with his talents for argument that he declared him "a very *formidable* adversary across a table." He now took to the study of the law in connection with his labors for the press, and never, probably, were his exertions greater or better directed than at this time, or more conducive to his intellectual improvement. Desultory reading and speculation without any definite object were the bane of his life; but he was now held to his daily task and, under the pressure of want, the encouragement of his friends, and the kindling delight which he felt in high literary excellence, he was daily forming those habits of rich and powerful composition for which he was afterward so much distinguished.

In 1791 he published his first great work, the "Vindiciæ Gallicæ," or "Defense of the French Revolution against the accusations of the Right Honorable Edmund Burke." It was a daring attempt for a young man of twenty-six to enter the lists with such an opponent, celebrated beyond any man of the age for his powers as a writer and regarded as an oracle by nearly all among the middling and higher classes, who looked with horror and dismay at the Revolution which this unknown adventurer came forward to defend. Not to have failed utterly in such an attempt was no mean praise. But he did more. He brought to the work an honest and dauntless enthusiasm; a large stock of legal and constitutional learning; a style which, though inferior in richness to that of his great antagonist, was not only elegant and expressive, but often keen and trenchant; and his success was far beyond his most sanguine expectations. Three editions were called for in rapid succession; Mr. Fox quoted the work with applause in the House of Commons, and even Mr. Burke, who had been treated by Mr. Mackintosh with the respect due to his great talents, spoke of its spirit and execution in the kindest terms. Mr. Canning, who was accustomed, at that period, to treat every thing that favored the Revolution with ridicule or contempt, told a friend that he read the book on its first coming out "with as much admiration as he had ever felt."

The Revolution turned out very differently, in most respects, from what Mr. Mackintosh had hoped, and he saw reason to change some of the opinions expressed in this work. He afterward made the acquaintance of Mr. Burke and remarked, in a letter to him about four years after, "For a time I was seduced by what I thought *liberty* and ventured to oppose, without ever ceasing to venerate, that writer who had nourished my understanding with the most wholesome principles of political wisdom. Since that time a melancholy experience has undeceived me on many subjects in which I was then the dupe of my own enthusiasm. I can not say (and you would despise me if I dissembled) that I can even now assent to all your opinions on the present politics of Europe.[1] But I can with truth affirm that I subscribe to your general principles and am prepared to shed my blood in defense of the laws and Constitution of my country."[2]

In the latter part of 1795, Mr. Mackintosh was called to the bar, and in 1799 he formed the plan of giving lectures on the Law of Nature and of Nations. The subject was peculiarly suited to his philosophical cast of mind and had long occupied his attention. Being in want of a hall for the purpose, he asked the Benchers of Lincoln's Inn to grant him the use of theirs, and when some demur was made on account of the sentiments expressed in his Vindiciæ Gallicæ, he printed the Introductory Lecture as a prospectus of the course. It was truly and beautifully said by Thomas Campbell, "If Mackintosh had published nothing else than this Discourse, he would have left a perfect monument of his intellectual strength and symmetry; and even supposing that essay had been recovered only imperfect and mutilated—if but a score of its consecutive sentences could be shown, they would bear a testimony to his genius as decided as the bust of Theseus bears to Grecian art among the Elgin marbles." The Lord Chancellor [Loughborough], ashamed of the delay among the Benchers, interposed decisively and procured the use of the hall, and the Prime Minister, Mr. Pitt, "always liberally inclined," as one of his opponents in politics has described him, wrote a private letter to Mr. Mackintosh, saying, "The plan you have marked out appears to me to promise more useful instruction and just reasoning on the principles of government than I have ever met with in any treatise on the subject." The lectures now went forward, and Lincoln's Inn Hall was daily filled with an auditory such as never before met on a similar occasion. Lawyers, members of Parliament, men of letters, and gentlemen from the country crowded the seats, and the Lord Chancellor, who, from a pressure of public business was unable to attend, received a full report of each lecture in writing and was loud in their praise.

In such a course of lectures the name of Grotius could not fail to have a prominent place, and the reader will be delighted with the following sketch of his character, which has rarely, if ever, been equaled by any thing of the kind in our language.

> So great is the uncertainty of posthumous reputation, and so liable is the fame, even of the greatest men, to be obscured by those new fashions of thinking and writing which succeed each other so rapidly among polished nations, that Grotius, who filled so large a space in the eyes of his cotemporaries, is now, perhaps, known to some of my readers only by name. Yet, if we fairly estimate both his endowments and his virtues, we may justly consider him as one of the most memorable men who have done honor to modern times. He combined the discharge of the most important duties of active and public life with the attainment of that exact and various learning which is generally the portion only of the recluse student. He was distinguished as an advocate and a magistrate, and he composed the most valuable works on the law of his own country. He was almost equally celebrated as a historian, a scholar, a poet, and a devine; a disinterested statesman, a philosophical lawyer, a patriot who united moderation with firmness, and a theologican who was taught candor by his learning. Unmerited exile did not damp his patriotism; the bitterness of controversy did not extinguish his charity. The sagacity of his numerous and fierce adversaries could not discover a blot on his character; and in the midst of all the hard trials and galling provocations of a turbulent political life, he never once deserted his friends when they were unfortunate, nor insulted his enemies when they were weak. In times of the most furious civil and religious faction he preserved his name unspotted, and he knew how to reconcile fidelity to his own party with moderation toward his opponents.

The Introductory Lecture closed in the following beautiful manner:

> I know not whether a philosopher ought to confess that, in his inquiries after truth, he is *biased* by any consideration, even by the love of virtue; but I, who conceive that a real philosopher ought to regard truth itself chiefly on account of its subserviency to the happiness of mankind, am not ashamed to confess that I shall feel a great consolation at the conclusion of these lectures if, by a wide survey and an exact examination of the conditions and relations of human nature, I shall have confirmed but one individual in the conviction that justice is the permanent interest of all men, and of all commonwealths. To discover one new link of that eternal chain, by which the Author of the universe has bound together the happiness and the duty of his creatures, and indissolubly fastened their interests to each other, would fill my heart with more pleasure than all the fame with which the most ingenious paradox ever crowned the most ingenious sophist.

Mr. Mackintosh now devoted himself to his profession with the most flattering prospects of success; but his thoughts were soon after directed to a judicial station, either in Trinidad or India, which he had the prospect of obtaining, and which he considered as more suited to his habits and cast of mind. While this matter was pending, he made his celebrated speech in favor of M. Peltier, which is given in this collection. The case was a singular one. Peltier was a French royalist who resided in London and published a newspaper in the French language in which he spoke with great severity of Bonaparte, then First Consul of France. It would seem hardly possible that a man like Bonaparte could feel the slightest annoyance at such attacks; but it is said to have been the weak point in his character, and that he was foolishly sensitive on this subject. At all events, as the two countries were then at peace, he made a formal demand of the English ministry to punish Peltier for "a libel on a friendly government." A prosecution was accordingly commenced, and Mr. Mackintosh, in defending Peltier, was brought into the same dilemma with that of Demosthenes in his Oration for the Crown. Equity was on his side, but the law was against him; and his only hope (as in the case of Demosthenes) was that of pre-occupying the minds of the jury with a sense of national honor and public justice and bearing them so completely away by the fervor of his eloquence as to obtain a verdict of acquittal from their feelings without regard to the strict demands of law. His theme was the *freedom of the English press*—its right and duty to comment on the crimes of the proudest tyrants; and he maintained (with great appearance of truth) that the real object of Bonaparte, after destroying every vestige of free discussion throughout the Continent, was to silence the press of England as to his conduct and designs. He told the jury, after dwelling on the extinction of the liberty of the press abroad, "One asylum of free discussion is still inviolate. There is still one spot in Europe where man can freely exercise his reason on the most important concerns of society—where he can boldly publish his judgment on the acts of the proudest and most powerful tyrants. The press of England is still free. It is guarded by the free Constitution of our forefathers; it is guarded by the hearts and arms of Englishmen; and I trust I may venture to say that if it be to fall, it will fall only under the ruins of the British empire. It is an awful consideration, gentlemen: every other monument of European liberty has perished: that ancient fabric which has been gradually reared by the wisdom and virtue of our fathers still stands. It stands (thanks be to God!) solid and entire; but it stands alone, and it stands amid ruins." Still, as the law was, the jury felt bound to convict Peltier.

We have hardly any thing in our eloquence conceived in a finer spirit, or carried out in a loftier tone of sentiment and feeling than the appeals made in this oration. It would have been just as sure to succeed before an Athenian tribunal as that of Demosthenes to fail in an English court of law. Lord Erskine was present during its delivery and before going to bed addressed the following note to Mr. Mackintosh:

> DEAR SIR,—I can not shake off from my nerves the effect of your powerful and most wonderful speech, which so completely disqualifies you for Trinidad or India. I could not help saying to myself, as you were speaking, *'O terram illam beatam quæ hunc virum acciperit, hanc ingratam si ejicerit, miseram si amiserit.'*[3] I perfectly approve the ver-

dict, but the manner in which you opposed it I shall always consider as one of the most splendid monuments of genius, literature, and eloquence.

Yours ever, T. ERSKINE.

When the speech was published, Mr. Mackintosh sent a copy to his friend Robert Hall and soon after received a letter, containing, among other things, the following passage: "Accept my best thanks for the trial of Peltier, which I read, so far as your part in it is concerned, with the highest delight and instruction. I speak my sincere sentiments when I say it is the most extraordinary assemblage of whatever is most refined in address, profound in political and moral speculation, and masterly in eloquence, which it has ever been my lot to read in the English language."

A few months after, Mr. Mackintosh was appointed Recorder of Bombay and at the same time received the honors of knighthood. He arrived in India about the middle of 1804 and spent eight years in that country, devoting all the time he could gain from the duties of the bench to the more congenial pursuits of literature. He wrote several interesting pieces during this period, and particularly a sketch of Mr. Fox's character, which will be found below, and which has always been regarded as one of the best delineations ever given of that distinguished statesman. His appointment to India was, on the whole, injurious to his intellectual growth. He needed beyond most men to be kept steadily at work, under the impulse of great objects and strong motives urging him to the utmost exertion of his powers. Had he remained at the bar, he might have surpassed Erskine in learning and rivaled him in skill as an advocate, while his depth and amplitude of thought would have furnished the richest materials for every occasion that admitted of eloquence. But he now relapsed into his old habits of desultory reading and ingenious speculation. He projected a number of great works and labored irregularly in collecting materials; but his health sunk under the enervating effects of the climate and he returned to England at the end of eight years, disappointed in his expectations and depressed in spirit, bringing with him a vast amount of matter for books which were never to be completed.

So highly were his talents appreciated that immediately after his return in 1812, he was offered a seat in the House of Commons by the government and also by his old Whig friends. He chose the latter and continued true to liberal principles to the end of his days.

In 1818 he was appointed Professor of Law and of General Politics at Haileybury College, an institution designed to prepare young men for the service of the East India Company. His lectures embraced a course of four years, extending through four months of each year. He endeared himself greatly to his pupils by his kind and conciliating manners, while his extraordinary learning and the high reputation he had with the public, made him the object of their respect and veneration. This situation he held nine years, and resigned it in 1827. During all this time he took an active part in politics, entering warmly into every important debate in Parliament and writing numerous articles for the Edinburgh Review. He also wrote, in 1829, a Dissertation on the Progress of Ethical Philosophy, which was first published as a supplement to the Encyclopedia Britannica, and soon after printed in an 8vo volume by itself. To these he added, in the three subsequent years, several volumes of an abridged history of England and a work on the Revolution of 1688, which was published after his death. Under the administration of Earl Grey, he was appointed a member of the Board of Control and took an active part in the great struggle for parliamentary reform.

As a speaker in Parliament he was instructive rather than bold and exciting. His residence in India had so debilitated his constitution, and his habits of speculation had so completely gained the ascendency, that he never spoke with that lofty enthusiasm and fervor of emotion which distinguished his defense of Peltier. He had, says an able cotemporary, "perhaps more than any man of his time, that *mitis sapientia* which formed the distinguishing characteristic of the illustrious friend of Cicero and which wins its way into the heart, while it at once enlightens and satisfies the understanding." He died on the 30th of May, 1832, in the sixty-seventh year of his age, perhaps more regretted and less envied than any public man of his age.[4]

GEORGE CANNING

GEORGE CANNING was born in London on the 11th of April, 1770. His father, who belonged to an Irish family of distinction, had been disinherited for marrying beneath his rank and was trying his fortune as a barrister in the English metropolis with very scanty means of subsistence. He died one year after the birth of his son, leaving a widow with three young children wholly destitute of property and dependent for support on her own exertions.

Under these circumstances, Mrs. Canning, who was a woman of extraordinary force of character, first set up a small school, and soon after attempted the stage. She was successful in her provincial engagements, especially at Bath and Exeter, and in the latter place she married a linen-draper of the name of Hunn, who was passionately attached to theatrical performances, and united with her in the employment of an actor. A few years after, she was again left a widow by the death of Mr. Hunn; but her profession gave her a competent independence, until she saw her son raised to the highest honors of the state and was permitted to share in the fruits of his success.[1]

George was educated under the care of his uncle, Mr. Stratford Canning, a London merchant, out of the proceeds of a small estate in Ireland which was left him by his grandmother. He was first sent to school at Hyde Abbey, near Winchester, where he made uncommon proficiency in the rudiments of Latin and Greek, and was particularly distinguished for his love of elegant English literature. On one occasion, when a mere child, being accidentally called upon to repeat some verses, he commenced with one of the poems of

Mr. Gray and never stopped or faltered until he had gone through the entire volume. His mother's employment naturally led him to take a lively interest in speaking and especially in acting dialogues, and in one instance, when the boys performed parts out of the Orestes of Euripides, previous to a vacation, he portrayed the madness of the conscience-stricken matricide with a force and tenderness which called forth the liveliest applause of the audience.

Before he was fifteen, George went to Eton and carried with him a high reputation for writing Latin and Greek verses, which always confers distinction in the great schools of England. He was at once recognized as a boy of surprising genius and attainments, and he used the influence thus gained in promoting his favorite pursuit, that of elegant English literature. When a little more than sixteen, he induced the boys to establish a weekly paper called the Microcosm, to which he contributed largely and acted as principal editor. Its pages bore such striking marks of brilliancy and wit as to attract the attention of the leading reviews, and the work became the means of training up some of the most distinguished men of the age to those habits of *early composition* which Sir James Mackintosh speaks of as indispensable to the character of a truly great writer.

His attention, while at Eton, was also strongly turned to extemporaneous speaking. He joined a society for debate, in which the Marquess of Wellesley, Earl Grey and other distinguished statesmen had gone before him in their preparation as orators and had introduced all the forms of the House of Commons. The Speaker was in the chair; the minister, with his partisans, filled the Treasury benches, and were faced by the most strenuous Opposition that Eton could muster. The enthusiasm with which Canning and his companions entered into these mimic contests was but little inferior to what they felt in the real ones that followed, and for which they were thus preparing the way. Canning, especially, showed throughout life the influence of his early habits of *writing* in conjunction with extemporaneous debate. His speeches bear proofs on every page of the effects of the pen in forming his spoken style. On every important debate, he wrote much beforehand,

and composed more in his mind, which flowed forth spontaneously, and mingled with the current of his thoughts, in all the fervor of the most prolonged and excited discussion. Hence, while he had great ease and variety, he never fell into that negligence and looseness of style which we always find in a purely extemporaneous speaker.

After standing foremost among his companions at Eton in all the lower forms, George became "captain" of the school and was removed to Christ Church, Oxford, in October, 1788. The accuracy and ripeness of his scholarship turned upon him the eyes of the whole University, and justified his entering, even when a *freshman,* into competition for the Chancellor's first prize, which he gained by a Latin poem entitled "Iter ad Meccam Religionis Causâ Susceptum." The distinction which he thus early acquired, he maintained, throughout his whole college course, by a union of exemplary diligence with a maturity of judgment, refinement of taste, and brilliancy of genius far beyond his years. In Mr. Canning we have one of the happiest exhibitions of the results produced by the classical course pursued at Eton and Oxford, which, "whatever may be its defects, must be owned," says Sir James Mackintosh, "when taken with its constant appendages, to be eminently favorable to the cultivation of sense and taste, as well as to the development of wit and spirit." The natural effect, however, of this incessant competition, in connection with the early tendencies of his mind and his remarkable success, was to cherish that extreme sensitiveness to the opinion of others, that delight in superiority, that quick sense of his own dignity, that sensibility to supposed neglect or disregard, which, with all his attractive qualities, made him in early life not always a pleasant companion and sometimes involved him in the most serious difficulties. But, though he never lost his passion for distinction, it was certainly true of him, as said by another, "As he advanced in years, his fine countenance, once so full of archness or petulance, was ennobled by the expression of thought and feeling; he now pursued that lasting praise which is not to be earned without praiseworthiness; and if he continued to be a lover of fame, he also passionately loved the glory of his country."

Mr. Canning left the University in the twenty-second year of his age and, after giving a few months to the study of the law, was invited by Mr. Pitt, who had heard of his extraordinary talents, to take a seat in Parliament as a regular supporter of the government. His first predilections were in favor of Whig principles. He had been intimate with Mr. Sheridan from early life, but differed from him wholly in respect to the French Revolution and was thus prepared to look favorably on the proposals of Mr. Pitt. After mutual explanations, he accepted the offer, and was returned to Parliament from one of the ministerial boroughs at the close of 1793, in the twenty-fourth year of his age.

Mr. Canning's maiden speech was in favor of a subsidy to the King of Sardinia and was delivered on the 31st of January, 1794. It was brilliant, but wanting in solidity and judgment, and in general it may be remarked that he rose *slowly* into those higher qualities as a speaker for which he was so justly distinguished during the later years of his life. He was from the first easy and fluent; he knew how to play with an argument when he could not answer it; he had a great deal of real wit, and too much of that ungenerous raillery and sarcasm by which an antagonist may be made ridiculous and the audience turned against him without once meeting the question on its true merits. There was added to this an air of disregard for the feelings of others, and even of willingness to offend, which doubled the sense of injury every blow he struck; so that during the first ten years of his parliamentary career, he never made a speech, it was said, on which he particularly plumed himself, without making likewise an enemy for life. He was continually acting, as one said who put the case strongly, like "the head of the sixth form at Eton: squibbing the 'doctor,' as Mr. Addington was called—fighting my Lord Castlereagh—cutting heartless jokes on poor Mr. Ogden—flatly contradicting Mr. Brougham—swaggering over the Holy Alliance—quarreling with the Duke of Wellington —perpetually involved in some personal scrape." These habits, however, gradually wore off as he advanced in life, and his early political opponents were warmest in their commendations of his conduct at the close of his political career.

In 1797, Mr. Canning projected the Anti-Jacobin Review,

in conjunction with Mr. Jenkinson and Mr. Ellis (afterward Lords Liverpool and Seaford), Mr. Frere, and other writers of the same stamp. Mr. Gifford was editor, and its object was to *bear down* the Radical party in politics and literature, and to turn upon them the contempt of the whole nation by the united force of argument and ridicule. It took the widest range, from lofty and vehement reasoning to the keenest satire and the most bitter personal abuse. It applied the lash with merciless severity to all the extravagances of the day in taste and sentiment—the mawkish sensibility of the Della Cruscan school, the incongruous mixtures of virtue and vice in the new German drama, and the various *improvements* in literature introduced by Holcroft, Thelwall, and others among the Radical reformers. Such an employment was perfectly suited to the taste of Mr. Canning. It was an exercise of ingenuity in which he always delighted; and a large part of the keenest wit, the most dextrous travesty, and the happiest exhibitions of the laughable and burlesque were the productions of his pen. The most striking poetical effusions were his. Among these, the "Knife-grinder," and the "Loves of Mary Pottinger," are admirable in their way, and will hold their place among the amusing extravangazas of our literature when the ablest political diatribes of the Anti-Jacobin are forgotten.[2]

In July, 1800, Mr. Canning married Miss Joan Scott, daughter of General Scott, and sister to Lady Tichfield, afterward Duchess of Portland. She had a fortune of £100,000, which placed him at once in circumstances of entire independence, while he gained an increase of influence by his family alliances.

In a sketch like this, only the leading incidents can be given in the political career of Mr. Canning. He was actively engaged in public life for nearly thirty-four years, eleven of which were spent in connection with Mr. Pitt. His first office was that of Under Secretary of State. He went out with his patron during Mr. Addington's brief ministry, and came in with him again, as Treasurer of the Navy, in 1804. On Mr. Pitt's death, early in 1806, he was not included (as he had reason to expect) in Lord Grenville's arrangements, and went into opposition. During his whole life, he was the ardent champion of the "Great Minister's" principles, and the defender of his fame. In the London Quarterly for August, 1810, he gave an estimate of Mr. Pitt's character and a defense of his political life, which for ingenuity of thought, richness of fancy, and splendor of diction, has never been surpassed in the periodical literature of our language. It came warm from his heart. He truly said to his constituents at Liverpool, "In the grave of Mr. Pitt my political allegiance lies buried."

On the accession of the Duke of Portland to power (March, 1807), Mr. Canning became Secretary of Foreign Affairs, and for the first time a member of the cabinet. But, at the end of two years, he had a personal altercation with Lord Castlereagh (then Secretary of War), resulting in a duel, which not only threw both of them out of office, but dissolved the Portland ministry.

Mr. Canning now remained out of power for some years, though regular in his attendance on Parliament. He took independent ground during Mr. Percival's ministry of a year and a half and delivered at this time his celebrated speech on the Bullion Question, exposing the current fallacy, "It is not paper that has fallen, but gold which has risen," and calling, in the strongest terms, for the resumption of cash payments. This speech, though interesting no longer to the general reader, has been truly characterized as "one of the most powerful and masterly specimens on record of chaste and reasoning eloquence." The question lay out of Mr. Canning's ordinary range of thought, and the ability with which he took it up proved (what his friends had always said) that no man could more promptly, or with greater effect, turn the whole force of his mind on any new subject, however foreign to his ordinary pursuits. Under his friend Lord Liverpool [Mr. Jenkinson], who followed Mr. Percival in June, 1812, he gave his cordial support to the ministry, though excluded from office by his views in favor of Catholic emancipation. To him especially, at this period, was Lord Wellington indebted for an enthusiastic support during his long and terrible conflict in Spain. It was under the policy and guidance of

Canning, as Secretary of Foreign Affairs in 1808, that this conflict commenced, and he never ceased to animate the country to fresh sacrifices and efforts in battling with Bonaparte for the rescue of the Peninsula. It was the first favorable opportunity ever presented for carrying out the continental policy of Mr. Pitt, and it was always the theme of Mr. Canning's proudest exultations. "If there is any part of my political conduct," said he, "in which I *glory*, it is that in the face of every difficulty, discouragement, and prophecy of failure, *mine* was the hand which committed England to an alliance with Spain."

In 1812, Mr. Canning was invited to stand as a candidate for Liverpool and, though powerfully opposed by Mr. Brougham, he carried his election and was again returned, on three subsequent occasions, with continually increasing majorities. Two speeches to his constituents at Liverpool will be found below; they are some of the best specimens of his eloquence.

In 1814, he was sent as embassador extraordinary to the court of Lisbon, and being attacked on this subject after his return to the House, in 1816, he made his defense in a speech of remarkable ability and manliness, which has, however, but little interest for the reader at the present day, because filled up chiefly with matters of personal detail. The same year [1816] he was made President of the Board of Indian Control and thus brought again into the ministry. From this time England was agitated for six or eight years by the rash movements of the Radical reformers, which led ministers to adopt measures of great, perhaps undue stringency, to preserve the public peace. Mr. Canning took strong ground on this subject and was severely attacked in a pamphlet understood to be from the pen of Sir Philip Francis. His extreme sensitiveness to such attacks showed itself in an extraordinary way. He addressed a private letter to the author of the pamphlet, through Ridgeway, the publisher, telling him, *"You are a liar and a slanderer, and want courage only to be an assassin."* Even on dueling principles, no man was bound to come forward under such a call, and the challenge which Mr. Canning endeavored to provoke was not given.

In 1822, he was appointed Governor General of India, but, at the moment when he was ready to embark for Calcutta, the office of Secretary of Foreign Affairs became vacant by the sudden death of the Marquess of Londonderry [Lord Castlereagh], and Mr. Canning was called to this important station on the 16th of September, 1822. It was a crisis of extreme difficulty. France was at that moment collecting troops to overthrow the constitutional government of Spain and was urging the other allied powers, then assembled in congress at Verona, to unite in the intervention. Mr. Canning instantly dispatched the Duke of Wellington to Verona with the strongest remonstrances of the British government against the proposed invasion of Spain and, at the opening of the next Parliament, explained and defended the views of the ministry in a manner which called forth the warmest applause of Mr. Brougham and most of his other political opponents. Early in 1825, Mr. Canning took the important step of recognizing the independence of the Spanish provinces in South America, a measure which made him deservedly popular in every part of the kingdom. In December, 1826, actuated by the same liberal sentiments, he made his celebrated speech on giving aid to Portugal, when threatened with invasion from Spain. It will be found below, and has been generally regarded as the master-piece of his eloquence, not only for the felicity of its arrangement and the admirable grace and spirit with which his points are pressed, but for the large and statesmanlike views he takes of European politics, and his prophetic foresight of the great contest of *principles* which was even then coming on.

As to all questions of foreign policy—the most important by far of any at that period—Mr. Canning was virtually minister from September, 1822, when he was appointed Secretary of Foreign Affairs. He had so entirely the confidence of Lord Liverpool that *his* intellect was the presiding one in the cabinet, and as Lord Liverpool's health began to decline, the burden of the government rested upon him more and more. In 1827, his Lordship died of a paralytic shock, and on April 12th of that year, Mr. Canning was made Prime Minister in form. The Duke of Wellington, Mr. Peel, and nearly all his Tory colleagues, threw up their places at once, out of hostility to Catholic emancipation, which they saw must prevail if he remained in power—the very men who, two years after, under the strong compulsion of public sentiment, carried that same emancipation through both houses of Parliament! But they sacrificed Mr. Canning before they could be made to do it. A keen and unrelenting opposition now sprung up, and some who, only a few months before had made him "the god of their idolatry," were foremost in denouncing him as "the most profligate minister that was ever in power." Unfortunately, at this crisis, his health failed him. He had been brought to the brink of the grave, at the commencement of the year, by an illness contracted at the funeral of the Duke of York, and with his peculiar sensitiveness, heightened by disease, he could not endure the bitter personal altercations to which he was continually exposed. He was singularly situated. Standing between the two great parties of the country, he agreed with the Whigs on the subjects of Catholic emancipation, foreign policy, and commercial regulation, while he differed from them as to parliamentary reform and the repeal of the Test Act. Still, they gave him a generous support; and he could rely on the wit of Tierney and the scathing eloquence of Brougham to defend him against the attacks of those who were so lately his servile dependents or his admiring friends. He had reached the summit of his ambition—but it was only to die! His ardent mind bore him up for a brief season, but was continually exhausting the springs of life within. His last act was one of his worthiest—that of signing the treaty of London for the deliverance of Greece. He transacted public business until a few days before his death and died on the 8th of August, 1827, in the fifty-eighth year of his age.[8]

As a fitting close of this memoir, the reader will be interested in the following beautiful sketch of Mr. Canning's character by Sir James Mackintosh, slightly abridged and modified in the arrangement of its parts.

"Mr. Canning seems to have been the best model among our orators of the adorned style. The splendid and sublime descriptions of Mr. Burke—his comprehensive and profound views of general principles—though they must ever delight and instruct the reader, must be owned to have been digressions which diverted the mind of the hearer from the object on which the speaker ought to have kept it steadily fixed. Sheridan, a man of admirable sense and matchless wit, labored to follow Burke into the foreign regions of feeling and grandeur. The specimens preserved of his most celebrated speeches show too much of the exaggeration and excess to which those are peculiarly liable who seek by art and effort what nature has denied. By the constant part which Mr. Canning took in debate, he was called upon to show a knowledge which Sheridan did not possess and a readiness which that accomplished man had no such means of strengthening and displaying. In some qualities of style Mr. Canning surpassed Mr. Pitt. His diction was more various—sometimes more simple—more idiomatical, even in its more elevated parts. It sparkled with imagery and was brightened by illustration; in both of which Mr. Pitt, for so great an orator, was defective.

"Had he been a dry and meager speaker, Mr. Canning would have been universally allowed to have been one of the greatest masters of argument; but his hearers were so dazzled by the splendor of his diction that they did not perceive the acuteness and the occasional excessive refinement of his reasoning; a consequence which, as it shows the injurious influence of a seductive fault, can with the less justness be overlooked in the estimate of his understanding. Ornament, it must be owned, when it only pleases or amuses, without disposing the audience to adopt the sentiments of the speaker, is an offense against the first law of public speaking; it obstructs instead of promoting its only reasonable purpose. But eloquence is a widely-extended art, comprehending many sorts of excellence, in some of which ornamented diction is more liberally employed than in others, and in none of which the highest rank can be attained without an extraordinary combination of mental powers.

"No English speaker used the keen and brilliant weapon of wit so long, so often, or so effectively, as Mr. Canning. He gained more triumphs, and incurred more enmity by it than by any other. Those whose importance depends much on birth and fortune are impatient of seeing their own artificial dignity, or that of their order, broken down by derision, and perhaps few men heartily forgive a successful jest against themselves, but those who are conscious of being unhurt by it. Mr. Canning often used this talent imprudently. In sudden flashes of wit, and in the playful description of men or things, he was often distinguished by that natural felicity which is the charm of pleasantry, to which the air of art and labor is more fatal than to any other talent. The exuberance of fancy and wit lessened the gravity of his general manner, and perhaps also indisposed the audience to feel his earnestness where it clearly showed itself. In that important quality he was inferior to Mr. Pitt,

> " 'Deep on whose front engraven,
> Deliberation sat, and public care;'[4]

and no less inferior to Mr. Fox, whose fervid eloquence flowed from the love of his country, the scorn of baseness, and the hatred of cruelty, which were the ruling passions of his nature.

"On the whole, it may be observed that the range of Mr. Canning's powers as an orator was wider than that in which he usually exerted them. When mere statement only was allowable, no man of his age was more simple. When infirm health compelled him to be brief, no speaker could compress his matter with so little sacrifice of clearness, ease, and elegance. As his oratorical faults were those of youthful genius, the progress of age seemed to purify his eloquence, and every year appeared to remove some speck which hid, or at least dimmed, a beauty. He daily rose to larger views, and made, perhaps, as near approaches to philosophical principles as the great difference between the objects of the philosopher and those of the orator will commonly allow.

"Mr. Canning possessed, in a high degree, the outward advantages of an orator. His expressive countenance varied with the changes of his eloquence; his voice, flexible and articulate, had as much compass as his mode of speaking required. In the calm part of his speeches, his attitude and gesture might have been selected by a painter to represent grace rising toward dignity.

"In social intercourse Mr. Canning was delightful. Happily for the true charm of his conversation, he was too busy not to treat society as more fitted for relaxation than for display. It is but little to say that he was neither disputations, declamatory, nor sententious—neither a dictator nor a jester. His manner was simple and unobtrusive; his language always quite familiar. If a higher thought stole from his mind, it came in its conversational undress. From this plain ground his pleasantry sprang with the happiest effect, and it was nearly exempt from that alloy of taunt and banter which he sometimes mixed with more precious materials in public contest. He may be added to the list of those eminent persons who pleased most in their friendly circle. He had the agreeable quality of being more easily pleased in society than might have been expected from the keenness of his discernment and the sensibility of his temper: still, he was liable to be discomposed, or even silenced, by the presence of any one whom he did not like. His manner in company betrayed the political vexations or anxieties which preyed on his mind: nor could he conceal that sensitiveness to public attacks which their frequent recurrence wears out in most English politicians. These last foibles may be thought interesting as the remains of natural character, not destroyed by refined society and political affairs.

"In some of the amusements or tasks of his boyhood there are passages which, without much help from fancy, might appear to contain allusions to his greatest measures of policy, as well as to the tenor of his life and to the melancholy splendor which surrounded his death. In the concluding line of the first English verses written by him at Eton, he expressed a wish, which has been singularly realized, that he might

" 'Live in a blaze, and in a blaze expire.'

It is a striking coincidence, that the statesman, whose dying measure was to mature an alliance for the deliverance of Greece, should, when a boy, have written English verses on the slavery of that country, and that in his prize poem at Oxford, on the Pilgrimage to Mecca—a composition as much applauded as a modern Latin poem can aspire to be—he should have so bitterly deplored the lot of other renowned countries now groaning under the same barbarous yoke,

" 'Nunc satrapæ imperio et sævo subdita Turcæ.'[5]

"To conclude: He was a man of fine and brilliant genius, of warm affections of a high and generous spirit—a statesman who, at home, converted most of his opponents into warm supporters; who, abroad, was the sole hope and trust of all who sought an orderly and legal liberty, and who was cut off in the midst of vigorous and splendid measures, which, if executed by himself or with his own spirit, promised to place his name in the first class of rulers, among the founders of lasting peace and the guardians of human improvement."[6]

LORD BROUGHAM

HENRY BROUGHAM is the last among the orators embraced in this collection; as he is still living, only a brief notice will be given of his life and character.

The family was one of the most ancient in Westmoreland, England. Brougham Castle is older than the days of King John, and the manor connected with it, after passing out of the family for a time, was regained by purchase and entailed on the oldest descendant in the male line. Toward the close of the last century, it fell to a young man who was studying in the University of Edinburgh and who married, while there, a niece of the celebrated historian, Dr. Robertson. The first-fruit of this union was a son named Henry, who was born at Edinburgh in 1779.

The family appear to have resided chiefly or wholly in the Scottish capital; the boy received the rudiments of his education at the High School of Edinburgh, under the celebrated Dr. Adam, and was even then distinguished for his almost intuitive perception of whatever he undertook to learn. "He was wild, fond of pleasure, taking to study by starts, and always reading with more effect than others (when he did read), because it was for some specific object, the knowledge of which was to be acquired in the shortest possible time." We have here a perfect picture of Lord Brougham's mode of reading for life. Eager, restless, grasping after information of every kind, he has brought into his speeches a wider range of collateral thought than any of our orators except Burke; and he has done it in just the way that might be expected from such a man, with inimitable freshness and power, but with those hasty judgments, that want of a profound knowledge of principles, and that frequent inaccuracy in details, which we always see in one who reads "for some specific object," instead of taking in the whole range of a science, and who is so much in a hurry, that he is constantly aiming to accomplish his task in "the shortest possible time."

He entered the University of Edinburgh in the sixteenth year of his age, and soon gained the highest distinction by his extraordinary mathematical attainments. He gave in solutions of some very difficult theorems which awakened the admiration of his instructors, and before he was seventeen, produced an essay on the "Flection and Reflection of Light" which was estimated so highly as to be inserted in the Edinburgh Philosophical Transactions. His supposed discoveries, so far as they were correct, proved, indeed, to have been anticipated by earlier writers; but they were undoubtedly the result of his own investigation; and they showed so remarkable a talent for mathematical research that he was rewarded, at a somewhat later period (1803), with an election as member of the Royal Society of Edinburgh. It is a curious fact that Lord Brougham has again taken up his favorite pursuits in optics at the age of seventy, and made recent communications to the French Institute, from his chateau at Cannes, in the south of France, on the same branch of science which called forth his early efforts in the University of Edinburgh.

Having completed his college course, Mr. Brougham entered with indefatigable zeal upon the study of the law, in conjunction with Jeffery, Horner, and several other young men, who, only a few years after, stood foremost among the leading advocates of the country. He had commenced the practice of extemporaneous speaking some years before in the Speculative Society, that great theater of debate for the University of Edinburgh. He now carried it to a still greater height in the immediate prospect of his professional duties and "exercised the same superiority over his youthful competitors (though some of them were then and afterward remarkable for their ability) which he held at a later period as Chancellor over the House of Lords." He was called in due course to the Scottish bar and commenced business in Edinburgh with the most encouraging prospects of success. In 1803, he published his first work, in two octavo volumes, entitled "The Colonial Policy of the European Powers," containing an immense amount of information and distinguished by the daring spirit of philosophical inquiry which he carried into this vast and complicated subject. He now removed to London and, in addition to his practice at the bar, entered warmly into politics, producing a volume on the "State of the Nation" which awakened the liveliest interest by its eloquent assertion of Whig principles and ultimately procured him a seat in Parliament by means of the Russell family.

Before his removal to London, he united with the companions mentioned above in establishing the Edinburgh Review. He was for nearly twenty years one of its most regular contributors, and to him more than any other man was the work indebted for its searching analysis, its contemptuous and defiant spirit, its broad views of political subjects, and its eloquent exposition of Whig principles. Its motto,[1] whether selected by him or not, was designed to justify that condemnatory spirit which is so striking a trait in his character. A great part of his life has been spent in *beating down;* in detecting false pretensions whether in literature or politics; in searching out the abuses of long established institutions; in laying open the perversions of public charities; in exposing the cruelties of the criminal code; or in rousing public attention to a world of evils resulting from the irregularities in the administration of municipal law. The reader will be amused to trace this tendency of his mind, in turning over the four octavo volumes of his speeches as edited by himself, and observing their titles. We have "Military Flogging," with an exposure of its atrocities—"Queen Caroline," defended at the expense of her husband—"The Durham Clergy," lashed unmercifully for their insulting treatment of the Queen—"The Orders in Council," with the folly of abusing the Americans because they had suffered from the abuse of France—"Agricultural Distress" and "Manufacturing Distress," as resulting from the rashness and incompetency of ministers—"Army Estimates," under which millions were lavished for mere military show in time of peace

—"The Holy Alliance," with its atrocious attack on the constitutional government of Spain through the instrumentality of France—"The Slave Trade"—"The Missionary Smith," murdered in Demerara under a false charge of having excited insurrection—"Negro Apprenticeship," its inadequacy and folly—"The Eastern Slave Trade," or the cruelty and guilt of transporting coolies from Hindostan to be made laborers in the West India Islands—"Law Reform"—"Parliamentary Reform"—"Education," and the abuse of Educational Charities—"Scotch Parliamentary and Burgh Reform"—"Scotch Marriage and Divorce Bill," showing that the existing laws are "the worst possible"—"The Poor Laws," with "the deplorably corrupting effects of this abominable system"—"Neutral Rights," exposing their invasion by Great Britain—"Administration of Law in Ireland," showing that "she had received penal statutes from England almost as plentifully as she had received blessings from the hands of Providence"—"Change of Ministry in 1834," with the gross, glaring, and almost incredible inconsistencies of Lord Wellington—"Business of Parliament," or "the abuses which prevail in the mode of conducting its business"—"Maltreatment of the North American Colonies"—"The Civil List," or men's voting an allowance to the Queen "under the influence of excited feelings, and without giving themselves time to reflect." No orator certainly, since the days of Pym and Charles I, could furnish such another list.

The character of his eloquence corresponds to the subjects he has chosen. "For fierce, vengeful, and irresistible assault," says John Foster, "Brougham stands the foremost man in all this world." His attack is usually carried on under the forms of logic. For the materials of his argument he sometimes goes off to topics the most remote and apparently alien from his subject, but he never fails to come down upon it at last with overwhelming force. He has wit in abundance, but it is usually dashed with scorn or contempt. His irony and sarcasm are terrible. None of our orators have ever equaled him in bitterness.

His style has a hearty freshness about it which springs from the robust constitution of his mind and the energy of his feelings. He sometimes disgusts by his use of Latinized English, and seems never to have studied our language in the true sources of its strength—Shakspeare, Milton, and the English Bible. His greatest fault lies in the structure of his sentences. He rarely puts forward a simple, distinct proposition. New ideas cluster around the original frame-work of his thoughts; and instead of throwing them into separate sentences, he blends them all in one, enlarging, modifying, interlacing them together, accumulating image upon image and argument upon argument, till the whole becomes perplexed and cumbersome in the attempt to crowd an entire system of thought into a single statement. Notwithstanding these faults, however, we dwell upon his speeches with breathless interest. They are a continual strain of impassioned argument, intermingled with fearful sarcasm, withering invective, lofty declamation, and the earnest majesty of a mind which has lost every other thought in the magnitude of its theme.

Lord Brougham has been in opposition during the greater part of his political life. He came in as Lord Chancellor with Earl Grey at the close of 1830, and retained his office about four years. Of late he has withdrawn, to a great extent, from public affairs, and spent a considerable part of his time on an estate which he owns in the south of France.[2]

The following comparison between the subject of this sketch and his great parliamentary rival will interest the reader, as presenting the characteristic qualities of each in bolder relief from their juxtaposition. It is from the pen of one who had watched them both with the keenest scrutiny during their conflicts in the House of Commons. The scene described in the conclusion arose out of a memorable attack of Mr. Canning on Lord Folkestone for intimating that he had "truckled to France." "The Lacedæmonians," said Mr. C., "were in the habit of deterring their children from the vice of intoxication by occasionally exhibiting their slaves in a state of disgusting inebriety. But, sir, there is a moral as well as a physical intoxication. Never before did I behold so perfect a personification of the character which I have somewhere seen described, as 'exhibiting the contortions of the Sibyl without her inspiration.' Such was the nature of the noble Lord's speech." Mr. Brougham took occasion, a few evenings after, to retort on Mr. Canning and repeat the charge, in the manner here described: but first we have a sketch of their characteristics as orators.

"Canning was airy, open, and prepossessing; Brougham seemed stern, hard, lowering, and almost repulsive. Canning's features were handsome, and his eye, though deeply ensconced under his eyebrows, was full of sparkle and gayety; the features of Brougham were harsh in the extreme: while his forehead shot up to a great elevation, his chin was long and square; his mouth, nose, and eyes seemed huddled together in the center of his face, the eyes absolutely lost amid folds and corrugations; and while he sat listening, they seemed to retire inward or to be vailed by a filmy curtain, which not only concealed the appalling glare which shot from them when he was aroused, but rendered his mind and his purpose a sealed book to the keenest scrutiny of man. Canning's passions appeared upon the open champaign of his face, drawn up in ready array, and moved to and fro at every turn of his own oration and every retort in that of his antagonist. Those of Brougham remained within, as in a citadel which no artillery could batter and no mine blow up; and even when he was putting forth all the power of his eloquence, when every ear was tingling at what he said, and while the immediate object of his invective was writhing in helpless and indescribable agony, his visage retained its cold and brassy hue, and he triumphed over the passions of other men by seeming to be without passion himself. When Canning rose to speak, he elevated his countenance and seemed to look round for applause as a thing dear to his feelings; while Brougham stood coiled and concentrated, reckless of all but the power that was within himself.

"From Canning there was expected the glitter of wit and the glow of spirit—something showy and elegant; Brougham stood up as a being whose powers and intentions were all a mystery—whose aim and effect no living man could divine. You bent forward to catch the first sentence of the one and felt human nature elevated in the specimen before you; you crouched and shrunk back from the other, and dreams of ruin and annihilation darted across your mind. The one seemed to dwell among men, to join in their joys, and to live upon their praise; the other appeared a son of the desert, who had deigned to visit the human race merely to make it tremble at his strength.

"The style of their eloquence and the structure of their orations were just as different. Canning arranged his words like one who could play skillfully upon that sweetest of all instruments, the human voice; Brougham proceeded like a master of every power of reasoning and the understanding. The modes and allusions of the one were always quadrable by the classical formulæ; those of the other could be squared only by the higher analysis of the mind; and they soared, and ran, and pealed, and swelled on and on, till a single sentence was often a complete oration within itself; but still, so clear was the logic, and so close the connection that every member carried the weight of all that went before and opened the way for all that was to follow after. The style of Canning was like the convex mirror, which scatters every ray of light that falls upon it, and shines and sparkles in whatever position it is viewed; that of Brougham was like the concave speculum, scattering no indiscriminate radiance, but having its light concentrated into one intense and tremendous focus. Canning marched forward in a straight and clear track: every paragraph was perfect in itself, and every coruscation of wit and of genius was brilliant and delightful—it was all felt, and it was felt all at once; Brougham twined round and round in a spiral, sweeping the contents of a vast circumference before him and uniting and pouring them onward to the main point of attack.

"Such were the rival orators, who sat glancing hostility and defiance at each other during the session of eighteen hundred and twenty-three—Brougham, as if wishing to overthrow the Secretary by a sweeping accusation of having abandoned all principle for the sake of office, and the Secretary ready to parry the charge and attack in his turn. An opportunity at length offered. Upon that occasion the oration of Brougham was disjointed and ragged and apparently without aim or application. He careered over the whole annals of the world and collected every instance in which genius had prostituted itself at the footstool of power, or principle had been sacrificed for the vanity or the lucre of place; but still there was no allusion to Canning and no connection that ordinary men could discover with the business before the House. When, however, he had collected every material which suited his purpose—when the mass had become big and black, he bound it about and about with the cords of illustration and argument; when its union was secure, he swung it round and round with the strength of a giant and the rapidity of a whirlwind, in order that its impetus and its effects might be the more tremendous; and while doing this, he ever and anon glared his eye, and pointed his finger, to make the aim and the direction sure. Canning himself was the first that seemed to be aware where and how terrible was to be the collision; and he kept writhing his body in agony and rolling his eye in fear, as if anxious to find some shelter from the impending bolt. The House soon caught the impression, and every man in it was glancing fearfully, first toward the orator and then toward the Secretary. There was, save the voice of Brougham, which growled in that under tone of muttered thunder which is so fearfully audible and of which no speaker of the day was fully master but himself, a silence as if the angel of retribution had been flaring in the faces of all parties the scroll of their personal and political sins. The stiffness of Brougham's figure had vanished; his features seemed concentrated almost to a point; he glanced toward every part of the House in succession, and, sounding the death-knell of the Secretary's forbearance and prudence with both his clinched hands upon the table, he hurled at him an accusation more dreadful in its gall and more torturing in its effects than had ever been hurled at mortal man within the same walls. The result was instantaneous—was electric. It was as when the thundercloud descends upon the Giant Peak; one flash—one peal—the sublimity vanished and all that remained was a small and cold pattering of rain. Canning started to his feet and was able only to utter the unguarded words, 'It is *false!*' to which followed a dull chapter of apologies. From that moment the House became more a scene of real business than of airy display and angry vituperation."

Notes

Index

NOTES

INTRODUCTION by A. Craig Baird

1. Chauncey Allen Goodrich, *Select British Eloquence* (New York: Harper & Brothers, 1852).
2. S. Austin Allibone, *Critical Dictionary of English Literature, and British and American Oratory* (Philadelphia: J. B. Lippincott Co., 1855–71), I, 700.
3. Richard Murphy, "Goodrich's *Select British Eloquence,* Microcard Edition," *The Central States Speech Journal,* IX (Fall 1957), 37–42. The present editor is indebted to Dr. Murphy for his interesting research and important criticism of this Goodrich publication.
4. *Ibid.*, 42.
5. William Norwood Brigance, "Whither Research?" *Quarterly Journal of Speech,* XIX (November 1933), 557.
6. Lester Thonssen and A. Craig Baird, *Speech Criticism* (New York: Ronald Press, 1948), p. 244.
7. Donald Bryant and others, "After Goodrich: New Resources in British Public Address—A Symposium," "Foreword," *Quarterly Journal of Speech,* XLVIII (February 1962), 1.
8. *Dictionary of American Biography* (New York: Charles Scribner's Sons, 1946).
9. *Ibid.* See also Anson Phelps Stokes, *Memories of Eminent Yale Men* (New Haven: Yale University Press, 1894), I, 222; and Charles E. Cuningham, *Timothy Dwight* (New York: Macmillan Company, 1942).
10. W. L. Kingsley, *Yale College* (New York: Henry Holt, 1879), II, 47–48.
11. *Dictionary of American Biography,* VII, 399.
12. T. D. Woolsey, *A Discourse on the Life and Services of the Rev. Chauncey Allen Goodrich, D.D.* (New Haven, 1860), pp. 9–10.
13. *Dictionary of American Biography,* XVIII, 338–39.
14. F. B. Dexter, editor, *Biographical Sketches of the Graduates of Yale College with Annals of College History* (New York: Henry Holt, 1885–90), VI, 323.

15. Woolsey, *op. cit.*, pp. 9–10.
16. *Ibid.*, p. 10.
17. J. W. Black, "Webster's Peroration in the Dartmouth College Case," *Quarterly Journal of Speech*, XXIII (December 1937), 636–42.
18. Kingsley, *op. cit.*, p. 50.
19. Dexter, *op. cit.*, VI, 332.
20. John Hoshor, "The Rhetorical Theory of Chauncey Allen Goodrich," unpublished doctoral dissertation, State University of Iowa, 1947. See the study as drafted for publication, "Lectures on Rhetoric and Public Speaking by Chauncey Allen Goodrich" *Speech Monographs*, XIV (1947), 1–37. See also John P. Hoshor, "American Contributions to Rhetorical Theory and Homiletics" in Karl Wallace (editor), *A History of Speech Education in America* (New York: Appleton-Century-Crofts, 1954), pp. 129–52.
21. Dexter, *op. cit.*, VI, 323; Kingsley, *op. cit.*, I, 112–24, II, 492 ff.; Timothy Dwight, *Theology Explained and Defended with a Memoir of the Author* (New Haven, 1818–19), pp. 86–87.
22. John Hoshor, dissertation (quoting from Goodrich's lectures at Yale), pp. 5, 238, 242.
23. *Ibid.*, p. 250.
24. Karl R. Wallace, "Tudor-Stuart Speakers," in Bryant and others, *op. cit.*, p. 2.
25. Loren Reid, "Speaking in the Eighteenth Century House of Commons," *Speech Monographs*, XVI (August 1949), 135–43.
26. Goodrich, *op. cit.*, p. 11.
27. *Ibid.*, pp. 149, 391, 528, 515, 825.
28. Cf., Thonssen and Baird, *op. cit.*, pp. 297–311.
29. *Ibid.*, pp. 8–14.
30. Cf., Carroll Arnold, "Goodrich Revisited," Bryant and others, *op. cit.*, p. 13. Arnold suggests that Goodrich wrote when Carlyle's *The French Revolution* and *Heroes and Hero Worship* and other works were especially influential.
31. Lloyd Watkins, "William Pitt," in Bryant and others, *op. cit.*, pp. 7–8.
32. Publications in the United States in recent decades that reflect thorough scholarship and comprehensive approach to the history and criticism of public address, include such works as W. N. Brigance, editor, *History and Criticism of American Public Address* (McGraw-Hill, 1943), 2 vols.; Marie Hoch-

muth and others, *History and Criticism of American Public Address,* Vol. III (Longmans, Green and Company, 1955).

33. Cf., Bryant and others, *op. cit.*, p. 1–14.
34. A. P. Samuels, *The Early Life, Correspondence and Writings of Rt. Honorable Burke* (Cambridge: Cambridge University Press, 1923).
35. Cf., Donald Bryant, "The Contemporary Reception of Burke's Conversation" in *Studies in Speech and Drama in Honor of Alexander M. Drummond* (Ithaca, New York, 1944), pp. 354–68; "Edmund Burke: New Evidence, Broader View," *Quarterly Journal of Speech,* XXXVIII (December 1952), 435–45; "Burke's Present Discontents: The Rhetorical Genesis of a Party Testament," *Quarterly Journal of Speech,* XLII (April 1956), 115–26.
36. *Quarterly Journal of Speech,* XLIII (December 1957), 357–64.
37. A doctoral dissertation in speech, privately printed at the State University of Iowa, Iowa City, 1932.
38. Karl Wallace, in Bryant and others, *op. cit.*, pp. 1–5.
39. Jerome Landfield, "Sheridan," in Bryant and others, *op. cit.*, 7.
40. Lloyd I. Watkins, "William Pitt," 7–10; Merrill T. Baker, "Lord Erskine," 10–13; and Carroll Arnold, "Goodrich Revisited," 13–14 in Bryant and others, *op. cit.*, 1–14.
41. John Hoshor, dissertation, p. 262.
42. *Ibid.*, p. 218.
43. Goodrich, *op. cit.*, p. 241.
44. John Hoshor, dissertation, p. 261.
45. Goodrich, *op. cit.*, p. 688.
46. John Hoshor, *op. cit.*, pp. 156, 157.
47. Goodrich, *op. cit.*, p. 173.
48. *Ibid.*, p. 241.
49. *Ibid.*, p. 295.
50. *Ibid.*, p. 271.
51. John Hoshor, dissertation, p. 352.
52. Goodrich, *op. cit.*, p. 628.
53. *Ibid.*, p. 25.
54. *Ibid.*, p. 394; cf., Richard Murphy, *op. cit.*, 40.
55. Thonssen and Baird, *op. cit.*, p. 461.

[*Professor A. Craig Baird, the editor of this volume, has in some cases added notes to Goodrich's own notes below.*

Such instances are distinguished by "ED." *at the end of the added material.*]

SIR JOHN ELIOT

1. "State of England," speech of June 3, 1628.

THE EARL OF STRAFFORD

1. This is shown at large by Mr. Forster in his Life of Strafford, which forms part of Lardner's Cabinet Cyclopedia.
2. Alluding to the threats of the Parliament being dissolved for their freedom of speech.
3. "Defense against impeachment for high treason," speech of April 13, 1641.—ED.

LORD DIGBY

1. "On bill of attainder against the Earl of Strafford," speech of April 21, 1641.—ED.

LORD BELHAVEN

1. "On union of England and Scotland," speech of November 2, 1706.—ED.

SIR ROBERT WALPOLE

1. "Reply to Sir William Wyndham," speech of March 13, 1734; "Against his own removal," speech of February 11, 1741. —ED.

WILLIAM PULTENEY

1. "The Army and the parliament," speech of 1746.—ED.

LORD CHESTERFIELD

1. "On the gin act," speech of February 21, 1743.—ED.

LORD CHATHAM

1. It is surprising that Charles Butler should insist, in his Reminiscences, that "it was the *manner,* and not the *words,* that did the wonder" in his allusion to Newcastle's overbearing influence with the King. Had he forgotten the jealousy of the English people as to their monarch's being ruled by a favorite? What changed the attachment of the nation for George III, a few years after, into anger and distrust, but the apprehension that he was governed by Lord Bute? And what was better calculated to startle the House of Commons than the idea of sinking, like the once free Parliaments of France,

"into a little assembly, serving no other purpose than to register the arbitrary edicts of *one* too powerful *subject?*"

2. It is not difficult to conjecture what were the "daggers" referred to by Mr. Pitt. The Stormont family, to which Murray belonged, was devotedly attached to the cause of James II. His brother was confidential secretary to the Pretender during the rebellion of 1745; and when the rebel lords were brought to London for trial in 1746, Lord Lovat, who was one of them, addressed Murray, to his great dismay, in the midst of the trial, *"Your mother was very kind to my clan as we marched through Perth to join the Pretender!"* Murray had been intimate, while a student in the Temple, with Mr. Vernon, a rich Jacobite citizen; and it was affirmed that when Vernon and his friends drank the Pretender's health *on their knees* (as they often did), Murray was present and joined in the act. When he entered life, however, he saw that the cause of James was hopeless and espoused the interests of the reigning family. There was no reason to doubt his sincerity; but these early events of his life gave Mr. Pitt immense advantage over him in such attacks. Junius cast them into his teeth sixteen years after. "Your zeal in the cause of an unhappy prince was expressed with *the sincerity of wine and some of the solemnities of religion.*"

   In quoting from Butler, I have modified his statement in two or three instances. By a slip of the pen he wrote *Festus* for Felix, and Solicitor for Attorney. He also makes Pitt say *"Judge* Festus," when Murray was not made judge until a year later. It is easy to see how the title judge might have slipped into the story after Murray was raised to the bench; but Mr. Pitt could never have addressed the same person as judge, and yet as prosecuting officer of the Crown.

3. A curious anecdote illustrates the ascendancy of Pitt over Newcastle. The latter was a great valetudinarian and was so fearful of taking cold, especially, that he often ordered the windows of the House of Lords to be shut in the hottest weather, while the rest of the Peers were suffering for want of breath. On one occasion he called upon Pitt, who was confined to his bed by the gout. Newcastle, on being led into the bed-chamber, found the room, to his dismay, *without fire* in a cold, wintery afternoon. He begged to have one kindled, but Pitt refused: it might be injurious to his gout. Newcastle drew his cloak around him and submitted with the worst possible grace. The conference was a long one. Pitt was deter-

mined on a naval expedition, under Admiral Hawke, for the annihilation of the French fleet. Newcastle opposed it on account of the lateness of the season. The debate continued until the Duke was absolutely shivering with cold; when, at last, seeing another bed in the opposite corner, he slipped in and covered himself with the bed-clothes! A secretary, coming in soon after, found the two ministers in this curious predicament, with their faces only visible, bandying the argument with great eagerness from one bedside to the other.

4. The Grecian chiefs, and Agamemnon's host,
   When they beheld the MAN with shining arms
   Amid those shades, trembled with sudden fear.
   Part turned their backs in flight, as when they sought
   their ships. * * * * Part raised
   A feeble outcry; but the sound commenced,
   Died on their grasping lips.

5. One of those brilliant sallies for which Mr. Pitt was distinguished occurred at this time, and related to Sir Edward Hawke. In proposing a monument for General Wolfe, Mr. Pitt paid a high compliment to Admiral Saunders: "A man," said he, "equaling those who have beaten Armadas—may I anticipate? those who *will* beat Armadas!" The words were prophetic. It was the very day of Hawke's victory, November 20th, 1759.

6. In his long and frequent interviews with George II, Mr. Pitt, though often commanded to sit while suffering severe pain from the gout, never obeyed. When unable any longer to stand, he always kneeled on a cushion before the King.

7. Annual Register for 1761.

8. Parliamentary History, xv., 1262. The report of this speech is too meager and unsatisfactory to merit insertion in this work.

9. Supposed to refer to Lord North and Mr. George Cooke, who were made joint paymasters.

10. There was a mystery connected with Lord Chatham's long confinement which has created many surmises. A writer in the London Quarterly Review for 1840 has endeavored to show that it was, to a great extent, a thing of pretense and affectation; that he was shocked at the sudden loss of his popularity after accepting the peerage; disconcerted by the opposition which sprung up; mortified at the failure of his attempts to strengthen his government; and that, under these circumstances, "he felt some reluctance to come forward in his new character, and perhaps clung to office only that he

might find some *striking and popular occasion for resignation.*" To an enemy of Lord Chatham's fame and principles this may seem probable; but it is a mere hypothesis, without the least evidence to support it. It is probably true that Lord Chatham's withdrawal from public business was not owing to *direct* sufferings from the gout during the whole space of two years. Lord Chesterfield, who was no friend of Chatham and not the least inclined to shelter him, attributed "his inactivity to the effects of the injudicious treatment of his physician, who had prevented a threatened attack of the gout by dispersing the humor throughout the whole system. The experiment caused a severe fit of illness, which chiefly affected his nerves." Whether this was the cause or not, it is certain that his nervous system was in a very alarming state, and that his mind became greatly diseased. He was gloomy in the extreme and perhaps yielded to unreasonable jealousies and suspicions. Such seems to have been at one time the opinion of Lord Camden, who says in a confidential letter, "Lord Chatham is at Hayes, brooding over his own suspicions and discontents—his return to business almost desperate—inaccessible to every body; but under a persuasion that he is given up and abandoned." But Lord Camden soon after received information which probably changed his views. "On his return to London," says his biographer, "he heard such an account of Lord Chatham as to convince him that the country was forever deprived of the services of that illustrious man." This refers, undoubtedly, to a report of his being *deranged,* which was then prevalent. It now appears that this was not literally the fact, though his mind was certainly in such a state that Lady Chatham did not allow him to be master of his own actions. It is, therefore, uncandid in the extreme to represent Lord Chatham as feigning illness in order to escape from the responsibilities of his station.

11. Though Lord Chatham had a high sense of Mansfield's learning and abilities, he continued to regard him with aversion and distrust on account of his extreme Tory sentiments. In reply to Mansfield, when the case of Wilkes again came up at a late evening session, he quoted Lord Somers and Chief-justice Holt on the points of law, and drew their characters in his own masterly style. He pronounced them "*honest* men who knew and loved the Constitution." Then turning to Mansfield, he said, "I vow to God, I think the noble Lord equals them both—*in abilities!*" He complained bitterly, in

conclusion, of the motion being pressed by Lord Marchmont and Lord Mansfield at so unreasonable an hour and called for an adjournment. "If the Constitution must be wounded," said he, "let it not receive its mortal stab at this dark and midnight hour, when honest men are asleep in their beds and when only felons and assassins are seeking for prey!"

12. Lord Chatham received numerous tokens of respect and gratitude from the colonies. At Charleston, S. C., a colossal statue of him, in white marble, was erected by order of the Commons, who say, in their inscription upon the pedestal,

TIME
SHALL SOONER DESTROY
THIS MARK OF THEIR ESTEEM,
THAN
ERASE FROM THEIR MINDS
THE JUST SENSE
OF HIS PATRIOTIC VIRTUE.

13. Lord Brougham speaks of him as having "a peculiarly defective and even awkward action." This is directly opposed to the testimony of all his contemporaries. Hugh Boyd speaks of "the persuasive gracefulness of action"; and Lord Orford says that his action, on many occasions, was worthy of Garrick. The *younger* Pitt had an awkwardness of the kind referred to; and Lord Brougham, who was often hasty and incorrect, probably confounded the father and the son.

14. Telum Oratoris.—Cicero. "You talk, my Lords, of conquering America; of your numerous friends there to annihilate the Congress; of your powerful forces to disperse her armies; *I might as well talk of driving them before me with this crutch.*"

15. Speeches as follows: "On the marriage of the Prince of Wales," April 29, 1736; "On the Spanish Convention," March 8, 1739; "On impressing seamen," March 6, 1741; "Reply to Horatio Walpole," March 6, 1741; "On the conduct of Sir Robert Walpole," March 9, 1742; "Second speech against Sir Robert Walpole," March 23, 1742; "On taking Hanoverian troops in the pay of Great Britain," December 10, 1742; "Thanks after the battle of Dettingen," December 1, 1743; "Right of taxing America," January 14, 1766; "Case of John Wilkes," January 9, 1770; "Spanish seizure of Falkland Islands," November 22, 1770; "Against quartering British soldiers in Boston," May 22, 1774; "Removal of British troops from Boston," January 20, 1775;

"Stopping hostilities in America," May 30, 1777; "Address to the throne," November 18, 1777; "Against adjourning parliament," December 11, 1777; "Last speech on America," April 7, 1778.—ED.

LORD MANSFIELD

1. Lord Hardwicke, father of Mr. Yorke.
2. Speeches: "On the right of taxing America," February 3, 1766; "When surrounded by a mob in the court of the King's Bench," June 8, 1768; "The case of Allan Evans, Esq.," February 4, 1767; "On depriving the Peers of certain privileges," May 9, 1770.—ED.

JUNIUS

1. A celebrated motto, *Stat nominis umbra,* was taken from the first book of Lucan's *Pharsalia,* line 135. The poet there speaks of Pompey, when he entered into the war with Cesar, as having his name, or reputation, chiefly in the *past,* and adds, in reference to this idea, "Stat magni nominis umbra"—He stands the shadow of a mighty name. When the author of these letters collected them into a volume, he beautifully appropriated these words to himself, with the omission of the word *magni,* and a change of application. He placed them on the title-page, in connection with the word JUNIUS, which "stands the shadow of a name," whose secret was entrusted to no one and was never to be revealed.
2. The following is a curious instance. About two years after these Letters were commenced, Garrick learned confidentially from Woodfall that it was doubtful whether Junius would continue to write much longer. He flew instantly with the news to Mr. Ramus, one of the royal pages, who hastened with it to the King, then residing at Richmond. Within two days, Garrick received, through Woodfall, the following note from Junius:

   "I am very exactly informed of your impertinent inquiries, and of the information you so busily sent to Richmond, and with what triumph and exultation it was received. I knew every particular of it the next day. Now, mark me, vagabond! keep to your pantomimes, or be assured you shall hear of it. Meddle no more, thou busy informer! It is in my power to make you curse the hour in which you dared to interfere with

   JUNIUS."

Miss Seward states, in her Letters, that on the evening after the receipt of this note, Garrick, for once in his life, played badly.

3. How much Junius relied for success on the perfection of his statement, may be learned from the following fact. When he had hastily thrown off a letter containing a number of coarse and unguarded expressions, of which he was afterward ashamed, he coolly requested Woodfall to say in a subsequent number, "We have some reason to suspect that the last letter signed Junius in this paper *was not written by the real Junius,* though the observation escaped us at the time!" There is nothing equal to this in all the annals of literature, unless it be Cicero's famous letter to Lucceius, in which he asks the historian to *lie* a little in his favor in recording the events of his consulship, for the sake of making him a greater man!
4. Voltaire somewhere remarks that the adjective is the greatest enemy of the substantive, though they agree together in gender, number, and case.
5. Referring to the story of the giant's tearing up mountains, and piling Pelion upon Ossa, in their contest with the gods.
6. It has been shown in the London Athenæum that the recent attempts to make the younger Lyttleton Junius, and also a Scottish surgeon named Maclain, are entire failures.
7. Charles Butler, in his Reminiscences, suggests a mixed hypothesis on this subject. He thinks that Sir Philip Francis was too young to have produced these Letters, which indicate very thorough and extensive reading and especially a profound knowledge of human character. He mentions, likewise, that Junius shows himself in the most unaffected manner, throughout his private correspondence with Woodfall, to have been not only a man of high rank, but of ample fortune—promising to indemnify him against any loss he might suffer from being prosecuted, a thing which Francis, with a mere clerkship in the War office, was unable to do. He therefore thinks that Sir Philip may have been the organ of some older man of the biggest rank and wealth, who has chosen to remain in proud obscurity. It is certain that some one acted in conjunction with Junius, for he says in his fifty-first note to Woodfall, "The gentleman who transacts the conveyancing part of this correspondence, tells me there was much difficulty last night." This person was once seen by a clerk of Woodfall, as he withdrew from the door after having thrown in a Letter of Junius. He was a person who

"wore a bag and a sword," showing that he was not a mere servant, but, as Junius described him, a "gentleman." It seems probable, also, that the hand of another was used in transcribing these Letters, for Junius says concerning one of them, "You shall have the Letter some time to-morrow; it can not be corrected and *copied* before"; and again, of another, "The inclosed, though begun within these few days, has been greatly labored. It is very *correctly* copied." This, though not decisive, has the air of one who is speaking of what another person had been doing, not himself. If this be admitted, Mr. Butler suggests that these Letters may actually have been sent to Woodfall in the handwriting of Francis, without his being the original author. Still, he by no means considers him a mere copyist. Francis may have collected valuable information; may have given very important hints; may even have shared, to some extent, in the composition or, at least, the revision of the Letters; for the writer was plainly not an author by profession. In short, Francis may have been to him, in respect to these Letters, what Burke was more fully to Lord Rockingham, and what Alexander Hamilton was at times to Washington. On this theory the government would have the same motives to buy off Sir Philip Francis, a thing they seem plainly to have done when these Letters stopped so suddenly in 1772. It may have been a condition made by Junius in favor of his friend. To have made it for himself seems inconsistent with his whole character and bearing, both in his Letters to the public and his confidential communications to Woodfall. The theory is, at least, an ingenious one, and has therefore been here stated. It has, however, very serious difficulties, as the reader will easily perceive.

8. Still rankles in his side the fatal dart.
9. Letters suggested for reading: "Letter to the printer of the Public Advertiser," January 21, 1769; "Letter to Sir William Draper," February 7, 1769; "Letter to Sir William Draper," March 3, 1769; "Letter to the Duke of Grafton," May 30, 1769; "Letter to the Duke of Bedford," September 19, 1769; "Letter to the King," December 19, 1769; "Letter to the Duke of Grafton," February 14, 1770.—ED.

EDMUND BURKE

1. Notwithstanding the extent of his reading in the classics, Mr. Burke (like many Irish scholars) paid but little attention to the subject of quantity, and a blunder in this respect which

was charged upon him in the House of Commons gave rise to one of his happiest retorts. In attacking Lord North for being in want of still larger supplies, in the midst of the most lavish expenditure, he quoted the words of Cicero, "Magnum vectigal est parsimonia," accenting the word *vectigal* on the first syllable. Lord North cried out in a contemptuous tone from the Treasury Bench, *vectigal, vectigal.* Mr. Burke instantly replied, "I thank the right honorable gentleman for his correction; and, that he may enjoy the benefit of it, I repeat the words, Magnum vectigal est parsimonia."

2. These early tendencies of Mr. Burke's genius explain a fact which has been spoken of with surprise by all his biographers; namely, that he preferred the Æneid of Virgil to the Iliad of Homer, though he admitted, at the same time, the superiority of the latter in invention, force, and sublimity. To a mind like his, so full of sentiment and philosophy, there is something more delightful in the description of the world of spirits, in the sixth book of the Æneid, and the almost Christian anticipations of the Pollio, than in all the battle scenes of Homer. His extravagant attachment to Young's Night Thoughts, in early life, may be accounted for in the same way.

3. Hamilton gained this title in the following manner. When Newcastle's administration was suffering from Lord Chatham's tremendous attacks in 1755, Hamilton (who voted with the ministry), finding their cause in extreme danger one evening, suddenly arose, though he had never spoken in the House before, and poured forth a speech of surprising cogency of argument and fervor of emotion with all the ease and self-command of a practiced orator. Every one expected that he would take his place at once among the leading debaters of the day. But, excepting a few words on the same subject soon after, he never made a speech of any length in the British Parliament, though he was a member for thirty years; nor did he speak elsewhere, except twice or three times, when compelled to do so, in the Irish Parliament. He was undoubtedly a man of talents; but, having gained so high a reputation by his maiden speech, he was afraid to make another—ever preparing, but never ready, for a second effort which should outdo the first. He left nothing as the result of sitting thirty years in the British Parliament except a meager treatise on parliamentary logic. His example furnishes one lesson to young orators, worth more than all the precepts of

his book, viz., *that he who would succeed as a speaker must be content sometimes to fail.*

4. Praise from the praised.
5. Milton.
6. Miscellanies, WARREN HASTINGS.
7. Parliamentary History, xxvi, 91.
8. See Mill's British India, v, passim.
9. The States-General resolved themselves into the National Assembly on the 17th of June, and the King and Queen were taken from Versailles to Paris on the 6th of October, 1789.

   The following extracts from the diary and correspondence of Mr. Gouverneur Morris, the American minister at Paris during the early stages of the Revolution, show that his views of the French people at this time coincided with those of Mr. Burke. "There is one fatal principle which pervades all ranks. *It is, a perfect indifference to the violation of engagements.* Inconstancy is so mingled in the blood, marrow, and very essence of this people that, when a man of high rank and importance laughs to-day at what he seriously asserted yesterday, it is considered the natural order of things."—Sparks' Life of Morris, vol. ii., p. 68. It is not, therefore, wonderful, that Mr. Morris had no faith in the Revolution. He told Lafayette, in reference to the leaders of it, "Their views respecting this nation are totally inconsistent with the materials of which it is composed, and the worst thing which could possibly happen would be to grant their wishes." Lafayette acknowledged the fact. "He tells me he is sensible that his party are mad, and tells them so."—Vol. i, 314. At a later period, speaking of Lafayette as commander of the National Guards, he says, "Lafayette has marched (to Versailles) by compulsion, guarded by his own troops, who suspect and threaten him. Dreadful situation! Obliged to do what he abhors, or suffer an ignominious death, with the certainty that the sacrifice of his life will not prevent the mischief."—Vol. i, 327. Mr. Morris seems to have anticipated from the first what happened at no very distant period, that Lafayette would be obligated to flee from France to escape the dagger of the assassin.
10. Wade's British History, p. 551.
11. It is stated in the London Christian Observer for 1807, which was edited at that time by Zachary Macaulay, Esq., father of the celebrated historian, "there seems to be but little doubt of the formation of a plan to raise an insurrection in

London about the close of 1792 or the beginning of 1793."

12. Parliamentary History, xxviii, 356.
13. Moore ascribes this to *jealousy*, a fault never before charged on Burke. Sheridan's *habits* were bad, and this made it easy for Burke to give him up.
14. Annual Register, xxxiii, 116.
15. Parliamentary History, xxix, 380.
16. The following speeches are suggested reading: "On American taxation," April 19, 1774; "On conciliation with America," March 22, 1775; "On the electors at Bristol," September 6, 1780; "On declining the election at Bristol," September 9, 1780; "On Mr. Fox's East India Bill," December 1, 1783; "On the Nabob of Arcot's debts," February 28, 1785; "Charges against Warren Hastings," February 19, 1788.—ED.

HENRY GRATTAN

1. The following speeches are suggested reading: "On moving a declaration of Irish right," April 19, 1780; "Second speech on Irish right," April 16, 1782; "Incentive against Mr. Flood," October 28, 1783; "Incentive against Mr. Corry," February 14, 1800.—ED.

RICHARD BRINSLEY SHERIDAN

1. The following lines of Tickell give the character of Brooks:

   And know, I've brought the best Champagne from Brooks;
   From liberal Brooks, whose speculative skill
   Is hasty credit and a distant bill;
   Who, nursed in clubs, disdains a vulgar trade,
   Exults to trust, and blushes to be paid.

   Nothing could be more convenient for a man of Sheridan's habits than so indulgent a creditor.
2. To exult in the applause of his *own* theater.
3. It was natural, in respect to such a speech, that some erroneous or exaggerated statements should have been given to the public. There is an anecdote related by Bissett, in his Reign of George III, which must be regarded in this light. Bissett says, "The late Mr. Logan, well known for his literary efforts and author of a masterly defense of Mr. Hastings, went that day to the House, prepossessed for the accused and against the accuser. At the expiration of the first hour, he said to a friend, 'All this is declamatory assertion without

proof'; when the second was finished, 'This is a wonderful oration'; at the close of the third, 'Mr. Hastings has acted unjustifiably'; the fourth, 'Mr. Hastings is a most atrocious criminal'; and at last, 'Of all monsters of iniquity, the most enormous is Warren Hastings!' "

Now the natural and almost necessary impression made by this story is that Mr. Logan, *previous* to hearing this speech, had written his "masterly defense of Mr. Hastings," and that, being thus "prepossessed" and committed in favor of the accused, he experienced the remarkable change of views and feelings here described. But the fact is, his defense of Hastings was written *after* the speech in question was delivered; and Mr. Logan therein charged the Commons with having acted, in their impeachment of Hastings, "from motives of personal animosity—not from regard to public justice." It is incredible that a man of Mr. Logan's character—a distinguished clergyman of the Church of Scotland—should have written such a pamphlet or brought such a charge only a few months after he had expressed the views of Mr. Hastings ascribed to him above. This anecdote must, therefore, have related to some other person who was confounded with Mr. Logan, and may be numbered with the many uncertainties which are current under the name of Literary History.

4. The Scottish members having deserted Mr. Addington in some debate about this time, Mr. Sheridan convulsed the House by suddenly exclaiming, in the words of the messenger to Macbeth, "*Doctor*, 'the THANES fly from thee!' "

5. Mr. Moore, in the following lines, gave vent to his feelings at the conduct of those who deserted Sheridan in his poverty, but crowded around his death-bed and flocked to his funeral with all the tokens of their early respect and affection:

How proud they can press to the funeral array
Of him whom they shunn'd in his sickness and sorrow—
How bailiffs may seize his last blanket to-day,
Whose pall shall be held up by nobles to-morrow!

Still, it should be remembered that such desertion is the inevitable fate of degrading vice, and especially of the beastly intemperance to which Sheridan had so long been abandoned. Large contributions had previously been made for his relief, but his improvidence knew no bounds; and he had for some time reduced himself to such a state that few of his old acquaintances could visit him without pain, or (it may be added) without the deepest mortification to himself, though they might wish, after his death, to do honor to his memory as a man of genius.

6. See *The Speeches of Richard Brinsley Sheridan* (London: Henry C. Bohn, 1842), 3 vols., especially "Against Warren Hastings," June 1788.—ED.

CHARLES JAMES FOX

1. I could not interest myself in them: they are absolutely deranged in their minds, and there is no hope of their recovery.
2. The reader will be interested in the following beautiful tribute to the memory of Lord Ashburton as an orator, from the pen of Sir William Jones: "His language was always pure, always elegant, and the best words dropped easily from his lips into the best places with a fluency at all times astonishing, and, when he had perfect health, really melodious. That faculty, however, in which no mortal ever surpassed him, and which all found irresistible, was his wit. This relieved the weary, calmed the resentful, and animated the drowsy; this drew smiles even from such as were the objects of it, and scattered flowers over a desert, and, like sunbeams sparkling on a lake, gave spirit and vivacity to the dullest and least interesting cause. Not that his accomplishments as an advocate consisted principally of volubility of speech or liveliness of raillery. He was endued with an intellect sedate yet penetrating, clear yet profound, subtle yet strong. His knowledge, too, was equal to his imagination, and his memory to his knowledge."—*Works,* iv, 577.
3. Age of Pitt and Fox, i, 145.
4. Fox's Speeches, ii, 39.
5. History of Party, iii, 316.
6. Memoirs, i, 269.
7. Vol. iv, 475.
8. Vol. v, 551.
9. Age of Pitt and Fox, i, 177.
10. Life of Sheridan, i, 215, Phila.
11. The bill for punishing mutiny in the army and navy is passed at each session for only one year. The power of withholding this bill and that which provides the annual supplies, gives the House of Commons, in the last extremity, an absolute control over ministers.

12. One of the speeches in this selection, that of December 17th, 1783, has been given with a particular reference to this point. The reader will be interested to remark how completely the matter of this speech is made up of just sentiments and weighty reasonings—contempt of underhand dealing, scorn of court servility, detestation of that dark engine of *secret influence,* which had driven Lord Chatham and so many others from power. All this is expressed with a spirit and eloquence which Chatham alone could have equaled, but coming from Mr. Fox, it availed nothing. He stood in so false a position that he could not even defend the popular part of the Constitution without turning the people more completely against him. The city of London, the most democratic part of the kingdom, thanked the King for that very interference which Toryism itself will not deny was a direct breach of the Constitution. But the people were taught to believe that Mr. Fox was aiming to make himself a "dictator" by the East India Bill, and they justified any measures which the King thought necessary for putting such a man down. Hardly any page of English history is more instructive than that which records the errors of Mr. Fox and the pernicious consequences both to himself and others.
13. Lord Eldon, speaking of this subject at a later period, said; "When the legality of the conduct of the High Bailiff of Westminster was before the House, all the lawyers on the ministerial side defended his right to grant a scrutiny. I thought their law bad, and I told them so. I asked Kenyon how he could answer *this*—that every writ or commission must be returned on the day on which it was made returnable. *He could not answer it.*"
14. See a paper of Lord Loughborough on this subject in Campbell's Lives of the Chancellors, vi, 195.
15. Speeches, iii, 401.
16. Id. ib., p. 407.
17. George III, throughout his whole life, believed that a conspiracy had been formed to prevent his remounting the throne. No explanations could ever relieve his mind from this error, and he always looked with abhorrence on those who resisted the limitations of the Regent's authority and the transfer of his person to the custody of the Queen. The feelings of the nation were strongly excited in his behalf. Without sharing in his error, they considered him as treated with disrespect and strongly condemned those who objected to

the restrictions mentioned above. It was in this way, as well as by his East India Bill and Coalition, that Mr. Fox did more than any other man in the empire to remove the unpopularity of the King, and to draw his subjects around him in support and sympathy.

18. Vol. xviii, 91.
19. Lives of the Chancellors, vi, 187.
20. Wraxall's Memoirs, ii, 277.
21. See Parliamentary History, xxxiii, 456.
22. Speeches suggested for reading: "On the East India Bill," December 1, 1783; "On secret influence," December 17, 1783; "On the Westminster scrutiny," June 8, 1784; "On Russian armament," March 1, 1792; "On parliamentary reform," May 26, 1797; "On rejection of Bonaparte's overtures for peace," February 3, 1800.—ED.

WILLIAM PITT

1. In America the word declaim is often used for recite in the English sense of the term; *i.e.*, to pronounce the speech of another when committed to memory. But in England it is very rarely used in this sense, and the context seems to show that such could not have been the meaning of Coleridge.
2. Mr. Pitt was seriously disposed during this debate and, as Mr. Wilberforce states, was "actually holding Solomon's porch door (a portico behind the House) open while vomiting during Fox's speech, to which he was to reply."
3. This was one of Mr. Pitt's severest sarcasms. Sir Cecil Wray, Mr. Powys, and others, who had long been connected with Mr. Fox as political adherents and personal friends, had put to him during this debate the most painful interrogatories respecting his coalition with Lord North and renounced all connection with him if that measure was consummated.
4. The reader cannot have forgotten the declaration of Mr. Fox, made only a few months before, that nothing could ever induce him to think of a coalition with Lord North, and that he was willing to be considered as *infamous* if he ever formed one.
5. While propitious, I praise her, and bless her glad stay;
   But if, waving her light wings, she flies far away,
   (Why, wrapped in my virtue), her gifts I resign
   And honest, though poor, I shall never repine.
6. More than twenty years after, Mr. Canning, while defending himself under circumstances somewhat similar, in respect to

Catholic emancipation, began to quote the passage so finely turned by Pitt; but as he uttered the words "Laudo manentem," it suddenly occurred to him how they had been used before, and he instantly varied them, in his graceful manner, saying, "or, rather, to use the paraphrase of Dryden,"

> "I can applaud her when she's king;
> But when she dances in the wind,
> And shakes her wings, and will not stay,
> I puff the prostitute away."

7. Age of Pitt and Fox, p. 155.
8. The reason which he was reported to have given, viz., that "he was married to his country," if not a mere jest, was probably, as Lord Brougham remarks, a fabrication of the day, like the words ("Oh, my country!") which were represented to have been the last that he uttered on his death-bed. "Such things," as his Lordship justly remarks, "were too theatrical for so great a man, and of too vulgar a cast for so consummate a performer, had he stooped to play a part in such circumstances."
9. Historical Memoirs, iv, 724.
10. Lord North felt this blow so keenly that Wraxall says, he had never but once seen him so much agitated during his whole parliamentary career.
11. The King's determination was again expressed in a letter to Mr. Pitt, written on the morning of the day when Lord Effingham moved a resolution in the House of Lords condemning the conduct of the majority in the Commons. "I trust," said he, "that the House of Lords will this day feel that the hour is come for which the wisdom of our ancestors established that respectable corps in the state, to prevent either the Crown or the Commons from encroaching on the rights of each other. Indeed, should not the Lords boldly stand forth, this Constitution must soon be changed; for if the two only remaining privileges of the Crown are infringed—that of negativing bills which have passed both Houses of Parliament and that of naming the ministers to be employed—I can not but feel, as far as regards my person, that I can be no *longer of utility to this country, nor can with honor continue in this island.*"
12. See the report of this debate, xxiv, 421–4.

13. Youth as I am, I will conquer the aged, if in nothing else, at least in modesty and command over my tongue.
14. The line is from Racine's Britannicus (Act i., Scene 1):

    I see my honors rise, my credit sink.

15. It was the *press,* to a great extent, which carried Mr. Pitt triumphantly through this struggle. The East India Company felt their existence to be staked on his success, and they spared no efforts or expense to rouse the nation in his behalf. From the day Mr. Fox introduced his bill into the House, a committee of the proprietors sat uninterruptedly at Leadenhall Street, for many weeks, sounding the alarm throughout the kingdom, and from that time to his final defeat in the general elections of 1784, they used every instrument in their power to defeat his designs. Among other things, caricatures were employed with great effect, some of them very ingenious and laughable. One of them, called the Triumphant Entry of Carlo Khan, represented Fox in the splendid costume of a Mogul emperor, seated on the body of an elephant, upon which was stuck the queer, fat, good-humored face of Lord North, while Burke strutted in front as a trumpeter with his instrument in full blast, sounding the praises of the Good Man. (See peroration of his speech on the East India Bill.)
16. Lives of the Chancellors, v, 566.
17. Lives of the Chancellors, v, 561.
18. Lord Campbell gives a letter from Lord Camden on this subject, which he says "Affords strong evidence of the Premier's sincerity." Lives of the Chancellors, v, 332.
19. Sketch of Pitt.—Statesmen of the Times of George III.
20. Lives of the Chancellors, v, 569.
21. Vol. i, 231.
22. See Prettyman's Life of Pitt, ii, 213; Belsham's Memoirs of the Reign of George III, iv, 123; Wade's British History, p. 558.
23. See Life, p. 125, Philadelphia edition.
24. Nicholl's Recollections of George III, p. 400.
25. Wade's British History, p. 572.
26. Lives of the Chancellors, vi, 254.
27. Id. ib., p. 266.
28. The following speeches are suggested reading: "Against the war in America," June 1781; "On an attempt to force his resignation," June 8, 1784; "On abolition of the slave trade,"

April 2, 1792; "On rupture of negotiations with France," November 10, 1797; "On Deliverance of Europe," June 7, 1799; "On refusing to negotiate with Bonaparte," February 3, 1800.—ED.

LORD ERSKINE

1. Lord Brougham speaks of him as having *"hardly any* access to the beauties of Attic eloquence, whether in prose or verse"; but Lord Campbell goes farther, and says, "he learned little of Greek *beyond the alphabet."*
2. The Rev. Dr. Emmons, one of the acutest reasoners among the divines of New England, was accustomed (as the writer is directly informed) to read the Massachusetts Reports as they came out, for the pleasure and benefit they afforded him as specimens of powerful reasoning. Would not our young divines find similar benefit from the study of great legal arguments like these of Erskine?
3. See Thomas Erskine, *Speeches of Lord Erskine* (London: J. Ridgway, 1810), 4 vols. The following are suggested reading: "On behalf of Lord George Gordon," February 5, 1781; "On rights of juries, case of Dean of Asaph," November 15, 1784; "In behalf of John Stockdale," December 9, 1789; "Defense of Tom Paine's Rights of Man," December 18, 1792; In behalf of John Frost," March 1793; "In behalf of Mr. Bingham," February 24, 1794; "In behalf of Thomas Hardy," November 1, 1794; "Against Thomas Williams for publication of Paine's Age of Reason," July 24, 1797; "In behalf of James Hadfield," June 26, 1800; "In behalf of Rev. George Markham," May 4, 1802.—ED.

JOHN PHILPOT CURRAN

1. Mr. Curran's feelings toward Mr. Boyse, who sent him to College, were expressed in a story he once told at his own table. "Thirty-five years after," said he, "returning one day from court, I found an old gentleman seated in my drawing-room, with his feet on each side of the marble chimney-piece, and an air of being perfectly at home. He turned—it was my friend of the ball-alley! I could not help bursting into tears. 'You are right, sir, you are right! The chimney-piece is yours, the pictures are yours, the house is yours: *you gave me all*—my friend, my father!' He went with me to Parliament, and I saw the tears glistening in his eyes when he saw his poor little Jackey rise to answer a *Right Honorable.* He is gone, sir. This is his wine—let us drink his health!"

2. Lord Avonmore, in whose breast political resentment was easily subdued by the same noble tenderness of feeling which distinguished Charles J. Fox upon a more celebrated occasion, could not withstand this appeal to his heart. The moment the court rose, his Lordship sent for his friend, and threw himself into his arms, declaring that unworthy artifices had been used to separate them and that they should never succeed in future.
3. See Washington Irving's story of the Broken Heart, in his Sketch Book.
4. The following speeches are suggested reading: "In behalf of Mr. Rowan," January 29, 1794; "In behalf of Finnerty," December 22, 1797; "Against the Marquess of Headfort," July 27, 1804.—ED.

SIR JAMES MACKINTOSH

1. Mr. Mackintosh here refers to Mr. Burke's views respecting the war with France, which he openly condemned in opposition to Mr. Burke; nor did he ever agree with him on a number of points mentioned in the sketch of Mr. Burke in this volume, p. 231. His change consisted mainly in withdrawing his defense of the Revolution as actually conducted, and agreeing with Mr. Burke that the nation was not prepared for liberty.
2. When Mr. Mackintosh visited Paris during the peace of Amiens, some of the French literati to whom he was introduced complimented him on his defense of their Revolution. "Gentlemen," said he, in reply, "since that time you have entirely *refuted me!*"
3. The words are taken from the peroration of Cicero's oration for Milo, in which he deplores the exile which must befall his client if he loses his cause.

   Happy the land that shall receive him! Ungrateful the country that shall cast him out! miserable if she finally lose him!
4. See James Mackintosh, *The Miscellaneous Works of the Right Honorable Sir James Mackintosh* (Philadelphia: Carey, 1848). Suggested reading: "On the trial of Jean Peltier," February 21, 1803.—ED.

GEORGE CANNING

1. It is a high testimony to Mr. Canning's manliness and warmth of heart, that he never attemped to throw any covering over

his mother's early history, but treated her openly throughout life with the utmost reverence and affection. He visited her at her residence in Bath as often as his public employments would permit, and never allowed any business, however urgent, to prevent him from writing to her every Sunday of his life. He obtained pensions for his mother and sisters; and when attacked on the subject, defended himself to the satisfaction of all by saying that, in retiring from his office of Under Secretary in 1801, he was entitled to a pension of £500 a year, and had only procured the settlement of a fair equivalent on his dependent relatives.

2. The reader may be pleased, as a specimen, to see Mr. Canning's sapphics on the Knife-grinder, intended as a burlesque on a fashionable poet's extreme sensibility to the sufferings of the poor, and his reference of all their distresses to political causes. It was also designed to ridicule his hobbling verse and abrupt transitions.

THE FRIEND OF HUMANITY AND THE KNIFE-GRINDER

Friend of Humanity.

Needy knife-grinder! whither are you going?
Rough is the road; your wheel is out of order;
Bleak blows the blast; your hat has got a hole in 't,
  So have your breeches!

Weary knife-grinder! little think the proud ones,
Who in their coaches roll along the turnpike-
Road, what hard work 'tis crying all day, "Knives and
  Scissors to grind O!"

Tell me, knife-grinder, how came you to grind knives?
Did some rich man tyrannically use you?
Was it the squire? or parson of the parish?
  Or the attorney?

Was it the squire, for killing of his game? or
Covetous parson, for his tithes distraining?
Or roguish lawyer, made you lose your little
  All in a lawsuit?

(Have you not read the Rights of Man, by Tom Paine?)
Drops of compassion tremble on my eyelids,

Ready to fall, as soon as you have told your
Pitiful story.

Knife-grinder

Story! why bless you! I *have none to tell,* sir;
Only last night a drinking at the Checkers,
This poor old hat and breeches, as you see, were
Torn in a scuffle.

Constables came up for to take me into
Custody; they took me before the justice;
Justice Oldmixon put me in the parish-
stocks for a vagrant.

I should be glad to drink your honor's health in
A pot of beer, if you will give me sixpence;
But, for my part, I never love to meddly
With politics, sir.

Friend of Humanity

I give thee sixpence! I will see thee hang'd first!
Wretch! whom no sense of wrongs can rouse to vengeance.
Sordid, unfeeling, reprobate, degraded,
Spiritless outcast!

(*Kicks the knife-grinder, overturns his wheel, and exit in a transport of republican enthusiasm and universal philanthropy.*)

3. "Canning," says a late writer, "would have attained to old age, but for his sleepless nights. Down to the year 1826, he had no organic disease whatever. His constitution was untouched; but his brain, at night, was active for hours after he retired to bed. He has himself, in a letter to Sir W. Knighton, given a graphic picture of a night of torture.
4. Paradise Lost, book ii.
5. Now to the satrap and proud Turk subjected.
6. Recommended speeches: "On the fall of Bonaparte," January 10, 1814; "On radical reform," March 18, 1820; "Speech at Plymouth on England in repose," 1823; "On granting aid to Portugal," December 12, 1826. R. Therry, ed., *Speeches of the Right Honourable George Canning* (London: Ridgway, 1828), 6 vols.—ED.

LORD BROUGHAM

1. "Judex damnatur dum nocens absolvitur," the judge is condemned when the guilty is suffered to escape.
2. Suggested speeches for reading: "On army estimates," March 11, 1816; "In behalf of Williams," August 9, 1822; "On French invasion of Spain," February 4, 1823; "On parliamentary reform," October 7, 1831; "Inaugural discourse," April 6, 1825. Henry Brougham, *Collected Works* (London: Griffin, 1856–62), 11 vols., and *Speeches* (A. & C. Black: Edinburgh, 1838), 4 vols.—ED.

INDEX